KU-671-218

The Dynamics of
Social Movement
IN HONG KONG

A new series on socio-economic and cultural changes in Hong Kong

HONG KONG CULTURE AND SOCIETY

Series Editors

Tai Lok LUI   Department of Sociology,
                            The Chinese University of Hong Kong

Gerard A. POSTIGLIONE   Department of Education,
                            The University of Hong Kong

Panel of Advisors

Ambrose KING   The Chinese University of Hong Kong

Alvin SO   The Hong Kong University of Science
                            and Technology

Siu Lun WONG   The University of Hong Kong

The Dynamics of Social Movement in Hong Kong

The contributors to this book are:

Stephen Wing Kai CHIU

Denny Kwok Leung HO

On Kwok LAI

Ching Kwan LEE

Benjamin K.P. LEUNG

David A. LEVIN

Tai Lok LUI

Ming SING

Pik Wan WONG

HONG KONG
Culture and Society

The Dynamics of Social Movement IN HONG KONG

Edited by
Stephen Wing Kai Chiu and Tai Lok Lui

香港大學出版社
HONG KONG UNIVERSITY PRESS

Hong Kong University Press
14/F, Hing Wai Centre
7 Tin Wan Praya Road
Aberdeen
Hong Kong

© Hong Kong University Press 2000

ISBN 962 209 497 X

All rights reserved. No portion of this publication
may be reproduced or transmitted in any form or
by any means, electronic or mechanical, including
photocopy, recording, or any information storage
or retrieval system, without permission in writing
from the Publisher.

Cover photo by Wong Kan Tai
Cover design by Lea & Ink Design

Printed in Hong Kong by Condor Printing Co. Ltd.

Contents

Series Foreword

Most past research on Hong Kong has been generally aimed to inform a diverse audience about the place and its people. Beginning in the 1950s, the aim of scholars and journalists who came to Hong Kong was to study China, which had not yet opened its doors to fieldwork by outsiders. Accordingly, the relevance of Hong Kong was limited to its status as a society adjacent to mainland China. After the opening of China, research on Hong Kong shifted focus towards colonial legitimacy and the return of sovereignty. Thus, the disciplined study of Hong Kong was hindered for almost half a century, and the richness of a society undergoing dramatic economic, social and political change within the contemporary world was not sufficiently emphasized.

The unfolding of culture and society in Hong Kong is no longer confined by the 1997 question. New changes are shaped by local history as much as by the China factor. Rather than being an isolated entity, Hong Kong is an outcome of interaction among local history, national context, and global linkages. An understanding of the future development of Hong Kong requires sensitivity to this contextual complexity.

The volumes in this series are committed to making Hong Kong studies address key issues and debates in the social sciences. Each volume situates Hong Kong culture and society within contemporary theoretical discourse. Behind the descriptions of social and cultural life is a conceptual dialogue between local agenda, regional issues, and global concerns.

This series focuses on changing socio-economic structures, shifting political parameters, institutional restructuring, emerging public cultures, and expanding global linkages. It covers a range of issues, including social movements, socialization into a national identity, the effect of new immigrants from the Mainland, social networks of family members in other countries, the impact of the colonial legacy on the identity of forthcoming generations, trade union organization within the shifting political landscape, linkages with Southeast Asian societies, Hong Kong's new role between Taiwan and the Chinese mainland, the transformation of popular culture, the globalization of social life, and the global engagement of Hong Kong's universities in the face of national integration.

Gerard A. Postiglione
Tai Lok Lui

Series general editors

Acknowlegements

The idea of developing an edited volume on the dynamics of social movement in Hong Kong was initiated by Ming Chan and Gerard Postiglione when they were general editors of the book series entitled *Hong Kong Becoming China: The Transition to 1997*. They have been very helpful and supportive throughout the years. A special note of thanks should be given to Ming Chan; without his added encouragement, this book project would not have been finished.

Earlier versions of the papers collected in this volume were presented at an informal workshop on social movements in Hong Kong, held at the Sociology Department of the Chinese University of Hong Kong in 1995. We would like to thank our department for having given us a small grant to organize the workshop and to cover the expenses for some preliminary editorial work.

Thanks are due to the anonymous reviewers and the editorial staff of Hong Kong University Press for their comments and editorial assistance respectively. We would also like to thank Amy Yuen for her work in compiling the Bibliography.

Stephen Wing Kai Chiu
Tai Lok Lui

Sociology Department
The Chinese University of Hong Kong

September 1999

Contributors

Stephen Wing Kai CHIU is an Associate Professor in the Department of Sociology at the Chinese University of Hong Kong. He is a co-author of *East Asia and the World Economy* and *City-States in the Global Economy: Industrial Restructuring in Hong Kong and Singapore*. His research interests are in the areas of industrial relations, social movement, and comparative studies of East Asian development.

Denny Kwok Leung HO is an Assistant Professor in the Department of Applied Social Studies at the Hong Kong Polytechnic University. He has written extensively on urban social movements, youth culture and popular culture in Hong Kong. His current research is on unemployment in Hong Kong and Beijing.

On Kwok LAI is an Associate Professor in the School of Policy Studies at Kwansei Gakuin University, Japan. He has written extensively on urban development, environmental politics, and social conflicts in Hong Kong.

Ching Kwan LEE teaches sociology at the Chinese University of Hong Kong. She is the author of *Gender and the South China Miracle* and a number of articles on labour and gender issues in China and Hong Kong. Her current research is on the recomposition of the Chinese working class in the reform era.

Benjamin K.P. LEUNG is an Associate Professor in the Department of Sociology, the University of Hong Kong. His major publications include *Social Issues in Hong Kong, 25 Years of Social and Economic Development in Hong Kong, Women in Hong Kong*, and *Perspectives on Hong Kong Society*.

David A. LEVIN is a Senior Lecturer in the Department of Sociology at the University of Hong Kong. He is co-editor of *Labour Movement in a Changing Society: The Experience of Hong Kong*.

Tai Lok LUI is an Associate Professor in the Department of Sociology, the Chinese University of Hong Kong. His publications include *Waged Work at Home, City-States in the Global Economy: Industrial Restructuring in Hong Kong and Singapore*.

Ming SING is an Assistant Professor in the Department of Public and Social Administration, City University of Hong Kong. He has published several book chapters, and articles in such journals as *Democratization, China Information, Journal of Contemporary Asia, International Journal of Public Administration,* and *Chinese Law and Government*. He is currently working on a book about Hong Kong's democratization.

Pik Wan WONG is a general education instructor at the Hong Kong Polytechnic University. She received her Ph.D. in Political Science from the University of California at Los Angeles.

1

Introduction — Changing Political Opportunities and the Shaping of Collective Action: Social Movements in Hong Kong

Tai Lok Lui and Stephen Wing Kai Chiu

The 1997 question brought Hong Kong under the spotlight of the international news media. The change in sovereignty over Hong Kong on 1 July 1997 was a world event of the 1990s. Largely due to such media attention, various aspects of Hong Kong politics — from tensions and conflicts in the diplomatic talks between China and Britain to the prospects of capitalist Hong Kong under 'one country, two systems' — have come to constitute topical issues for academic discussion as well as journalistic reporting. However, despite growing interests in Hong Kong politics, more attention has been given to diplomatic conflicts and their consequences (such as confrontations brought about by the political reform proposals put forward by Chris Patten) than the structuring of politics within Hong Kong society. And when the domestic political arena is under scrutiny, the focus is always placed on institutional politics, more precisely activities in the legislature, and not actions and contentions in the broader political context. Few people bother to ask: what is the role of the Hong Kong people in this extended period of transition? Other than talks about the threat to freedom of press (or differently put, the fear of political censorship as well as self-censorship), the future of pro-democracy political groups and post-1997 changes in social and political environment, few attempts have really been made to probe the shaping and reshaping of politics from below before and after 1997.

The chapters in this volume serve the purpose of redressing this imbalance and set out to examine the development of various kinds of social movement in contemporary Hong Kong.

Such a neglect of people's collective action and popular mobilization in the structuring of Hong Kong politics is no accident. Indeed, in the eyes of many observers of Hong Kong politics, the central question of their study has always been the stability of the anachronistic colonial political system. King discusses the problem of political integration in a colonial city under rapid urbanization and suggests that the 'administrative absorption of politics' is 'the way Hong Kong's political system has coped with the problem of stability'.[1] Kuan directly addresses the issue of political stability and notes that '[t]he persistence of the colonial constitutional order has been accompanied by remarkable political stability. Hong Kong has never experienced any large-scale revolt or revolution. On the contrary, it is reputed for its lack of serious disputes'.[2] Lau describes 'the existence of political stability under highly destabilizing conditions' in Hong Kong as a 'miracle' of the twentieth century.[3] In his depiction of Hong Kong politics:

> [c]onflicts and violence ... did occur in 1956, 1966 and 1967. Except for the last one, they were primarily social conflicts not directed specifically against the government .... Moreover, all three instances of conflict were, relatively speaking, small or moderate in scale. And, what is more significant, their political reverberations were minimal .... [T]he staggering inequality in the distribution of income in Hong Kong would have the potential of generating class conflict and industrial hostilities, which she can ill afford to have. Nevertheless, none of these potential conflicts have materialized.[4]

Leung rounds up this discussion of political stability and remarks that '[a]lthough a rapidly modernizing society under colonial rule, Hong Kong has been exceptional in having been spared the frequent turmoil and instability that have plagued other countries of a similar socio-economic and political status. Since they have not been a particular salient feature of the society, social conflict and social movements have rarely been the subject of inquiry in studies of Hong Kong society'.[5]

Of course, few observers of Hong Kong politics would deny the existence of social conflict and social movements in contemporary Hong Kong. Rather, they argue that 'conflicts will be confined in scale because, under normal conditions, it is extremely difficult to mobilize the Chinese people in Hong Kong to embark upon a sustained, high-cost political movement'.[6] In this vein, observers of Hong Kong politics downplay the significance of social conflict and social movement in Hong Kong's political life. Given that most local collective actions have not been able to present a forceful challenge to the colonial state and thus do not constitute a serious threat to the stability of the political order, social conflict and social movement are relegated to secondary importance, if not total insignificance, in the analysis of Hong Kong politics.

However, while observers of Hong Kong politics are busy with the construction of explanations of political stability, waves after waves of collective actions — from student activism to urban protests and organized actions of civil service unions — have been witnessed in this so-called politically quiescent society since the 1970s. The emergence of protest action and social movement since the early 1970s indicates a change in the parameters of the political arena under the colonial rule. Whereas it is reasonable to say that these collective actions have not shaken the social basis of political stability in Hong Kong, it is quite another thing to assume (or even to assert) that such popular mobilization is of limited significance to the political life of the colony. As we shall see in subsequent discussion, the impacts of these collective actions are not confined to those issues which originally generated such conflicts.[7] They have wider repercussions to the constitution of Hong Kong politics.

❑ Changing Political Opportunities and Popular Mobilization

In this introduction, which is intended to provide the historical backdrop for the discussion of various kinds of social movement in subsequent chapters, we shall analyse the development of social movements in the context of changing political opportunities. By social movement, we mean 'a collectivity acting with some degree of organization and continuity outside institutional channels for the purpose of promoting or resisting change in the group, society, or world order of which it is a part'.[8] Our approach to the study of social movements in Hong Kong is informed by the recent 'political process model' in the social movement literature, which emphasizes the importance of broader political institutions in giving rise to a structure of opportunities for the occurrences and patterns of collective action.[9] Particularly, we emphasize that:

1. social movements are structured by the institutional environment wherein they are embedded;
2. their development is both constrained and enabled by the existing political opportunity structures; and
3. they interact with the broader political environment and, in their turn, are able to impact on the institutional setting and create opportunities for collective action.

In conceptualizing the political context of mobilization, Kriesi et al. point to four components of the political opportunity structure: national cleavage structures, institutional structures, prevailing strategies, and alliance structures.[10] First, very briefly, the cleavage structure refers to the national-specific political cleavages, which are often 'rooted in the social and cultural cleavages of a given society' which serve as the basis of mobilization. In Hong Kong, for example, the KMT-CCP rivalry was once the dominant political cleavage in much of the post-war years. Since the 1980s, however, the contradictions between the various pro-China organizations and social forces on the one hand, and those who advocated faster democratization and higher autonomy for Hong Kong tend to structure social and political mobilization. Second, the formal institutional structures of the political system, such as laws, electoral rules, party systems and relationship between various branches of the government also shape the course of development of social movements. An issue that preoccupies many researchers on developing countries, for example, is the effect of democratization on social movements. A key question relevant to our discussion here concerns the impacts of the 'opening up' of the political opportunity structure (e.g. election to the legislature) on social movements.[11] Third, 'prevailing strategies' mean the more informal strategies followed by authority against social movements or those adopted by social movement organizations. In Hong Kong, as mentioned, the colonial state's strategy of 'administrative absorption' has often been emphasized. Finally, the concept of alliance structure highlights the more interactional aspect of the political process when actors formed alliances among themselves. For example, in the last years of colonial rule, the colonial state often formed temporary and shifting alliance with the pro-China groups or the democrats on different issues. Grass roots organizations also have forged an uneasy alliance with the middle-class democrats.

Our adoption of the political process model is a flexible one, taking it more as a useful set of conceptual tools for our examination of the Hong Kong cases than a theoretical strait-jacket. In the following chapters, authors are given the autonomy to be selective in their focus of the institutional configuration of the concerned social movements. For example, while democratization and changes in the formal political institutions appear to be a common theme in most essays, the shifting alliance structure and its effect on social movements are highlighted in only a few of them (e.g. Ho's treatment of alliances among movement organizations on housing issues in chapter 6). It is also not our intention to argue that the political and institutional structuring of collective action is adequate to answer all the questions related to our understanding of social movements. Indeed, we do not pretend to be exhaustive in our treatment of social movements in Hong Kong. First, the types of social movement covered in this volume are selective; the selection is informed by our judgment of their relevance to social and political changes in contemporary Hong Kong. Second, the emphasis of our discussion is placed primarily on the institutional configuration of the developmental paths of various kinds of social movement. At the expense of leaving out some interesting topics (such as culture and social movement) in our discussion, we believe that such an emphasis on the institutional structuring of and the course of development of social movement will help illustrate how various social movements are constituted by the changing social and political environment, and how they, in turn, constitute the social and political space for popular mobilization and collective action.

In our review of the development of social movements in contemporary Hong Kong, we suggest that the emergence of collective actions in the 1960s and 1970s was largely an outcome of social and political changes within Hong Kong society. Subsequent development in the 1980s and 1990s, especially changes brought about by the process of decolonization, has significantly politicized popular mobilization and collective actions. However, as we shall point out in this introduction, and equally emphasized by the contributors of this volume, the impacts of politicization vary among different social movements. While some social movements find the new openings in the political structure opportunities for bringing their demands to institutional politics, other encounter competition for resources and leadership of popular mobilization. The effects of politicization are more complex than those of straightforward political empowerment. Organizers and leaders of social movements in Hong Kong find both new opportunities and constraints in the period of transition to 1997.

❏ The Rise of Social Movements in a Politically Stable Colony

As we have pointed out in the above section, political stability is widely accepted as the central question for the study of Hong Kong politics. Although many researchers on this topic have made significant contributions to the study of political life in Hong Kong,[12] their focus on political stability has narrowed the scope of political analysis. The major problem of the binary concept of political stability and instability is that it leads researchers to look for political turmoil, disorder and collapse of authority. Any situation of social conflict which is not in a state of revolution, internal war or dramatic change in political control and state power falls out of the scope of their analysis. Social movements, before they have been changed into contentious struggles for political power and becoming capable of challenging the existing political order, are perceived as unimportant or simply irrelevant. The quotations we have cited in the above section should be adequate to illustrate this point. There are two consequences. First, social movements in Hong Kong are under-researched. As Chiu and Hung argue, the early generation of sociologists had a rather high threshold of instability.[13] Any collective action which fell short of challenging the entire social and political system would be deemed as insignificant and not worthy of studying. The paradigmatic concern of systemic equilibrium in this sense is self-reinforcing. By pinning their focus on the sources of social and political stability, they invariably overlooked the diverse forms of protests and resistance at the grass roots. Furthermore, when collective actions were included into political analysis, they were often taken as sporadic, unorganized actions expressing hidden angers and discontents but void of political meanings. Such a conception of collective action directed researchers' attention towards the breakdown of the normative and political order and away from the structural cleavages and the processes of mobilization and organization in the making of collective action. So, for example, the 1966 Kowloon riots were conceived as outcomes of communication failures between government and people,[14] problems of political integration[15] and generation gap.[16] Few attempts had been made to look at the riots in the light of social cleavages, people's grievances and popular mobilization. As a result, social movement was largely eclipsed as a research topic of local political analysis in the 1970s.

But there are exceptions. Two major studies of industrial relations in Hong Kong[17] cover the issue of industrial conflict.[18] To be fair to these authors, it should be noted that industrial conflict and strike activity are only parts of their overall analyses of industrial relations in Hong Kong. They did not set out to test any explanation of strike pattern or to explain the rise and fall of industrial action. Their research addresses the broader issue of how various social factors shape management-labour relations in the colony. Although they approach their questions differently, they come to a similar observation that the trade union movement has only a marginal influence at the workplace, industry and societal levels. England and Rear put considerable stress on the nature of worker orientation in combination with the structure and functioning of the labour market as a major determinant of the ineffectiveness of trade unionism.[19] Turner and his colleagues underline the orientation of union organization in their explanation of why local unions remain marginal in capital-labour bargaining at the workplace. While these two major works on industrial relations are relevant to our understanding of the labour movement in Hong Kong, they, by themselves, do not directly analyse industrial conflict and action as a kind of social movement.

But then the emergence of collective actions in the 1970s poses new questions, though very often being ignored, to the observers of Hong Kong politics. The rise of the student movement,[20] urban protests[21] and civil service unionism[22] illustrates the restructuring of the political arena after the two riots in 1966 and 1967. This restructuring process worked at two levels. At the level of identity formation and consciousness, the two riots had tremendous impacts on the 'post-war baby-boomers'. The proliferation of literary clubs in the 1960s was part of this 'conscientization' process. It expressed the dissatisfaction of the colonial social and political order, mainly in the form of a search of the Chinese cultural root among the younger generation. This subsequently developed into two strands of social participation — on the one side, university students actively participated in local social affairs (organizing the university reform campaign, visiting and delivering services to poor households, supporting protest actions, and launching a mass campaign calling for the adoption of Chinese as an official language) and on the other, a search of cultural identity (organizing visits to mainland China and organizing the 'Defend Diaoyutai Movement'). The former brought university students to encounter the restricted space of social and political participation under the colonial administration. The latter was later developed into nationalistic fervour. Under the political parameters of colonial rule, at the early stage of the student movement, the two strands coexisted and together had the chemical effect of boosting student activism. Experience of confronting the colonial government in the process of social participation reinforced the students' critique of colonialism and directed their attention to the look for an alternative. In the context of the early 1970s, this alternative was communist China — representing an alternative to both capitalism and colonialism.[23]

At the level of the institutional configuration of political participation, the 1966 and 1967 riots alerted the colonial administration of the potential outburst of popular discontents among the local Chinese. In response, the colonial administration carried out various programmes of reform, including the establishment of the City District Officer (CDO) Scheme, changing labour legislation, and provision of youth services. This, without bringing about major changes in the institutional structure of the existing polity, had provided more room in the public sphere for open discussion and criticism of government policies.[24] This new 'political climate' provided room for manoeuvre for advocates and community organizers to initiate organized actions to protest against government policies in the early 1970s. Furthermore, the triumph of the colonial authority over the pro-China groups in 1967 also led to the decline in significance of primary political cleavage in early postwar Hong Kong: the rivalry between the pro-China and pro-Taiwan groups. By attacking the colonial system, and failed, the pro-China groups began a protracted process of organizational and ideological reconstruction. The pro-Taiwan groups, on the other hand, chose to align with the colonial government during the struggles, and they also experienced a gradual decline in the 1970s, perhaps owing to the absence of an active enemy in sight. While much of the collective actions before the 1970s were instigated by the pro-China faction against the pro-Taiwan faction or vice versa (in Lee's description, 'Chinese politics on Hong Kong soil'),[25] the decline in the salience of the left-right political cleavage created new space for the more locally oriented social movements.[26] Politics in Hong Kong became localized in the 1970s.

❑ Challenges to the Colonial Administrative State

The early 1970s witnessed several waves of collective action. While the student movement addressed broader ideological and political issues of that period, urban protests and industrial actions in the public sector were driven by community-based and work-related interests. Here we shall not go into the details of these social movements.[27] Rather, we would like to discuss the major characteristics of social movement in this period. First, most of the collective actions of these social movements were expressed in the form of protest actions.[28] This partly reflected the limited resources of the movement organizations and participants — the main strategy of their action was to rally support of a third party for the purpose of exerting pressure on the government, showing their relatively weak bargaining position *vis-à-vis* the colonial state and limited resources for mass mobilization. Second, it was an outcome of the institutional configuration of political action under the so-called 'consultative democracy' political arrangement. Prior to the reform of local administration (i.e. the establishment of district boards and the related local elections) in the early 1980s, the channels of open political participation were confined to (through election) the Urban Council. More importantly, within this so-called 'consultative democracy' framework, the administrative state was politically insulated from society, and depoliticization was the ruling strategy of the colonial government.[29] In this context, while the elitist interest groups could access to the government through the appointment to consultative bodies and exerting political influence on the bureaucrats, political demands made by the general public were channelled to the non-institutional arena. Simply put, the design of the colonial state and the political representation system drove political claims and demands to assume the form of protest action.[30]

By the end of the 1970s, some signs of a 'social movement industry' was in formation. The proliferation of different types of collective action had greatly broadened the scope of contentious politics. A variety of interests and latent groups had been mobilized and became recognized political claims and demands. Protest groups and pressure groups were formed to sustain mobilization.[31] In a way, the early activism of the student movement in mobilizing collective action and its subsequent decline in importance in leading popular mobilization revealed the growth of social movement organizations and the formation of a 'social movement industry'. The growing importance of pressure groups like the Hong Kong Professional Teachers' Union and the Society for Community Organization in events like the Golden Jubilee Secondary School Incident (actions triggered by alleged corruption in a secondary school and protests against government intervention in closing that school) and the Yaumatei Boat People Protests (a series of protests demanding resettlement in land temporary accommodation), and the formation of an ad hoc alliance for joint action of mobilization under the leadership of these pressure groups illustrated a change towards consolidation of social protest through pressure group politics.

Our earlier discussion of the institutional configuration of social protest can also be applied to our understanding of the rise of pressure group politics in the late 1970s and early 1980s. In essence, pressure group politics was more of a continuation than a discontinuity of protest actions found in the early 1970s.[32] Despite that some of them were coopted into the colonial administrative system through appointment to advisory committees, most of the pressure groups were active mainly outside formal institutional politics.[33] Indeed, the fact that most pressure groups were 'outsiders' of institutional politics helped create some kind of tacit understanding among pressure groups, social movement organizations, and grass roots protest groups. In the joint actions organized in the late 1970s and early 1980s, pressure groups, social movement organizations, and grass roots protest groups could easily come together and formed an ad hoc organization for a common cause. Though ideological differences among different groups still mattered, on the whole they had little difficulties in making common demands and staging jointly organized protest actions. The affinity among these groups was largely a consequence of the restricted opportunity of political participation in that period. The closed political system created common understanding among the activists — they had the shared experience of being rejected, sometimes repressed, by the Hong Kong government and in the process of staging their protests, confronting a bureaucratic, colonial administrative state. Restricted entry into the formal channels of the polity 'created' an oppositional force being active in the non-institutional political arena.[34] Some of these groups (such as university students' organizations) were critical of colonialism and/or capitalism. Others (for example, residents' organizations) did not have elaborated ideological programmes, but were equally critical of the bureaucratic colonial administration which was not responsive to their demands. By the early 1980s and on the eve of the Sino-British negotiations over Hong Kong's future, there existed a loosely knitted network of pressure groups, social movement organizations and grass roots protest groups playing the role of an oppositional force to the colonial administration.

Studies of social movements in the late 1970s and early 1980s reflected an academic recognition of the relevance of social movement to the study of Hong Kong politics. Early attempts to analyse the development of social movements in the 1970s were mainly informed by Marxist political economy.[35] More systematic studies of social movement came at a later stage; their focus was no longer structural analysis at the level of political economy. Leung's study of the student movement is an application of resource mobilization theory to an understanding of the student activists.[36] Lui's analysis of housing protests offers a historical account of the development of housing protests in Hong Kong and how the form of collective action is shaped by the political institutions and organizational mobilization.[37] Chiu also analyses strike activity from a historical perspective and highlights the interactions of economic, institutional and organizational factors in shaping the variation in strike level.[38] The commonality of these studies lies in the rejection of a simplistic conception of structure and action and an attempt to probe the institutional configuration of collective action and the process of movement mobilization. More importantly, a common concern of these writers is to debunk the myth of 'stability' espoused in earlier studies. By painstakingly documenting a rich tradition of collective actions among local residents and workers, Lui and Chiu[39] provide ample evidences to the empirical inadequacies and historical myopia in the studies like Lau's, King's and Miners'.[40]

❏ Social Movements in the Process of Decolonization

The Sino-British negotiations over Hong Kong's future and the subsequent agreement between the two governments on returning the colony to China on 1 July 1997 brought a drastic change in both the political agenda and parameters of Hong Kong. The settlement signalled the beginning of the decolonization process. Whether the initiation of political reforms (from the establishment of district boards to the introduction of popularly elected members to the Legislative Council) was part of the British government's preparation for decolonization or otherwise is beyond the scope of our discussion here. Without going into the background of different phases of political reform carried out in the 1980s, it is safe to say that changes in the political design have restructured the political arena. Though initially pressure groups, social movement organizations and grass roots protest groups had shown signs of reservation about participating in formal institutional politics,[41] they were quickly drawn into electoral politics, first at the levels of election to district boards and Urban and Regional councils and later in direct and indirect elections to the Legislature. The new agenda then was that of politics in the transitional period. At the same time, the academic discussion of Hong Kong politics shifted from the question of political stability to that of opportunities and institutional constraints encountered by local strategic elite in this transitional period.[42] The new question was: how a new political order is to be made within the parameters of 'decolonization without independence' and the diplomatic politics between Britain and China?[43] Again, the question of political development, whether formulated in terms of political participation, democratic transition or political reintegration, attracted most of the attention. The study of popular mobilization and social movement was once again being left out. Meanwhile, in the realm of *realpolitik*, the 1980s was a period of political struggle through electoral politics.

In the studies of social conflicts in 1975–91, it is shown that there has been a drastic increase of conflicts related to political issues (i.e. those concerning constitutional matters and issues about political and civil rights) since 1984.[44] Before 1984, constitutional matters rarely appeared on the agenda of local social movements. This, of course, was not because of political indifference among the activists. Rather, it was because, prior to the political reforms in the 1980s, the question of democratization was simply seen as remote — an issue unlikely to have any practical meanings in the face of a closed colonial administration. This growing importance of political issues in social conflict reveals the opening of new political opportunities brought about by decolonization and also a shift of attention to political participation in formal institutional politics by pressure groups, social movement organizations, and grass roots protest groups. The struggle for democracy, both for deepening political reform before 1997 and for democratizing the political structure after the handover, became the major concern of the activists in the 1980s and 1990s (for a discussion of the democracy movement, see chapter 2).

The opening of new political opportunities driven by decolonization has a double-edged effect on the development of social movement in Hong Kong. On the one side, there are now new opportunities for political intervention in the sphere of electoral politics and in the process of designing the future political structure of Hong Kong. After a short spell of initial reservation, activists from pressure groups, social movement organizations and grass roots protest groups quickly came to form new political groups for the purposes of preparing for elections at different levels and articulating political programmes for expressing to the Chinese government their opinions on blueprints of transitional arrangements and post-1997 administration.[45] The proliferation of political groups in the 1980s can be seen as a response to the new political environment triggered by decolonization. Many of them actively participated in the democracy movement for securing the establishment of a more democratic political structure before 1997. Sing's study of the democracy movement in the 1980s (see chapter 2) best illustrates how former pressure groups, social movement organizations and newly formed political groups have come to develop a loosely defined group of democrats on the basis of previous collaborative experience and some tacit understanding of the need of fighting for the democratic cause. The opening of political opportunities has brought about the further politicization of pressure groups and social movement organizations. Political parties were formed for consolidating the existing network of activists and concerned groups.

On the other hand, participation in formal institutional politics had given rise to divisions among the loosely connected active groups in local social movements. The twists and turns during the Sino-British talks about Hong Kong's political reforms and the post-1997 political arrangements and the emphasis on convergence towards a social and political system which China would find acceptable posed new questions to the political groups and social movement organizations. The choice between pragmatism (accepting the parameters prescribed by China) and continuing to play the role of an oppositional force (especially after the June 4 Incident in 1989) created divisions among these active groups. The loosely formulated consensus found among active groups in the 1970s had lost its relevance, and the solidarity among the so-called democrats was weakened. Previous informal political networking was replaced by formalized party participation and inter-organization linkages.

At the same time, electoral politics and party politics became the focus of contentious politics in the transitional period. Discussions about the decline of grass roots protest groups reflected the gradual separation of grass roots mobilization and community action on the one side, and party politics on the other.[46] After a short period of active participation in local elections, grass roots protest groups had changed their strategy and assumed a low profile in the 1991 and 1995 elections to the Legislative Council.[47] This changing relationship between social movement and party politics is an issue worth further investigation. Indeed, the discussion about the incorporation of popular mobilization and protest action into party and electoral politics reflects the peculiarities of social movement and political groups in Hong Kong.[48] Related to our discussion of the development of social movements, most of the present leaders of the democrats started their political careers in organizing protest actions and social movements in the 1970s and 1980s. Their close connections with social movement organizations created expectations from the grass roots that they would continue to play the role of leading popular mobilization against government policies. Indeed, their experience in organizing social movements and their role as oppositional force led them to assume a double role in Hong Kong politics — they were both the leaders of protest actions and the oppositional politicians in the elected bodies at different levels.

Nevertheless, it was also becoming clear that the politics of grass roots mobilization was different from that of election. The rapid development of electoral politics and the concentration of efforts in parliamentary struggle had led to a 'hollowing out' of political organization at the grass roots level. This was not just an issue for community groups. The same phenomenon of leaving behind workplace-organizing and jumping onto electoral competition was also found among local unions (Chiu and Levin in chapter 4). Lai's study of the protests against hazardous installations on Tsing Yi Island in the 1980s (chapter 9) also illustrates very well how electoral politics shaped community-based social movements. Since the development of local elections in the early 1980s, protests groups in Tsing Yi soon became deeply involved in electoral politics and gradually stayed away from noninstitutional collective actions.

The mass mobilization before and after the June 4 Incident did not really change the picture portrayed above. While a huge crowd had joined the street rallies and marches protesting against the suppression of the student movement in Beijing, the pro-Chinese democracy movement quickly fell from the peak after the crackdown (Wong in chapter 3). The longer-term impact of the June 4 Incident is found not in sustained mobilization of mass action but in the introduction of a moral dimension (how one positions oneself in the judgement of the crackdown at Tiananmen Square after 1989) into the political discourse — continuation of support of the pro-Chinese democracy movement is often seen as a sign of daring to stand firm against the authoritarian regime of China. In this way, the 'China factor' (in terms of one's political position in the question of Chinese democracy) is brought closer to democratic politics in Hong Kong. Meanwhile, controversies about the political reform programme put forward by Chris Patten also had not triggered another round of pro-democracy popular mobilization. As Hong Kong approached 1997, it became increasingly difficult to mobilize the public and to stage open confrontational action against China.

❏ New Social Movements

The 1980s and 1990s also witnessed the emergence of new social movements in Hong Kong. Environmental issues at community level had led to a number of collective actions in the 1980s.[49] However, unlike the development of green politics in industrialized countries, apart from the anti-Daya Bay Nuclear Plant movement, most of the environmental actions were not articulated to a wider political agenda (Lai in chapter 9). Many of these organized actions were based on the concerns of individual communities and best characterized by the 'not-in-my-backyard' mentality — a mentality which took environmental issues as matters of protecting one's own community from environmental hazards and not universal problems of human development. Also, there were signs of the development of the institutionalization of the environmental movement. With government and corporate supports for environment education, some NGOs concentrated on the promotion of environmental consciousness as a lifestyle, staying aloof from the real political and economic problems which brought about the degradation of our environment (Lai in chapter 9).

We also saw the development of grass roots-oriented women's groups in the 1980s. Lee's study of the women's movement in Hong Kong (chapter 8) argues that since the 1980s, there has been an emergence of feminist politics. In her words, 'the women's movement in Hong Kong over the years created a new collective actor'. Women's struggle now works on this new identity — women's claims are no longer put in a language of familial/maternal welfare but that of their rights, independence and gender equality.

How the women's movement would further make an impact on the political arena is an issue for future research. While the environmental movement seems to be confined to consciousness-raising and environment education and becomes more dependent of state and corporate supports, the women's movement is expected to put more efforts in changing policies for the promotion of gender equalities. The democratization of the legislature has helped bring gender issues to public debate.

❏ Social Movements in the Post-1997 Milieu

As a result of the confrontation between Britain and China precipitated by the proposals for political reform put forward by Chris Patten, the original idea of a 'through-train' arrangement (i.e. continuity in terms of major political institutions) had been revoked. Lu Ping, then director of the State Council's Hong Kong and Macau Affairs Office, expressed the opinion of 'abandoning of the illusion of co-operation from Britain during the transition to Chinese rule'.[50] China moved on to set up the 'second stove' by forming the Preparatory Committee and set out to put the Provisional Legislative Council in operation before 1 July 1997. Various moves initiated by China to redefine the political parameters after the political transition, with the clear objectives of upsetting the implementation of Patten's political reform and pre-empting pro-democracy groups from gaining a foothold in the future political system, met criticisms and oppositions from different sectors of the local population. Negative public response notwithstanding, China cleared its way of ensuring a convergence of Hong Kong's political structure into an institutional arrangement that it found acceptable.

In a sense, these moves did not mark a departure from China's original vision of 'Hong Kong people ruling Hong Kong'. As put by Xu Jia-tun in his personal memoir, 'the essence of the future "Hong Kong people ruling Hong Kong" arrangement is a cross-class united government under the leadership of the bourgeoisie'.[51] As shown in the processes of electing the Chief Executive, the formation of the Provisional Legislative Council, and the adoption of new voting methods for the election of the first SAR legislature in 1998, both pro-China groups and business interests had been well taken care of. Although there is still room (yet significantly circumscribed by changes in the arrangements of the election process) for the democrats to manoeuvre in electoral politics, the SAR government had largely established a governance structure which is executive-led, pro-business, accommodating to China's influence. And the style of governance would be, as repeatedly hinted by Tung Chee-hwa, conservative and paternalistic.

Meanwhile, the tensions between China and Hong Kong, mainly the fear of political intervention, continued to be one of the key concerns of the local population. In recent years, oppositions to China's policies over Hong Kong, from questions concerning future constitutional arrangements to the increasingly authoritarian posture about social and political control, had become one of the major concerns of local demonstrations and protest actions. From 1993 to 1996, protests outside the Xinhua News Agency increased from 100 to 175. Police records of the number of marches also showed a jump from 285 in 1993 to 405 in 1995.[52] In fact, people's concerns about the 'China factor' in Hong Kong's social life were not confined to political matters. The public outcry against the open attack on RTHK, the government broadcasting station, made by Mr Xu Ximin, a senior Chinese People's Political Consultative Conference delegate, revealed how nervous Hong Kong people were about a tightening of social and political control through disciplining the mass media. While the fear of China's intervention continues to haunt the public (disputes concerning the ruling of the Court of Final Appeal on Mainland children's right of abode is just another case at stake), with a drastic downturn of confidence in Hong Kong's economy since late 1997, people's attention has shifted to livelihood issues, particularly those of rising unemployment and the effects of the plunge in property prices.

The effects of a restructured economy (particularly pertinent here was the declining manufacturing sector) and vibrant speculations in the stock market and property market emerged in the context of speculators' attack on the Hong Kong currency and the financial chaos in the East and Southeast Asian region. In the first quarter of 1998, for the first time in the past 13 years Hong Kong experienced negative economic growth. Unemployment rate shot up dramatically and continued to rise. The stock market was volatile and property prices once fell some 40% within a year's time.[53] Meanwhile, the income gap between the rich and the poor widened. In 1996, the Gini Coefficient was 0.518, a significant jump from the 0.453 in 1986. More people began to feel the heat of a depressing economy; even white-collar employees were also driven out of their previously rather stable jobs. The unemployment problem was no longer an issue confined to those middle-aged former (male and female) manual labourers. The extended period of rapid growth in the postwar decades seemed to have come to a close. There witnessed the rise of protest actions organized by those lower-middle- and middle-class people who were angry with the government's imposition of the new mother-tongue language education programme (thus affecting their children's opportunity of receiving English education), those suffered from the collapse of small stockbrokers' agencies triggered by the drastic downturn in the stock and property markets, or those badly hit by the plunge in property prices and becoming owners of negative assets.

Can the self-acclaimed paternalistic, executive-led, pro-business SAR government be able to handle various demands from local people in the midst of rapid changes in the economic environment and psychological pessimism worrying about rising economic hardship? Can it turn the clock back (reinstating 'administrative absorption of politics' by strengthening the appointment system and the advisory machinery and playing down the significance of electoral politics) and reconstitute a paternalistic bureaucratic state, after intense politicization in the decolonization process and in the face of emerging conflicts between civil servants and Tung Chee-hwa? Questions concerning the prospect of further democratization, the protection of Hong Kong from Beijing's political intervention and monitoring government's performance remain the overarching concerns.

Tung Chee-hwa was eager to depoliticize what he saw an overpoliticized environment. There would not be major changes in the existing political system before 2007, as stipulated in Annex II of the Basic Law. More than once, Tung had tried to show in public his style of paternalistic and bureaucratic governance. However, after a series of events happened after the handover (from the bird flu to the government's slow reactions to the impacts of the economic turmoil in the region, to Tung's inconsistency in handling the housing issue, to the airport fiasco, just to name a few examples), public confidence in the SAR government dropped to a record low. The government was widely criticized for its incapability in dealing with problems arising from crisis situations. Yet, most of the recent protest actions and popular mobilization were taken over by political parties of different orientations. The need of securing electoral support drove political parties of diverse political persuasions to assume a more active role in interest articulation and popular mobilization. On the one hand, more resources were available to collective action-organizing. On the other hand, popular discontents and demands for policy change were quickly subordinated to the political struggle in institutionalized politics. Differently put, political struggles for further democratization and power-sharing had overshadowed social movements.

❑ Contextualizing Hong Kong's Social Movements

The contributors of this volume emphasize that social movements in Hong Kong predated the political transition triggered by the 1997 question. Indeed, one of their central arguments is that a useful handle to start our analysis of social movements in Hong Kong is to look at the effects of the long-term changes of the political opportunity structure on their course of development. In this regard, the contributors have tried to give historical and developmental accounts of social movements in Hong Kong. Decolonization and the resultant politicization of social conflict are no more than parts of the larger, macro-structuring of political opportunity for collective actions. It is interesting to observe that, as shown in the studies of different social movements reported by our contributors, there is no single, homogeneous '1997 effect' on social movements. China's intervention into Hong Kong's social and public affairs, while no doubt always bring about the politicization of social issues, does not necessarily create more opportunities for social movement organizations. As we shall see in the following chapters, the '1997 effect' varies and the impacts of decolonization and China's intervention have been differently appropriated by different types of social movement.

The other common theme in the following chapters lies in the emphasis that a more adequate understanding of the structuring of social movements requires us to look into social movement organizations and the process of mobilization for collective action. While our contributors examine the macro-structuring of the trajectories of social movements and thus will not be able to probe the issue of organizational development in adequate depth, they have discussed the responses of social movement organizations to the changing political environment.

All the chapters in this volume look at longer-term development of social movements in Hong Kong. This, we hope, will help redress the imbalance we find in journalistic accounts of social and political development in many 1997 special issues of newspapers and magazines. Hong Kong society and its politics have much broader relevance than merely another case of political transition. The same is true for our study of social movements in Hong Kong.

Notes

1. King, 'Administrative absorption of politics in Hong Kong', p. 129.
2. Kuan, 'Political stability and change in Hong Kong', p. 146.
3. Lau, *Society and politics in Hong Kong*, p. 1.
4. Ibid., pp. 2, 4.
5. Leung, *Perspectives on Hong Kong society*, p. 159.
6. Lau, *Society and politics in Hong Kong*, p. 20.
7. See also Cheung, 'The rise of the new middle class and its political implications', and Lui, 'The path of development of Hong Kong's popular movements'.
8. McAdam and Snow, 'Social movements: conceptual and theoretical issues', p. xviii.
9. Tilly, *From mobilization to revolution*, McAdam, *Political process and the development of Black insurgency 1930–1970*, and McAdam, McCarthy and Zald, *Comparative perspectives on social movements: political opportunities, mobilizing structures, and cultural framing*.
10. Kriesi et al., *New social movement in Western Europe: a comparative analysis*.
11. See, for example, Canel, 'Democratization and the decline of urban social movements in Uruguay: a political-institutional account'.
12. One example is the proliferation of research on the cultural foundation of the existing political order. See, for instance, Hoadley, 'Hong Kong is the lifeboat: notes on political culture and socialization', King, 'The political culture of Kwun Tong', and Lau and Kuan, *The ethos of the Hong Kong Chinese*.

13. Chiu and Hung, 'The colonial state and rural protests in Hong Kong'.

14. Hong Kong government, *Kowloon disturbances 1966: report of Commission of Inquiry*.

15. King, 'Administrative absorption of politics in Hong Kong'.

16. Jarvie, 'A postscript on riots and the future of Hong Kong'.

17. England and Rear, *Chinese labour under British rule* and *industrial relations and law in Hong Kong*, and Turner et al., *The last colony: but whose?*

18. These two studies of industrial relations were expanded and updated in the 1980s. See England, *Industrial relations and law in Hong Kong*, and Turner, Fosh and Ng, *Between two societies: Hong Kong labour in transition*.

19. It is interesting to note that England also formulates his research question in a format rather similar to the studies of political stability. England, *Industrial relations and law in Hong Kong*, p. 1, writes: '[v]iewed against the potential for conflict which exists in Hong Kong, the miracle of social order should be placed alongside its acknowledged economic miracle. The question arises then as to how the potential power of working-class action in a capitalist society has been diffused. Has it been achieved by the removal of sources of disaffection, by the development of an armoury of repression, or by directing grievances into constitutional or administrative channels?' But given his research interest in management-labour relations, England does not stop at pointing out the existence of industrial peace. He moves on to ask what are the factors that bring about the demobilization of the working class.

20. See The Hong Kong Federation of Students, *Hong Kong's student movement*.

21. Lui, 'Urban protests in Hong Kong', and Lui and Kung, *City unlimited: housing protests and urban politics in Hong Kong*.

22. Ho, 'The government and the clerical workers: a case study of labour-management conflicts in the Hong Kong civil service'.

23. The ideological struggle between the pro-China faction and the social actionist faction within the student movement in the mid-1970s is a topic worth more serious research. The rise and fall of the pro-China faction can be seen as a change in the direction of self-searching among the young people in the 1970s. The formation of a local identity and the gradual articulation of localism make the search of a culturally Chinese identity less appealing and even obsolete among the second or third batch of the baby-boomers.

24. See, for instance, *The Urban Council White Paper 1971*.

25. Lee, 'Hong Kong identity — past and present', p. 158.

26. Lui, 'The path of development of Hong Kong's popular movements'.

27. On the student movement, see The Observers of Far Eastern Affairs, *The student movement*, The Hong Kong Federation of Students, *Hong Kong's student movement*; on urban social movement, see Lui, 'Urban protests in Hong Kong', Lui and Kung, *City unlimited: housing protests and urban politics in Hong Kong*;' on public sector unionism, see Ho, 'The government and the clerical workers: a case study of labour-management conflict in the Hong Kong civil service'.

28. See Lui and Kung, *City unlimited: housing protests and urban politics in Hong Kong* for elaboration; also consult Lipsky, 'Protest as a political resource'.

29. Harris, *Hong Kong: a study in bureaucratic politics*.

30. Lui, 'Urban protests in Hong Kong', Lui and Kung, *City unlimited: housing protests and urban politics in Hong Kong*. Also see Jenkins and Klandermans, *The politics of social protests*.

31. On the formation of protest groups and pressure groups concerning community politics, see The Hong Kong Council of Social Service, *Community development resource book*, various years.

32. Lui, 'Pressure group politics and political participation'.

33. The best example showing the attitude of the colonial administration towards local pressure groups is the comments made in the report of the SCOPG. See Lee, 'Pressure groups and party politics', p. 134.

34. Compare with Tilly, *From mobilization to revolution*, and Gamson, *The strategy of social protest*.

35. Wu, 'The political conjuncture of contemporary Hong Kong and development of popular movements', and Tsang, 'An exploratory analysis of Hong Kong's class structure'.

36. Leung, 'Who protests'.

37. Lui, 'Urban protests in Hong Kong'.

38. Chiu, 'Strikes in Hong Kong'.

39. Ibid., and Lui, 'Urban protests in Hong Kong'.

40. Lau, *Society and politics in Hong Kong*, King, 'Administrative absorption of politics in Hong Kong', and Miners, *The government and politics of Hong Kong*.

41. Lui, 'Pressure group politics and political participation', and 'The path of development of Hong Kong's popular movements', and Lui and Kung, *City unlimited: housing protests and urban politics in Hong Kong*.

42. Lau, 'Political reform and political development in Hong Kong', 'Decolonization without independence', and 'Basic Law and the new political order of Hong Kong'.

43. While Lau, 'Decolonization without independence' and 'Basic Law and the new political order of Hong Kong', directly addresses the issue of the formation of a new political order in the transitional period and looks for a new mode of political integration, Scott, *Political change and the crisis of legitimacy in Hong Kong*, raises the question of legitimation crisis and suggests that this is the fundamental problem of the future SAR government.

44. Cheung and Louie, 'Social conflicts in Hong Kong, 1975–1986', and Chui and Lai, 'Patterns of social conflicts in Hong Kong in the period 1980 to 1991'.

45. Cheng, *Hong Kong: in search of a future*.

46. Leung, 'Community participation: the decline of residents' organizations', Lui, 'Back to basics: rethinking the roles of residents' organizations', and Ho in Chapter 6.

47. Lui, 'Two logics of community politics'.

48. Lui, 'What is to be done?'

49. Chan and Hills, *Limited gains*.

50. Quoted from Sida, *Hong Kong towards 1997*, p. 409.

51. Xu, *The memoirs of Xu Jiatun on Hong Kong*, p. 121.

52. Gilley, 'Jumping the gun', p. 16.

53. Elliott, 'The numbers don't lie'.

2

Mobilization for Political Change —
The Pro-democracy Movement in Hong Kong
(1980s–1994)

Ming Sing

❏ Introduction: Democratization and Pro-democracy Movement

In the late twentieth century, one of the most significant and widespread phenomenon in the world has been the global process of democratization.[1] Between 1974 and 1991, 40 countries in the world became significantly democratized.[2] The wave of democratization started with the toppling of Western Europe's last three dictatorships in Greece, Spain and Portugal. It then turned to Argentina, Bolivia, Chile and Uruguay in Latin America, before spreading to Asia, Eastern Europe, the former Soviet Union and Africa. In Asia, the overthrow of Marcos in the Philippines in 1986, the abolition of martial law in Taiwan and the fall of Chun Doohwan of South Korea in 1987, testified to a democratic turn away from their authoritarian traditions.[3]

While no single factor has yet been found to be necessary or sufficient for explaining democratization,[4] a most commonly mentioned one has been the vibrancy of pro-democracy movements from civil society. Organized social movement organizations, encompassing labour unions, religious organizations, women's associations, student unions and other intermediate groups in civil society, spanning from Poland, Hungary, Czechoslovakia and Yugoslavia in Eastern Europe, through Taiwan, South Korea, Philippines and Thailand in Asia, to those in Latin America and Southern Europe, have undermined the authoritarian states and facilitated democratization.[5]

In Hong Kong, during the 1980s, there were both heated debates and fervent mobilizations concerning democratization. The period was hallmarked by the most vibrant and organized pro-democracy movement since 1945. The flourishing movement carries double significance. First, its persistent popular mobilizations in support of democracy, and its accusations of China's violation of the Sino-British Joint Declaration, did not only keep the issue of democratization alive among the public, but also strengthen a pro-democracy political culture in Hong Kong. Second, the cooperation among various organizations in the movement during the 1980s encouraged them to institutionalize their pro-democracy opposition by forming political parties during the early 1990s. These political parties subsequently won a sweeping electoral victory at the maiden direct elections of 1991 for Hong Kong's legislature. Given the significance of the pro-democracy movement, this chapter probes the formation and development of the movement between the 1980s and the early 1990s. I will argue that between early 1980s and 1994, the pro-democracy movement from groups in civil society went through the following phases:

1. Formative phase (1982–86): an alliance championing the movement was formed in 1986.
2. Conflicting phase (1987): it engaged in severe conflicts with other political forces.
3. Decisional phase (1990): it finalized its blueprint of democratization.
4. Declining phase (1991–94): the alliances behind the movement were weakened in strength and size.

In this chapter, the main focus will be placed on the pro-democracy activities of civil society directed against the state, i.e. political opposition in civil society.[6] I will analyse the developmental path of the pro-democracy movement in an environment of political transition.

❏ Phase I — The Formative Phase of the Pro-democracy Movement Alliance in Hong Kong (1982–86): Political Opportunity Structure for Formation of Democratic Movement Expanded

Crisis and Changing Stances of Britain and China Towards Democratization

The Chinese Communist Party (CCP) has put national reunification and modernization of China as its major priorities ever since Deng came to power in 1978. Because of these concerns, the CCP decided to recover Hong Kong's de facto sovereignty in 1997 and promised Hong Kong a high degree of autonomy under the precept of 'one country, two systems'. After two years of thorny talks, a draft Sino-British Agreement was released on 26 September 1984. It stated that the sovereignty and administration of Hong Kong would revert to China on 1 July 1997. From then on, under the precept of 'one country, two systems', Hong Kong would become a highly autonomous Special Administrative Region. Despite the eventual Agreement, the prospect of reverting to communist China triggered off a very severe 'confidence crisis' for Hong Kong people between 1982 and 1984. People had very pervasive and deep fears of losing their cherished lifestyles, freedom and prosperity after 1997.[7]

China's reaction to the crisis has to be understood in terms of three issues it has harboured with respect to Hong Kong. The three issues have been, first, to maintain Hong Kong's pragmatic value for China; second, to achieve national unity by regaining Hong Kong and using it to lure Taiwan into unity; and third, to preclude Hong Kong from a rapid democratization which would undermine CCP's control over it and its hegemony in China.

To alleviate the 'confidence crisis' and avoid having the above interests undermined, it endorsed the following provisions in the Sino-British Agreement concerning Hong Kong's post-1997 political institutions:[8]

1. The chief executive shall be appointed on the basis of the results of elections or consultations to be held locally.

2. The legislature shall be constituted by elections.

Those democratic provisions, in the light of recent findings, were inserted only after being insisted upon by Britain at the closing stage of Sino-British talks.[9] As early as 1985, China began to obstruct Hong Kong's democratization to alleviate their worries that anti-Communist and pro-British forces might evolve in Hong Kong in the process of democratization.[10] Nevertheless, to maintain Hong Kong's pragmatic value, achieve national unity and use Hong Kong to lure Taiwan into unity, China needed to engineer its obstruction of democratization in Hong Kong as skilfully as possible. However, it had repeatedly aired warnings of dismantling any excessively democratic structure in 1997 as it saw fit.

In the face of Chinese opposition, how did Britain react? Britain had had two major interests with regard to Hong Kong:

Since Hong Kong would be decolonized without independence and, as a result, would be under the governance of a socialist state, the British government was under pressure to indemnify itself against attack by opposition parties at home and against international condemnation. Britain's foremost interest was to leave the colony as gracefully as possible. This meant securing China's cooperation during the run-up to 1997 in order to guarantee British administration over Hong Kong up to then. It also implied maintaining the continuity of Hong Kong's prosperity, stability and basic free lifestyles. Democratization of Hong Kong could make the British public and international communities feel that Hong Kong would be better protected from future adverse interference from China if no grave instability or economic crisis was engendered. Nevertheless, the timed reversion of the colony's sovereignty entailed that China, the future master of the colony, could pose real threats to Hong Kong's stability and prosperity if it was determined to dismantle any quickly installed democratic institutions in or after 1997.

To avert the above threats to Hong Kong's economy and stability, the British and the Hong Kong governments took a cautious and incremental 'testing' approach. The Hong Kong government did persist with plans for indirect election into the legislature in 1985, and recommended in the same year that direct election of legislators would be feasible in 1988. There were thus expanded political opportunities for bottom-up democratization in 1984–85 (Table 1):

Table 1: Expanded Political Opportunity for Democratization following the Crisis

Political Opportunity Structure	Constraint	Opportunity
China and the UK seemingly offer prospects of regime-led, top-down democratization by the Joint Declaration and political reform	No independence of Hong Kong	Push for further democratization by mobilizing social forces by pressure groups and three quasi-parties

Seizing the apparent opportunity of an apparently 'regime-led' democratization, as many as 95 organizations (Appendix 1, pp. 47–9), ranging from three quasi-parties, through dozens of social movement organizations in educational, religious, social welfare, housing and labour sectors, to district bodies, coalesced into a pro-democracy alliance in late 1986. The alliance championed a Hong Kong-wide democratic movement to promote democratization.[11]

Table 2: Nature of Constituent Organizations of the JCPDG

Nature of Groups	%
Community organizations	58.9
Political groups	11.6
Labour organizations	7.3
Student bodies	7.3
Social services	4.3
Educational bodies	4.2
Religious bodies	4.2
Total	100

Formation of a Pro-democracy Alliance — Joint Committee On the Promotion of a Democratic Government (JCPDG)

Besides the conducive political opportunity structure, the existence of a pre-existing loose alliance and communication network via former cooperation, the sharing of common goals and the formation of a conservative business alliance were also crucial to the formation of the JCPDG.

Concerning their previous cooperation, ever since the 1970s, some key social movement organizations on the JCPDG, plus the three quasi-political parties, which together constituted the mainstays of the JCPDG, had on many occasions cooperated in campaigns concerning social issues (Table 3).

Table 3: Past Cooperation of Some Key JCPDG Members, 1973–86

Campaign	Social Movement Organizations*
1. Campaign for Chinese as an Official Language (early 1970s and 1980s)	HKPTU, HKFSU
2. Anti-corruption (1973)	HKFSU, HKCIC
3. Improve boat people's living conditions (1978–79)	HKFSU, HKSWGU, HKCIC, Society for Community Organization
4. Campaign against the rise of bus fares (1980–81)	HKPTU, FCSU, HKFSU, HKCIC, HKSWGU, HKCC
5. Against Japan's revision of its textbooks about invading China in World War II	HKPTU, FCSU, HKFSU, HKCIC, HKSWGU
6. Campaign for curbing general rises in prices of public utilities (1985)	HKPTU, FCSU, HKFSU, HKCIC, HKSWGU, HKCC, People's Council on Public Housing Policy (PCPHP)
7. Power and Privilege Ordinance (1985)	Meeting Point, HK Affairs Society (HKAS), HKPTU, FCSU, HKFSU, HKCIC, HKSWGU, HKCC
8. Shelve the construction of Daya Bay Nuclear Plant (1986)	HKPTU, FCSU, HKFSU, HKCIC, HKSWGU, PCPHP, Meeting Point, HKAS

* For full names of these social movement organizations, see Table 4.

Source: interviews by author, and documentary survey

Their past cooperation, as evident in the above table, highlighted that the groups involved shared three kinds of goals: nationalist sentiments, concern for the welfare of the lower class and emphasis on human rights.[12] These goals forged the bond and communication network among them before 1986 that enhanced their coalescence into the JCPDG in 1986.

In addition, they had also formed a prototype alliance in 1984 cooperating in a political reform. It was a predecessor of the pro-democracy alliance that emerged in 1986.

Expansion in Hong Kong's political opportunity structure since the early 1980s invited corresponding changes in the arena of cooperation among the pro-democracy social movement groups. Their mutual support transcended mere ad hoc alliances. The perceived expanded opportunity for democratization disposed some of these groups' leaders to shift their concern from social policies to political reforms. The Green Paper issued by the Hong Kong government in 1984, and the Sino-British Agreement, both seemingly held out the promise of opening up the political structure in Hong Kong.

Some social movement group leaders became the core leaders that formed the three quasi-political parties. Besides, when the Hong Kong government invited opinions on its Green Paper of 1984, various social movements and quasi-parties demanded a much faster timetable of democratization than the one suggested in the Green Paper (Table 4). Noticeably, the government suggested there should be 48 and 50 seats in the legislature in 1985 and 1988 respectively.

The demands of various pressure groups, quasi-parties and community groups for a directly elected legislature culminated in a joint conference of over 50 organizations, and subsequently, the launching of a mass assembly in September 1984. The legislature, they asserted, should be the body with the highest power in future. It was their belief that only through direct election could the ideal of 'Hong Kong people ruling Hong Kong' promised by China for the post-1997 Hong Kong be realized.

The glaring presence of the pro-democracy ad hoc joint conference, however, threatened and propelled some anti-democracy bourgeoisie into forming another alliance.

The Presence of a Reinforcing Factor

The preparatory steps towards forming a more organized pro-democracy alliance became known to some conservative business people and professionals in the Basic Law Consultative Committee (BLCC),[13] who reacted by coalescing into a group of 57 members (the Business and Professional Group, BPG). The presence of pro-democracy activists had made them apprehensive about increasing instability and welfarism if full democracy was installed. The BPG published their own conservative blueprint for democracy on 21 August 1986, suggesting that 25% of the legislature in 1997 be directly elected. The hostile stance of the BPG forced the prototype alliance, formed by the democratic activists in 1984, to become more organized. The formation of the JCPDG and the BPG thus reinforced each other in a spiral of mobilization and polarization.[14]

Table 4: Proposed Schedules of Democratization by Key Members of the JCPDG in Response to the Green Paper of 1984

Name	Suggested Democratization in 1988	Other Suggestions on Democratization
Hong Kong Christian Industrial Council (HKCIC)	Not available	Leg: 100% DR before 1997
Hong Kong Professional Teachers' Union (HKPTU)	Leg: DR to increase from 1988 to 1994; replace all appointed and functional constituencies seats; has some policy-making power	Leg: 100% DR
Hong Kong Federation of Students Union (HKFSU)	Leg: 1/3 DR in 1986 Ex: elected from Leg	Leg: at least 50% DR in 1990; at least 2/3 DR in 1993; ministerial system
Federation of Civil Service Unions (FCSU)	Leg: 12 seats by DR Ex: elected from Leg and evolve into ministerial system	Leg: 50 seats by DR in 1994; 60 seats by DR in 1997 (assuming 60 seats in total)
Hong Kong Christian Council (HKCC)	Leg: 15 seats by DR Ex: elected from Leg	Leg: 100% DR in 1997 Ex: elected from Leg
New Hong Kong Society	Leg: 12 seats by DR	in early 1990s, Leg elects Governor, and then Governor appoints senior officials
HK Social Work General Union	Leg : 10 seats by DR; evolves into highest-power body	Leg: 19 seats by DR in 1991; 38 seats by DR in 1994; 50 seats (100%) by DR in 1997 Ex: elected by public when ripe
Meeting Point	Leg: 20 seats by DR and evolves gradually	

Leg: Legislature; DR: Direct Election; Ex: Chief Executive

Source: *HKPTU News*, 22 September 1984; *Wah Kiu Yat Po*, 4, 12 September 1984, 13 August 1984, p. 2; *Wen Wei Po*, 14 July 1984, 6 August 1984; *Hong Kong Daily News*, 22 September 1984

Democratic activists' attempt to organize and to shape democratization (mid-1986)

⇓

Formation of BPG and release of their blueprint (21 August 1986)

⇓

Release of an initial platform by 19 pro-democracy BLCC members (22 August 1986)

⇓

Formation of the JCPDG (27 October 1986) and mobilization for the Ko Shan Meeting (2 November 1986)

⇓

Press conference of BPG (3 November 1986)

⇓

Debates and mobilizations with increasingly sharp-worded recriminations

---

⇓ : temporal order

Figure 1 Spirals of Mobilization and Counter-mobilization between the JCPDG and BPG

In short, the political opportunity structure alone did not directly determine the formation of the JCPDG. The pre-existing loose alliance and communication network, the sharing of common goals, the formation of a conservative business alliance, and the urgency of the situation had been intervening events of a political process triggered by the crisis and changing political opportunity structure, which later speeded up the formation of the JCPDG.

Perceived Political Opportunity Structure and Strategic Calculations of Pro-democracy Activists

Finally, concerning the formation of the JCPDG, a micro process of the strategic political calculations on the part of the pro-democracy activists was also pertinent. The overall political opportunities in late 1986 were not especially conducive to rapid and full democratization, given the incipient opposition from China and a business alliance and the pull-back of Britain. Why did they organize the JCPDG at all?

Against the backdrop of the above political environment, leaders of the JCPDG had the following perceptions of the political opportunity structure before they decided on its formation:

Table 5: Perceived Constraints/Facilitations of the Political Opportunity Structure Among JCPDG Leaders, 1985–86

Political Opportunity Structure	Constraints and Facilitations
China	China as final decision-maker over political structure • Antagonistic to relatively faster democratization and intent on controlling Hong Kong. • Only few political models will be considered and the deadline for considering them was near.
UK	• Different perceptions of Britain's sincerity and ability in democratizing Hong Kong, with most of them distrustful. • Under additional time pressure to reach an internal compromise for shaping the debate on political reforms initiated by the Hong Kong government in 1987.
57 Conservative Business People and Professionals	• Perceived as a powerful, aggressive and anti-democratic bloc intent on maintaining their own interests. • Had good access and connections with China's senior officials.
Public	• Knew little about democracy; frail support for democratic campaigns.

JCPDG's leaders answered in interviews that the stipulation in Joint Declaration concerning the elective element of the legislature in 1997, and the political reform launched by the Hong Kong government in 1984, had granted them the golden opportunity of pressuring the two governments to democratize Hong Kong. They therefore decided to get organized to launch various social mobilizations and protests, in order to expand further the political opportunities for a more rapid democratization. Thus, the will of the activists did matter. They endeavoured to shape the political opportunity structure by coalescing into an alliance, with the perceived opportunities for bottom-up democratization arising from the Joint Declaration and the Hong Kong government's reforms. After its formation, what actions did the alliance launch to fulfil its goals?

❑ Phase II — Conflicting Phase (1987): Increasing Conflicts Over the Desirability of Holding Direct Elections in 1988

The Significance of Holding Direct Elections in 1988 for Political Reform

Unlike those impoverished authoritarian states in Latin America, the opposition in civil society as led by the JCPDG could not simply mobilize public support in Hong Kong on the cleavage of inequality, in face of the general improved standard of living after 1945. Given the meagre financial resources of its constituent members and other organizations, it had to mobilize for collective actions to impose costs on anti-democracy forces.

To highlight the dynamics of and constraints on oppositional activities, the debate concerning the holding of direct elections in 1988 has been an illuminating case.

Between 1987 and early 1988, the debate on whether some seats in the legislature should be directly elected in 1988 triggered popular mobilizations both by the pro-democracy JCPDG, and the anti-democracy CCP and conservative business alliance. As CCP's appointed body would announce in 1988 the first draft of the post-1997 mini-constitution for Hong Kong, and that China repeatedly demanded Britain to converge to the draft in designing the political structures in and after 1997, the holding of the elections would be the last chance for the British government to exercise a relatively free hand.

Against this backdrop, the JCPDG worked to mobilize public support to press for direct elections in 1988 for 25% of the seats for the legislature on several grounds:

First, the imperative of 'convergence' meant that once the first draft of the Basic Law was announced in 1988, China could exercise more control over Hong Kong's future political structure. Hence, the JCPDG was highly motivated to win public support for direct elections, in order to shape the future political structure.

Second, immediately after the formation of the JCPDG in late 1986, it pronounced a proposal of having 50% of legislators directly elected by 1997. The JCPDG could smooth the democratic transition from the late 1980s to 1997 by demanding that 25% of legislators be directly elected in 1988.

Third, the JCPDG's high-profile mobilization for direct elections in 1988 could demonstrate its seriousness about the democratic model to opponents. It could prompt opponents to take the model as its real baseline.

Dynamic Contests for Public Support

To counter the JCPDG, the BPG and China needed to assail the value of greater and faster democratization. Thus, while the JCPDG acted as a 'social movement alliance' (SMI), presenting the ideology of democracy to the public and mobilizing support for democratization, the BPG and China figured as counter social movement groups (CSM),[15] presenting a counter-ideology and engaging in counter-mobilizations to prevent fast and full democratization. The roles and relationship of the five political forces during most of the period 1986–90 could be characterized as the picture in Figure 2.

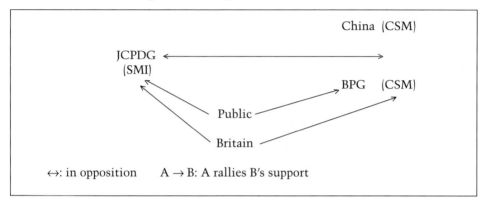

Figure 2 Mobilization and Counter-mobilization for and against Democratization

What follows is an elucidation of the strategic interactions, mobilizations and counter-mobilizations of those forces.

During most of 1987, Chinese senior officials repeatedly and openly opposed to a directly elected legislature in 1988, even on a limited scale. A justification China cited was that as the first draft of the post-1997 mini-constitution would be announced a few months after the Hong Kong government's political review, should the Hong Kong government approve direct elections in 1988 and contradict the mini-constitution, the political structure of Hong Kong would risk being dismantled by China after its resumption of sovereignty. In short, China used convergence between the Basic Law and the political review to hamstring the British Hong Kong government's leverage over democratization. The holding of direct elections in 1988, China feared, would create 'snowballing' demand for faster democratization in 1997, and render the future political structure less amenable to China's control. Consequently, pro-China labour unions, banks, secondary schools, kinship associations and women's clubs were mobilized against holding direct elections in 1988.[16]

The emergence of the BPG in Hong Kong in August 1986 marked the beginning of the internal, polarized conflicts over democratization. Some BPG members were leading tycoons or representatives of big business interests in Hong Kong; others occupied important positions in the four influential business chambers of Hong Kong.[17] Their primary interest was to keep intact Hong Kong's internationally renowned non-intervention, low-taxed economy and their predominant proportions in the two most powerful political institutions. The introduction of direct elections in 1988 might lead to greater demands for faster and more democratization well before 1997, and then dramatically expand social welfare, business profit taxes and political tensions. Hence, the local bourgeoisie tried to legitimate an elitist political system to counteract the power of the JCPDG. They pointed out that the lack of civic education, of participant culture and of good political leadership implied that direct elections in 1988 would spell adversarial politics and threats to prosperity.[18]

Given the implications of direct elections in 1988, winning public backing was crucial in order to gain the upper hand in bargaining over democratization. The most important weapon on which the pro-democracy activists could rely was the winning of public support. A successful mobilization of mass support for democracy could impose costs on the Chinese and British governments by destroying the credibility of 'one country, two systems', thwarting China's appeal to Taiwan for reunification and preventing Britain's graceful departure. The JCPDG, as suggested by the strategic choice analysis, had devised many means to increase the perceived costs of its opponents.

Modify Opponents' Perceptions of Costs by Mass Mobilizations

Exploit Political Opportunities and Promote the Agenda of Political Transition by Democratization

To raise the stakes perceived by the Chinese and British governments in resisting democratizing Hong Kong, like their counterpart in Taiwan that accused the state of reneging on promises democratization,[19] the JCPDG first of all exploited the political opportunities open to it by publicizing the substantial agenda of transition initiated by the Joint Declaration. The Joint Declaration stipulated that the post-1997 legislature should be elected and composed of local inhabitants, whereas the Chief Executive 'shall be selected by election or through consultations held locally and be appointed by the Central People's Government.'[20] Chinese senior officials in 1984 at least twice endorsed direct elections and 'democracy' in Hong Kong, and promised Hong Kong people a 'high degree of autonomy' with 'Hong Kong people ruling Hong Kong'. The Hong Kong government also stressed in its 1984 political review the possibility of direct elections in future. Thus, the JCPDG attempted to whip up public support for democratization by referring to those promises.

Appeal to Popular Fear of Communism and Persuade Public to Accept Democracy

Confronted with the prospect of communist rule, Hong Kong people were widely apprehensive. They displayed a gamut of reactions ranging from fatalism through 'wait-and-see' to emigration. Faced with vast uncertainties, Hong Kong people needed a coherent interpretative framework to inform them of what was happening and how to cope with the future.

To persuade the public to accept democracy, the JCPDG tried to assuage public fear and distrust of communist China with the notion of 'democracy'. Democracy, they contended, could reduce Chinese erosion of Hong Kong's stability, prosperity and civil liberties, and a high degree of autonomy. As direct election was integral to democracy, they called for public support for it.

In addition, the JCPDG always emphasized their cherished basic values of 'political equality', 'political competition', 'human rights'. Stress on the equal and inalienable political rights of every human being might appeal to ordinary people. The more they could appeal to the public, the better they could dispute the legitimacy of the undemocratic structures proposed by the BPG and China, thus raising the costs of authoritarian rule and encouraging hopes of realizing a credible democratic alternative.[21]

Persuasion and Dynamic Counter-attacks to Mobilize Public Support

Besides sending two delegations to lobby the British and Chinese governments,[22] the JCPDG mainly channelled energies into a large number of talks, debates and forums, which appeared in the mass media, in an effort to sway public opinion and keep the issue of political reform in the spotlight. The process was dynamic and the JCPDG seized as many chances as possible to assail their antagonists' stance while propagating their own:

Table 6: JCPDG's Counter-attacks and the Dynamic Process of Persuasion

Against 1988 DR	Pro-1988 DR (JCPDG or its member organizations)
1. 14 February 1987 China first showed open opposition to 1988 DR. It demanded that HK's political reform be decided only after the release of the BL in 1990.[23] DR in 1988 risked being dismantled later if the BL disagreed with pre-1990 DR.	14 February 1987 Time for learning democracy wasted; accuse their moulding of public opinions before HK government's opinion consultations.[24] It strengthened the 'lame duck' image of HK government and reduced HK elites' confidence in 'one country, two systems'. Similar public views on the BL and HK government's review would mean the 'convergence' of the BL and political review.[25]
2. 17 March 1987 The local conservatives contended that the middle and upper classes were	17 March 1987 Both direct and indirect elections should be practised for equal

unprepared to gain power through elections in 1988. In the past, they were guaranteed predominant power through government's appointments and consultations. Such unpreparedness would polarize conflicts among strata and injure stability and prosperity.[26] For fairness, if the HK government insisted on having the 1988 DR, the electoral college system should also be allowed.[27]

competition of different interests and long-term stability.[28] To assess public opinions, they suggested conducting HK-wide scientific surveys.

3. 17 April 1987
    Deng Xiaoping stressed that only those who 'loved HK and China' should govern HK, and general elections might not guarantee such results.[29]

27 April 1987
HK had enough socio-economic requisites for democracy; 'Love HK and China' was ambiguous. China should not set up criteria to screen out people for election. Besides, most HK people supported China's modernization, sovereignty and the Joint Declaration.[30]

4. 26 April 1987
    A senior member of the Executive Council stressed HK's political reform is not determined just by its own people's wishes. He hinted the new sovereign master of HK (China) would constrain HK's political reform and DR in 1988. It was also China that decided on the level of 'autonomy' HK could get through the BL.[31]

27 April 1987
The most senior member of the Executive Council could not determine HK's political structure[32] by yielding to China's interference.

5. 19 June 1987
    China accused the Green Paper of violating the Joint Declaration. Only necessary changes stipulated by the Joint Declaration should be made. Other changes between 1984 and 1977 should be minimum.

20 June 1987
As only a few months had elapsed between the announcement of the HK government's results of political review and the first draft of the BL, the same public opinions ensured the convergence.

DR: Direct Election

BL: Basic Law

Use of Different Symbols, Sites and Campaign Strategies for Rallying Support

Being a minority in the institutionalized power structures like the Legislative Council and the BLCC, the pro-democracy activists mainly launched their campaigns outside them. They launched exhibitions and forums and distributed pamphlets.

Table 7: Activities Launched by JCPDG to Promote Direct Elections in 1988

Date	Activities
2 November 1986	Ko Shan rally: around 1 000 participants
18–20 April 1987	Cartoon exhibitions in New World Centre (shopping mall)
28 June 1987	Printing and distribution of cartoon newspapers for democracy
4 July 1987	A political forum and distribution of pamphlets
27 September 1987	Victoria Park rally: 5 000 participants

Second, they set up their own independent survey office to gauge public opinion on the issue of direct elections in 1988. This acted as a watchdog on Hong Kong government's public consultation, and threatened it with future condemnation later if its results differed from their own.

Moreover, the JCPDG demonstrated its political muscle to make its implicit threats efficacious. It mounted a signature campaign, gathering 230 000 signatures on two Sundays in support of the '1988 direct election'. A mass rally was their last show of strength before the political review ended.

Despite the popular mobilizations of the JCPDG, popular support for pro-democracy activities, like protests, sit-ins and mass gatherings, was lacking. For instance, only about 5 000 to 8 000 people attended its most important public rally. The failure of the JCPDG to mobilize more public participation curtailed its bargaining power with both the British and the Chinese governments. Why had public support for direct elections been so limited?

Weak Public Support

In early 1986, i.e., immediately before the pro-democracy alliance was formed, shaped by the previously discussed long-term historical and institutional parameters, the public tendered generally strong, though not uncomplaining, support for the existing quasi-bureaucratic political system. They remained equivocal towards democracy and lacked ideological commitment to any political system. Such attitudes boded ill for the support needed for a quickly paced democratization.[33]

Between 1987 and early 1988, the debate on whether some seats in the legislature should be directly elected in 1988 triggered popular mobilizations by both camps. On the surface, those who supported holding direct elections in 1988 overwhelmed those who opposed it.[34] Nevertheless, the moderate public support at an attitudinal level was not matched by behaviour. China's oppositions and threats of dismantling 'overly' democratic structures in 1997 had intensified the already strong pervasive sense of political powerlessness, bred under the above-mentioned long-term factors. Sixty-three percent of respondents of a survey did in 1987 cast doubt on the usefulness of public opinions in shaping the development of Hong Kong's representative government.

Lack of knowledge also diminished public support for holding direct elections in 1988. Only 23.2% of the public regarded direct elections as a necessary condition for democracy, despite its popular appeal.[35] Generally, large-scale popular participation in the campaign for holding direct elections in 1988 was lacking. The support also appeared ambiguous among Hong Kong's middle class.

Ambivalent Middle Class Support for Democratization

Like any middle class elsewhere, Hong Kong's seemed to be more supportive than other classes of having a directly elected legislature in 1988. However, surveys conducted by 13 middle-class professional organizations revealed that the 'caring professionals' as journalists, teachers, social workers, doctors, town planners, nurses and lawyers supported direct elections more than the practical and business-oriented ones, including surveyors, engineers, accountants and computing experts.[36]

In short, the relatively larger but less than overwhelming support of the public for direct elections, the political powerlessness of the grass roots and the middle class, and the lack of knowledge of and commitment to a democratic system, all limited support for an early set-up of a partially directly-elected legislature. Nonetheless, such domestic constraints rapidly disappeared in mid-1989. Between mid-1989 and 1990, there was a surging and outpouring of support for democratic movement.

❑ Phase III — Decisional Phase (May 1989 - early 1990): Political Opportunity Structure for Sharply Rising Support for Democratic Movement Further Expanded

China in Tumult 1989: A New Crisis for Hong Kong

China's turmoil in 1989 erupted in mid-April and climaxed on 4 June, when a massacre of pro-democracy campaigners was reported. An unprecedented outpouring of support from millions of Chinese people for democratizing socialist China was relentlessly quashed by the government.

The suppression in China posed an alarming 'threat' to Hong Kong's prosperity, stability, civil liberties and lifestyle after 1997, if not even earlier. A conspicuous tumble in people's confidence in the successful implementation of 'one country, two systems' was unambiguously registered. It could be shown by contrasting three Hong Kong-wide representative sample surveys done in September 1988, late May 1989 and October 1989.

Table 8: How Confident Are You that the Basic Law Will Make Sure the 'One Country, Two Systems' Promise Will be Kept?

	September 1988	May 1989	October 1989
Confident	44%	33.6%	25%
Not confident	36%	55.1%	69%

Source: *Ming Pao Daily News* and various reports[37]

According to a longitudinal survey assessing Hong Kong people's political confidence, the index recorded an all-time low in June 1989. Another strong indicator of 'crisis' was behavioural. Quite a significant portion of the local population, particularly the middle class, sought safety outlets by trying to obtain foreign passports. In the third quarter of 1989, 43.6% of Hong Kong people hoped to emigrate, while those who did not fell short of half the population for the first time. Another representative sample survey conducted between 6 and 9 June 1989 indicated that 58% of Hong Kong people, who were extremely pessimistic if not desperate about their future, wanted a passport allowing them right of abode in another country.[38]

The average citizen, lacking expertise, capital or kin already settled abroad, had nowhere to turn to but Britain. In response, the British government repeatedly ruled out the possibility of granting the right of abode to 3.25 million British Hong Kong passport-holders.[39] Britain did not think it feasible to renounce the Joint Declaration or enter into new negotiation with China. With hopes of emigration dashed and the fate of reversion to China incontrovertible, the crisis triggered heightened demands for faster democratization in Hong Kong.

Rapidly Expanding Political Opportunity Structure — Increasing Demands for Democratizing Hong Kong After China's Chaos

Increased Public Support for Faster Democratization

By all indicators, demands for faster and greater democratization had started to 'increase rapidly' since May 1989. With two peaceful protest marches each joined by a record of over one million citizens,[40] a general demand for greater democratization was unmistakably attested.

Table 9: Rising Public Support for Greater Democratization in Hong Kong

Question	Rate
Thinking about the events in China, I agree the next draft of the Basic Law for Hong Kong should contain more provisions for democracy after 1997.	92.1%

Source: *South China Morning Post*, 25 May 1989

To be more specific, 74% of respondents wanted Hong Kong's first Chief Executive after 1997 to be directly elected by the public, rather than by the electoral college.[41] Those with higher income and level of education were more likely to be supportive of directly electing the Chief Executive.[42]

Unofficial Members of Hong Kong's Executive and Legislative Council (OMELCO) and the Hong Kong Government: Demand for Faster and Full Democracy

Events in China also prompted the Executive and Legislative councils to be more united on democratization. They sought to strengthen public confidence by subscribing to faster democratization.

After internal debates an 'OMELCO model' was agreed, stipulating that one-third, not less than half and all of the legislators be directly elected in 1991, 1995 and 2003 respectively. In addition, they demanded that the Chief Executive be directly elected by 2003. Given that over half of the legislators had opposed the introduction of direct elections in 1988, the turmoil in China had clearly prompted a U-turn among them. In response, though failing to give a firm commitment, the top Hong Kong government officials openly pledged support for the OMELCO model.[44]

The BPG Split and Its Major Wing Proposed the '4–4–2' Model

The conservative BPG was split after China's political turmoil. Its dominant wing, led by Lo Hon Shui, demanded accelerated democratization and proffered a new '4–4–2' model in response to Hong Kong's crisis. They proferred that 40% and 60% of seats in the legislature be directly elected in 1997 and 2001 respectively. In 2005, the Special Administrative Region would decide if the legislature should be fully directly elected. It was suggested that the Chief Executive be directly elected in 2005. The leaders of this majority wing of the BPG had at least two grounds for their decision. First, their concessions were made in order to build up a badly needed consensus with other local political forces to weather the crisis, and save Hong Kong's prosperity and stability.[45] In addition, Hong Kong people had raised their demand for democracy since the chaos in China. Some leading members of the BPG commended that pro-democracy activists were able to behave responsibly when leading the two mass rallies and other demonstrations in May 1989.[46]

China: Warned About Hong Kong's Subversion and Thwarted Hong Kong's Democratization

Soon after the June 4 massacre, the CCP regained its grip over China and began verbal attacks on Hong Kong.[47] For the CCP, the danger of Hong Kong's pro-democracy movement 'subverting' China had become immensely larger, given the large overlap in leadership between the JCPDG and the Alliance in Support of the Patriotic Democracy Movement (ASPDM), the body that organized protests against China's tough suppression.[48]

China refused to consider the OMELCO model in the drafting of the Basic Law and denigrated it as the brainchild of an unrepresentative colonial institution.[49] Above all, the Chinese leaders actively and openly threw their weight behind a very conservative political blueprint called the Bicameral Model.

Thus the unexpected political chaos in China had plunged Hong Kong people's confidence in their future to a critically low level. The scope of support for expediting democratization became unprecedentedly large. Nevertheless, the Chinese government made very clear its rejection of faster democratization in Hong Kong. Against this new backdrop, the JCPDG decided to replace its first constitutional model with a new one.

Perceived Political Opportunity Structure and Strategic Choices of the JCPDG: Promulgation of Two New Constitutional Blueprints

Choice of a Second Constitutional Platform (New 190) in July 1989 for Faster Democratization

In July 1989, the JCPDG designed a new constitutional blueprint demanding a very rapid democratization called the 'new 190'. It set out that the legislature and Chief Executive be fully directly elected in as early as 1995 (see Table 10).

Table 10: Timing and Contents of the Three Constitutional Blueprints Suggested by the JCPDG — Perceived Political Opportunity Structure and Calculations

Year	1st: 'Old 190' (Nov. 1986)	2nd: 'New 190' (July 1989)	3rd: '4–4–2' (Sept. 1989)
1991		Leg: 50% DR	
1995		Leg: 100% DR Ex: directly elected	
1997	Leg: 50% DR Ex: directly elected		Leg: 40% DR, 40% FC, 20% EC, Ex: elected by Election Com.
2001			Leg: 60% DR, 40% FC Ex: elected by Election Com.
2005			Ex: directly elected

Leg: Legislative Council
DR: Direct Election
Ex: Chief Executive
FC: Functional Constituencies
EC: Electoral College
Election Com: Election Committee

The JCPDG favoured much faster democratization, chiefly because they capitalized on the surging societal demands; that could impose more costs on China and thus heighten its own bargaining power. In face of the CCP's intransigence, most JCPDG leading members were not optimistic of their new constitutional blueprint. However, many of them feared that without coining such a progressive blueprint as 'new 190', the JCPDG would see its leading role in championing the democratic movement vitiated. In addition, while the Basic Law that would dictate the schedule of post-1997 democratization would not be announced till only April 1990, the JCPDG expected in July that the implicit bargaining over democratization would drag on for quite some time. Hence, many JCPDG's leaders endeavoured to bid a higher price, so that they could seek compromise with other local forces later, before the promulgation of the Basic Law.

Nevertheless, in face of the CCP's mounting attacks, the JCPDG eventually entered into explicit bargaining with the organized business interests and reached a compromise model ('4–4–2') in September. Of the three constitutional models endorsed by the JCPDG, the last one, i.e., the '4–4–2' model, aroused most internal controversy. It should be noted that the '4–4–2' model stipulated that only 40% of the seats in the 1997 legislature be directly elected. Why did the JCPDG abandon their two earlier faster-paced blueprints and make a genuine compromise?

As the consultation period for the last version of the Basic Law drew to an end in late 1989, the JCPDG could maintain 'a tough reputation' by holding fast to their radical and new blueprint only at the expense of reaching a compromise with domestic forces. It could then weaken pressure on China. Seeing the 'support' from average people alone as too weak a force to compel China to give way, the JCPDG was motivated to ally itself with the organized bourgeoisie to increase its own power over the final schedule of democratization, before the consultative period of the final draft of the Basic Law ended in October 1989.

Nevertheless, given JCPDG's need to coalesce with other political forces, why did it compromise with the BPG on the '4–4–2' model and not with the 'OMELCO model' or others?

Most leaders of the JCPDG believed that as China had flatly dismissed many times the OMELCO model as the brainchild of the British, there was no prospect for it to be accepted by China. They consented to the '4–4–2' model partly in a bid to build a possibly long-term cooperative relationship with the business sector and to avoid political isolation.

What were the effects of these strategic choices on the final schedule of democratization when the Basic Law was decided on in April 1990?

Effects on Britain's and China's Calculations and the Basic Law

After the Tiananmen Square Incident, well aware of the confidence crisis, the British government pushed for faster democratization to meet the sharply rising aspirations of the Hong Kong community. It demanded 33.3% and 40% of total seats, i.e., 20 and 24 out of 60, in the legislature be directly elected in 1991 and 1995 respectively.[50] The British Foreign Secretary, Douglas Hurd, stressed that the demand had been based on the aspirations of Hong Kong's business community and moderate people. He was clearly pressing China to accept a revised '4–4–2' model that had won the support of the JCPDG, Hong Kong's public and the major wing of the BPG.

Faced with the potentially catastrophic, massive emigration of professionals and the persistent popular upsurge for faster democratization, China was hard pressed to placate Hong Kong with at least a little faster democratization, so as to contain damage to Hong Kong's prosperity, to China's modernization as well as reunification with Taiwan. The British support for a smooth transition and alleviation of the crisis was also badly needed during that critical juncture. Consequently, the Chinese government suggested it would concede Britain to dramatically increase the number of directly elected seats in the legislature from 10 to 18 in 1991. It yielded to public demand by permitting a steady progression towards full democracy after 1997. It also allowed the possibility of full democracy in 2007, four years ahead of what had been suggested in the earlier draft of the Basic Law. Thus, China had probably responded to pressure from the implicit alliance of the British government, the JCPDG, the BPG and the public, by slightly increasing the pace of democratization.

The above-mentioned limited concessions made by China between late 1989 and early 1990 showed that while China's strong opposition had been the most important factor in explaining the slow pace of the actual and scheduled democratization between 1986 and 2007, it was not a sufficient explanation. Given that Hong Kong people and pro-democracy forces had posed a threat to the CCP in 1989, and that China still made limited concessions in early 1990, a more early-formed, sustained and broad-based alliance of the bourgeoisie, middle class and average public and other political forces could have forced China to concede at least some more.[51]

❑ Phase IV – Declining Phase (1990–94): Decline of Democratic Movement in Civil Society and Its Replacement by Political Parties

Crisis of Tiananmen Square Incident and Formation of Political Parties

With the outpouring of public support for democracy and the holding of direct elections in 1991, two members of the JCPDG, i.e., Meeting Point (MP) and Hong Kong Association for Democracy and People's Livelihood (HKADPL), transformed themselves from political groups into political parties in early 1990s. Another political group, the United Democrats of Hong Kong (UDHK), a new one amassing the greatest number of leaders and activists of over 600 members from the pro-democracy camp from both within and without the JCPDG, was also formed in 1990. Their formation and the dissolution of the JCPDG in 1991 set a new stage for the democratic movement in civil society, i.e., its decline.

After the introduction of direct elections in 1991 and the formation of the three pro-democracy parties, the pro-democracy organizations in civil society precipitously declined in number of members, resources and vibrancy. That this followed the heels of Britain's renewed attempt to democratize Hong Kong since 1992, made the phenomenon particularly intriguing.

Expanded Political Opportunity for Building Representative Institutions and Decline in Civil Society

Popular reactions to the Tiananmen Square Incident strengthened Britain's determination to widen Hong Kong's electoral base in due course after the event, to honour their obligation to millions of Hong Kong people and gracefully retreat from the colony.[52] The coming of Chris Patten in late 1992 as Hong Kong's governor and his unveiling of a package of democratic reform in October 1992 marked a new phase of Hong Kong's democratic transition. He stood for the last-ditch top-down attempt of the British government to democratize Hong Kong before its imminent departure in 1997. The reform endeavoured to boost Hong Kong's democratization without violating the future mini-constitution dictated by China by exploiting the grey area that the constitution embodied.

From the CCP's vantage point, the unanticipated British endeavour to introduce top-down democratic reform might forebode one of many plots in the West to subvert its political system incrementally. Besides, any significant expansion of electoral base would render Hong Kong less controllable after 1997, especially so in the wake of the maiden direct elections of legislators in 1991. The sweeping electoral victory of the three pro-democracy parties in the maiden direct elections of 1991, and the renewed British efforts at democratization in 1992, had afforded a new round of expanding political opportunity for pro-democracy opposition since late 1992. Yet, surprisingly, the two new alliances of local pro-democracy political opposition between 1992 and 1994, i.e., the JAPOD (Joint Association of People's Organizations) and FD (Full Democracy in 1995), composed of mainly urban social movement groups in civil society, had been far weaker than the JCPDG in the 1980s. The JAPOD and FD formed a narrower base of only about 50-plus movement organizations altogether, less than the 90-strong-member organization alliance of the JCPDG formed in 1986.

The JAPOD was constituted in late 1992, soon after the Governor of Hong Kong announced his package of political reform. It consisted of the HKPTU, CIC, UDHK and 30 more other small movement bodies. It demanded half of the seats in the legislature be directly elected in 1995 and 1997 and openly pledged its support behind the Governor's package as its baseline. Concerning the FD, it was formed in the middle of 1993, headed by an outspoken legislator and critic of the Chinese government, Ms Emily Lau. Dissatisfied with the relatively 'conservative' stance of the three political parties and the JAPOD, the FD, consisting of 20-plus more 'progressive' movement bodies including the HKFSU, demanded a more radical blueprint of having a fully directly-elected legislature installed in 1995.

The strength of the two alliances relative to that of the JCPDG was far more feeble, indicated by the number of their constituent organizations, the maximum number of activists they could mobilize and the highest level of political mobilization they had ever achieved:

Table 11: Decline in Political Opposition of Civil Society, 1992–94

	JCPDG (1985–91)	JAPOD (1992–94)	FD (1992–94)
No. of constituent organizations	95	33	fewer than 20
No. of activists	few hundreds	few dozens	few dozens
No. of participants during the biggest political mobilization	5 000	400	400

Source: Interviews by author and minutes of those bodies

The formation of political parties, and the political divisions between civil society and parties had been the main causes for the ebb in the democratic movement of civil society.

Tension Between Democratic Movement in Civil Society and Political Parties

Why had the formation of parties contributed to a decline in the oppositional forces of civil society? In Hong Kong, where a strong state and a politically weak civil society had been in long existence, popular leaders of social movement organizations or pro-democracy forces had been scarce. Most of those leaders and activists of the JCPDG had joined the UDHK.[53] Consequently, excepting one or two figures of FD, the informal opposition of FD and JAPOD had been short of enough well-known political activists, not to mention experienced ones. The dearth of leadership and the accompanying paucity of mobilization skills and networks had severely discouraged media reports and consequently, depressed their political mobilizations.

In addition, like Mexico and Spain,[54] the formation of parties, especially the relatively dominant one of UDHK, had alerted some cautious activists in the informal alliances of JAPOD and FD to take precaution against the domination of parties over them. As they were charged with a mission to hold both government and parties publicly accountable, they took collective steps to prevent the leaders of parties from controlling alliances.[55]

Lastly, the stances of the two alliances (JAPOD and FD) were obviously more radical than the parties' (Figure 3). Political parties have the imperative to secure their institutionalized role and influences in the state structure. They thus become more pragmatic, far-sighted, accommodating and instrumental in their political platforms *vis-à-vis* informal and loose social movement alliances.

HKADPL ——— MP ——— UDHK ——— JAPOD ——— FD
conservative   radical

Figure 3   Relative Stance of Different Groups on Political Reform

Hence, the institutionalization of parties that contributed to the moderation of political parties had set them further apart from the informal political opposition and compounded the difficulty of unity.

Constraints on Democratic Movement between 1992 and 1994

In the extended row over the Governor's political reform, major battles had been fought between Britain and China in a protracted series of negotiations and propaganda wars since 1992. The public in Hong Kong was sidelined, pervaded by a paralyzing sense of impotence to exert any substantive effect on the final outcome. Surveys conducted in this period also testified that public support for Patten was subdued by China's recurrent threats of demolishing the political structure of Hong Kong in 1997 if reform would be implemented, even though the relative majority of the public stood for the reform.[56] The middle class in Hong Kong who expectedly would loathe to see a destabilizing Hong Kong and a bruised economy, faced with incessant vocal threats, did not tender support for the reform any more than other groups.[57] Faced with the lukewarm and wavering backing from the average public and middle class, the two already frail alliances in civil society, i.e., JAPOD and FD, had to abandon mass mobilizations in their fight for the cause. Instead, the former staged a number of street dramas and drew up caricatures to mock at the antagonists to the reform. The latter held regular forums in various districts to arouse community awareness of and media attention to their campaigns. However, the small-scaled public participation in those events had robbed them of the chances of being given adequate spotlights in media reports, which highlighted the general decline in democratic movement of civil society.[58]

❏ Conclusion: Democratic Transition and the Contribution of the Pro-democracy Movement in Hong Kong

In the last few sections, the vicissitudes of the local democratic movement have been elaborated. The developmental path of the movement was partly a result of the changing political opportunity structure, and partly of the participants' own creative and pro-active strategic choices.

Hong Kong's pattern of democratic transition was very special. As it was a British colony scheduled to be decolonized not by becoming independent, but by reversion to another regime, its democratic transition was largely dependent on two external regimes. In addition, as the departing regime attempted to democratize Hong Kong without support from the incoming regime, the democratic transition was marked by inter-regime conflicts, not found in conventional typologies of democratic transition.[59] Yet, during most of the 1980s, since the British climb-down in the face of Chinese threats in 1987, the major source of pressure for democratization had been the internal force of the pro-democracy alliance. The democratic transition in Hong Kong was a 'limited democratization of a dependent polity during decolonization.'

The Hong Kong pro-democracy movement was faced with strong opposition from China and the organized local bourgeoisie, while it enjoyed only limited public support before mid-1989 from a politically weak and divided civil society. Judging from the wide gap between its first constitutional blueprint and the finalized Basic Law, the achievement of the Hong Kong pro-democracy movement was limited.

However, the persistent mobilization of the JCPDG in support of democracy kept the issue of democratization alive among the public in 1984–90. It thus played an important part in enhancing the political consciousness of the public during the critical years of Hong Kong's political transition.[60]

❑ Appendix 1: Members of the JCPDG

Total number: 95 in November 1986

Political Groups (11)

Association for Democracy and People's Livelihood
Association for Democracy and Justice
China-Hong Kong Society
Christian Communist Critics
Hong Kong Affairs Society
Hong Kong Policy Viewers
Hong Kong for the Advance of Justice
Meeting Point
New Hong Kong Society
Pei Shum Society
Sam Fong Society

Educational Bodies (4)

Education Action Group
Hong Kong Association of Professional Teachers
Hong Kong Education Research Group
Technical Institute Teachers' Association

Unions and Labour Organizations (7)

Association of Government Land and Engineering Surveying Officers
Association for Accident Victims
Federation of Civil Service Unions
Government Construction Technology and Survey
Government Cookers' Association
Government Surveyor Association
Hong Kong Christian Industrial Committee

Religious Bodies (4)

Hong Kong Christian Sentinels
Kowloon West Community Church
Kwun Tong Community Church
Public Policy Committee, Hong Kong Christian Council

Students Bodies (7)

Current Affairs Committee, Students Union, CUHK
Current Affairs Committee, Students Union, HKP
Current Affairs Committee, Students' Union, HKU
Hong Kong Federation of Students
Hong Kong Students Christian Movement
Social Services Group, Student Union, She Yan College
Students Union, HKBC

Social Services and Social Workers' Unions (6)

Hong Kong Social Workers General Union
Kwun Tong Methodist Community Centre
Methodist Epworth Village Community Centre
On Wing Social Services Centre
Salvation Army Employees' Association
Workers Association, Hong Kong Federation of Youth Groups

Community Organizations (56)

Association for Better Living in Butterfly Bay
Cha Kwoa Lane THA Residents' Association
Choi Hung Estate Residents' Association
Concern Group for Development of Southern District
DB* Member's Office, Chan Chi Keung
DB Member's Office, Chan Yuen Sum
DB Member's Office, Cheng Kam Wah
DB Member's Office, Cheung Ka Man
DB Member's Office, Choi Cheung Yuet Lan
DB Member's Office, Choi Wai Sek
DB Member's Office, Hung Wing Tat
DB Member's Office, Lai Kwok Hung
DB Member's Office, Lee Chi Fai
DB Member's Office, Lee Wah Ming
DB Member's Office, Lee Yuk Wah
DB Member's Office, Liu Shing Lei
DB Member's office, Luk King Shing
DB Member's Office, Luk Shun Tim
DB Member's Office, Mok Ying Fan
DB Member's Office, Ng Kin Sang
DB Member's Office, Ng Wai Jo

DB Member's Office, Shin Chung Kai
DB Member's Office, Tang Sun Wah
DB Member's Office, Tse Man Kai
DB Member's Office, Tsui Kim Ling
DB Member's Office, Wong Chi Kwan
DB Member's Office, Wong Chung Chuen
DB Member's Office, Wong Yiu Chung
DB Member's Office, Yeung Mei Kwong
DB Member's Office, Yin Tin Sang
DB Members' Office, Chan Mo Pau and Yeung Shuk Chuen
DB Members' Office, Chu Wai Bun and Ng Ming Yan
Hong Kong Society of Community Organization
Joint Committee of Community Organization Concerning Basic Law
Kowloon City Development Council
Lai King Estate Residents Association
People's Council of Public Housing Policy
RC* Members' Office, Tsang Kwong Yuen
RC Members' Office, Wong Man Tai
RC, DB Member's Office, Chan Wai Yi
RC, DB Members' Office, Lai Kam Cheung and Lee Ho Fai
RC, DB Members' Office, Lai On kwok and Lee Wing Tat
Research Centre on the Development of Central and Western District
Shamshuipo Development and Service Centre
Shamshuipo People's Livelihood Concern Group
Shatin Concern Group
Society for the Rights of Butterfly Bay's Residents
Tsing Yi Concern Group
Tuen Mun People's Livelihood Concern Association
Tuen Mun Tsuen Wai Voluntary Society
UC* Member's Office, Fok Pui Yee
UC Member's Office, Lam Chak Pil
UC Member's Office, Lee Chik Yuet
UC Member's Office, Tong Kam Bill
UC, DB Members' Office, K.K. Fung, K.T. Leung, K.K. Tam
Yaumatei Community Research Group

* DB: District Board
  RC: Regional Council
  UC: Urban Council

Notes

1. Definitions of democracy abound. Dahl's is the most popular version, it can be crystallized into political opposition, political participation in selecting leaders and policies via elections and enjoyment of basic civil and political liberties. Democratization means the process of building up democracy. See O'Donnell, Schmitter and Whitehead, *Transitions from authoritarian rule: prospects for democracy*. In Hong Kong, it refers to the pace and extent of having the Chief Executive and seats in the legislature directly elected. For Robert Dahl's definition, see *Polyarchy: participation and opposition*, p. 3.

2. Diamond, 'Global economic transformation and less developed countries', pp. 31–70.

3. For recent works on democratic transitions in Asia, see Morley, *Driven by growth: political change in the Asian-Pacific region*, Scalapino, 'Democratizing dragons: South Korea and Taiwan', and Robinson, *Democracy and development in East Asia*.

4. For a diverse range of factors causing democratization, see Huntington, *The third wave: democratization in the late twentieth century*, pp. 37–8.

5. See White, 'Civil society, democratization and development: clearing the analytical ground', Neher, *Southeast Asia in the new international era*, Stepan, 'On the tasks of a democratic opposition', and Rueschemeyer, Stephens and Stephens, *Capitalist development and democracy*.

6. 'Civil society' here refers to the 'realm of organised social life that is voluntary, self-generating, (largely) self-supporting, autonomous from the state and bound by a legal order or set of shared values...it involved citizens acting collectively in a public sphere to express their interests, passion..., make demands on the state and hold state officials accountable. Civil society differs from political society, which consists of political parties, in an important sense that the former does not intend to win the formal power or office in the state. See Diamond, 'Toward democratic consolidation'.

7. Cheng, *Hong Kong: in search of a future*.

8. Ibid., pp. 14–5.

9. See the valuable research on Sino-British talks by Cottrell, *The end of Hong Kong*. See also Thatcher, *Thatcher's memories, the Downing Street years*.

10. According to recent memories of the most senior former China's representative stationed in Hong Kong, those worries had been harboured by Deng Xiaoping and become the cornerstone for drafting the post-1997 mini-constitution of Hong Kong. See Xu, *Memories of Hong Kong*.

11. The three quasi-political parties — the Meeting Point, Hong Kong Affairs Society, as well as Hong Kong Association for Democracy and People's Livelihood — were all established in the early 1980s in the midst of the talks over returning Hong Kong to China.

12. The major beneficiaries of the third, fourth and sixth issues in the table were the lower class. Such issues registered the pressure groups' concerns for the welfare of that particular target group of people. The seventh one, concerned the pressure groups' perceived indignation at the infringement of human rights following the expanded power and privileges of the legislature. The eighth issue was unique in two ways: as most of the Hong Kong people opposed China's building a nuclear plant in Daya Bay, very close to Hong Kong, the pressure groups and quasi-parties

were fighting for the welfare of all classes. It also marked the first head-on conflict between Hong Kong's liberal pressure groups and quasi-parties with China.

13. Cheung et al., *No change for fifty years? The wrestle among China, Britain and Hong Kong for the Basic Law.*

14. Spirals of mobilization, counter-mobilization and rising polarization have been discussed in the literature of social movements. Zald and Useem, 'Movement and countermovement interaction: mobilization, tactics and state involvement'.

15. Ibid., pp. 247–88.

16. *South China Morning Post,* 7, 16 September 1987.

17. For instance, five members of the BPG were directors and/or general managers of six companies, which were among the top ten in terms of their total share values in Hong Kong between 1984 and 1986.

18. For the view of members of the BPG, see *Ta Kung Pao,* 28 April 1987, 30 May 1987; *South China Morning Post,* 6 November 1986. On 23 June 1987, they released a new blueprint which stated that in 1992, 25% of the legislature should be directly elected (*Hong Kong Economic Journal,* 24 June 1987).

19. See Cheng, 'Democratizing the quasi-Leninist regime in Taiwan', p. 481.

20. *A draft agreement between the government of the United Kingdom of Great Britain and Northern Ireland and the government of the People's Republic of China on the future of Hong Kong,* pp. 14–5.

21. Stepan, 'On the tasks of a democratic opposition', pp. 41–9.

22. *Ming Pao Daily News,* 27 November 1987.

23. *South China Morning Post,* 14 February 1987; *Wah Kiu Yat Po,* 15 February 1987.

24. *South China Morning Post* and *Hong Kong Daily News,* 14 February 1987.

25. Lee Shun Wai, *Ming Pao Daily News,* 17 March 1987.

26. Tsui Si Hung, ibid.

27. *Ming Pao Daily News,* 3 April 1987.

28. Ibid.

29. Deng Xiaoping, *South China Morning Post,* 17 April 1987.

30. Yeung Sum, *Hong Kong Daily News,* 27 April 1987.

31. *Oriental Daily News,* 24 April 1987; *Ta Kung Pao,* 2 May 1987.

32. *Oriental Daily News,* 27 April 1987.

33. The public's ambivalence towards democracy was underscored by the agreement on the statement that 'although the political system of Hong Kong is not perfect, it is the best we can have under existing circumstances'. The lack of pervasive commitment to democracy was shown by less than half of the respondents agreeing that elected political leaders could outperform the incumbent Hong Kong government. Lastly, 61% of the public endorsed that 'whichever kind of government is immaterial, provided a minimum standard of living can be safeguarded for myself', indicating a lack of any commitment to a specific type of political system. Lau and Kuan, *The ethos of the Hong Kong Chinese,* p. 74.

34. A longitudinal survey was conducted at four time-points during the heated debates of 1987. General endorsement of direct elections in 1988 stood at 54%, 54%, 49% and 46%, more than double those who disagreed with direct elections. See Public Opinion Surveys on Green Paper: The 1987 Review of Developments in Representative Government Survey 4, SRH.

35. Lau and Kuan, *The ethos of the Hong Kong Chinese,* p. 75.

36. Sing, *The democracy movement in Hong Kong 1986–1990.*

37. See *Ming Pao Daily News,* 29 September 1988, for the 1988 survey. For the other

two, refer to the survey reports conducted by Inrasia Pacific Ltd. H-03 May 1989; OP 19, 29 October 1988).

38. See *South China Morning Post*, 19 June 1989.

39. See *Ming Pao Daily News*, 6 July 1989; *Hong Kong Economic Journal*, 15 June 1989.

40. See *South China Morning Post*, 21 May 1989 and 28 May 1989.

41. Survey report done by Inrasia Pacific Ltd. (OP 6a, August 1989).

42. Respondents in the highest income category, i.e., those with $15 000 or above, favoured universal suffrage for electing the first Chief Executive in 1997, which was the highest percentage among all income groups. Of respondents with primary, secondary and tertiary education, 72%, 77% and 70% respectively agreed on using universal suffrage to select the Chief Executive in 1997. The results came from a representative sample of 619 persons interviewed by telephone by Inrasia Pacific Limited. See the Poll Release for publication, August 1989.

43. Even the pro-China Hong Kong Federation of Trade Unions urged faster democratization than the draft Basic Law suggested. On 5 July 1989, it proposed that 40% of the seats in the legislature be directly elected in 1997.

44. See *South China Morning Post*, 16 November 1989, for the interview with the Chief Secretary of Hong Kong.

45. See *Ming Pao Daily News*, 13 October 1989, for an interview with a member of the BPG, Mr Chan Wing-kee. See Fung, *Approaching 1997*.

46. The minority wing of the BPG, led by Tak Shing Lo, formed a new organization called the New Hong Kong Alliance. It proposed a conservative political structure called the Bicameral Model, in which only 25% of legislators would be directly elected before 2005 (Appendix 5). Each chamber in the bicameral structure would have the veto power *vis-à-vis* the other. The Chief Executive would not be directly elected before 2005.

47. For the second time in three days, China condemned Hong Kong people for supporting the democracy movement in China and branded them as 'counter-revolutionaries' (*South China Morning Post*, 16 June 1989). A few days later, a senior Chinese official warned against Hong Kong people interfering with China's political institutions (*Hong Kong Economic Journal*, 22 June 1989). On 11 July, the General Secretary of the Chinese Communist Party, Mr Jiang Zemin, said that Hong Kong people should not transplant capitalism and democracy into China (*South China Morning Post*, 12 July 1989).

48. Among 22 of ASPDM's Executive Committee members, no less than 13 belonged to the JCPDG (document of ASPDM).

49. *South China Morning Post*, 7 September 1989.

50. These were shown in letters revealed in late 1992 simultaneously by the two governments, in the midst of the argument between them over Hong Kong's democratization (source: Hong Kong Government Office, London).

51. Side by side with those concessions, China also tightened some controlling measures over Hong Kong in the final draft of the Basic Law: final right of interpreting the Basic Law rested with the National People's Congress of China and no more than 20% of legislators shall be foreign nationals.

52. In her memories, Margaret Thatcher mentioned the British government's resolve to democratize Hong Kong even more after the Tiananmen Square Incident, though not immediately in 1989 to avoid provoking China (*Sunday Morning Post* Magazine, 17 October 1993). Her successor, John Major, had pledged a moral duty to the Hong

Kong people on the part of the British government during his visit to Hong Kong. The growing interference of China into Hong Kong after 1989, the endurance of the stalemate over Hong Kong's new airport project despite his flying to Beijing and the proven widening popular support for greater democracy after 1989, had all enhanced the British resolve to further democratize Hong Kong.

53. Martin Lee was of such an example. He had been both an influential leader of the JCPDG and the chairperson of the UDHK.

54. Foweraker, 'Popular political organization and democratization: a comparison of Spain and Mexico', p. 227.

55. They asked for 20 seats to be directly elected in 1995, the same number set down in the Basic Law for 1997 and the expansion of electorate base in both the election committee and functional constituencies.

56. Chung, 'Public opinion'.

57. See ibid. and Sing, *Survey report on the public towards Chris Patten's reform.* Tests of associations were conducted from two data-sets. The first was generated from Sing's survey conducted in June 1994 and the second from Chung's surveys done between 1992 and 1994. No positive association was found between class and attitudinal support for Patten's reform.

58. Such data of their activities were based upon the minutes of the two alliances gathered by the author.

59. For example, Share's typology of democratic transition assumes the presence of only one regime. Similarly, inter-regime conflicts are not the main type of democratic transition in the typology of O'Donnell's work. See Share, 'Transitions to democracy and transition through transaction', and O'Donnell, Schmitter and Whitehead, *Transitions from authoritarian rule: prospects for democracy.*

60. Lau et al., *Indicators of social development: Hong Kong 1988.* A total of 37.9% of respondents in a representative sample survey conducted in 1988 expressed an increase in their political interests, whereas only 8.2% indicated a decrease, compared with three years earlier. The younger and more educated ones were more likely to report an increase in political interest.

The Pro-Chinese Democracy Movement in Hong Kong

Pik Wan Wong

❏ Introduction

The 1989 pro-democracy movement in China triggered worldwide pro-Chinese democracy movements, in Hong Kong and in many other cities throughout the world.[1] The strong ethnic, cultural, economic and political ties between Hong Kong and China made the pro-Chinese democracy movement (PCDM) in Hong Kong the largest such movement in all the overseas Chinese communities in the world.[2] In addition, the number of participants in Hong Kong's PCDM in mid-1989 was also the largest among all social movements in the territory during its entire history. Above all, the movement had a significant impact on political culture, party development and democratization in Hong Kong. Given the enormous political significance of the PCDM, especially in 1989, the development of the movement in Hong Kong is worth studying.

Though it was reported that over one million Hong Kong people, one-sixth of the Hong Kong population, participated in the actions of the PCDM in mid-1989; between 1976 and early 1989, only a handful of university students and radical socialist groups supported the cause. The local movement also saw a sharp decline in participation in July 1989, only one month after the explosive upsurge of popular support for the movement. Why did the movement attract such lukewarm support between 1976 and early 1989? Why was there an explosion of popular support for it in mid-1989? And finally, what explains the dramatic downfall in participation shortly after the unprecedented upsurge in

July 1989? To answer these questions, this chapter seeks to explain the emergence and decline of the PCDM focusing on the period 1976–95.

Contrary to recent literature on social movements that stresses the importance of domestic factors in explaining the emergence of social movements,[3] I argue that an external factor — the rise of a massive pro-democracy movement in China — was the major catalyst for the development of the Hong Kong PCDM. Hence, this chapter contends that the interaction between external and domestic factors explains the ebb and flow of the PCDM in Hong Kong.

To account for the evolution of the PCDM, this chapter adopts a macro-micro synthetic approach to the analysis of the development of the social movement. The framework comprises three levels of analysis:

1. a macro political analysis which emphasizes broad societal conditions such as external events and domestic political conditions;
2. an organizational-level analysis which focuses on the perceptions, strategic calculations and national sentiments of various pro-democracy groups; and
3. a micro level of analysis which stresses the identity, perceptions and emotions of the Hong Kong people.

In view of the significance of external factors in the evolution of the PCDM in Hong Kong, the chapter will first review pro-democracy movements on the Mainland since 1976 to provide a background for subsequent analysis. Next, I shall analyse in three phases the emergence and development of the PCDM in Hong Kong since 1976. Lastly, the chapter will conclude with the theoretical implications of the PCDM, as well as an assessment of the achievements and limitations of the movement.

❑ An Historical Overview of the Pro-democracy Movement in China

April Fifth Tiananmen Incident and the Democracy Wall Movement (1976–81)

Several pro-democracy movements have taken place since the foundation of the People's Republic of China (PRC) in 1949. Early pro-democracy activities include the Hundred Flowers Movement (1956–57) and the posting of the *Liyizhe dazibao*[4] on a wall in Guangzhou in November 1973. The first Tiananmen incident took place on 5 April 1976. In memory of the recently deceased premier Zhou Enlai, students and tens of thousands of Beijing citizens turned out at Tiananmen Square in Beijing in late March 1976. Bearing thousands of wreaths, memorial poems and posters, they staged a public mourning ceremony and held demonstrations in the square. In their speeches and poems, the demonstrators criticized Chairman Mao Zedong and the Gang of Four (*sirenbang*).[5] On the morning of 5 April, when the demonstrators found that all their wreaths and poems had been removed from the square, a major confrontation between demonstrators and police took place. Similar protests also took place in Nanjing, Shanghai, Wuhan, Hangzhou and Kunming, marking the first popular protest against the Gang of Four and the repressive post-1949 regime. The CCP labelled the April Fifth Movement a 'counter-revolutionary movement'. The CCP suppressed all demonstrations, arrested thousands of demonstrators and dismissed Deng Xiaoping from all his party and government posts.[6]

By December 1978, two years after the death of Chairman Mao on 9 September 1976 and the arrest of the Gang of Four, Deng Xiaoping was rehabilitated and the CCP formally announced a 'reversal of the verdict' on the April Fifth Tiananmen Incident. Socialist democracy was written into the 1978 state constitution. As a reaction to the open policy of the CCP initiated by its vice-chairman and deputy premier, Deng Xiaoping, another pro-democracy movement took place. It took the form of putting up 'big-character posters' (*dazibao*) on the Democracy Wall (*minzuqiang*) at Xidan, close to Tiananmen Square in downtown Beijing. Others organized an open democracy forum (*minzu luntan*) in Beijing. At first, the pro-democracy movement gained the blessing of Deng Xiaoping and flourished for one year. Many pro-democracy journals (*minkan*), such as 'Exploration' (*Tansuo*), 'Beijing Spring' (*Beijing zhi chun*), 'Enlightenment' (*Qimeng*) and 'April Fifth Forum' (*Siwu luntan*), as well as a number of mimeographed periodicals sprang up in cities around the country. The demand for democracy was best expressed by a young electrician who worked in the Beijing Zoo, Wei Jingsheng. In a famous poster, Wei called for a 'Fifth Modernization', saying that without democracy the other four[7] would be impossible and inadequate. Nevertheless, the burgeoning Democracy Wall movement[8] came to an end in April 1981, when Deng had the wall moved to a relatively inaccessible location and arrested Wei Jingsheng and numerous pro-democracy activists.

Students' Pro-democracy Protests in 1986

The issue of political reform was raised again in 1986. On 5 December 1986, more than 2 000 students from the Chinese University of Science and Technology in Hefei, Anhui, took to the streets to protest against their exclusion from the process of electing the head of their student union, as well as the undemocratic nature of the election of the provincial People's Congress. Students in more than a dozen cities *(shi)*, including Shanghai and Nanjing, followed suit. The pro-democracy student protests lasted for one month and were eventually suppressed by the Chinese government. Partly as a result of these protests, the liberal reform leader and party general secretary, Hu Yaobang, was forced to step down. At the same time, the CCP also launched a campaign against 'bourgeois liberalization' and prohibited public discussion of political reform.[9]

The 1989 Chinese Democracy Movement and the June 4 Incident

On 6 January 1989, the political dissident and astrophysicist Fang Lizhi wrote a letter to Deng Xiaoping, asking for the release of Wei Jingsheng[10] and other political dissidents. Thirty-three Chinese intellectuals signed the letter and demanded democratic reforms and improvement in the human rights situation in China.[11] The intellectuals' appeal, however, received no response from the government. On 16 April, a student-led pro-democracy movement erupted in Beijing and lasted for 56 days. The students first demanded an end to government corruption and called for political as well as economic reforms. Their demands evoked wide popular support and the student protests eventually developed into a nationwide pro-democracy movement. On 17–18 May, over one million people, including workers, intellectuals and ordinary citizens, marched through the streets of Beijing in support of student hunger strikers.

The scale of the 1989 democracy movement was much larger than that of any previous pro-democracy protest. Though it originated in Beijing, the movement spread in May to other major cities in China. Among the 434 cities in China, 107 reported student pro-democracy protests and 32 of which also reported workers' participation in the movement.[12] The massive pro-democracy movement was eventually suppressed by the CCP when the Chinese government decided to 'clear' Tiananmen Square, where thousands of students and workers had occupied for seven weeks. During the night of 3–4 June 1989, tens of thousands of troops together with armoured military vehicles started moving into the capital to enforce martial law. According to a report published by Amnesty International, at least 1 000 civilians were killed and several thousand injured by troops firing into crowds in Beijing between 3 June and 9 June.[13]

The following section will explore how the Hong Kong Chinese responded to the Chinese democracy movement during three phases: (1) the pre-June 4 phase (1976–88); (2) the June 4 phase (January-June 1989); and (3) the post-June 4 phase (July 1989–95). I will focus on the second and third phases, which comprise the peak periods of the PCDM and the subsequent decline of the movement in Hong Kong following the crackdown on the democracy movement in China.

❏ The Emergence and Development of the Pro-Chinese Democracy Movement in Hong Kong (1976–95)

Pre-June 4 Phase: Historical Context and Initial Mobilization of the Pro-Chinese Democracy Movement (1976–88)

During the initial phase of the PCDM, most social movement organizations, mainstream pro-democracy groups, as well as the public in Hong Kong showed little interest in joining the movement. Major players in this phase included a handful of university students and radical socialist groups such as the Revolutionary Marxist Coalition *(Geming Makesi zhuyizhe tongmeng)*.

Student Activism and the PCDM

The student movement in Hong Kong emerged in the late 1960s and grew rapidly in the 1970s. In its early stage, the movement had a strong anti-colonialist, anti-capitalist and nationalist character. In the early 1970s, university students began to participate in various social movements. Some of these movements, such as the Anti-Corruption Campaign (1973) and the Anti-Inflation Movement (1974) addressed social injustice in Hong Kong and expressed the grievances of the general community. Other movements, such as the Campaign to Make Chinese an Official Language (1968–71), Defend Diaoyutai Movement[14] (1970–71), were coloured by nationalism. Through these nationalistic campaigns and by organizing China Week *(Zhongguo zhou)* on college campus, the students were able to make public their concern for China. The spread of nationalist sentiments among college students set the stage for student participation in the Chinese democracy movement.

The April Fifth Movement was the first Beijing incident to trigger student reactions in Hong Kong. In April 1976, some university students began to take an interest in the Tiananmen Incident. Student unions of the University of Hong Kong and the Chinese University of Hong Kong, together with two other college student unions, organized an open forum on the Tiananmen Incident to discuss what stand they should take. The debates among the students were fierce. The pro-China faction *(Guocui pai)*[15] supported the Chinese government, while other students were critical of the Chinese government's repressive actions and supported Beijing Spring.[16] Besides holding debates and seminars and expressing their opinions in Hong Kong, no concrete action was taken to give actual support to the pro-democracy movement on the Mainland.[17]

With the collapse of the pro-China faction after the death of Mao and the downfall of the Gang of Four, university students in Hong Kong began to adopt a more critical attitude towards the CCP, and many gradually reached a consensus that the Chinese democracy movement was worthy of support.

Beginning in the second half of 1979, Beijing Spring drew greater attention from university students in Hong Kong who organized various study groups and seminars to publicize the development of the Democracy Wall movement. This preliminary interest paved the way for students' further participation in the PCDM during the 1980s. In August 1980, eight student organizations submitted a petition to the National People's Congress in Beijing to protest the party's crackdown on pro-democracy journals and to demand the release of pro-democracy activists. In late 1980, students from the Chinese University of Hong Kong also launched a signature campaign in support of the draft Publication Law *(Chubanfa caoan)* proposed by Beijing students.[18]

Since the early 1980s, university students had been active in expressing their opinions on democratic development in China and had taken an active part in the PCDM. This took the form of demanding the release of various political dissidents in China and of the Hong Kong pro-democracy activist, Lau Shan-ching.[19] Students also issued public statements and petitions to Chinese senior officials and organized various fact-finding missions to Guangzhou, Shanghai and Beijing to learn about the fate of pro-democracy activists who had been arrested.[20] Some university students even sought to establish networks in China and to hold dialogues with pro-democracy activists in different parts of China.[21]

During the 1986 student movement, the Hong Kong Federation of Students sent a delegation to Shanghai to support the student protests. Soon after this, however, the Chinese student movement was suppressed. Hong Kong students, who participated in the movement, began to wonder whether they should continue to send delegates to the Mainland to support the students there.[22] Yet they continued to show their support of the democracy movement on the Mainland on the ground that it could contribute to China's democratization.

Trotskyites and Radical Socialists

Besides university students, other groups that participated actively in the PCDM prior to 1989 were a number of radical socialist groups. These included, for example, the Revolutionary Marxist Coalition, the October Review Association *(Shiyue pinglun she)*, the Socialist Youth Association *(Shehuizhuyi qingnian she)*, Youth Fighters *(Qingnian zhanshi)* and the *Zhanxun.*[23] These organizations were mainly composed of intellectuals and young workers who supported socialism and opposed colonialism and capitalism. They believed in socialist democracy and strongly opposed the corrupt and oppressive bureaucracy in China.[24] Moreover, they believed that a democratic China could provide a solid foundation for a democratic Hong Kong.

Like the university students, the radical socialist groups were pioneers in supporting the Chinese democracy movement. One month after the April Fifth Movement (1976) in Beijing, four radical socialist groups, including the Socialist

Youth Association and the Revolutionary Marxist Coalition, held an open forum in Hong Kong's Victoria Park to discuss the Tiananmen Incident.[25] Following the Chinese government's crackdown on the Beijing Spring Movement, the radical socialist groups frequently protested against the CCP's arrest and suppression of pro-democracy activists, and petitioned for the release of pro-democracy activists.[26] In addition, some travelled to the Mainland to show their support for the Chinese democracy movement.

Lau Shan-ching was a leading pro-democracy activist who made 14 trips to mainland China between October 1979 and December 1981. His purpose was to extend his network of personal contacts, initiate dialogues with pro-democracy activists on the Mainland, provide them with spiritual and material support, and exchange publications.[27] Nevertheless, Lau's direct participation in the Chinese democracy movement proved to be risky and short-lived. In December 1981, Lau was arrested in Guangzhou and was sentenced to ten years imprisonment because of his active involvement in the pro-democracy movement in southern China.

In the 1980s, the PCDM focused on trying to free Lau Shan-ching and other political dissidents who had been jailed for their activities. A Committee for the Rescue of Lau Shan-ching was formed in February 1982.[28] Several labour unions, student organizations, women's groups and religious organizations also rendered their support and pressed for Lau's release.[29] Yet, in the face of the bureaucratic authoritarian regime in China, the radical socialist groups were not effective in obtaining the release of political dissidents. In sum, from 1976 to the 1989 Beijing student protests, the PCDM mainly appealed to college students and radical groups and failed to attract popular support.

Explaining the Lack of Popular Support for the PCDM Prior to 1989

Macro Political Analysis: Weak External Stimulation and the Depoliticization of Hong Kong

Prior to 1989, the low level of mobilization of the pro-democracy movements in China had little impact on Hong Kong. Moreover, only limited information about the Chinese democracy movement was publicly available in Hong Kong. For example, the few pro-democracy journals that circulated in Hong Kong were read by a handful of university students and members of the radical socialist groups mentioned above. Most Hong Kong citizens were unaware of the pro-democracy movement in China. Hence, the Chinese democracy movement could not have a significant effect across the border.

In addition to the weak external stimulation received from China, the political character of Hong Kong society also imposed negative constraints upon the mobilization of the PCDM. Prior to the 1980s, Hong Kong was an apolitical immigrant society. The government's ruling strategy of depoliticization, the lack of civic education, and the generally undemocratic political structure made

Hong Kong an 'economic city', leaving little room for political participation and mobilization. Although several social movements had taken place since the early 1970s, the political mobilization of social movements was subject to harsh political control. The Hong Kong government sought to control collective action and political mobilization through such measures as the repressive Public Order Ordinance, which imposed stern restrictions on public demonstrations and the formation of political organizations.

Besides these structural and political factors, the perceptions and strategies of various pro-democracy groups in the territory also weakened the effectiveness of the PCDM between 1976 and 1988.

Organizational-Level Analysis: Perceptions and Strategic Calculation of Pro-democracy Groups

Organizational-level analysis is directed at both mainstream and non-mainstream pro-democracy groups. During the pre-June 4 phase, non-mainstream pro-democracy groups were the major organizations supporting the PCDM. University students and leftist groups such as the April Fifth Action Group (AFAG) insisted that the democratic future of Hong Kong was closely tied to the prospects of democratization in China. They believed that without a democratic China, it would be impossible to have a democratic Hong Kong, as the sovereignty of Hong Kong was to revert to China in 1997.[30] However, these non-mainstream organizations failed to trigger wide social support in Hong Kong. The marginalization of radical socialist groups restricted the development of the PCDM. The fragmentation of the student movement in Hong Kong also weakened students' support of the PCDM in the 1970s. There was no consensus among university students as to how to evaluate the nature of the pro-democracy movement in China, as well as what role they should play in it. This fragmentation further constrained the mobilization of the PCDM.

Although a local pro-democracy movement emerged in Hong Kong in the mid-1980s, most mainstream pro-democracy groups decided to keep their distance from the Chinese democracy movements. Most local leaders of the pro-democracy movement consciously separated the Hong Kong democracy movement from that in China. Only a few members of the leading democratic alliance, the JCPDG, addressed the need for democratization in China or participated in the Chinese democracy movement. This low level of participation can be explained as follows: Firstly, the pro-democracy movement in Hong Kong had few resources and was weak in terms of political mobilization. Hence the JCPDG could not afford to spend its scarce resources in support of the pro-democracy movement on the Mainland. Secondly, mainstream democrats were afraid that integrating the local democracy movement with that in China would upset the Chinese government and reduce the chances of increasing the pace of democratization in Hong Kong. Thirdly, mainstream democrats also believed that Hong Kong was not in a position to trigger or mobilize the pro-democracy movement in China. They contended that it was impossible for Hong Kong to be directly involved in the pro-democracy movement in China.[31] Consequently, the goals, agendas and activities of the local pro-democracy movement were confined to democratic development in Hong Kong. Local democrats, especially mainstream democrats led by the JCPDG and its core political organizations, channelled all their resources and energy into speeding up the pace of democratization in Hong Kong.[32]

Micro Level of Analysis: Perceptions and Identity of the Public

Prior to the mid-1980s, Hong Kong people displayed a remarkable degree of political apathy. Hong Kong developed quite differently from China, and thus avoided the tragic Cultural Revolution and numerous political campaigns that took their toll on China's society and economy. Having emigrated from China after World War II as refugees, many Hong Kong citizens strongly distrusted the CCP and disassociated themselves from the political turmoil and oppression on the Mainland.[33] Hong Kong people's political culture was characterized by low political interest and a strong sense of political powerlessness.[34] Moreover, the severe punishment of political dissidents on the Mainland, as well as the imprisonment of Hong Kong pro-democracy activist Lau Shan-ching, also suggested that involvement in the PCDM could be risky. Therefore, few Hong Kong people participated in the PCDM during the pre-June 4 phase.

In addition, unlike many university students, few Hong Kong people had a strong sense of national identity. Based on a survey conducted in 1988, when asked to choose between 'Hongkongese' and 'Chinese' as their primary identity, 63.3% of interviewees chose 'Hongkongese' and only 28.8% chose 'Chinese'.[35] The national sentiment of most Hong Kong Chinese was usually subdued and rarely manifested prior to the June 4 phase.[36]

June 4 Phase: Massive Upsurge of the PCDM (January-June 1989)

This section examines the massive upsurge of the PCDM by focusing on the formation of the leading umbrella organization—the Hong Kong Alliance in Support of the Patriotic Democratic Movements of China (hereafter the Alliance). Both the mobilization process, the social basis of support, and the organizational aspects of the movement, as well as the goals and actions of the Alliance during the June 4 phase will be analysed.

Process of Mobilization and Social Basis of Support

The 1989 Chinese democracy movement and the June 4 massacre in Beijing triggered an unprecedentedly large and popular movement in Hong Kong. In early 1989, a small-scaled PCDM was led by university students and radical socialist groups. In memory of the tenth anniversary of the Beijing Spring, the AFAG—a newly formed radical group—held a signature campaign on 26 February to petition the Chinese government for the termination of one-party control, for freedom of expression and publication, as well as for the release from jail of pro-democracy activists.[37] Two student groups from the Students' Union of the University of Hong Kong also launched a signature campaign to demand the release of pro-democracy activists.[38] On 29 March, seven Hong Kong citizens attempted to take petitions bearing a total of 24 163 signatures to Beijing, but Chinese customs officials in Tianjin seized the documents before the group reached Beijing.[39] Radical groups such as the AFAG and the Sun Mui Group (Xinmiao she) continued to protest against the repressive action of the CCP and lobbied for the mainstream democrats' support in March and April.[40]

On 20 April, the Hong Kong Federation of Students (HKFS) sent four delegates to Beijing to observe the student movement. Bearing in mind their negative experience in the 1986 student movement, the student representatives were determined to observe the situation in Beijing rather than participate directly in the pro-democracy movement. Nevertheless, the HKFS's delegates changed their mind and decided to support the Beijing students after they arrived in Tiananmen Square and heard the Beijing students' appeal. To support the Beijing students, the HKFS began to raise funds and held a May Fourth student demonstration in Hong Kong. Several students from the Chinese University of Hong Kong also went to Beijing and joined the student protests. On 14 May, the HKFS sent another group of representatives to China to further explore their role in supporting the Chinese democracy movement. In addition to raising funds and holding student demonstrations in Hong Kong, some Hong Kong students also provided Beijing students with current Hong Kong newspaper reports concerning information of the pro-democracy movements in Hong Kong and China.[41] The mainstream democratic alliance, the JCPDG, took no action until May 1989. Nevertheless, on 4 May, 14 member organizations of the JCPDG, including the Hong Kong Professional Teachers' Union, the Christian Industrial Committee, Meeting Point,[42] the Association for Democracy and People's Livelihood, the Hong Kong Social Workers General Union and the Federation of Civil Service Unions, issued a public statement in support of the student-led pro-democracy movement in China. Szeto Wah, one of the leading democrats of the JCPDG, stated that the pro-democracy movement in Hong Kong and that in China should interact and support each other.[43] The JCPDG took no further action until 16 May, when during a general meeting, the JCPDG decided to mobilize the organization's resources to support the Chinese students' patriotic and democratic movement.[44] This date marked the beginning of the 'integration' of the two movements, as well as the beginning of cooperation among university students, radical groups and mainstream democrats.

On 15 May, more than 20 Hong Kong students staged a sit-in and hunger strike outside the New China News Agency (NCNA), China's representative office in Hong Kong, to show their support for the student protests in China. On 17 May, 6 000 students from 14 universities and post-secondary colleges gathered in Victoria Park in support of the Beijing students. However, owing to students' inexperience in leading territory-wide mass movements, the leadership of the PCDM was taken up by the secretariat of the JCPDG from 20 May onwards. Other social groups, including some pro-PRC organizations,[45] also joined the PCDM. From 21 May, the movement was transformed into a popular movement and grew speedily under the leadership of the JCPDG and the newly formed umbrella organization—the Hong Kong Alliance in Support of the Patriotic Democratic Movements of China.

From 21 May to 4 June 1989, three mass demonstrations, each with an estimated number of participants of over one million, or one-sixth of the Hong Kong population, took place in Hong Kong: at first to show support for the student-led democracy movement in Beijing; and later, in protest against the crackdown in Tiananmen Square. This extraordinary outpouring of emotion left many Hong Kong people teary-eyed. For details of major collective action during the June 4 phase, see Table 1.

Besides organizing large-scale solidarity activities and raising funds in Hong Kong, student bodies and the Alliance also sent delegates to Beijing. A Hong Kong Resources Distribution Centre *(wuzi zhuanyun zhan)* was set up in Tiananmen Square in Beijing to coordinate the distribution of resources collected in Hong Kong in support of the Beijing student movement. Participation by the Hong Kong Chinese became visible in the square.

To pledge their support for the Chinese democracy movement and to express their anger at the military crackdown, people of all ages and from all walks of life joined the popular movement. The new-found solidarity did not end in the streets. People from a variety of backgrounds also filled the pages of Hong Kong newspapers with political advertisements or public statements in support of the students in Beijing. From 24 April through 2 October, a total of 1 616 advertisements were published in Hong Kong's Chinese-language newspapers, including *Ming Pao Daily News, Wen Wei Po, Express News* and others.[46] The publishing dates of these advertisements demonstrated two peaks in mass mobilization activity. As shown in Figure 1, the first peak took place during 23–27 May, when a total of 627 political advertisements were published. The second peak occurred after the June 4 massacre. During 6–8 June, a total of 539 advertisements were published.

Unlike the pre-June 4 phase, the social basis of support for the PCDM expanded significantly during the June 4 phase. An examination of political advertisements published during the June 4 phase demonstrates popular support for the PCDM throughout the territory. People from all walks of life joined the movement: student organizations and educational bodies, religious and

Table 1: Mass Mobilization of the PCDM During the June 4 Phase

Date	Major Collective Action	Estimated Number of Participants
20 May	JCPDG holds a mass rally in Victoria Park in support of the pro-democracy movement in China.	50 000
21 May	JCPDG holds the first territory-wide procession. The Alliance is formed.	1 000 000
24 May	The Alliance holds a rally in Victoria Park to demand the resignation of Li Peng.	100 000
26 May	A Christian group, Breakthrough, holds a youth mass rally in support of the Beijing student movement.	200 000
27 May	The Alliance holds a fund-raising pop concert in Happy Valley racecourse.	200 000
28 May	The Alliance holds the Worldwide Chinese March.	1 500 000
4 June	The Alliance holds the Mourning Sit-in.	1 500 000

Source: The Alliance, *Annual report of the first general committee of the Alliance*, November 1990, p. 9. Number of participants as estimated by the Alliance.

community organizations, trade unions and labour organizations, traditional residents' organizations, political groups, professional groups, business enterprises, groups of journalists and artists, youth groups, women's groups, socialists and revolutionary Marxist groups, as well as pro-Taiwan organizations and pro-PRC organizations.

Participation by the pro-PRC sector was remarkable during the peak June 4 phase. To name a few participants, the left-wing Pui Kiu Secondary School mobilized students to join demonstrations. The pro-PRC Federation of Education Workers urged the Chinese government to meet the students' demands. The 170 000-strong Hong Kong Federation of Trade Unions, in a telegram to Beijing, also praised the hunger-striking students as patriots. Local delegates to the Chinese National People's Congress (NPC) issued a letter to the NPC standing committee urging party leaders to help end the hunger strike.[47] About 30 Hong Kong delegates to the Chinese People's Political Consultative Conference (CPPCC) also cabled Beijing to express their support for the Beijing

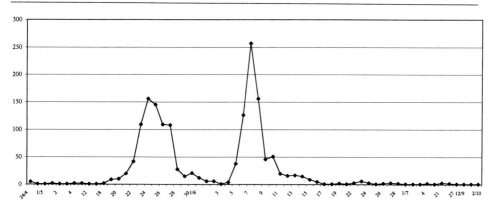

Source: Chinese Democracy Movement Information Centre, Newspaper advertisements
on the democratic movements in China '89, May, p. 199, Appendix 1

Figure 1 Pro-democracy Movement Advertisements Published in Hong Kong
Newspapers, 24 April – 2 October 1989

demonstrators' demand for a dialogue with the nation's leaders.[48] Most surprising
of all, employees of the NCNA and the territory's leading pro-PRC newspapers,
Wen Wei Po and *Ta Kung Pao*, also joined the growing legions of supporters of
the pro-democracy protests.[49] Nevertheless, the pro-PRC sector's participation
was short-lived and receded soon after the crackdown on the movement.

Since several major collective actions were organized by the Alliance, the
following section will examine the formation and goals of this umbrella
organization.

Formation, Goals and Activities of the Alliance

After 20 May, when the student-led PCDM grew into a popular movement, the
umbrella organization—the JCPDG—was unable to attract support across a wide
political spectrum. Furthermore, the local pro-democracy elite perceived that
China was in crisis. They felt strongly that all concerned Hong Kong people
should form a united front to deal with this national crisis. On 20 May, the
preparatory committee of the Alliance issued a public statement asking all Hong
Kong citizens to join the Alliance and support the mainland Chinese and their
long-term struggle for a democratic China.[50] In light of this, on 21 May, the
Hong Kong Alliance in Support of Patriotic Democratic Movements of China
was finally founded in a territory-wide mass rally.

The prior existence of a democratic alliance—the JCPDG—was crucial to
the formation and initial mobilization of the Alliance. Though the Alliance
was organizationally independent of the JCPDG, the leadership and member

organizations of the two organizations overlapped to a large extent. Szeto Wah and Martin Lee, the leading figures in the JCPDG, were elected as the first chairperson and vice-chair respectively of the Alliance. The secretariat of the Alliance's General Committee was made up of core members of the secretariat of the JCPDG.[51]

Formed in 1989 at the height of the PCDM, the Alliance remains the largest political organization in Hong Kong. During its first year of existence, the Alliance comprised 216 member organizations (see Appendix 1, pp. 80–6), representing a wide spectrum of social groups. Some were newly formed pro-Chinese democracy groups which emerged during the June 4 phase. Others included student and educational bodies, political organizations, religious organizations, unions and labour organizations, community and grass roots organizations and cultural organizations (see Table 2). Although two dozen organizations quit the Alliance during the first year of its existence, an equal number of organizations later joined the Alliance.

Table 2: Social Grouping of Member Organizations of the Alliance

Type of Social Groups	Number of Organizations
Pro-Chinese democracy groups	12
Student and educational bodies	12
Political organizations	17
Religious organizations	12
Unions and labour organizations	49
Community and grass roots organizations	104
Cultural organizations	10
Total	216

Source: Based on Appendix 1 — Member Organizations of the Alliance, November 1990

The Alliance had five major goals: to officially acknowledge the 1989 pro-democracy movement as a patriotic movement *(pingfan bajiu minyun)*; to release all pro-democracy activists who had been arrested *(shifang beibu minyun renshi)*; to demand that those responsible for the June 4 massacre be made accountable for their actions *(zhuijiu tucheng zeren)*; to terminate the 'one-party dictatorship' on the Mainland *(jieshu yidang zhuanzheng)*; and to create a democratic China *(jianshe minzhu Zhongguo)*. Over the past few years, major activities of the Alliance focused on the first two short-term goals rather than the other three long-term goals.[52]

Since its formation in 1989, the Alliance has been active in providing moral and material support for the pro-democracy movement in China through various

means. Major activities of the Alliance regarding the June 4 massacre included:
— to provide humanitarian support to political dissidents and their families, and to help hundreds of them flee China and seek political asylum abroad;
— to organize collective action and demand the release of pro-democracy activists;
— to promote democratic and patriotic education in Hong Kong;
— to contact foreign pro-democracy groups and provide them with information and resources;
— to hold annual candlelight vigils to commemorate the June 4 Incident; and
— to disrupt the nationwide official news blackout in China by sending newspapers, letters, facsimiles and videotapes depicting the June 4 massacre to people all over China.[53]

Explaining the Emergence of a Massive Upsurge in the PCDM During the June 4 Phase

The citizens of Hong Kong usually reserve their deepest passions for business, not politics. In a territory noted for its political apathy and reticence, the number and range of Hong Kong citizens who took part in the PCDM during the June 4 phase are astonishing. What explains the sudden explosion of popular support for the movement during the June 4 phase?

Macro Political Analysis: External Factors and Domestic Political Climate

The PCDM in Hong Kong during the June 4 phase was unprecedented in scale in the history of the territory. Unlike other local social movements, the PCDM was triggered predominately by external factors. The massive pro-democracy movement in China was the major catalyst for the massive upsurge in the local PCDM. On 2 May, students from several Beijing universities issued a letter of appeal to the citizens of Hong Kong asking for their solidarity and support.[54] Having received a direct appeal from Beijing, students in Hong Kong began to organize their first collective action on 4 May. As shown in Table 3, several of the major massive mobilizations in Hong Kong that occurred during the June 4 phase were responses to major events which took place in Beijing, including the students' hunger strikes and mass demonstrations, the declaration of martial law, and of course the June 4 massacre. These major events as well as the military crackdown on the movement played a major role in catalysing the popular movement in Hong Kong.

What set off this contagious effect? Unlike previous pro-democracy movements in China, news of the 1989 Chinese democracy movement spread to Hong Kong and the outside world immediately through the mass media. During the June 4 phase, television news in Hong Kong interrupted regular programming and presented updates on the Beijing student movement. Through television, people in Hong Kong were in contact with the Beijing student leaders

**Table 3: Major Events in Beijing and Their Catalysing Effects
on Hong Kong's PCDM During the June 4 Phase**

Date	Major Events in Beijing	Date	Mass Mobilization in HK
4 May	60 000 students, 400 journalists and many workers march in Beijing to call for an end to dictatorship	4 May	more than 3 500 students join the march and democracy rally
13 May	over 200 students begin a hunger strike in Tiananmen Square	15 May	more than 20 students hold a hunger strike
17 May	over one million people march in Beijing in support of demands for more democracy		
18 May	over one million Beijing citizens, students, workers and soldiers turn out to demonstrate	18 May	more than 6 000 people from all walks of life gather at Victoria Park to support the Beijing students
20 May	Beijing government proclaims martial law	20 May	50 000 people join a mass rally in Victoria Park to support the democracy movement in China
21 May	over one million Beijing residents protest against martial law	21 May	one million Hong Kong residents join a pro-democracy march
23 May	over one million demonstrators, including officials and staff members of party and government organizations, march in Beijing to demand the resignation of Li Peng	24 May	100 000 people join the 'down with Li Peng rally'
28 May	more than 100 000 students and citizens hold a 'Worldwide Chinese March' in Beijing	28 May	1.5 million people join the Worldwide Chinese March
4 June	military crackdown in Tiananmen Square	4 June	1.5 million people join the mourning sit-in at the Happy Valley racecourse

Source: Wong, ed., *Guonan, minyun, xinyang fansi* (Some Christian reflections on the June 4 massacre and the democratic movement), Appendices 1 and 2; and Landsberger, 'Chronology of the 1989 student demonstrations'.

and the hunger strikers. Deeply shocked by the bloody scenes of the Tiananmen massacre, people from all walks of life were galvanized to join the movement. Moreover, journalists, student representatives, labour unions and the Alliance also played an important role in transmitting information, establishing cross-border networks and linking the local PCDM to the pro-democracy movement on the Mainland. In sum, there was extensive contact between the pro-democracy movement in China and the PCDM in Hong Kong during the June 4 phase.

The declaration of martial law threw China into a national crisis. As Hong Kong was to revert to Chinese sovereignty in 1997, most Hong Kong people were unable to remain emotionally detached from the crisis in China. A vastly expanded window of political opportunity emerged for the PCDM. Employers, teachers and community leaders in Hong Kong publicly expressed their sympathy for the students in Beijing and for those who participated in the PCDM. A cross-social sectors alliance was formed in support of the pro-democracy movement in China. Facing a national crisis, people in Hong Kong were willing to donate money and other resources to support the mass mobilization in the territory and students' protest in China. In other words, the rapidly changing political opportunity made various kinds of fund-raising activities more effective than ever before (see Table 4).

Table 4: Major Fund-raising Activities in Support of the PCDM During May-June 1989

Fund-raiser	Date	Amount Collected (HK$)	Source
HK Federation of Students	May	700 000	*
HK Federation of Education Workers	19 May	1 300 000	*SCMP* (23 May)
The Alliance	27 May	14 442 000	#
HK Catholic Diocese	29 May	683 400	*Wen Wei Po* (2 June)
HK Christian Alliance in Support of the Chinese Patriotic and Democratic Movement	24 May-9 June	347 000	@
HK Red Cross	1 June	1 370 000	*Wen Wei Po* (2 June)
April Fifth Action Group	June-15 August	269 200	**

* *The truth of fire and blood: a documentary on the pro-democracy movement in mainland China in 1989*, Section 3, p. 17
# The Alliance, *Annual report of the first general committee of the Alliance*, November 1990, p. 12
@ Newsletter of the HK Christian Alliance in Support of the Chinese Patriotic and Democratic Movement 2 (15 June 1989), p. 4
** April Fifth Action Group, Financial Report, 16 August 1989

The colonial government was also highly tolerant of the mass demonstrations. Many collective activities were held peacefully without obtaining prior police permission that would normally have been required by the Public Order Ordinance. Yet, there were no arrests in this respect during the June 4 phase.

The national crisis not only broadened the political opportunity for the PCDM, but also had a vital impact on the mainstream pro-democracy groups in the territory. What follows is an organizational-level analysis focusing on the JCPDG, a major pro-democracy alliance in Hong Kong.

Organizational-level Analysis: Perceptions and National Sentiment of Pro-democracy Groups' Elites

Beginning on 16 May, the pro-democracy activists in the JCPDG decided to change their strategy by integrating the local democracy movement with that on the Mainland. On that day, the JCPDG released a statement which included the following:

> JCPDG believes that Hong Kong is a part of China that will revert to Chinese sovereignty in 1997. Hence, the fate of China and the fate of Hong Kong are tied to each other. Today, we support the Chinese democracy movement, as a way of pursuing a democratic Basic Law in Hong Kong... the JCPDG believes that democracy is an irreversible historical trend and the common desire of Chinese and Hong Kong citizens... JCPDG fully supports the Chinese students' patriotic and democratic movement and will join hands with other democratic forces to fight for a democratic Hong Kong, as well as a democratic China. [Author's translation.][55]

What explains the change in the JCPDG's strategy? Based on a series of interviews[56] with leaders of the local pro-democracy movement conducted by the author in April and May 1991, it was shown that the national crisis that China underwent during the June 4 phase played a significant role in shaping the perceptions and strategies of the JCPDG's leaders. Below is a sampling of statements made by these pro-democracy activists:

> During the June 4 crisis, I realized that without a democratic China, it was impossible to have a democratic Hong Kong. Given such a national crisis, democrats had no other choice but to become involved in the PCDM.

> I violated my own personal rule and became involved in the Chinese democracy movement owing to the June 4 crisis... Eventually emotion dominated my rationality and I began to participate in the PCDM, something for which I have no regrets.

> In the beginning, I felt dubious as to whether all democrats should participate in the movement, but finally we all became involved. Being a Chinese, we all have the responsibility of supporting the PCDM. Besides, the demands of the Chinese students were quite reasonable and deserved our support.

> The JCPDG unanimously agreed to support the PCDM owing to the specific political context of the June 4 period, and because we were emotionally driven by the entire student movement in Beijing.

> The 1989 Chinese democracy movement came as a big shock to the Hong Kong people. This shock was strong enough to dispel all your existing fears and thus enable you to participate in the movement.

In sum, the attitudinal and behavioural breakthrough of the mainstream democrats during the June 4 phase can be explained by two major factors. Firstly, by 1989, most democrats agreed that the democracy movements in Hong Kong and China could not be separated, and what they needed were suitable political opportunities and resources. Secondly, the national crisis in China that followed the student hunger strike created a new political opportunity which changed the perception of local elites, and triggered strong national sentiment among local democrats.

But without the support of the general public, the participation of the pro-democracy groups could not constitute a popular movement. A micro-level analysis focusing on the perceptions, identity and emotions of the Hong Kong people is in order.

Micro-level Analysis: Perceptions, Identity and Emotions of the Public

Karl-Werner Brand, a new social movement theorist, suggests that 'the openness to and dependence upon changing social moods has substantially influenced the development and the public resonance of the social movement.' For him, 'social mood' or 'cultural climate' of a given period means 'the specific configuration of world-view, thoughts and emotions, fears and hopes, beliefs and utopias, feelings of crisis or security, of pessimism or optimism, which prevail in this period.' According to Brand, this social mood directs patterns of political behaviour and lifestyles; it channels psychosocial energies outward into the public sphere or inward into the private sphere and thus provides or deprives social movements of essential public response.[57] Although it is difficult to measure 'social mood' and how it changes over time, this analytical perspective directs our attention to the 'emotions' and the social psychology of Hong Kong society.

The emergence of the mass pro-democracy movement in China unleashed the suppressed sense of Chinese national identity and the patriotic sentiments of many Hong Kong Chinese. This 'reactive' nationalism was an important driving force in mass mobilization, galvanizing Hong Kong people to stand shoulder to shoulder with the Chinese people and to oppose the repressive communist regime by peaceful means. Some of the most popular songs in Hong Kong during the June 4 phase included 'Brave Chinese' *(Yonggan de Zhongguo ren)* and 'Descendant of the Dragon' *(Long de chuanren).* This was the first time many Hong Kong citizens felt proud to be Chinese, despite their profound dislike of the CCP.

The televised images of peaceful pro-democracy marchers and hunger strikers in Beijing being suppressed violently by the Chinese government generated what Edward J. Walsh called 'suddenly imposed grievances'[58] and left the Hong Kong people horrified and stunned. The mass turnout of protesters reflected the deep shock and sorrow set off by the violent repression in China. Most of the pro-democracy political advertisements published after 4 June also reflected the sorrow, pain, sadness and wrath of the Hong Kong people. After the bloody crackdown, retailers expressed their sorrow by displaying black ribbons or posters in their shop windows. Many Hong Kong people wore black clothing and wept in public, as if they were mourning for their family members.

The unprecedented outcry also reflected Hong Kong's growing anxiety over its post-1997 fate. Hong Kong residents scrutinized the crisis in China for clues to their own fate under communist rule. One banner held up at the front of the parade in Hong Kong on 23 May read: 'Today's China is Hong Kong's tomorrow.' This was not merely an expression of anger against the hardliners in Beijing, but an expression of solidarity in the face of a perceived threat common to Hong Kong and China, which had generated strong impetus for social insurgency in Hong Kong. The pre-existence of JCPDG and many social movement organizations provided vigorous organizational support by giving direction to these impulses and feelings and venting them through collective action.

Post-June 4 Phase: Decline of the Mass PCDM (July 1989–95)

Mobilization Declined

Fervour among the Hong Kong Chinese in support of China's pro-democracy movement receded quickly after July 1989. The PCDM declined in three respects. Firstly, as shown in Figure 1 (p. 67), the number of pro-democracy movement advertisements declined dramatically after mid-June 1989. Secondly, although several mass rallies were held after the June 4 phase, none of them matched the scale of the earlier rallies. For example, in terms of participation in mass collective actions, there had been a sizable and constant decrease in annual June 4 candlelight vigils since 1990. As shown in Table 5, crowd estimates on the first anniversary were as high as 150 000. In 1995, only 35 000 people joined the candlelight vigil (see Table 5).

Thirdly, the social basis of support had been shrinking rapidly in the post-June 4 phase. The pro-PRC sector in Hong Kong withdrew its participation one month after the military crackdown. For example, the Hong Kong Federation of Education Workers and the Hok Yau Club, a pro-PRC youth group, quit the Alliance on 11 July 1989 and on 9 January 1990 respectively.[59] The Hong Kong Federation of Trade Unions also terminated all activities related to the PCDM.

Table 5: Number of Participants at the Annual June 4 Candelight Vigils in Victoria Park (1990–95)

Year	No. of Participants (estimates supplied by the Alliance)
1990	150 000
1991	100 000
1992	80 000
1993	40 000
1994	40 000
1995	35 000

Source: *Ming Pao Daily News*, 5 June 1992 and 5 June 1995; and the Alliance, ed., *Annual report of the general committee of the Alliance*, 1990, and Annual reports, 1991–94.

The two pro-PRC newspapers, *Wen Wei Po* and *Ta Kung Pao*, underwent personnel changes in their editorial staff and began to toe the party line in late June 1989.[60] In addition to the pro-PRC sector's withdrawal, four Catholic organizations also withdrew their membership from the Alliance since August 1989.[61] Several business and professional elites called for the dispersal of the Alliance. In 1994, among the 217 organizations in the Alliance who maintained their membership, only 20 were active participants in the PCDM.[62]

The ensuing section explores why participation in the PCDM declined after the June 4 phase.

Explaining the Decline of the PCDM During the Post-June 4 Phase

Macro Political Analysis: External and Domestic Factors Reduced Political Opportunities for the PCDM

The preceding section has demonstrated that the local pro-Chinese democracy movement depended on and was driven by the pro-democracy movement in China, and that the PCDM shrank rapidly after the military crackdown in Beijing. During the crackdown, the Chinese government declared all autonomous student organizations and worker organizations 'counter-revolutionary' and 'anti-government', and banned them accordingly. Workers, intellectuals and students became targets of the post-June 4 crackdown. The suppression of the pro-democracy movement in China changed the domestic political context, the strategy of pro-democracy organizations and the social mood in Hong Kong.

Repression in China, the CCP's strategic reactions in Hong Kong and the increasing control of pro-democracy demonstrations by the Hong Kong government after the June 4 phase, had restructured the political opportunity and significantly inhibited the mobilization of the PCDM.

Firstly, Beijing reasserted its control over its Hong Kong-based pro-PRC organizations after the June 4 Incident. The pro-PRC sector followed the official party line and withdrew its support accordingly, which weakened the social basis of support for the PCDM.

Secondly, the Chinese government also intensified its attacks on and intimidation of Hong Kong people, and the Alliance in particular, in the post-June 4 phase. In mid-June, the CCP's official mouthpiece, the *People's Daily* and China Central Television, accused Hong Kong people of the serious crime (regarded so in China) of taking part in illegal activities aimed at subverting the Chinese government.[63] On 21 July, an editorial commentary in *People's Daily* accused the Alliance of being 'subversive' and 'counter revolutionary', which in China was punishable by death. It also accused the Hong Kong government of turning a blind eye to the Alliance, which the paper asserted was planning to turn the territory into 'a base for overthrowing the Chinese government'. It was also understood that Chinese officials privately asked the British government to disband the Alliance. Such requests, however, were rejected by the British side.[64] In November 1989, Zhou Nan, the newly appointed director of the NCNA, warned local pro-democracy activists against using the territory as an 'outpost' *(qianshao jidi)* through which to seek to change the Chinese socialist system.[65] The CCP continued to issue such accusations and threats over the next six years.

Thirdly, apart from verbal attacks, the Chinese government also took other measures to intimidate Hong Kong people. On 6 June 1989, Lee Cheuk-yan, a unionist and a representative of the Alliance who had been sent to Beijing, was arrested at Beijing Capital Airport while boarding a flight bound for Hong Kong. Lee was released on 8 June after signing a confession. Yao Yongzhan, a Chinese citizen and Hong Kong resident who was a student at Fudan University in Shanghai and had played an active role in the pro-democracy movement in Shanghai, was also arrested and detained in Shanghai for one year. Other pro-democracy activists in Hong Kong took this as a warning that they too could be arrested and charged if they set foot on the Mainland. In fact, the Chinese government rejected applications by several key members of the Alliance and the Democratic Party,[66] such as Martin Lee, Cheung Man-kwong, Tsang Kin-sing and To Kwan-hang, to visit China.

Fourthly, the Hong Kong government tightened controls on pro-Chinese democracy protests during the post-June 4 phase. On 23 October 1989, the political adviser to the Hong Kong government, William Ehrman, issued a letter to the director of foreign affairs of the NCNA. In the letter, which was leaked to the press, the Hong Kong government assured the NCNA that it would not allow Hong Kong to be used as a base for subversive activities.[67] One of the major signs of increasing police control was the arrest of members of the AFAG protesting outside the venue of a Chinese National Day (1 October) reception and their subsequent charge of having committed public order offences.[68]

Moreover, police protection for the NCNA headquarters had also been strengthened. Confrontations and scuffles between police and pro-democracy activists occurred on anniversaries of the April Fifth Movement and the June 4 massacre, and on Chinese National Day.[69] For example, on the third anniversary of the June 4 Incident in 1992, a confrontation occurred when 200 university students marched to the NCNA to protest against the Tiananmen massacre. Four student leaders were charged by the police for having organized an illegal public gathering.[70] These official measures in Hong Kong inhibited the political mobilization of the PCDM.

Organizational-level Analysis: Perceptions and Strategic Calculation of Various Groups

Sociologist J.M. Barbalet suggests that social movements as agents of social and political change necessarily create problems for the state. Hence, 'the strategy adopted by the state in dealing with these will have an influence on the orientation, structure, composition, and future development of the social movement'.[71] The post-June 4 phase of the PCDM reflected the impact of the state on the elites' perceptions and strategies. Directed by Beijing, pro-PRC organizations withdrew their support for the PCDM. Cheng Kai-nam, the leading figure in the pro-PRC Federation of Education Workers, quit the standing committee of the Alliance one month after the June 4 event, so as to maintain a good relationship with the Chinese government and educational organizations in China. Maintaining such a position in a 'subversive' organization would hamper his federation's relationship with China.[72]

Other social groups also had more important goals than supporting the PCDM. For example, in order to maintain good relationships with the incoming sovereign power and to further their economic and political interests, many business professionals withdrew their support quickly after the military crackdown as the costs and risks of participating in the movement increased. The Catholic Church in Hong Kong was poised to play a pivotal role in re-establishing relations between the Vatican and Beijing that had broken off in 1957. In September 1989, the Catholic Church ordered all Catholic groups to quit the Alliance.[73] The withdrawal of the four Catholic organizations from the Alliance and the softened stance of the Catholic Church towards China reflected the internal struggle and strategic calculation of the Catholic Church in Hong Kong.

Pro-democracy groups had different perceptions and strategies which led to different approaches towards the PCDM. Non-mainstream democrats, such as university students and the AFAG, continued to 'integrate' the two pro-democracy movements despite continuous threats from Beijing and increased police control in Hong Kong. Their motivation was definitely non-materialistic. The mainstream democrats adopted an ambiguous attitude towards the two pro-democracy movements. The JCPDG and mainstream democrats such as

Martin Lee began to withdraw their attention and resources from the PCDM and concentrate on the local pro-democracy movement and the formation of a new political party—the United Democrats of Hong Kong (UDHK)—during the post-June 4 phase. Others, such as Szeto Wah, preferred an 'integrative approach' and remained active in both leading the Alliance and participating in the formation of the UDHK. In 1990, 7 out of the 20 general committee members of the Alliance joined the UDHK and were elected to the central committee.[74] Once some of the leading mainstream democrats shifted their attention to domestic politics in Hong Kong, resulting in a lack of consensus on how to deal with Chinese officials, the united front among the democrats was weakened accordingly.

Micro Level of Analysis: Perceptions and Emotions of the Public

In Hong Kong, the strong emotions and national sentiment fired by the events in China did not last long. Indeed, these feelings began to subside almost immediately after 4 June. The 'social mood' or 'cultural climate' in Hong Kong changed dramatically within one month after the bloody crackdown on the movement in China, as fervent threats and warnings were issued by the Chinese government. The dispersal of the democracy movement on the Mainland, the restructuring of political opportunity, the rising personal cost of participation in the PCDM, as well as the loss of people's confidence in the successful implementation of the 'one country, two systems' policy, had given rise to greater pessimism over the future of Hong Kong. The goal of democratizing China seemed too remote and arduous to achieve. Disillusionment with CCP leaders and widespread fear of losing prosperity, stability, civil liberties and Hong Kong's prevailing lifestyle after 1997 triggered a strong social demand for 'political exits'. Hong Kong people sought safe havens by trying to obtain foreign passports. According to a survey conducted in the third quarter of 1989, 43.6% of Hong Kong people hoped to emigrate, a larger number than ever before.[75] The Campaign to Demand the Right of Abode in the United Kingdom began one month after the crackdown on the democracy movement. Instead of directing their attention to democratizing China, Hong Kong people made 'saving Hong Kong' and seeking foreign passports for 'self-protection' their immediate concerns. Pessimism and frustration were just two of the psychological factors that explained the rapid decline of the popular movement in the post-June 4 phase.

❑ Conclusion

This chapter examines the ebb and flow of the PCDM in 1976–95. Inspired by the pro-democracy movement on the Mainland, the PCDM in Hong Kong emerged in the 1970s. During the pre-June 4 phase, only non-mainstream pro-democracy groups such as university student bodies and radical socialist groups took part in the PCDM. Only during the June 4 phase did a popular pro-democracy movement in Beijing transform the small Hong Kong PCDM into an unprecedentedly large popular movement. The social basis of support for the PCDM expanded tremendously during May and June 1989. A cross-social sectors alliance was formed and various groups raised a total of over $30 million in a short period of time to support the movement. During the most active period of mobilization of the PCDM, three separate demonstrations, each attracted over one million people, took place in Hong Kong. Nevertheless, one month after the crackdown on the democracy movement in China, the PCDM experienced a dramatic decline in support.

Although the popularity of the PCDM had been in decline, it continued to have an impact on politics in Hong Kong. Firstly, the PCDM had a major transformative effect on Hong Kong politics. It reinforced a sense of Chinese identity in many Hong Kong people and aroused their interest in Chinese affairs. There was an enormous demand among young adults to learn about contemporary Chinese politics, as well as current affairs on the Mainland, immediately after the June 4 Incident and through late 1989.[76] Though this demand abated gradually after 1989, over the next few years, the Alliance had funded various civic education projects to promote patriotism and foster a greater understanding of both democracy and contemporary China.[77]

Secondly, the PCDM also reinforced the existing 'anti-communist China sentiment'[78] of the Hong Kong people. This sentiment affected voting in the Legislative Council (Legco) elections held since 1991, leading to electoral victory by pro-democracy electoral candidates. For instance, in 1991, two years after the Tiananmen massacre, over 60% of voters supported liberal and pro-democracy candidates. In the 1995 Legco election, held six years after the Tiananmen massacre, about the same proportion backed pro-democracy candidates.[79] Candidates' positions on the June 4 Incident continued to impact on voters' perception of their political commitment.

The annual march and candlelight vigil to commemorate the June 4 Incident, which were held in May and June 1999, continued to attract a large crowd. So far, the Chinese government and the SAR government have kept a low profile in this issue. Political activists closely associated with the Alliance are still avoided by the two governments. Meanwhile, it is quite clear that pro-Chinese democracy activities are still able to find local supporters. Some are very critical of the authoritarian rule in China. Others quietly show their opposition to oppressive measures used by the Chinese government against dissidents. In short, the June 4 Incident and the concerns for democracy in China will continue to be important aspects in the political life in Hong Kong.

❏ APPENDIX 1: Member Organizations of the Hong Kong Alliance in Support of Patriotic Democratic Movements of China (November 1990)

Pro-Chinese Democracy Groups (12)

1. Democratic Forum
2. Compatriot Memorial Committee
3. Shatin Coalition in Support of Democratic Movement
4. Democratic Martyrs Memorial Organization
5. Shatin Joint Committee for the Promotion of the Democratic Movement
6. Joint Committee of Hong Kong Women in Support of Democratic Movement of China
7. Committee of Hong Kong Press in Support of Beijing Student Movement
8. La Salle College Alumni Concerning the Patriotic and Democratic Movement Group
9. Yellow River Association in Support of Democracy
10. Joint Committee of the Performing Arts in Support of Patriotic and Democratic Movement of China
11. Democratic and Patriotic Staff Association of the Chinese University of Hong Kong
12. Association of Overseas Students in Australia Concerning Democratic Movement of China

Student and Educational Bodies (12)

13. Student Union of Chung Chi College, the Chinese University of Hong Kong
14. Secondary Student Group of Chinese Language Movement
15. Autonomy Association of Overseas Secondary Students in Canada
16. Student Union of Golden Jubilee Precious Blood School
17. Student Union, the Chinese University of Hong Kong,
18. Hong Kong Secondary Student Association for Promoting Democracy
19. Hong Kong Federation of Students
20. Hong Kong Polytechnic Student Union
21. Preparatory Committee of Lau Wong Fat Secondary School in Support of Student Movement
22. Union of Shue Yan College in Support of Patriotic and Democratic Movement
23. Education Action Group
24. Hong Kong Autonomous Association of Tertiary Education Teachers

Political Organizations (17)

25. Meeting Point
26. Hong Kong Association for Democracy and People's Livelihood
27. Hong Kong Affairs Society
28. Hong Kong Association for the Promotion of Justice
29. Hong Kong Association for the Promotion of Democracy and Autonomy
30. Hong Kong Policy Viewers
31. Hong Kong Forum
32. Joint Committee of Grassroots Units Concerning Political Development
33. Association Struggling for Democracy
34. Friends of Singapore
35. Sam Fong Society
36. New Hong Kong Society
37. Xinhua May Seventeenth
38. October Review Association
39. April Fifth Action Group
40. Revolutionary Marxist Coalition
41. Sun Mui Press

Religious Organizations (12)

42. Hong Kong Diocesan Chinese Priest Association
43. Hong Kong Catholic Youth Council
44. Social Concern Group, Lower Kwai Chung St. Stephen Parish
45. Cathedral of the Immaculate Conception Parish Council
46. Social Concern Group, St. Lawerence Parish
47. Social Concern Group, St. Margaret's Parish
48. Hong Kong Christian Alliance in Support of Patriotic and Democratic Movement
49. Student Christian Movement — Hong Kong
50. Hong Kong Christian Institute
51. Hong Kong Women Christian Council
52. Hong Kong Christian Sentinels
53. Christian Labour Church

Unions and Labour Organizations (49)

54. Association for the Rights of Industrial Accident Victims
55. Chinese and Western Food Workers' Union
56. Federation of Civil Service Labour Unions
57. Swire Bottlers Ltd. Staff Union

58. Clerical Grades Civil Servants General Union
59. Urban Taxi Driver Association Joint Committee
60. Traffic Services Employees Association
61. Mass Transit Railway Operating Department Staff Union
62. Clothing Industry Workers General Union
63. Government School Non-Graduate Teachers' Union
64. Union for Environmental Management Section of Hong Kong Housing Department
65. House Managerial Staff Union of Hong Kong Housing Department
66. Housing Department Foremen Association
67. Government Chainmen Union
68. Association of Government Land and Engineering Surveying Officers
69. Association of Government Technical and Survey Officers
70. Association of Government Estate Surveying Officers
71. Government Electrical and Mechanical Works Supervisor Craftsmen and Workmen Association
72. Association of Government Nursing Staff
73. Laundry Trade Employees' Union
74. Hong Kong Liaison Office, Federation of Food Workers' Unions
75. Hong Kong Labour Union Education Center
76. Hong Kong Civil Servants General Union
77. Federation of Hong Kong Transport Workers Organizations
78. Hong Kong Social Workers' Association Ltd.
79. Hong Kong Social Workers' General Union
80. Hong Kong Air-Conditioning and Refrigerating Trades Workers General Union
81. Staff Association of the Hong Kong Federation of Youth Groups
82. Hong Kong Storehouses and Transportation Staff Association
83. Christian Industrial Committee
84. Hong Kong Professional Photographers Union
85. Hong Kong Salvation Army Employees' Association
86. Hong Kong Professional Teachers' Union
87. Cotton Industry Workers' General Union, Hong Kong
88. Union of Hong Kong Post Office Employees
89. Federation of Hong Kong Employees' Unions
90. Union of Officers of Cross-Harbour Tunnel Co. Ltd.
91. Education Department, Government Grant-in-Aid, Subsidized and Private Schools Junior Staff Union
92. Industrial Relations Institute
93. Hong Kong and Kowloon Trade Union Council
94. Hong Kong and Kowloon Gold Ornaments and Jewellery Trade Workers' Union

95. Hong Kong and Kowloon Life Guards Union
96. Hong Kong and Kowloon Union of Workers in Wine, Spirit, Tinned Provisions and Food Shops
97. Federation of Hong Kong and Kowloon Labour Union
98. Hong Kong and Kowloon Electronics Industry Employees' General Union
99. Hong Kong and Kowloon Electrical Engineering and Appliances Workers' Union
100. Food and Beverage Management and Professional Staff Association
101. Theatres and Amusement Parks Workers' Union
102. Hospital and Clinic Nurses Association

Community and Grass Roots Organizations (104)

103. Tai Hang Tung and Nan Shan Estate Residents' Association Ltd.
104. Shui Pin Wai Estate Residents' Service Association, Yuen Long
105. Siu Ping House Mutual Aid Committee
106. Siu Fai House Mutual Aid Committee, Siu Hong Court
107. Kowloon City Development Association
108. Tai Hing Residents' Service Association
109. Shan King Service Association
110. Central and Western District Development and Research Centre
111. Yuen Long Community Development and Service Centre
112. Long-ping Estate Residents Service Association, Yuen Long
113. Tuen Mun Yau Oi District Residents' Service Association
114. Tuen Mun Town Centre Residents' Service Association
115. Tuen Mun Forth Viewers
116. Association for Tuen Mun People's Livelihood
117. Shek Yam Concern Group
118. Shek Lei People's Livelihood Concern Group
119. On Man Social Service Centre
120. On Wing Social Service Centre
121. Western Kwai Chung Residents' Service Centre
122. Shatin District Joint Committee for the Concern of the Basic Law
123. Leung Tin District Service Association
124. Northern-East Kwai Chung Residents' Association
125. Youth Mutual Aid Association
126. Tsing Yi Concern Group
127. Southern District Development Concern Group
128. Tsuen Wan Labour Service Centre
129. Association for Tsuen Wan People's Livelihood
130. Sham Shui Po People's Livelihood Concern Group
131. Sham Shui Po Development and Service Centre

132. Bauhinia Service Association
133. Association of Cross-Country and Recreation
134. Kwai Tsing Council
135. Butterfly Bay Inhabitants Association
136. Butterfly Bay Residents' Welfare and Rights Promotion Association
137. Association for Kwun Tong People's Livelihood
138. People's Council on Public Housing Policy
139. Society for Community Organization
140. Wong Tai Sin Residents' Rights Promotion Committee
141. Office of District Board (D.B.) member, Mr TING Yin-wah
142. Office of D.B. member, Mr Paul LEUNG Ying-yeung
143. Office of D.B. members, Mr LEE Yiu-hung and Mr YIM Tin-sang
144. Office of Urban Council (U.C.) member, Mr MAN Sai-cheong
145. Office of D.B. member, Mr WONG Shui-lai
146. Office of Mid-Levels and Central District Board Members
147. Office of Legislative Council (L.C.) member, Mr SZETO Wah
148. Office of U.C. member, Mr LAM Chak-piu
149. Office of Regional Council (R.C.) member, Mr NG Ming-yum
150. Office of D.B. member, Dr Anthony NG Shun-man
151. Office of D.B. member, Mr NG Wai-Cho
152. Office of D.B. member, Mr LEE Wing-tat
153. Office of D.B. member, Mr LI Yuk-wa
154. Office of D.B. member, Mr Desmond LEE Yu-tai
155. Office of D.B. member, Mr LEE Chi-fai
156. Office of L.C. member, Mr Martin LEE Chu-ming, J.P.
157. Office of D.B. member, Mr LEE Shun-wai
158. Office of D.B. member, Mr LI Po-ming
159. Office of D.B. members, Ms SHA Mi-ching and Mr TAM Kwok-kiu
160. Office of D.B. member, Mr YUEN Bun-keung
161. Office of R.C. member, Mr CHOW Yick-hay
162. Office of L.C. member, Mr Ronald CHOW Mei-tak
163. Office of U.C. member, Mr CHOW Wai-keung
164. Office of D.B. members, Mr CHOW Kwok-leung and Mr LEUNG Kam-tao
165. Office of D.B. member, Mr LAM Kui-shing, J.P.
166. Office of D.B. member, Mr Steven HUNG Chung-fun
167. Office of D.B. member, Mr Billy HUNG Ying-ho
168. Office of D.B. member, Mr Gerry WAI Ka-Cheung
169. Office of D.B. member, Mr WAI Hing-Cheung
170. Office of D.B. members, Mr TSUI Pak-lam and Mr LEUNG Yiu-chung
171. Office of D.B. member, Mr CHUI Kim-ling
172. Office of D.B. members, Mr MA Lee-wo, Ms HA Wing-wun and Ms YAU Lai-wo

173. Office of D.B. member, Mr MA Yun-kwong
174. Office of D.B. member, Mr LEUNG Kwong-cheong
175. Office of D.B. member, Madam WONG Kwai-wan
176. Office of D.B. members, Mr Kwok Ngai-kuen and Mr LEE Kin-sang
177. Office of D.B. member, Mr Timothy CHAN Kar-kok
178. Office of D.B. member, Mr CHAN Choi-hi
179. Office of R.C. member, Mr Albert CHAN Wai-yip
180. Office of D.B. member, Ms Esther CHAN Wai-fong
181. Office of D.B. member, Mr Sumly CHAN Yuen-sum
182. Office of D.B. member, Mr LUK King-shing
183. Office of D.B. member, Mr TSANG Kwong-yuen
184. Office of D.B. member, Mr CHING Cheung-ying
185. Office of D.B. member, Mr FUNG Chi-wood
186. Office of U.C. member, Mr Frederick FUNG Kin-Kee
187. Office of R.C. member, Mr WONG Man-tai
188. Office of D.B. members, Mr Johnston WONG Hong-chung and Mr LAU Kong-wah
189. Office of D.B. member, Mr WONG Yu-cheung
190. Office of D.B. member, Mr Zachary WONG Wai-yin
191. Office of D.B. member, Mr George WONG Fuk-wha
192. Office of D.B. member, Mr WONG King-cheung
193. Office of D.B. member, Mr WONG Yiu-chung
194. Office of D.B. members, Mr YEUNG Shuck-chuen and Mr CHAN Mo-pow
195. Office of D.B. members, Mr CHUNG Man-fai and Mr SIN Chung-kai
196. Office of D.B. member, Mr HUNG Wing-tat
197. Office of D.B. member, Mr CHIANG Sai-cheong
198. Office of D.B. member, Mr CHOY Kan-pui, J.P.
199. Office of D.B. member, Mrs CHOI CHEUNG Yuet-lan
200. Office of D.B. member, Mr CHENG Shui-tai
201. Office of D.B. member, Mr Joseph LAI Chi-Keong
202. Office of D.B. member, Mr LAI Kwok-hung
203. Office of D.B. members, Mr Michael LAI Kam-cheung and Mr LEE Ho-fai
204. Office of D.B. member, Mr CHUNG Kwai-ping
205. Office of D.B. member, Mr TAM Tai-on
206. Office of D.B. member, Mr KWONG Fu-sam

Cultural Organizations (10)

207. Cultural Development Forum in Asia Co. Ltd.
208. Si Lin Association
209. Hong Kong University Staff Committee on Current Affairs in China

210. Teachers' and Staff Concern Group on Current Affairs in China, City Polytechnic of Hong Kong
211. Hong Kong Current Affairs Association
212. Hong Kong Media Association
213. Concern Group on Current Affairs in China — Teachers and Students of the Social Work Department, University of Hong Kong.
214. Association of Contemporary China
215. Le Qun Society
216. Yi Shi Tong Yuan Guan

Notes

1. For example, pro-Chinese democracy protests occurred in Macau, Taipei, Tokyo, Melbourne, Sydney, Auckland, London, Paris, Vancouver, Toronto, and many cities across the United States. For details of overseas pro-Chinese democracy movements, see the Chinese Democracy Movements Information Centre, *Bajiu Zhongguo minyun tuanti zhuanji* [Concerned organizations on Chinese Democratic Movement '89], February 1991.
2. On 4 June, while over one million people mourned publicly in Hong Kong, fewer people attended pro-democracy activities in other cities. For example, in San Francisco, an estimated 20 000 people joined the march. Demonstrations also were held in New York, Chicago, Houston, Los Angeles, Vancouver, and London, with the number of participants ranging from 1 000 to 6 000. For details, see *New York Times*, 5 June 1989, and *Washington Post*, 5 June 1989.
3. See, for example, McAdam, McCarthy and Zald, 'Social movements', pp. 698–716.
4. *Liyizhe dazibao*', a big-character poster, written by Wang Xizhe and three other persons, was addressed to Mao Zedong and the Fourth National People's Congress. The *dazibao* suggested that China should establish democracy and a legal system under socialism. It also suggested that the general public should oversee cadres' performance and they should have the right to dismiss senior cadres who lost the trust of the people.
5. The 'Gang of Four' refers to four Politburo members who played an active role during the Cultural Revolution: Mao's wife Jiang Qing, Wang Hongwen, Zhang Chunqiao and Yao Wenyuan.
6. Concerning the April Fifth Movement, see Yip, *Where is China heading?*, chapter 3; and Yan, *Toward a democratic China*, chapter 5.
7. The four modernizations include: modernization of agriculture, industry, science and technology, and national defence.
8. 'Beijing Spring', 'April Fifth Movement' and the 'first Tiananmen incident' are different names for the same movement. For details of the Democracy Wall movement, see Nathan, *Chinese democracy*, pp. 3–30, and Baum, *Burying Mao*, pp. 69–79.
9. For details of the student movement in 1986 and the campaign against bourgeois liberalization, see ibid., pp. 201–21.
10. Wei Jingsheng had served 14.5 years of a 15-year sentence and was released in September 1993, but his release was short-lived. On 13 December 1995, the 46-year-old Wei Jingsheng was jailed for another 14 years owing to his pursuit of human

rights and democracy in China. For details, see *South China Morning Post*, 14 December 1995.

11. See *Cheng Ming*, March 1989, p. 22.

12. Here, 'workers' participation' refers to the reported existence of independent workers' organizations. Concerning workers' participation as well as the spatial distribution of the movement, see my unpublished paper, 'Workers' participation in the 1989 Democracy Movement in China', and Tong, *1989 democracy movement in China: a preliminary spatial analysis*.

13. See 'People's Republic of China: preliminary findings on killings of unarmed civilians, arbitrary arrests and summary executions since 3 June 1989', *Amnesty International*, 14 August 1989, p. 273. Reprinted at the Chinese Democratic Movement Information Centre, ed., *Bajiu Zhongguo minyun jianzheng baogao zhuanji* [Witness reports on the democratic movement of China '89], May 1990.

14. The Diaoyutai Islands are near the northeast coast of Taiwan. For details concerning the sovereignty of the islands, as well as the early phase of the student movement in Hong Kong, see chapter 7 in this volume.

15. In the early 1970s, the student movement in Hong Kong was divided into three different factions: the pro-China faction *(guocui pai)*, the social action faction *(shehui pai)* and the liberal democratic faction *(ziyou minzhu pai)*. For details of the Hong Kong student movement, see chapter 7 in this volume.

16. See Chan, 'Yu wusheng chu ting jinglei—Xianggang xuejie canyu Zhongguo minzhu yundong de huigu' [A review of the Hong Kong students' participation in the Chinese democracy movement], p. 6.

17. Concerning students' opposing views on the first Tiananmen incident, see Leung, *Xueyun chunqiu: Xianggang xuesheng yundong* [The annals of the student movement: the student movement in Hong Kong], p. 12.

18. See Chan, 'A review of the Hong Kong students' participation in the Chinese democracy movement', pp. 11–2.

19. Lau San-ching, a Hong Kong citizen who graduated from the University of Hong Kong in 1976, worked as a computer sales engineer before his disappearance in Guangzhou at Christmas, 1981. He was detained and sentenced for ten years' imprisonment due to his active participation in the Chinese democracy movement. For details of Lau's story and his participation in the Chinese democracy movement, see Lau, 'A journey without regret'.

20. For details, see *October Review* 8, no. 5/6 (1 June 1981), p. 18; ibid., 9, no. 5 (30 May 1982), p. 7; and *The Nineties*, July 1989, p. 52.

21. Ibid., p. 6.

22. See ibid., July 1989, p. 52.

23. See *October Review*, 20 June 1976, p. 4; and Lau, 'A journey without regret', *Hong Kong Economic Journal*, 17 February 1992.

24. See the Editorial Committee of *October Review*, 'Our opinion concerning the Tiananmen Incident: speech delivered in Victoria Park on 16 May', 20 June 1976, p. 3.

25. See ibid., 20 June 1976, p. 4.

26. See ibid., 30 November 1979, pp. 2–3; 15 January 1980, pp. 4–5; and 1 June 1981, p. 22.

27. See Lau, 'A journey without regret', *Hong Kong Economic Journal*, 12 February 1992.

28. Lau was finally released on 26 December 1991 after serving ten years in prison. The rescue action did not shorten his imprisonment in China.

29. See *October Review*, 31 December 1984, pp. 9, 11.
30. See Wong, 'Nationalism and the democracy movement in Hong Kong', pp. 104–5.
31. See ibid., pp. 102–4, 108–12.
32. For details of the pro-democracy movement in Hong Kong, as well as the goals and strategy of the JCPDG, see chapter 2 in this volume.
33. See Lau, *Society and politics in Hong Kong*, and Lau and Kuan, *The ethos of the Hong Kong Chinese*.
34. For details, see Hoadley, 'Hong Kong is the lifeboat: notes on political culture and socialization', and King, 'The political culture of Kwun Tong: a Chinese community in Hong Kong'.
35. See Lau et al., *Indicators of social development: Hong Kong 1988*, p. 177.
36. Except for several occasions such as the 1967 riot, the campaign to make Chinese an official language (1968–71), the movement in defence of the Diaoyutai Islands (1970–71). For further details on nationalistic movements in Hong Kong, see Wong, 'Nationalism and the democracy movement in Hong Kong', pp. 38–41.
37. A total of 12 859 signatures were gathered during the campaign. For details, see *October Review*, 25 April 1989, p. 17.
38. Ibid., p. 27.
39. The seven delegates included journalists and representatives of religious groups. See ibid., p. 7, and *The truth of fire and blood: a documentary on the pro-democracy movement in Mainland China in 1989*, Section 3, pp. 4–5.
40. Ibid., pp. 23, 25, 33.
41. See *The Nineties*, July 1989, pp. 52–3, and Shanzhong Ren, 'The Chinese University of Hong Kong and the 1989 democracy movement'.
42. On 5 March 1989, Meeting Point wrote a letter to Chinese senior officials to ask for the release of Wei Jingsheng and demand democratic reform in China. For details, see *October Review*, 25 April 1989, p. 24.
43. See Wong, 'Nationalism and the democracy movement in Hong Kong', p. 26.
44. See the minutes of no. 38 general meeting of the Joint Committee on the Promotion of Democratic Government, 16 May 1989 (unpublished internal document).
45. 'Pro-PRC' organizations also refer to 'pro-China' or 'pro-Beijing' organizations, those organizations in Hong Kong whose political stances are close to those of the Chinese government, or those organizations under the direct control of the Chinese government.
46. Information based on the Chinese Democracy Movements Information Centre, *Newspaper advertisements on the democratic movements of China '89*.
47. See *South China Morning Post*, 18 May 1989, pp. 1, 12.
48. See ibid., 19 May 1989, pp. 1, 13.
49. Concerning the reaction of *Wen Wei Po* during the 1989 Chinese democracy movement, see Chan and Lau, 'Dilemma of the communist press in a pluralistic society'.
50. See 'The statement of the preparatory committee of the Alliance', 20 May 1989, republished in the Hong Kong Alliance in Support of the Patriotic Democratic Movements of China, *Annual report of the first general committee of the Alliance*, p. 34, Appendix 10.
51. See ibid., November 1990, pp. 2–3.
52. *United Daily News*, 3 June 1994.
53. See the Hong Kong Alliance in Support of the Patriotic Democratic Movements of China, *Annual report of the first general committee of the Alliance*, November 1990, pp. 3–6.

54. See Students of the Capital, p. 14.
55. See Joint Committee on the Promotion of Democratic Government, 'An urgent statement concerning the students' hunger strikes in Beijing and in Hong Kong' (unpublished statement made by the JCPDG), 16 May 1989.
56. These interviews were conducted as part of my research for my M.Phil. thesis, 'Nationalism and the democracy movement in Hong Kong'. I conducted 15 in-depth interviews with pro-democracy leaders, including core members of the secretariat of the JCPDG 1986–91; leading figures of major political groups such as Meeting Point, the Hong Kong Affairs Society, Association for Democracy and People's Livelihood, the United Democrats of Hong Kong, the Alliance, as well as the April Fifth Action Group; and leaders of university student bodies 1987–91.
57. See Brand, 'Cyclical aspects of new social movements: waves of cultural criticism and mobilization cycles of new middle-class radicalism', pp. 27–8.
58. See Walsh, 'Resource mobilization and citizen protest in communities around Three Mile Island area'.
59. See the Hong Kong Alliance in Support of the Patriotic Democratic Movements of China, Annual report of the first general committee of the Alliance, November 1990, p. 8.
60. See Chan and Lau, 'Dilemma of the communist press in a pluralistic society'.
61. The four Catholic organizations are: Catholic Institute for Religion and Society, Hong Kong Catholic Social Communications Office, Hong Kong Central Council of Catholic Laity, and the Pomtisical Foreign Mission Institute-Concern Group. See the Hong Kong Alliance in Support of the Patriotic Democratic Movements of China, Annual report of the first general committee of the Alliance, November 1990, p. 8.
62. See Wah Kiu Yat Po, 3 June 1994, speech made by Cheung Man-kwong, member of the General Committee of the Hong Kong Alliance in Support of the Patriotic Democratic Movements of China.
63. See Hong Kong Standard, 17 June 1989, p. 4.
64. See Ming Pao Daily News, 25 July 1989, p. 1.
65. See Ming Pao Daily News, 30 November 1989.
66. In October 1994, the United Democrats of Hong Kong and the Meeting Point merged and formed a new political party—the Democratic Party, which became the largest political party in Hong Kong after the Legislative Council election held on 17 September 1995.
67. See the Hong Kong Alliance in Support of the Patriotic Democratic Movements of China, 'Statement concerning Mr William Ehrman's Letter', in Annual report of the first general committee of the Alliance, p. 40.
68. See The other Hong Kong report, 1990, p. 185.
69. See South China Morning Post, 1 October 1994 and 6 April 1995; and Ming Pao Daily News, 6 April 1995.
70. See Sing Tao Daily, 29 October 1992.
71. See Barbalet, 'Social movements and the state: the case of the American labor movement', p. 258.
72. Interview by Mei-po Chow, reporter of University Line, November 1995.
73. See South China Morning Post, 19 May 1989; and Oriental Daily News, 28 October 1989 and 3 May 1994.
74. See the Hong Kong Alliance in Support of the Patriotic Democratic Movements of

China, *Annual report of the first general committee of the Alliance*, November 1990, p. 2.

75. See *Ming Pao Daily News*, 29 August 1989.
76. For example, the Hong Kong Christian Institute, a member organization of the Alliance, organized two civic education courses in July-August 1989, to analyse the pro-democracy movement in China. Over 800 applicants applied for each course within a short period after the programmes were advertised. Other organizations such as Democracy University also received remarkable responses.
77. From 1989 to 1991, the Alliance spent over HK$311 109 to support local civic educational programmes. See the first and the second annual reports of the General Committee of the Alliance.
78. For a detailed analysis on the 'anti-communist China syndrome' and its impact on the 1991 Legislative Council election, see Leung, 'The "China factor" in the 1991 Legislative Council election: the June 4th Incident and anti-communist China syndrome'.
79. See *Eastern Express*, 2 October 1995, p. 2.

4

Contestatory Unionism: Trade Unions in the Private Sector[1]

Stephen Wing Kai Chiu and David A. Levin

❏ Introduction

In the early 1980s, studies by England and Rear, and Turner et al. of Hong Kong's postwar industrial relations concluded that the local trade union movement had only marginal influence at the workplace, industry and societal levels. Their explanations for this marginality differed however. England and Rear put considerable stress on the nature of worker orientations in combination with the structure and functioning of the labour market as a major determinant of the ineffectiveness of the union movement.[2] Turner et al. by contrast put more weight on the influence of internal organizational factors within the numerically dominant union federation as the key cause of the movement's marginality.[3]

Both studies did however reach similar conclusions about the union movement's future. England and Rear predicted that the 'lack of employee organization at the workplace level will continue to be a major characteristic, alleviated only by the appearance in disputes of ad hoc representatives and outside "advisers" '.[4] Civil service unions might persist in pursuit of their sectional interests but with limited repercussions outside this context. Turner et al. also held a pessimistic view of the movement's ability to play a more dynamic role in protecting and advancing the interests of private sector workers. They proposed the creation of a system of workplace councils as 'a substitute, but non-competitive, equivalent to a normal labour movement when the major trade union organization is inhibited from acting as one.'

These observers hedged their bets however in light of the turmoil in public sector labour relations in the late 1970s. This turmoil suggested to Turner et al.[5]

> ... new reluctance on the part of younger and better educated employees to accept existing relationships equably, if in a limited context so far; but this dissent may well extend in future to the territory's rather notable degree of general inequality.

The past 'comparative docility' of the labour force was likely to be further undermined, they argued, by inflationary pressures and strains on state welfare service delivery due to the large surge of immigration in the late 1970s. England and Rear outlined a possible scenario of cumulative tensions in industrial relations as the private sector unions and the unorganized followed the lead of public sector unions in pushing for sectional interests.[6]

But these were minor qualifications. The principal expectations of these observers with respect to the future of the trade union movement were twofold. First, the movement would undergo little change. It would remain largely confined to its existing organizational boundaries, with continuing fragmentation and marginal influence in the wider society. Second, labour unrest could well spread in the private sector. If it did, the question then became whether it could be contained in the general absence of institutionalized procedures for conflict regulation at the enterprise level.

The aim of this chapter is to assess the validity of these predictions in light of developments in the trade union movement since the early 1980s. The key question is whether changes in the movement's economic, political and social environments since the early 1980s have further reinforced its marginality, or whether these changes are inducing the union movement to re-invent itself so that it can become a major player in shaping Hong Kong's future development. More specifically, is private sector unionism in Hong Kong emerging from its historical encapsulation in a rhetorical form of political unionism towards one or more of the types found in other industrialized or developing countries — economic unionism, political unionism or social movement unionism?[7]

In pursuing this aim, we borrow insights from social movement theories to interpret and explain continuities and discontinuities in the character of the Hong Kong union movement. We believe that these theories can enrich our understanding of how and why union movements change, through their sophisticated approach to the analysis of the cultural bases of collective organization and action, and their sensitivity to the impact of the changing structure of political opportunities on movement orientations and strategies.[8] For analytical purposes, a distinction is made between trade unions in the 'private' and the 'public' sectors for two reasons. First, unionism in the public sector (including the civil service and related social service sectors, such as education, social welfare and health, which are heavily subsidized by government revenues and enjoy terms of employment much in line with the civil service) demonstrates a very different pattern of development since the 1980s. Second, key variables such as changes in the labour market that have influenced union development in the private sector are much less significant in explaining the course of development of public sector unionism.

The first section below reviews briefly the historical and institutional context for the development of the private sector union movement from the early postwar period up to the early 1980s, and it is followed by a discussion of changes in the economy and their effects on labour during the 1980s. The second section turns to continuities and changes in selected characteristics of the labour movement from the 1980s. The third section focuses on a description and assessment of the activities of private sector unions outside the workplace, in politics and in community-wide issues. The fourth section analyses the role of the labour market, culture and the political opportunity structure in reinforcing on the one hand the marginal status of the union movement in the workplace, but enhancing on the other hand its participation in Hong Kong's political and social life since the early 1980s. We argue that these changes work in tandem to push and pull the union movement towards a more 'normal' type of political unionism, but that evidence for the emergence of a new social movement unionism is weak. The final section offers some tentative judgements about the future effectiveness of the Hong Kong union movement.

❏ The Historical and Institutional Context

Among the factors contributing to the marginality of the private sector union movement from the 1950s through the 1970s, three are discussed here: the labour policy of the colonial state, the crystallization of the movement's welfarist orientation, and the failure of the movement to make substantial inroads in organizing the emerging industrial working class.

In the context of considerable tensions in labour relations in the early postwar years, the colonial government through both legislative and administrative means set two basic institutional rules governing the behaviour of unions and employers. The first was that unions (and also employer associations) were required to register, which enabled the government to regulate their objects and internal administration. The role of the Registrar of Trade Unions was primarily to monitor the registration process and the internal administration of unions. The second was that it was left to employers and unions to decide among themselves how to regulate their relationships. In line with the influence of the British 'voluntarist' tradition, employers were not legally required either to recognize unions or to negotiate with them. The Trade Unions and Trade

Disputes Ordinance of 1948 'gave the Governor the power to refer trade disputes, with the agreement of both involved parties, to voluntary arbitration', but this provision was invoked only once, in 1950.[9]

The goals and methods of the two early postwar union federations — the Hong Kong Federation of Trade Unions (FTU) and the Hong Kong and Kowloon Trades Union Council (TUC) also crystallized about this time. One goal was political, not in the sense of pursuing power and influence in the Hong Kong polity, but rather in terms of expressing and mobilizing support for the policies of the PRC and Taiwan respectively. A second goal was to expand their influence among workers, which required demonstrating a concern for workers' welfare. This did not however take the form of seeking systematic bargaining with employers. After the early 1950s, the FTU became less overtly involved in industrial actions against major employers, and began to concentrate more on building up worker support through expanding educational, cultural and welfare services to members. The TUC adopted a similar strategy.

The organizational features of the union movement solidified and changed little between the early 1950s and the mid-1960s, even though Hong Kong was undergoing a major economic transformation from a predominantly commercial and trading colony to an export-oriented industrial colony. The number of unions remained at around 240 for most of this period and declared union membership in 1966 — 171 623 — was roughly comparable with that of the early 1950s. Most unions were small.[10] The FTU became the numerically dominant federation, accounting for some 60% of declared union members in 1966, compared with 23% for the TUC and 17% for neutral (unaffiliated) unions.[11] Neither the FTU nor TUC managed to make substantial inroads into the growing industrial working class. Of the 512 000 persons in manufacturing in 1961 (about 43% of the total working population), only about 10% were union members, compared with 40.6% in utilities and 78% in transport, storage and communication.[12]

Following mass social disturbances in 1966 and 1967, a new wave of unionization began.[13] One dimension of this wave was membership growth among private-sector unions. Those in manufacturing added 52 000 members and those in transport, storage and communication added 38 000 between 1968 and 1978.[14] The FTU-affiliated unions recorded very large gains, with their combined membership more than doubling from 96 062 in 1968 to 214 858 in 1978. A qualitatively new dimension to this wave was the proliferation of unions and growing union membership among non-manual occupational groups in community and social services. This included the civil service where the number of registered unions more than doubled from 34 to 93 over the period 1967/68–1977/78.[15] New unions were also formed by non-civil service employees in health, education and welfare. Of the 95 345 union members in community, social and personal services in 1978, about half were in public administration and one-third from social services. These new unions were distinctive in another way: nearly all of them remained independent of both the FTU and TUC. Still, when observers in the early 1980s wrote about the Hong Kong union movement, they emphasized primarily its continuing numerical weakness relative to employment, especially in manufacturing, its various forms of fragmentation, and its allocation of resources mainly to providing welfare benefits rather than to collective bargaining with employers.

❑ The Changing Economy and Labour Market

By the early 1970s, Hong Kong was a uniquely industrial colony in terms of its economic structure and labour force distribution.[16] It retained this character into the early 1980s but the economy was shortly about to undergo major structural changes. Three key dimensions of these changes are the slackening in economic growth rates, the declining levels of capital investment, and de-industrialization. The trigger for the overall deceleration of Hong Kong's economy was the drifting of the Western economies into recession. The weakness of the US economy in the 1980s, Hong Kong's largest market, posed the biggest hindrance to the expansion of the local economy. Increased competition from low-cost industrializing countries in the region also added to Hong Kong's troubles.

The hyper-growth record of the 1960s and 1970s tapered off during the 1980s. The average annual growth rate of real gross domestic product (GDP) in the 1980s was 7.5% compared with 9.4% in the 1970s. An even starker contrast with the 1970s was the slumping rate of investment, indicating a lack of confidence among capitalists in future business prospects (reinforced by the uncertainty in the early 1980s over Hong Kong's political future). Gross domestic capital formation (GDCF) increased only 5.2% annually in the 1980s compared with 12.4% in the 1970s. Growth rates in real GDP and GDCF clearly show a downward trend, with both series fluctuating around narrower margins at a lower base in the 1980s.[17] The share of manufacturing in both total employment and national product declined in the 1980s relative to other sectors. In absolute terms, the number of workers employed in manufacturing was nearly halved from 907 463 in 1980 to 483 628 in 1993 as the tertiary sector overtook manufacturing as the high-growth sector.

Along with these structural changes was a trend towards greater inequality in the distribution of income. The Gini ratio increased from 0.43 in 1971 to 0.46 in 1986, and then to 0.48 in 1991.[18] The ratio of profits to employee compensation in national income also showed a long-term rising trend as employees' share of Hong Kong's total income fell steadily during the 1980s.[19] The stagnation in real wage growth was a vital sign of a weakening in workers' market position despite apparent full employment. Whereas in the 1970s the average annual growth in real wages for all employees was 4.2% (despite the severe depression caused by the oil crisis), during the 1980s, the average annual growth in real wages fell sharply to 1.5%. In some manufacturing sectors such as garment-making real wages barely grew in the 1980s and even began to fall in the late 1980s.

Another indicator of structural changes in the economy is the figures on company liquidations and dissolutions (noncompulsory liquidations). The average annual numbers of company liquidations and dissolutions were 52.7 and 542.3 respectively in the 1970s. The comparable figures in the 1980s jumped to 221.6 and 1767.4. Economic instability inevitably affected the lives and experiences of workers. Growing job insecurity was reflected in the fact that the most common cause of industrial disputes other than strikes in the 1980s was a cluster of issues connected with employment security, including dismissals, redundancies, lay-offs and claims against bankrupt employers.[20] The number of industrial disputes caused by company insolvencies and closures shot up from 21 in 1981 to 59 in 1982. It increased to 88 in 1983 and stayed at over 80 per year subsequently.

The impact of this structural transformation was felt most acutely in the manufacturing sector. After three decades of rapid growth, manufacturing witnessed a real decline in the 1980s as plants were relocated to the South China region or neighbouring Southeast Asian countries where land and labour were much cheaper than in Hong Kong. Many manufacturing firms which had not yet closed down their production facilities in Hong Kong by the early 1990s were planning to do so.[21] In line with the relocation of manufacturing production to low-cost countries, the number of workers engaged in manufacturing, as reported by the General Household Survey, was almost halved from 918 600 in 1987 to 558 300 in 1994. Real wages grew at a slow rate for craftsmen and operatives and actually declined in 1991 and 1994. Middle-level employees such as clerical and sales workers enjoyed a healthier growth, but for both categories, real wage growth lagged substantially behind real GDP growth. A high inflation rate was also a drag on the growth of real wages in spite of almost double-digit annual money wage increases. In the 1990s, some sectors including manufacturing and restaurants and hotels have actually seen negative real wage growth.[22]

In sum, due to slackening growth and de-industrialization as well as relatively high inflation rates, real improvements in workers' pay and living standards were more difficult to sustain than in earlier decades. The relocation of labour-intensive production to the Mainland and elsewhere also reduced demand for less skilled workers whose only alternative was lower paid and more insecure jobs in the service sector. The income gap between them and the better educated and qualified employees widened. The lower stratum of the labour market also saw jobs filled in the late 1980s by an increase in imported labour. Calls for unemployment and retirement benefits were repeatedly rejected by the government. Given the deteriorating labour market position of many workers during the 1980s, we would expect a higher level of economic grievances compared with the 1960s and 1970s when higher growth rates had produced rising real wages and near-full employment. Here, it seemed, was a tailor-made opportunity for the private sector union movement to capitalize on workers' grievances arising from growing employment insecurity and declining growth in the level of real wages. To what extent then had the private sector union movement responded to workers' needs by playing a more active role in defending and advancing labour's employment interests in both the economic and political arenas? In the next section we focus on signs of change in the private sector labour movement by focusing on membership trends, the movement's external structure, the orientations of the main federations and internal union organization.

❏ The Private Sector Labour Movement Since the 1980s

Numerical Strength

The number of private sector unions increased in the 1980s from 206 in 1981 to 255 in 1997 or by nearly 25%.[23] The biggest increase was in 1991 when 11 new unions were registered. As Figure 1 shows however, the overall numerical strength of the union movement in the private sector, as indicated by declared membership, was roughly constant over the 1980s. In 1980, private sector unions accounted for just over 250 000 members. Union membership fell sharply between 1980 and 1981 and subsequently stabilized until the late 1980s when it began to climb again, exceeding the 1980 figure only in 1993.[24] Between 1994 and 1997, however, there was a sharp rise from about 260 000 members to 297 347.

Reliable estimates of private sector employment have been available only since 1981 to enable us to calculate accurate union density figures.[25] In contrast with the steady growth of overall union density (including both public and private sectors) since 1981, private sector union density dropped slightly. For the union movement as a whole, around one in five workers was a union member in 1995. When the public sector is excluded, union density in the private sector drops to 10% (Figure 2). In contrast therefore to the rapid growth in union membership in the public sector, private sector unionism had been barely able to keep up with the growth in employment. While union membership rebounded from its trough around mid-1980s, the unionization rate in the private sector had seen less than a 1% increase.

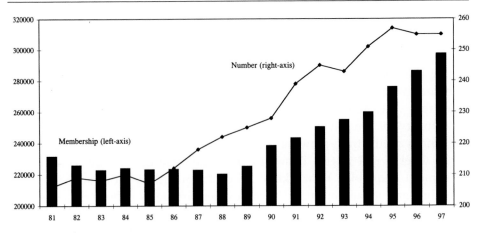

Source: Trade Union Dataset

Figure 1 Membership and Number of Private Sector Unions, 1981–97

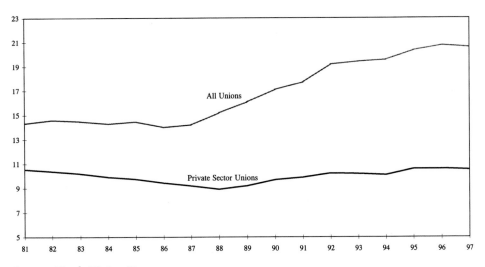

Source: Trade Union Dataset

Figure 2 Union Density, 1981–97 (in percentages)

The steady trend in aggregate union density masks the divergent trends across different sectors. As shown in Table 1, commerce (wholesale, retail and import/export trades, restaurants and hotels), transport and communication, and financial and business services registered a drop in union density between 1981 and 1995. Conversely, manufacturing, construction and private sector services experienced an increase in union density over the same period mainly due to the surge of union membership from the late 1980s.

Table 1: Private Sector Union Density by Sectors, 1981-97 (in percentages)

	manufacturing	construction	wholesale, retail and import/export trades, restaurants and hotels	transport, storage and communication	finance, insurance, real estate and business services	private community, social and personal services	others	total
1981	6.8	7.2	9.5	46.6	14.3	3.5	5.3	10.5
1982	6.8	6.7	8.7	43.4	12.5	3.9	5.3	10.4
1983	6.7	6.5	8.5	41.8	12.3	4.1	5.8	10.2
1984	6.2	7.0	8.0	40.7	13.0	4.1	5.2	9.9
1985	6.2	6.9	7.6	39.4	12.4	3.8	3.8	9.7
1986	6.5	6.5	6.8	37.7	11.3	3.6	3.9	9.4
1987	6.7	6.3	6.4	34.9	10.6	3.5	3.9	9.2
1988	7.0	5.9	6.2	31.0	9.8	3.4	4.5	8.9
1989	7.6	6.4	6.0	30.2	9.5	3.5	5.3	9.2
1990	8.2	10.3	5.9	29.8	9.5	3.2	6.3	9.7
1991	8.9	10.6	5.9	29.3	9.3	3.6	7.2	9.9
1992	10.1	9.3	6.0	27.2	11.3	3.6	7.7	10.2
1993	11.3	9.0	5.9	25.6	9.7	3.6	8.1	10.2
1994	12.1	8.4	5.9	23.9	9.3	3.7	8.2	10.1
1995	13.5	9.9	6.3	25.1	9.7	3.5	8.1	10.6
1996	15.2	9.0	5.9	26.4	9.7	3.3	8.4	10.6
1997	16.4	8.3	5.5	28.0	8.9	3.4	8.5	10.5

Source: Trade Union Dataset, *Hong Kong Annual Digest of Statistics*, various years

Membership declines in manufacturing in the first half of the 1980s reflect in part the shifting employment structure discussed above. Manufacturing's share of the working population fell from 44.8% in 1976 to 31.9% by the third quarter of 1988.[26] In some industries such as textiles, employment declined due to a combination of factors such as technological change, relocation of manufacturing operations to the special economic zones of China and other countries, and competition from other developing countries. Since the textile industry had been an union stronghold within manufacturing, its decline had a major impact on the union density rate in this sector. In the case of transport, Ting attributed declining membership of the Seamen's Union to containerization and rationalization in the shipping industry.[27]

Although non-manual occupational groups in the public sector have shown a propensity to join unions, this is not the case for the private sector. For example, union density in the financial sector has declined over the past decade despite the rebound in union membership in the late 1980s. With the tremendous expansion of employment in the financial and business services sector, growth in union membership simply could not keep pace with the growth in employment.

External Union Structure

Two main developments in the 1980s were the continuing proliferation of unions and the formation of new federations. There were 160 more registered trade unions in 1995 than in 1981. As in the 1970s, the majority of these new unions were formed in the service sector, mainly within the civil service. The only other sector to record a substantial increase was transport, storage and communication. This proliferation had a mixed effect on the size distribution of unions. In 1981, about one-tenth of all unions had 50 members or below; in 1997, the proportion of unions in this size category had increased to about 23% (see Table 2). At the other extreme, the proportion of all unions accounted for by the largest unions (those with over 1 000 members) dropped slightly. In terms of the share of union membership however, unions with more than 1 000 members continued to account for the bulk of union members, over 80% in both 1981 and 1997. The share of the smallest unions in total union membership was still insignificant (0.6% of total in 1997).

In the 1970s there was little formal integration among the independent unions, but between 1979 and 1991 they had formed three new federations, listed in Table 3.

Though not a trade union, the Hong Kong Christian Industrial Committee (CIC) has also become a highly visible actor on the labour scene since the 1970s. The CIC considers itself to be a specifically Christian labour organization and a pressure group committed to fighting for workers' rights and promoting unity

Table 2: Size Distribution of Private Sector Trade Unions, 1981, 1986, 1991

Size		1981	% of total	1991	% of total	1997	% of total
50 or below	membership	740	0.3	1 348	0.6	1 674	0.6
	number	20	9.7	45	18.8	57	23.4
51 to 100	membership	3 563	1.5	3 340	1.4	2 598	0.9
	number	45	21.8	46	19.2	35	14.3
101 to 500	membership	18 651	8.1	18 806	7.7	16 619	5.6
	number	70	34.0	74	31.0	69	28.3
501 to 1 000	membership	17 239	7.4	19 347	8.0	21 894	7.4
	number	24	11.7	27	11.3	29	11.9
over 1 000	membership	191 319	82.6	200 509	82.4	252 019	85.5
	number	47	22.8	47	19.7	54	22.1
Total	membership	231 512		243 350		294 804	
	number	206		239		244	

Source: Registrar of Trade Unions, various years

among labour groups through education, organizing and action.[28] It is not a trade union but does advise workers with employment problems and encourage workers to join unions, and has assisted in the formation of a number of trade unions, including in 1987 a new industry federation among independent unions in the transport sector, the Federation of Hongkong Transport Workers' Organizations. The CIC has also functioned as a 'linking pin' over the past decade in bringing together reform-oriented organizations to lobby government on issues of broader public concern. In 1991, the CIC again served as the stimulus to the formation of a new federation of politically independent unions, the Hong Kong Confederation of Trade Unions (CTU).

As a result of the above changes, there has been a shift in the relative distribution of private sector unions and union members among the FTU, TUC and those outside the two older federations, as shown in Table 4. The new independent unions have altered the balance of power within the trade union movement as a whole. In the past, the major division within the movement

Table 3 Membership of Peak Labour Federations, 1994

Name of Federation	Year of Registration	Number of Affiliated Unions (1994)	Membership of Affiliated Unions (1994)
Hong Kong Federation of Trade Unions (FTU)	1949	91	200 300
Hong Kong and Kowloon Trades Union Council (TUC)	1949	65	30 600
Hong Kong Confederation of Trade Unions (CTU)	1991	28	78 500
Joint Organization of Unions—Hong Kong (JOU)	1979	16	9 000
Federation of Hong Kong and Kowloon Labour Unions (FLU)	1984	23	19 400

Source: Daryanani, *Hong Kong 1995: a review of 1994*, p. 133

was between the pro-China FTU and the pro-Taiwan TUC. With the waning of the influence of the TUC, the principal groupings are now the FTU and the independent sector of the trade union movement (primarily the CTU). As the independent unions have grown, conflicts have occasionally erupted with established FTU unions where both have organized in the same workplace.[29]

Orientations of the Federations

In some respects, the orientation of the FTU has changed considerably since the mid-1970s. In 1976, during the Cultural Revolution in China, the FTU's policy statements reflected the world-view of the Chinese leadership at that time: liberating Taiwan, participation in the anti-US and anti-USSR movements, criticizing Confucius, combating rightist elements in the CCP, supporting socialist revolution and construction, and strengthening nationalism and anti-imperialism among the working class. In practice, it drew sharp boundaries between itself and other organizations. The FTU and its affiliates at that time refused to cooperate with other unions or to participate in elections to the Labour Advisory Board, the institutional channel created by the Hong Kong government for trade unions to advise on labour policy.

With the downfall of the Gang of Four and the new policy of the four modernizations in China, the FTU's rhetoric and policies began to change. The 1984 Sino-British agreement on the future of Hong Kong as well as local political

Table 4: Private Sector Unions by Affiliation, 1981–97

	FTU		TUC		CTU*		Others	
	Membership	Number	Membership	Number	Membership	Number	Membership	Number
1981	162 057	68	32 956	73	5 092	7	31 407	58
1982	155 972	68	32 672	73	5 351	7	31 830	61
1983	153 183	68	31 527	71	5 926	8	32 186	61
1984	151 916	68	31 162	71	7 295	9	33 656	62
1985	153 128	66	30 532	68	7 526	10	31 999	63
1986	157 036	70	27 628	66	7 784	10	30 922	66
1987	157 505	73	25 449	66	7 775	10	32 014	69
1988	154 402	73	26 408	66	7 214	10	32 161	73
1989	153 879	74	27 192	66	9 354	12	34 720	73
1990	154 724	75	26 876	65	13 293	12	43 420	76
1991	158 647	78	26 988	65	14 156	14	43 559	82
1992	167 149	79	27 022	65	14 978	18	41 274	83
1993	173 726	81	27 145	62	14 843	18	39 235	82
1994	179 517	83	27 601	63	14 482	18	38 168	87
1995	189 579	83	27 406	63	13 773	18	45 188	93
1996	195 847	83	26 362	60	14 087	19	49 881	93
1997	204 308	83	26 171	55	14 024	19	52 848	98

*   The CTU was established in 1991. Its membership before 1991 is calculated by
   adding membership of affiliates which predated the federation.

reforms further stimulated a rethinking of the FTU's role. In 1985, the FTU's
chairman stated that 'while fighting for, and protecting, workers' rights, [the
FTU] also participates actively in social affairs and democratic political activities,
and works together with all social strata for the progress and stability of Hong
Kong.' This is indicative of the new orientation of the FTU towards politics,
labour-management relations and other sectors of the union movement.
Regarding politics, the FTU's role was to encourage active participation in the
drafting of the Basic Law (the post-1997 mini-constitution for Hong Kong) and
in local elections. The building-up of good labour-management relations was
seen to be important for maintaining Hong Kong's prosperity and stability. Thus,

although contradictions between labour and management still had 'an objective existence in a capitalist society', they could be 'easily resolved' through mutual concession, negotiation and consultation. While recognizing that unions held 'divergent political beliefs and viewpoints', nevertheless they also had a 'common aim in fighting for workers' rights and benefits.' The basis for inter-union cooperation was 'seeking common points while tolerating differences'.[30]

In contrast with the FTU and the independent unions, the TUC is a declining organization. Both its membership and number of affiliates are shrinking. In contrast with the FTU where a second generation of younger members have moved into leadership positions, the leadership of the TUC and its affiliates is aging (although efforts are being made to rejuvenate the leadership). The TUC's political allegiance to the Nationalists in Taiwan is increasingly seen as a liability in recruiting new members.[31] Moreover, many of the TUC affiliates are traditional craft unions which have suffered from diminishing employment in their industries. Even their leaders have doubts about whether the TUC will be allowed to exist China now that has resumed sovereignty over Hong Kong.[32]

While the newer federations are concerned with members' sectional interests, they also tend to define their mission in broader social terms. The Joint Organization of Unions—Hong Kong (JOU), for example, has taken the view that trade unions should not fight solely for their own sectional interests, but should play an active part in promoting social development. The new CTU has also professed its orientation to include participating actively in broader social issues and, as we shall see below, in political affairs.

Internal Union Structure

Turner et al. commented a decade ago that 'the internal organization of Hong Kong unions appears flimsy: union staffs, branch and workplace organization appear skeletal and — outside the civil service, at least — direct member participation in union management seems low.'[33] Given that most unions are small and cannot afford full-time officials, their internal weakness is unsurprising. The largest trade unions are however able to devote some resources to strengthening internal administration. In the 1980s, the FTU sought to strengthen its internal organization and administration through sponsorship of training courses for union personnel and shop stewards and by a more modernized management style in the handling of union affairs. In the 1994 general assembly, the FTU also resolved to establish a training centre for trade union and affiliated welfare agency personnel.[34] Union affiliates also enjoyed a wide range of welfare facilities provided by the federations to attract members.

Solid data on changes in rank-and-file membership participation in union activities are lacking. Turner found from his 1985 survey that indicators of participation in union activities among those who did report belonging to trade unions was 'high by comparison with the record of trade unions in other capitalist economies.'[35] For example, 35% of union members reported attending meetings occasionally and 11% regularly, 43% reported joining in unions' social activities and 10% reported attending union courses or study groups.

The extent to which members are able to voice their preferences and influence union leadership decisions is not known. In the case of older unions, especially those affiliated to the FTU and TUC, outsiders have criticized their oligarchic tendencies.[36] In 1989, signs surfaced of rank-and-file discontent with the accommodative stance of the FTU leadership in negotiations with the two bus companies. In one case, rank-and-file members compelled the more moderate leadership of a bus company branch of the FTU-affiliated Motor Transport Workers General Union to launch a strike that paralyzed public transport for two days. At another bus company, over 200 members of the same union took out a newspaper advertisement to announce their withdrawal from the union, citing as their reason the union leadership's acquiescence to the company.[37] The FTU is not alone in facing internal dissension. In 1988, the largest affiliate of the TUC pulled out, reportedly because leaders of much smaller (and largely moribund) affiliates had been appointed to top positions in the TUC while leaders of the larger unions were excluded.[38] The independent unions seem to be run in a more democratic manner, as indicated by the ability of the members to replace leaders. In 1989, for example, the chairman of the Federation of Civil Service Unions was voted out on the grounds that he had made several decisions without adequate consultation and discussion with affiliates. Nonetheless, even among the independent unions, the typical organizational pattern is still a top-heavy structure.

Workplace Activities and Industrial Action

The commonly accepted assessment of trade unions in the early 1980s — their weakness at the workplace level — on the whole still applies to the private sector. Collective bargaining resulting in written agreements at the enterprise or industry level is rare. Wage levels are normally fixed by individual agreement between employers and workers.[39] It has been estimated that only about 4% of the labour force is covered by collective agreements, but even the nature of these agreements is often not in a detailed form.

In some trades with long guild traditions, general wage agreements are negotiated on an annual or periodic basis between craft unions and employers' associations. However, these agreements are often ritualistic, focusing mainly on minimum pay rates and overtime payments, but lacking detail on procedural matters or on other substantive terms of employment, and having little effect on the actual practices of individual employers. An exception is the printing industry where there is an established union tradition, and open-ended agreements exist between the FTU-affiliated union and an employers' association covering holidays and workers' compensation. The closest approximation to the Western practice of collective bargaining in the private sector is the case of Cable and Wireless Ltd. where in the early 1970s, following a bitter industrial dispute, management extended voluntary recognition to a staff union as the legitimate bargaining agent for employees.[40]

In major manufacturing sectors such as clothing and electronics, union membership is low and collective bargaining apparently non-existent. However, 'quasi-bargaining' took place in cotton textiles where unions existed since the 1950s. A similar situation exists in the restaurant trade where unions and an employers' association have reached agreements on standards defining the provision and arrangement of annual leave and other holidays for restaurant workers. Occasional bargaining over employment conditions occurs in some of the larger companies, such as the bus companies, where trade unions have an established position. Negotiations also take place between unions and management in a few of the large companies such as Cathay Pacific.

While many employers are undoubtedly opposed to collective bargaining, there are other reasons for its underdevelopment. The more powerful FTU affiliates such as the Seamen's Union prefer not to negotiate over wages and conditions of employment, but to handle grievances that arise over the interpretation of crew agreements unilaterally drawn up by management.[41] What little direct evidence there is suggests a persistent weakness in the role of trade unions at workplace level. In Turner's 1985 survey, of those respondents who reported being involved in disagreements with their employers over the previous five years, 'in no single case reported was a trade union involved in the workers' representation'.[42]

There seems to be little pressure from employees for labour-management relations to take the form of collective bargaining. In both his 1976 and 1985 surveys, Turner asked respondents to indicate their preferences among various methods of job improvement. Trade union negotiation was preferred by only 12% in 1976 and 9% in 1985. Government legislation was preferred by 32% in 1976 and 25% in 1985, but formal joint consultation by 31% in 1976 and 36% in 1985. Further evidence that trade union negotiation is not considered as a route to job improvements comes from a 1986 survey of 481 female factory workers in Tsuen Wan (an industrial district in the New Territories). Respondents were asked the following open-ended question: 'In your opinion, what is the best way to increase your income?' No respondent mentioned explicitly the possibility of trade union negotiation.[43]

Added to this is the low level of industrial actions. As Visser points out, there is no automatic link between union membership and militancy, but in Hong Kong it seems that both membership and militancy have been low.[44]

Contrary to the expectations of observers in the early 1980s, the level of manifest industrial conflict as measured by the number of strikes or working days lost due to strikes did not rise. If anything, as shown in Figure 3, strikes (in the private sector) seemed to be withering away. The decline was most noticeable in the manufacturing sector. In the early 1980s the annual frequency of strikes was around 30 but by the late 1980s it had plummeted to fewer than ten per year. The frequency of strikes in the non-manufacturing sector also declined but less sharply.

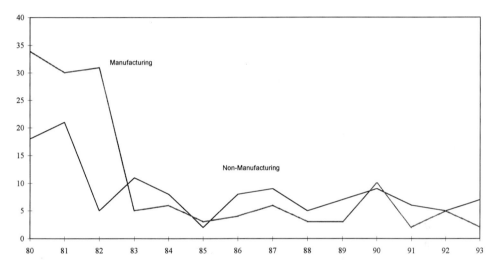

Source: Unpublished Labour Department records

Figure 3   Strikes in Manufacturing and Non-manufacturing Sectors, 1980–93

Chiu found a drop in the aftermath of the 1967 disturbances in participation by organized labour in strikes.[45] During 1968–70 only 36% of strikes involved labour organizations and during 1971–75 only 21%. Over the decade 1978–88, however, over 40% of all strikes involved at least one labour organization although not always trade unions. In the 1990s, some 74% of all strikes had unions or other labour organizations involved but, as in the past, such involvement was usually no more than offering post-hoc advice to strikers or representing them in negotiations.[46] The character of union involvement in industrial action when it occurs can best be described as 'defensive economism' in that most actions do not touch on issues relating to job control, but focus on matters relating to wages or fringe benefits. Unions' defensiveness is also suggested by the fact that their involvement tends to ebb and flow in a counter-cyclical manner. Chiu's study found a strong inverse relationship between the business cycle and the proportion of strikes in which labour organizations were involved.

Another form of collective action is the 'trade' or labour dispute which usually involves conflicts between an employer and a group of workers (though not necessarily a trade union) who may have resorted to some form of industrial action. The causes of these disputes are classified officially under such categories as employer insolvency or cessation of business for other reasons, prolonged lay-off, removal of factory, redundancy or retrenchment, dispute between principal contractor and subcontractor, changes of terms of employment and dismissal. The number of industrial disputes jumped after the mid-1980s, and the number of cases in which unions and labour organizations were involved also increased. Nevertheless, we should not construe this as a sign of an increase in labour militancy since such trade disputes were no more than a record of the grievances that workers sought to redress through an institutional channel. Collective organization and militancy are not necessary ingredients in trade disputes.

❑ Towards a New Type of Unionism?

While private sector trade unions' workplace economic activities appear to be waning, they have found new roles in the wider community. Before the 1970s, as mentioned above, the orientation of Hong Kong's labour movement was fundamentally political in a special sense. It was basically an extension of the CCP-KMT political rivalry on the Mainland. The FTU and TUC pledged loyalty to the CCP and the Kuomintang (KMT) respectively. Their political activities in postwar Hong Kong were directed primarily at each other. The FTU unions occasionally confronted the colonial state, the most striking example being the 1967 riots. Apart from a few incidents however, both the FTU and the TUC unions did not attempt to alter Hong Kong's political power structure and seldom sought the improvement of working class conditions through legislative channels.

By the 1980s, however, a new form of political unionism was developing. Rather than engaging in political struggles largely outside the arena of institutional politics as they used to do, local unions began to become more active inside it. Not only were unions becoming major forces in the political arena, they were also forging crucial alliances with political parties and forming competing coalitions for the control of legislative power. This became increasingly evident in the 1980s in the context of two major political developments — the Sino-British agreement on the future of Hong Kong and the opening up of the local political system to wider participation. The labour movement's new propensity to realize its objectives through political and legislative channels is suggested by the struggle for a central provident fund. Finally, unions have come to participate more actively in issue-oriented social movements. This suggests they may be taking on the characteristics of social movement unionism. We illustrate these developments below.

The Drafting of the Basic Law[47]

The dominant political development of the 1980s was the agreement reached in 1984 between the governments of the UK and the PRC on the future of Hong Kong under which China would resume sovereignty over Hong Kong on 1 July 1997. Under the terms of the agreement, Hong Kong as a Special Administrative Region (SAR) of China is supposed to enjoy a high degree of autonomy after 1997, except on matters concerning foreign affairs and defence.[48] In 1985 China created the Basic Law Drafting Committee (BLDC) to draft Hong Kong's post-1997 mini-constitution. It appointed 69 members to the BLDC including 23 Hong Kong members of whom only 2 were trade unionists. In 1986, another body, the BLCC, was appointed with 180 members, including 13 representing labour organizations, comprising 6 from civil service unions and 7 from other labour organizations. The nomination of these seven members was to become a source of controversy within the labour movement.

Prior to the formation of the BLCC, the Joint Conference of Labour Groups on the Basic Law was formed in September 1985, open to all trade unions, to collect and express the views of labour on the Basic Law, and by October some 167 organizations had joined. The Joint Conference was allowed to nominate seven members to the BLCC while the civil service unions were asked to nominate six. It was agreed that these nominees would be decided by election. Because the TUC unions had refused to participate in the Joint Conference, the FTU affiliates had a majority of votes in the election on a one-union one-vote basis.[49] Concerned that the FTU group would command a majority in the election, the CIC and some other labour organizations bargained for the allocation of one of the seven BLCC seats to be a representative from the CIC, two to be from the FTU group, and two each to represent independent labour federations and independent unions. Just before the election, the CIC's director was informed that some of the FTU members unions would not support him in the election. Two unions close to the CIC then withdrew from the Joint Conference and they were followed by another 20 civil service unions in protest against what was perceived as manipulation and discrimination against the independent unionists. In the October election for labour nominees to the BLCC, three of the seven elected were from the FTU group, three from independent unions, and one from an independent labour federation.[50]

This split over labour representation on the BLCC highlights the cleavages that have long beset Hong Kong's union movement. Another example involves attitudes towards political change. The independent unions have generally lobbied for a more democratic political framework for the future SAR as well as more substantive rights for labour. They have demanded a higher proportion of representatives to be elected by universal suffrage in the future legislation and had called for inclusion of such labour rights as organization, bargaining and social security in the Basic Law. The FTU and its affiliates, although largely concurring with demands for labour's substantive rights, part ways with the independent unions on the future political system. Echoing the line of China's leaders that the primary task is to maintain Hong Kong's stability and prosperity, they rallied for moderation in the pace and degree of democratization in Hong Kong's political development. In 1988, the FTU proposed a blueprint for the future SAR legislature in which 45% of the seats would be allocated to representatives from functional groups, 40% filled by direct elections and 15% from an electoral college, with all representatives sitting in a single chamber.[51]

Following the June 1989 events in China, China's leaders became strongly suspicious of Hong Kong because of the support many Hong Kong people gave to the students and democratic movement in China. The Chinese government considered it necessary to install checks and balances in the future political system for Hong Kong in order to prevent it from becoming a 'base of subversion'. A so-called 'One Council, Two Chambers' or bicameral model was then proposed by local political groups said to have close connections to the Chinese government. Chinese officials quickly expressed their support for the scheme.

China's changing position on the future political system created a dilemma for the FTU. On the one hand, shocked by the Tiananmen student massacre, the FTU publicly condemned the suppression of the democratic movement.[52] Towards the end of 1989 however, the FTU backtracked on its earlier proposal for the future SAR legislature and now proposed a model that bore a strong similarity to the 'One Council, Two Chambers' model supported by China. It was not known whether the FTU's new proposal was influenced by the preferences of the Chinese government. The FTU leaders had maintained that it was the product of consulting their members and opinions from wider society. However, some members of FTU affiliates issued public statements criticizing the FTU's support for the bicameral model and pointed out that rank-and-file members had not been consulted before the FTU announced the proposal.[53]

The final draft of the Basic Law, ratified by China's National People's Congress in early 1990, permitted tentative evaluation of the efficacy of union participation in the drafting process. On the future political framework, trade union assessments of the Basic Law varied. The FTU and its affiliates considered it acceptable as doing 'justice to the interests of all circles'. Independents were disappointed with the outcome while the TUC remained silent. While it is difficult to assess how much influence the union movement as a whole has had in the drafting of the Basic Law, their limited influence does surface in those areas that most unions agree upon. The right to strike and to participate in trade unions are included in the Basic Law, as is reference to legal protection of 'welfare benefits and retirement security of the labour force'.[54] However, demands from both FTU and independent unions also included the right of recognition from employers and the right of collective bargaining. On this score, even the FTU leaders expressed reservations about the provisions in the Basic Law.

Some political commentators had considered the union movement largely irrelevant to the drafting process. The major players were the CCP, the British government and the capitalist class in Hong Kong.[55] Unionists were a minority on the BLCC and had only token representation on the BLDC. On the other hand, members of Hong Kong's capitalist class had visited Beijing frequently and the CCP leaders had been well versed in their needs and worries. Under these circumstances, it was not surprising that unions had only a marginal influence in shaping their own political future.

Participation in Electoral Politics

The Hong Kong government's moves during the 1980s in the direction of a more representative political system began with the opening to election in 1982 of some positions previously filled by nomination on the Urban Council and District Boards. Following the 1984 White Paper on 'The Further Development of Representative Government in Hong Kong' a system of indirect elections to the legislature was implemented. In place of a legislature comprised solely of official members (civil servants) and appointed unofficial (non-civil service) members, the composition of the Legislative Council from late 1985 was restructured to include 12 members elected by an electoral college (comprised of all members of District Boards, the Urban Council and a new Regional Council), 12 members elected by nine functional constituencies, 22 appointed by the Governor, and 10 official members. Of the nine functional constituencies, three — the commercial, industrial and labour — returned two members each.

This corporatist form of political representation thus opened a new institutional channel for organized labour to participate in the making of public policy. The electorate for the Labour functional constituency was the same as for the LAB — all registered employee trade unions — with each union that registered as an elector entitled to one vote. Only individuals substantially connected with the Labour functional constituency could stand for election (the exception was civil servants who were not permitted to run) and they should be nominated by at least ten unions to become a candidate. A preferential voting system applied to the election of the two candidates.

With the exclusion of civil servants as candidates, this left the potential field for election from the Labour constituency open only to non-civil servants.

In the first election in 1985 only two candidates were nominated, one from the FTU and the other from the TUC.[56] However, the influence of elected labour representatives on the legislature was structurally limited since they were outnumbered by those from the government, business and professional classes.

The FTU encouraged members to register as voters in the 1985 District Board elections and the 1986 Regional Council elections. In the District Board elections, the FTU claimed that 10 out of a total of 525 candidates were from member unions, of whom 5 were elected. The TUC reportedly put up seven, with two elected. By comparison, members of the Professional Teachers' Union (PTU) reportedly won 24 seats on the District Boards. Both the FTU and TUC were also reported to have drawn up lists of candidates whom members were asked to support.[57]

After the June 4 Incident, local 'patriotic' political forces loyal to the CCP formed the Democratic Alliance for the Betterment of Hong Kong (DAB). The DAB had close relations with the FTU whose leaders played key roles in the new political party. On the other hand, the diverse political bodies formed by the liberals also consolidated into a political party, first in the United Democrats of Hong Kong (UDHK) and then the Democratic Party (DP). Both the UDHK and DP have close ties to the CTU, the new independent union federation. Lau Chin-shek, a leader of the CTU, played an active part in the formation of the UDHK. DP leaders like Szeto Wah, Cheung Man-kwong and Ho Mun-ka are leaders of unions affiliated to the CTU.

Unions were being pulled more strongly into electoral politics over the course of political transition. In the 1994 District Board and Urban Council election, the FTU, along with the Democratic Alliance, launched itself into electoral politics on a grand scale. The FTU 'supported' a total of 50 candidates in the District Board election. Two CTU organizers also participated in the DB election. Union-supported candidates scored a remarkable success in the DB elections since 30 out of 52 candidates won seats.[58] In the 1995 Legco election, apart from the trade union functional constituencies and other professional functional constituencies such as social services, teachers and nurses, union activists contested a large number of seats in the newly established sectoral functional constituencies. The CTU forged a 'Democratic Workers' Front' to support six candidates in the new functional constituencies election. Among these six, four were selected from the CTU's own affiliates, one was its ally from a local workers' organization, and the last one from the Democratic Party. Not to be outdone, the FTU fielded the same number of candidates. Between the two federations, they accounted for 34% of the 35 candidates competing for the nine seats in the new functional constituencies. One of CTU's leaders, Lau Chin-shek, competed in one of the geographical constituencies. Two FTU candidates in turn competed in the geographical direct elections. By all standards, trade unions had done very well in the 1995 election. Out of a total of 60 seats, trade unionists won

9.[59] In the new 'universal' functional constituencies, they won four out of the nine seats.

Electoral participation by trade unions continued after the handover, although changes in electoral rules had become less favourable to them. In the 1998 Legislative Council elections, four prominent trade unionists who headed the list of candidates for their political parties in certain geographical constituencies won seats. They were Tam Yiu-chung, a vice-chairman of the FTU, from the DAB list for New Territories (NT) West; Lee Cheuk-yan, General Secretary of the CTU, from The Frontier list for NT West; Lau Chin-shek, Chairman of the CTU, from the DP list for Kowloon West; and Chan Yuen-han, a vice-chairman of the FTU, from the DAB list for Kowloon East. Leung Yiu-chung, a labour activist, was elected under the Neighbourhood and Workers' Service Centre banner in NT West. Szeto Wah, a past president of the PTU, was returned from the DP list for Kowloon East. Due to the narrowing of the electorate for the functional constituencies representing major economic groupings (e.g. manufacturing) to include only corporate members of major organizations, labour activists did not compete for election from these constituencies in 1998. But three individuals from the union movement were returned for the three Labour functional constituency seats, and the successful candidates for the Education (Cheung Man-kwong) and Health Services (Ho Mun-ka) constituencies (both running under the DP banner) came from a trade union background. Thus, 11 of the 60 Legco seats in the first post-handover elected legislature were occupied by individuals who were either currently or previously active in labour affairs.

Using Legislative Channels

Apart from active participation in electoral politics, the 're-politicization' of the labour movement can also be observed in organized labour's efforts to seek improvements in labour conditions through legislative channels. From the 1980s onward, trade unions have concentrated much effort on lobbying and campaigning for legislative improvements of labour conditions. Much of their attention has been devoted to three major issues involving the state and the labour market. The first concerns the importation of foreign workers and the retraining of local workers to alleviate the 'shortage' of labour. The second centres on the debate over the establishment of a central provident fund and related forms of retirement and old-age benefits. The third issue concerns the discrimination faced by women in the labour market and the demand for equal opportunity legislation. We address only the first two issues here since the third is discussed in chapter 8.

From the early 1980s, business organizations began to highlight the labour shortage problem in order to pressure the government for possible solutions at the community level.[60] Two industries that earlier on encountered serious recruitment problems were textiles and clothing whose ability to relocate to China was limited by country-of-origin rules and quota availability. In 1987 the Standing Committee on Textiles of the Federation of Hong Kong Industries submitted proposals to the government to alleviate the labour shortage, including allowing the importation of contract labour from China, the creation of a special processing zone in the New Territories near the border with China so that PRC workers could cross the border to work in the zone during the day and return to China in the evening after work, and using Vietnamese refugees confined to closed camps. The Federation also called for a government/industry working group to study the problem. Trade associations in construction, textiles and hotels as well as the Chinese Manufacturers' Association and the Chinese General Chamber of Commerce conducted surveys of the labour shortage problem faced by their members and also proposed solutions.[61] A number of leading business and employer federations then formed the Joint Associations Working Group and commissioned a consulting firm to produce a report. The resulting 1989 *Report on Hong Kong's Labour Shortage* recommended that 'the Government should urgently re-examine its labour policy and adopt a more flexible attitude towards the importation of contract labour from outside Hong Kong', and warned of the dire consequences for failing to do so, such as rising inflation impairing Hong Kong's international competitiveness, and slower economic growth.

Initially the government resisted calls for labour importation. In his October 1988 address at the opening of the 1988/89 session of the Legislative Council, the Governor acknowledged tightness of the labour supply situation over the previous year, but he believed the long-term solution lay in 'increased automation, greater productivity and improved wages and working conditions which attract more people to seek employment'. To allow contractors to import workers for specific projects 'would interfere with the normal adjustment process within the economy ... [and] would also conflict with [the] aim of allowing the workforce to share the benefits in good years as they share the difficulties in lean years'.[62] This official policy had the support of the trade unions which were strongly opposed to allowing the importation of workers because of perceived threats to their own employment and standards of living.[63]

In April 1989 however, as pressure from private business organizations mounted, the government reversed course and announced it would adopt a more flexible stance on importation of labour. During 1989, some 11 409 professionals and other persons having technical expertise or administrative and managerial skills from over 30 countries were admitted for employment. In addition, due to the general shortage of skilled labour in the local market, a special scheme allowing employers to recruit skilled workers from outside Hong Kong was introduced in May 1989. The scheme provided for the importation of 3 000 workers at technician, craftsman and supervisory levels on contracts not exceeding two years. In 1990, the government decided to allow employers to recruit from outside Hong Kong up to 2 700 skilled workers at the technician, craftsman and supervisory levels, 10 000 workers at the experienced operative level and initially 2 000 construction workers to facilitate the construction of the new airport and related projects. Under the new scheme, 4 524 applications involving 57 558 workers were received. After vetting, 12 389 workers were found eligible for entry under the scheme.[64] In late 1991, the government announced that it was considering further expanding the labour importation scheme to allow the importation of up to 25 000 skilled and semi-skilled foreign workers but without specification or allocation of quotas to any particular industry. In spite of strong opposition from organized labour, the Executive Council in early January 1992 approved the scheme.[65]

Despite their ideological differences, the major trade union federations in Hong Kong shared in common opposition to labour importation and called for the schemes to be scrapped. When the Executive Council in early January 1992 approved a scheme to allow the importation of up to 25 000 skilled and semi-skilled foreign workers (doubling the previous ceiling of 12 500), six employee representatives on the Labour Advisory Board and two members of the Legislative Council who represented the Labour functional constituency issued a joint statement demanding abolition of the scheme. Individual unions and union federations joined in the attack, arguing that imported labour would suppress local wages and hurt those dismissed due to lack of work, factory closures and relocations. Moreover, unions believed that an expanded quota was the thin edge of the wedge and that more labourers would be brought in to work on the massive airport core projects. Despite attempts by the Secretary for Education and Manpower to reassure union activists of government measures to protect the interests of local labour by setting wage levels for imported labour, imposing heavy penalties on employers who exploit these workers and creating a retraining fund financed through a levy on imported workers, organized labour had remained adamantly opposed to the policy of labour importation.

Following the Executive Council's decision in early 1992 to increase the quota of imported labour, a coalition of 219 labour unions representing some 200 000 members from both the left and right wings of the union movement was formed. In mid-January the Joint Committee Against Importation of Labour was established and a decision was made to set up a strike fund.[66] Plans were made for a mass rally and demonstration outside the Legislative Council chamber in late January when labour representatives on the Legislative Council planned to move a motion debate on the issue. A signature campaign, public hearings and demonstrations were also planned to maintain momentum. Despite labour's mobilization, the motion in Legislative Council calling for shelving of labour importation schemes was defeated by a vote of 35 to 23. No general strike followed however. This was not surprising since, first, it was not clear whether substantial numbers of workers would respond to a call to strike over the imported labour issue, and second, the threat of a general strike was probably intended more as a signal to the government and business of the potential loss of labour's good will and of future labour relations problems if the labour importation scheme were to be expanded further. What organized labour had succeeded in achieving was to sensitize the government to the potential explosiveness of policy changes that did not take into account the interests of labour.

Partly to pacify the unions over the imported labour issue, the government announced in 1992 a plan to retrain unemployed workers previously employed in manufacturing. Prior to that, the government had denied that displaced workers faced problems finding jobs elsewhere because the overall unemployment rate was very low and demand for workers in the services sector had been expanding rapidly. While it had preferred to let the market mechanism operate to transfer human resources from one sector to another, it could no longer do so once it had chosen to intervene by enlarging the supply of low-cost labour through the importation scheme. When non-interventionism became indefensible, the government established the Employees Retraining Board (ERB) to provide training to workers adversely affected by the industrial restructuring. It offered career counselling, job placement service and retraining programmes to teach workers new skills in such areas as hotel room service, Chinese computer input and retail sales.

In 1993, the 'On-the-Job Training Scheme' was launched to subsidize employers who hired and provided training to retrainees. Employers participating in the scheme could then pay retrainees below going market rates with the shortfall covered by a retraining allowance paid by the ERB. By the end of 1993, 342 employers had joined the Scheme which offered more than 4 200 vacancies.[67]

Unions continued to criticize the Scheme for its inability to counteract the effects of competition from imported labourers and sexual and age discrimination in the labour market.[68] They preferred a large-scale system of unemployment benefits to be installed to give displaced manufacturing workers a reasonable standard of living while they were looking for other jobs. Moreover, they favoured establishing retraining programmes on a much larger scale and administered by the public sector (with union participation) to ensure more useful new skills were provided to workers. Finally, unions contended that all retraining efforts would be in vain if middle-aged and female workers forced out of manufacturing were being discriminated against by prospective employers on the basis of their age and gender. They thus advocated the introduction of equal opportunity legislation. The government argued that the Scheme was a model for public-private cooperation in tackling the retraining problem. It was determined to avoid transforming retraining into a disguised form of unemployment benefit, and claimed a centralized state-administered scheme would be too inflexible to keep up with the constantly changing demand for new skills.

A second issue that preoccupied unions in the 1980s was the debate over a central provident fund (CPF). Demands for a scheme that would provide retirement benefits to workers were first raised in the 1980s, with the FTU being one of the earliest proponents, but the Hong Kong government's position had been to encourage voluntary retirement schemes. The result was that only a minority of workers enjoyed a pension or other form of retirement benefit schemes, notably civil servants and employees of major public utilities. During the 1980s, the three major union blocs had come out in support of the establishment of a CPF. It was a feasible objective for the FTU to pursue because it enabled the FTU to demonstrate its efforts on behalf of the working class while avoiding the thorny issue of democratization. The independent unions, led by the CIC, were a spearhead in putting pressure on the government to take action. The TUC also supported it, being content to deal with an issue not connected to the Basic Law.

The independent unions and the FTU nevertheless differed on their preferred pace for establishing a CPF. The FTU, with its greater concern over maintaining Hong Kong's stability and prosperity, was ready to accept a watered-down government proposal in 1985 for a long-service payment scheme compensating dismissed workers with long tenure as a first step towards the eventual establishment of a CPF. The independents were less compromising and staged a protest in front of the Legislative Council when the bill on a long-service payment scheme was passed.[69] The FTU was also more inclined to work within the institutional framework and largely abstained from the protests of the independent unions and other labour organizations. For the latter group, mobilization of the public, arousing public consciousness and directing protest actions were the key methods of struggling for their objectives.

Despite the trade unions' united front on the CPF, the interests of the capitalist class prevailed. In 1987, consistent with the position of employers, the Governor announced the rejection of the proposal for a CPF on the grounds that it would adversely affect the local economy. The government was also concerned about its own financial solvency and additional fiscal burdens of a CPF.[70] Thus, the fundamental nature of Hong Kong's political economy and the imbalance of class power frustrated the unions' effort to seek some safeguards for the working class.

In the 1990s however, the CPF issue was resurrected by the colonial government presumably due to its concern with maintaining popular support in preparation for a 'honourable retreat' in 1997. The local business elite also became somewhat more receptive to the idea of having some form of retirement schemes for employees. Major companies in particular were favourable to a compulsory contributory pension scheme simply because most of them already had their own schemes. The government's initial proposal however was not a pay-as-you-go CPF, but a standard payment to all senior citizens paid out of a fund to which both employers and employees were to contribute. It differed from the CPF or private pension scheme because the payment would be the same for all senior citizens regardless of their past contribution. Instead of a compulsory saving scheme envisaged in a CPF programme, it was a type of disguised tax involving the redistribution of income from employers and high-income earners to low-income earners.

The proposal met with opposition from almost all key social groups although for different reasons. Liberals and trade unionists supported the scheme's redistributive thrust, but objected to the government's limited financial commitment to the scheme and demanded the government make a matching contribution to the pension fund. The business class resented of course the principle of income redistribution underlying the scheme and feared the scheme would open the floodgates to a public retirement benefits scheme as a welfare entitlement. The Chinese government also opposed the scheme from concerns that it could be a forerunner of a welfare state for Hong Kong, and would lead to a deterioration of the business environment by adding to business operating costs.

Facing concerted opposition and divided opinions, the government then made an about-face and scrapped the old-age payment scheme in favour of a mandatory private pension scheme. Under the new proposal, all companies would have to set up a pension scheme for their employees. Both employers and employees would be required to contribute and the pension funds would be managed by private fund managers who in turn would be monitored by a new central regulatory agency. Trade unionists opposed this mandatory private pension scheme because it would mean even less governmental financial commitment since the government would not underwrite the risk of mismanagement and low returns by private fund managers. They were also dissatisfied because the proposed scheme would in effect exclude low-income workers from benefiting by allowing them to be exempt. Once again due to the concerted opposition of the business elite and the Chinese government, as well as the factional dissension within the labour movement, the struggle for legislative stipulation of retirement benefits resulted in a less desirable outcome (a mandatory private pension scheme instead of the CPF) from labour's point of view.

Trade Union Participation in Social Protest

During the 1970s, trade union participation in social protest was fairly muted. The lack of involvement by the FTU and TUC in social issues was not due to indifference but was a matter of 'whether involvement can gain any political privilege by, say, discrediting the Government or conversely, supporting the

Government, in the light of the action of the rival camp.'[71] From the late 1970s however, some labour organizations and trade union leaders began to participate more visibly in community protest movements. The organizational form of these protest movements was that of temporary alliances among labour and other community groups for limited purposes as a means of putting more effective pressure on the government. The CIC had served as one of the linking pin organizations in bridging different groups and coordinating their actions.

In the late 1970s, a campaign was launched to promote industrial safety and improvements in employees' compensation. This resulted in a statement signed by 41 unions, including 13 belonging to the FTU and 2 to the TUC, together with other labour groups. In 1981, the Coalition Against Bus Fare Increase was formed and included leaders of the PTU and initially the FTU, as well as church and student groups. During the later stages of this campaign, some civil service unions also became involved. In 1982, the Coalition for the Monitoring of Public Utility Companies was formed after utility companies had raised charges. Trade unionists from the PTU, the FTU, the Hong Kong Social Workers' General Union and several civil service unions joined with church and student activists in this coalition. This campaign was effective in that for the first time the government agreed to publish the scheme of profit control for seven utility companies. The coalition subsequently mobilized other pressure groups to petition the Governor in late 1982 on the setting up of a central provident fund scheme. A signature campaign and lobbying among unofficial members of the Executive and Legislative councils followed.[72] Since then, the CIC and later the CTU had taken an active part in successive campaigns against price increases by public utilities.

On May Day, 1983, in the context of a deteriorating economy, rising indirect taxes, a fall in real wages and a relatively low pay increase granted to civil servants, a mass rally was organized that involved some 300 representatives from 80 labour organizations. A petition was submitted to the Governor for a comprehensive social security plan, laws to protect workers from unfair dismissals, the setting up of a wages compensation fund, and making Labour Day a paid legal holiday. Proposals by the Hong Kong government for political reforms stimulated another trade union joint venture when, in September 1984, unions formed the Joint Conference on Representative Government. Some 88 organizations participated, including 17 independent unions.[73] Trade unionists who had played a leading role in earlier protest movements were among the principal leaders.

In the aftermath of the June 4 Incident, trade unionists participated actively in organizations supporting the democratic movement in China. Unionists were involved, for example, in the formation of the Hong Kong Alliance in Support of Patriotic Democratic Movements of China.[74] The FTU-affiliated unions joined ranks initially with other groups to show their support for the students. The long-term consequence of this incident was the reinforcement of the split within the labour movement along the lines of whether unions should support the Chinese government. FTU unions were quickly drawn back into the 'patriotic' front supporting the Chinese government's policies while many unions affiliated to the CTU remained sympathetic to the Chinese democratic movement.[75]

Towards the late 1980s, trade unions began participating more in wider social and community affairs only indirectly related to labour issues. Both the FTU and the CTU had set up social affairs committees focusing on involvement in social and community issues. For instance, the CTU's Social Affairs Committee has since 1994 joined forces with women's concern groups to raise public awareness over sexual harassment and in 1994 lobbied over the discriminatory rules of inheritance among indigenous New Territory residents.[76] In the first quarter of 1994, the FTU's Social Affairs Committee petitioned the Secretary for Transport and the Legco respectively against an increase in bus fares and for the freezing of a proposed increase in rates. It also held a press conference to present its view towards the new government budget. With its more abundant organizational and financial resources, the FTU had also been able to establish local branches as a way of showing its commitment to community-based issues. These local branches organized signature campaigns against a rates' increase and had formed alliances with local pro-China political organizations and residents' groups to expand the influence of the 'patriotic popular front' and compete for local support.[77]

The widening scope of unions' involvement in broader community-based issues and their growing cooperation with community-based protest movements appear to signal the emergence of 'social movement unionism' found in some developing countries.[78] As in other Third World countries, problems arising from the provision of urban public goods — housing, medical services, environment and transport — have now been incorporated into the unions' agenda, especially those of the major federations. It is premature however to claim that a new form of social movement unionism is emerging in Hong Kong. The participation of the labour movement in community struggles has been limited in both frequency and depth. Local unions have not established the kind of organic links with community organizations found elsewhere and have been at best marginally involved in community mobilization.

Union intervention in community issues is best interpreted as fundamentally political in character in that union local community activities are often geared more towards building local support for the major union federations. In this respect, the FTU has been executing this strategy to greater effect and does not hesitate to acknowledge the electoral function of its local branches.[79] Furthermore, the style of union involvement in local issues is not substantially different from that of other political pressure groups. The dominant repertoire consists of a signature campaign, a very small opinion survey, a press conference, meetings with officials and petitions submitted to the government. The primary objectives seem to be limited to raising the level of public concern over the issue, exerting pressure on the government to do something about the situation, and above all enhancing public recognition of unions' active participation in local affairs. The type of active participation in community organization and mobilization seen elsewhere is conspicuously absent in Hong Kong. For example, Seidman has described how Brazilian and South African unions have been willing, in alliance with community-based protest groups, to engage in broad community campaigns targeting the state and employers to provide a decent standard of living to workers and community residents.[80]

❑ Explaining Continuing Stagnation and the New Politicization

The preceding discussion has stressed three points about the union movement since the early 1980s:

1. its continuing stagnation in numerical terms;
2. the growing politicization of movement strategies; and
3. its still limited influence on important issues affecting the future of the working class.

This section seeks to account for this situation by synthesizing three different strands of analysis: economic-structural, cultural and political.

The Labour Market

A well-rehearsed line of argument is that the particular pattern of Hong Kong's postwar industrialization has been a major hindrance to a stronger labour movement. After World War II, the emergence of a new international division of labour in the capitalist world and the incorporation of Hong Kong into this network of exchange and production transformed Hong Kong from a trading port to an industrial city.[81] This led to a rapid change in the contours of the union movement. Previous union strongholds such as ship-building and ship-repairing declined. The emergence and expansion of export-oriented light industries set in motion a process of 'structural demobilization' of labour that worked against effective organizing:

> ... it is clear that the preponderance of industrial jobs in the light-industry export sectors characterized by low-skill, minimal advancement opportunities, and job insecurity, along with a workforce dominated by young women who do not anticipate long-term industrial employment, militate against effective class politics or organization.[82]

The proletariat class created by Hong Kong's postwar industrialization consequently differed qualitatively from its pre-war counterpart.

As demand for labour soared in the labour-intensive manufacturing sector from the late 1950s and competition for labour intensified, workers discovered that they could get higher pay through individual action via exit (or the threat of exit). The feasibility of the exit option was enhanced by the spatial density of firms as they rapidly proliferated (especially in clothing, toys and plastics, and electronics), by the low level of skill required in these industries, and by the widespread use of piece-rate systems of pay. Because market forces led to continuous rises in real wages, 'labour mobility has been an acceptable alternative to collective wage bargaining and grievance resolution'.[83] Furthermore, the combination of a tight labour market and the familial ethos among workers had also enabled the working class family to pursue a strategy of survival and mobility by pooling family resources. In particular, the patriarchal arrangements in the Chinese family had allowed working class families to appropriate the income of their unmarried working daughters.[84] In brief, Hong Kong's particular pattern of industrialization had engendered structural forces that in turn triggered off a vicious circle of individual (or familial) strategies of market behaviour and weak class formation among the industrial working class. This process had inhibited union growth in the manufacturing sector, and the union movement as a whole stagnated as manufacturing became the largest employment sector in the economy.[85]

If a tight labour market for semi-skilled labour was at least partly responsible for a weak labour movement in the earlier decades, the slackening in the growth of the economy in the 1980s had paradoxically contributed to its continuing stagnation in the private sector. The decline of traditional manufacturing industries such as textiles which had been union strongholds contributed to the sharp drop in union membership. The process of industrial restructuring also heightened workers' sense of labour market insecurity as firms closed their local operations and relocated elsewhere. Participation in trade unions simply would not help them to cope in this situation. The mass exodus of workers from manufacturing to other sectors also accentuated labour market competition among workers and weakened the appeal of collective organization. For instance, in the growing industries, like commerce, transport and financial services, union density declined over the 1980s. Only in the older industries such as manufacturing and construction had unions through their organizing efforts from the late 1980s been able to recuperate some of the earlier losses. As employment in these sectors declined rapidly, union density actually rose in the early 1990s. Consistent with the arguments of the resource mobilization approach, the weakening in workers' bargaining power in the labour market has had a dampening effect on workers' tendency to embrace collective organizations such as trade unions.

The Role of Culture

Another stock answer to the question of why unions remain weak in Hong Kong's private sector stresses cultural values, in particular the impact of the 'refugee mentality' on workers' industrial attitudes and behaviour. A substantial portion of the rapid growth of the Hong Kong population after World War II was comprised of refugees fleeing from the political turmoil and changes in China.[86] These refugees encountered in Hong Kong a laissez faire economy and had to depend to a large extent on the familial group for economic survival. A consequence was an ethos of 'utilitarianistic familism' in which familial interests tended to take precedence over societal or other group interests.[87] This type of familism, combined with a strong motivation to seek individual economic advancement and a desire for a stable political environment, was said to generate psychological resistance to trade unions, which were seen to be extensions of Chinese politics. The impact of the refugee mentality in preventing union growth should not be exaggerated however. It cannot explain the widely divergent fortunes of unions across different economic sectors. Employees in the public sector, as we shall show in the next chapter, were not encumbered by the refugee mentality in joining trade unions. Moreover, if the refugee mentality were operative, it would be difficult to explain why so many workers had joined the politically oriented FTU and TUC. Finally, even if a refugee mentality were influential in the early postwar decades, it has gradually faded away as the local-born generation has come of age. Recent surveys show the postwar generation to be much less apathetic towards social affairs and much more willing to protect their own interests by collective action.[88]

  This does not mean culture is irrelevant, only that the affective or normative effects of culture should not be overstated. Cultural values do not dictate uniform patterns of action. Rather, culture 'is more like a "tool kit" or repertoire from which actors select differing pieces for constructing lines of action'.[89] This imagery alerts us to how rational social actors respond to different circumstances by drawing on their cultural repertoires of strategies. The familial ethos and the refugee mentality did impact on workers' orientations, but the prevalence of individualist modes of action at the expense of collective ones has to be accounted for by how different contexts activated different responses from among a broader set of cultural repertoires. This point suggests the importance of taking into consideration the economic and political contexts of action. What needs to be highlighted is not cultural values per se, but how the structural contexts interact with workers' cultural predispositions. What needs to be explained therefore is the sensitivity of union movement development to changes in the labour market. Why did the union movement seem so adversely affected by the downturn in the labour market?

  One theoretical strand of new social movement theory highlights how structural changes in a capitalist society generate new forms of social movements as indicated by their values, action forms and constituencies.[90] The changing locus of collective identities for example can shift the loci of social protests from the arena of production to consumption, from the political arena to the civil society, from class and nation to other multifarious social contradictions previously marginalized. From this perspective, if there has been the 'colonization of life-worlds' by the spread of technocratic administrative rationality in advanced European societies, what we have seen in Hong Kong is the triumph of market rationality. Workers' sensitivity to market forces is thus a manifestation of this market rationality.

We contend that this sensitivity reflects a culturally dominant instrumental orientation to work that is rooted in the structural and institutional constitution of Hong Kong society and economy. While cost-benefit calculations may be universal, institutional variables can mitigate or enlarge labour-capital power differentials in situations where market relations are mediated by the collective organization of the working class or state policies. This in turn induces fluctuations in levels of working class collective action by shaping the perceptions of the likelihood of success. In Hong Kong however, the market reigns supreme. Workers have to confront the market directly in the absence of a legally stipulated minimum wage, protection against unfair dismissal and meagre unemployment benefits. In other words, the Hong Kong colonial government has not offered much institutional sheltering from the swings in the labour market compared with other industrial countries.

Unions also became largely ineffective after the 1960s in offering protection to workers due to their small size, organizational fragmentation and their detachment from the shop-floor. The Hong Kong labour market, especially in the manufacturing sector, has also not been conducive to the formation and maintenance of workplace solidarity. Most rank-and-file industrial workers are female whose attachment to work is often secondary to their family obligations.[91] Others argue that familism is a dominant normative orientation of Hong Kong workers irrespective of sex.[92] A high rate of labour turnover is also inimical to the forging of strong cohesive work groups on the shop-floor. While survey data show that Hong Kong workers have a high level of awareness of socio-economic inequality, class does not form a salient basis for the formation of collective identity.[93] Unions were deeply involved historically in political struggles between the Chinese Nationalists and the Communists and were unable to articulate a collective identity capable of capturing the imagination of the postwar locally born generation who lack identity with this historical political schism. In any case, unions are too weak organizationally to be the carrier for the formation of a collective identity among the Hong Kong working class. Before 1968, unions were strong enough to mobilize a substantial minority of workers on the basis of Chinese nationalism to participate in a number of militant and often-politicized strikes. Following the defeat of FTU unions after the 1967 political strikes and the political changes in China after the Cultural Revolution, cultural themes of nationalism and patriotism were unable to take root among the working class.

The net result of this structural constitution of the Hong Kong economy is a high level of instrumentalism and materialism among workers in the sense that 'they emphasize material rewards and underplay the intrinsic qualities of work'.[94] A high level of instrumentalism does not mean workers do not take their work seriously. While lacking moral or emotional attachment to their jobs, they do see working as part of their long-term quest for their own and their families' well-being. A mixture of instrumentalism and a strong drive for economic advancement thus characterizes workers' orientations towards their work. In other words, Hong Kong workers have a high level of instrumental commitment to their work (as a means to personal and familial advancement) but low moral commitment.

These cultural values shape not only workers' perceptions of work but also their propensity to engage in collective actions over workplace issues. Since orientations to work are essentially instrumental and calculative, the impact of market forces on decisions to join unions can be readily comprehended. Participation in collective organization is perceived in terms of its consequences for personal advancement.[95] Hong Kong workers are not therefore culturally predisposed to be individualistic, as England and Rear for example have argued, but when they do participate in collective action they need to be sure that it is to their advantage to do so.[96] In practice, 'they may be prepared to adopt both individual or collective means for protecting or advancing their status, depending on what seems to be the most effective strategy in the circumstances'.[97] Given the pre-existing weakness of the union movement in sectors adversely affected by the economic changes since the 1980s, participation in trade unions is therefore perceived by most workers to be largely irrelevant in advancing or protecting their interests. The majority apparently considered union participation to be of little benefit as manufacturing employment declined sharply after the mid-1980s. When unions stepped up their organizing efforts in the 1990s, they did so by offering immediate and tangible benefits to workers in the form of an array of service and welfare provisions.

The Structure of Political Opportunity

If the structure of the economy was a major impediment to a more viable union movement, political factors including the role of the colonial state, the China factor, and the changing domestic structure of political opportunities since the mid-1980s had also exacerbated the difficulties for union organization.

The colonial state had occupied a peripheral position in the postwar structure of accumulation. It supplied the infrastructural support, maintained law and order and provided some basic social services, but it had not become involved directly in production unlike the experiences of many late industrializers in the Third World. Private entrepreneurs rather than the state played the pivotal role in economic development. In conjunction with this arm's length approach to the economy, the colonial government had followed the British voluntarist tradition in industrial relations.[98] Given the power imbalance in the workplace, this served to buttress managerial prerogatives rather than facilitate labour organization. Though the government did not intervene in labour relations directly, it had not always been a neutral referee. When union actions took on political and anti-colonial overtones in a number of industrial conflicts in the early 1950s, militant workers were arrested and union leaders deported. During the 1967 disturbances involving FTU unions and workers, the government once again did not hesitate to crack down on these unions. Unlike states in many other developing countries however, the Hong Kong colonial government did not adopt direct political repression as its principal strategy for controlling labour.

After the disturbances of 1966 and 1967, the government took on a more active role in labour relations and began to compete with the unions in rendering assistance to workers in settling individual and collective disputes with employers.[99] The rising expenditures by the government since the late 1960s on public goods — housing, education, welfare — may have undermined unions by providing an alternative source of tangible benefits to those offered by some unions.[100] The government's housing policy also had an unintended adverse effect on the union movement by disrupting working-class communities that formed in the immediate postwar period in squatter areas. As workers in these areas were dispersed among different housing estates, the spatial basis for reinforcement of group cohesion and collective consciousness was undermined. The pace and extent of this change seriously outstripped the unions' ability to organize them.[101]

The key political influence crippling the union movement was not however the colonial state but the China factor. Nationalist sentiments were a stimulus to working-class organization before World War II. However, the civil war between the Communists and the Nationalists created a permanent division within Hong Kong's union movement. Competition and infighting among TUC and FTU unions not only caused the proliferation of unions, but also facilitated the divide-and-rule strategy used by employers and the state.[102] This rivalry was fizzling out with the declining status of the right-wing unions, but the June 4 Incident suddenly created a new rift between the FTU and some of the independent unions because of the latter's involvement in protests supporting the Chinese democracy movement.

Lange and Ross argue that critical events in the early stage of union development often have a long-lasting effect on subsequent evolution.[103] This point applies to the Hong Kong union movement. The impact of its political orientation from its early stages became inscribed into its organizational structure. The political divisions within the union movement foster fragmentation, and the political purpose for which unions were established typically induces a top-heavy structure.[104] In order to sustain the unions' political objective, rank-and-file participation is not overly encouraged and workplace organization is given a low priority. Bargaining is not a major objective of union activities; welfare activities instead become the paramount strategy to attract a following.[105] While welfare activities and other union services have been able to attract more workers to join unions, whether genuine and meaningful participation in union activities and a strong sense of union loyalty follow are questionable. Many white-collar employees for example join unions to take advantage of discount prices in the union supermarket and for self-improvement courses in union education centres, but the union itself is rarely considered relevant to their workplace needs.

Changes in the structure of political opportunity from the 1980s have also shaped union orientations and strategies. Lui points out that Hong Kong's popular movements are in a sense 'lost' amid the rapid changes on the political scene.[106] While his comment is not specifically directed to organized labour, it can be argued that, as in the case of other social movement groups, the unprecedented expansion in opportunities for political participation has induced unions to focus on electoral politics — lobbying for legislative changes, heightening awareness and visibility of union activities in local communities, and galvanizing support in elections for union-supported candidates. Rather than concentrating on workplace organizing (which is costly and arduous) and mobilizing for protest action (save for such forms of actions as petitions and signature campaigns), trade unions have been transformed into a prominent vehicle in electoral competition, hence the alliance between unions and political parties, the predominance of welfare and service provisions as an organizing strategy, the establishment of local branches, the frequent intervention in local issues related to people's livelihood, and ultimately the launching of union-supported candidates in elections.

One important and long-run consequence of this election-oriented strategy could be the attenuation of the salience of unions to members and wider public. Many unions now appear to members to act more like welfare and cooperative institutions, rather than as institutions designed to protect and advance employee interests in the labour market and enterprise. Union-provided self-improvement courses, credit cards and discount shopping figure prominently in decisions to join a union. To the average citizen-voter, trade unions have come to appear as just another pressure group cum political organization with the professed objective of advancing grass roots interests and competing for electoral support.

We believe that recent unions activities bear out this interpretation but a few caveats are in order. First, not all unions are electorally oriented; the intensity of this orientation varies from one union to another. The FTU appears to be the most devoted to pursuing this strategy while the CTU appears to remain committed to shop-floor organization and bread-and-butter issues on top of its electoral appeal. Second, we are not suggesting that unionists are merely 'posturing' and 'jockeying' for seats in representative assemblies and thereby manipulating union membership to promote their own personal status. Our interpretation of union strategies need not be construed as a pejorative one. The election-oriented and pressure group strategy may well be a rational response given the various environmental and cultural obstacles to effective shop-floor organization. This strategy might also yield greater dividends in the long run in terms of advancing workers' interests. Third, the effectiveness of this new political unionism is in jeopardy so long as union blocs compete for influence rather than developing genuine and long-lasting forms of inter-organizational cooperation. While the TUC is gradually phasing out, the political and organizational division between the FTU and the CTU is clearly minimizing the impact of their lobbying and electoral efforts in terms of improving working-class conditions. The cacophony of their often-conflicting messages and demands is far from creating a genuine 'voice' of and for the working class.

❏ Conclusion

We began this chapter by referring to two predictions by observers in the early 1980s about the future of the Hong Kong trade union movement. The first was that the union movement would continue to be confined to its existing organizational boundaries with continuing fragmentation and marginal influence on the wider society. Events since the 1980s have only partially confirmed this prediction for the private sector. Although private sector union membership, especially of FTU affiliates, has risen in the 1990s, the increase is not substantial. Union workplace organization remains weak while collective bargaining is rarely practised. Yet unions have made major headway in the political arena, emerging as a force to be reckoned with on both sides of the political spectrum, especially during elections. On the other hand, the second prediction about labour unrest spreading is roundly contradicted by the evidence. Strikes have largely withered away owing to a slump in manufacturing strikes.

Why did observers get it wrong? One answer is that they failed to anticipate the radical changes in the economy and the political arena and the paradoxical effects they had on the capacity for collective organization and action. A corollary of these changes is a subtle long-term shift in the very conception workers have of unionism. That is, it appears that the significance of belonging to a union has changed. Union density in the early postwar years was not particularly high, yet joining a union then signified an important part of a worker's identity. It is questionable whether this is still the case. Since the 1980s there has been a tendency for the process of the 'professionalization' of social movement organization to spread within the established sections of the Hong Kong union movement. This carries the danger that what McCarthy and Zald call 'paper membership' — membership implying little more than allowing one's name to be used on membership rolls — will become increasingly more common as union activities are conducted increasingly away from the shop-floor and instead at union headquarters.[107] Less time, money and resources are demanded from rank-and-file members while a small core of activists or professional organizers play a more important role in running the unions. The union federations have also become more significant actors than their individual affiliates.

These processes of organizational centralization and professionalization are in many respects inimical to grass roots activism or development of shop-floor bargaining, but they appear to suit the unions' new political strategy.[108] This is not surprising as elsewhere, '[u]nions are capable of mobilizing considerable energies and exerting significant presence even with small fluctuating memberships when they are seen as crucial intermediation for public policies or important contributors to political and social equilibria'.[109] The union federations and their headquarters now perform a lot of the political tasks of lobbying legislators and government officials for legislative improvements benefiting the working and middle classes. The top-heavy structure is also appropriate for the building of electoral support for candidates supported by the unions or their political allies. Union federations have taken up a wide range of issues and attempt to mobilize 'moral support' from the public (instead of actually mobilizing them to participate in protests) through such devices as signature campaigns, press conferences and petitions.

Although union members account for only a minority of employees, the union platform seems to be convincing voters that they are the best representatives of grass roots interests. Furthermore, given the high degree of public awareness of union-affiliated candidates and abundant media exposure, trade unions were in an advantageous position to attract support among the highly diversified and amorphous electorate in the new functional constituencies. This perhaps was a clear confirmation of the rationality of the unions' electoral orientation and offer great hope that trade unions would be able to make use of legislative channels to deliver what they have long promised the working class. With support from other legislators sympathetic to grass roots interests, trade unionists began to capitalize aggressively on their newly won legislative muscle to improve workers' lot. For example, almost immediately after the 1995 Legislative Council election, trade union legislators moved to introduce bills that would terminate the labour importation programme once and for all. This in turn prompted the government to introduce bills of its own to scale down, but not phase out, the importation of foreign workers.[110]

Nevertheless, there are limits to the effectiveness of the political strategy. Institutionally, Hong Kong under the SAR administration is still an executive-led polity. Even if those supportive of labour's interests were to comprise a majority of the legislature, there is no guarantee that they could push through legislation that the executive branch opposes. More importantly, the unions' political strategy also has an unintended consequence on their ability to influence events in the future. Trade unions appear to have abdicated control of the shop-floor to employers and to have bet on their capacity to exert a greater degree of influence over governmental policy in the future. Sheer numbers and public demonstration of activism may be adequate for this purpose. Yet it is not inconceivable that while unions' political influence could increase, its long-term mobilizational capacity might face a terminal decline.

Seen in this light, Hong Kong's labour movement appears to fit what Valenzuela characterizes as the 'contestatory' type of unionism 'that is divided politically and ideologically, with an important segment linked to the Communist Party.'[111] His analysis highlights the risks of the current strategy pursued by the local trade union movement in the private sector:

> Given the combination of union weakness, the tendency towards demand escalation that stems from the competition between different segments of leadership, and the great capacity to formulate comprehensive programmes for change that comes from the ideologically charged environment, this form of unionization typically generates a large gap between what it proposes and what it obtains. It easily articulates a critical discourse regarding social and economic ills that should be corrected, but it lacks the necessary strength (except during extraordinary periods of mobilization) to pressure employers and the state effectively.[112]

Politically and organizationally divided, with a small membership base and without a strong presence in the workplace, it will be difficult for the union movement to transcend its current role as simply another interest group in Hong Kong's society and polity. While this sounds like an imprudent judgement on the local labour movement especially given its recent flurry of political activities, it is put in this way because we believe that trade unions remain the most effective institution for defending working-class interests in Hong Kong despite all their limitations. It will be tragic if the labour movement fails to realize its potential to become the authentic collective voice of working people.

❏ Acknowledgements

We gratefully acknowledge support for this and the next chapter from the Hong

Kong Research Grants Council for an earmarked research grant for the project 'Hong Kong Trade Unions Bracing for the Future: Environmental Changes and Organizational Dynamics' (HKU 391/96H).

Notes

1. Parts of this chapter are drawn from our earlier writings, especially Levin and Chiu's 'Dependent capitalism, a colonial state, and marginal unions: the case of Hong Kong'.
2. See England and Rear, *Industrial relations and law in Hong Kong*.
3. See Turner et al., *The last colony: but whose?*
4. See England and Rear, *Industrial relations and law in Hong Kong*, p. 378.
5. See Turner et al., *The last colony: but whose?* p. 159.
6. See England and Rear, *Industrial relations and law in Hong Kong*, p. 378.
7. All labour movements face problems of defining their objectives and deciding whether to pursue these objectives in the economic arena, the political arena, or both. While in a broad sense all decisions about objectives and the context in which to pursue them may be construed as political, we limit the use of the concept of political strategy to refer to all forms of labour movement action aimed at the state and its policies. For a discussion of the historical experience of Hong Kong in this respect, see Levin and Chiu, 'Decolonization without independence: political change and trade unionism in Hong Kong'. While the political/economic distinction dominates in the postwar literature on union strategies, the idea of social movement unionism is more recent. This refers to trade unions acting more like social movement organizations in that they become involved in community struggles not directly related to the workplace nor to enhancing representation of labour in the political arena.
8. In contrast with the social movement approach, Dunlop's industrial relations systems approach views the problem of explaining change in terms of adaptation by system actors — organized labour, employers, government — to changes in their economic, technological and/or political environments. This approach lacks in our view a well-developed theory of the causal mechanisms that link environmental changes to changes in industrial relations institutions and practices. See Dunlop, *Industrial relations systems*. The concept of 'strategic choice' is one attempt to overcome this limitation. See Kochan, Katz and McKersie, *The transformation of American industrial relations*, pp. 3–21.
9. See England and Rear, *Industrial relations and law in Hong Kong*, p. 318.
10. In 1966, 121 of the 240 unions had between 50 and 250 members, 71 between 251 and 1 000, and 30 more than 1 000. Of this 30, only 7 had over 5 000 members, 5 of them affiliates of the FTU.
11. The FTU's strength was mainly in its industrial union affiliates in transport, parts of manufacturing, utilities and the service sector, while the TUC's base was in smaller trades, construction and the restaurant industry.
12. See Chiu, 'Strikes in Hong Kong: a sociological study', p. 205.
13. Scott, *Political change and the crisis of legitimacy in Hong Kong*, pp. 81–126; and England and Rear, *Industrial relations and law in Hong Kong*, pp. 17–23, discuss these disturbances, the role of the FTU unions in the events of 1967, and the effects of these disturbances on government social policy.

14. See England and Rear, *Industrial relations and law in Hong Kong*, p. 148.
15. See Arn, 'Public sector unions', pp. 238–9.
16. See Hopkins, *Hong Kong: the industrial colony*.
17. See Chiu, 'The reign of the market: economy and industrial conflicts in Hong Kong'.
18. See Tsang, 'Income distribution', p. 363.
19. See Turner, Fosh and Ng, *Between two societies: Hong Kong labour in transition*, p. 16.
20. See ibid., p. 71.
21. See Lui and Chiu, 'Industrial restructuring and labour-market adjustment under positive noninterventionism: the case of Hong Kong'.
22. Census and Statistics Department, *Hong Kong annual digest of statistics*.
23. The statistics on trade unions presented below in this chapter and the next one are generated by a computer database containing the information on individual employee unions and their membership reported in the Registrar of Trade Unions' annual reports. Our figures do not necessarily conform to the aggregate statistics presented in the annual reports mainly because of the different accounting procedures used. For example, in the case of unions which have been reclassified as 'mixed' unions of employers and employees, their record is removed from the database because including them would distort over time comparisons.
24. The decline between 1980 and 1981 was mainly due to the reclassification of the Hong Kong Graziers' Union from an employees' union to a mixed organization of employers and employees because its membership (22 655 in 1981) was comprised of persons working in jobs related to agriculture, many of them self-employed and small employers. In calculating total union membership, we have excluded the Hong Kong Graziers Union.
25. Union density is calculated as union membership divided by total number of employees. Private sector employment is estimated by deducting employment in community, social and personal services from labour force statistics collected from the General Household Surveys.
26. See Hong Kong government, *Hong Kong 1989: a review of 1988*, p. 95.
27. See Ting, 'The impact of containerization on seamen's employment: the Hong Kong experience', pp. 120–3.
28. See Leung, 'Promoting workers' interests outside the trade union system: the experience of the Christian Industrial Committee', p. 117.
29. One reported case occurred in 1983 at the Hongkong International Terminals Ltd. between employees belonging to the Union of Godown and Wharf Workers, affiliated to the FTU, and another belonging to an independent union, the Storehouses and Transportation Staff Association. Another involved two Hong Kong Post Office unions, the FTU-affiliated Postal Workers' Union and the Hong Kong Union of Post Office Employees (UPO) over support for UPO's call for industrial action for improved working conditions. A representative from the independent Association of Government Nursing staff reported conflicts with an FTU-affiliated union over a ten-year period. See Leung and Leung, *At the crossroads: Hong Kong's independent trade union movement and the international trade secretariats*, pp. 28–30.
30. See Cheng, 'The role of a trade union centre in a changing society: the case of the Hong Kong Federation of Trade Unions', pp. 114–5.
31. See Li, 'The tension in labour relations is about to explode'.
32. See 'The inevitable trend of union participation in politics', *Sing Tao Evening News*, 10 February 1989; and Li, 'The tension in labour relations is about to explode'.

33. See Turner et al., *The last colony: but whose?* p. 30.
34. See 'Welcoming the arrival of a new era', *FTU Monthly*, June 1994, pp. 6–7, in Chinese.
35. See Turner, 'The prospects for trade unions in Hong Kong', pp. 183–4.
36. Yeung ('Looking at the trade union movement as a social movement', p. 21), for example, has commented as follows: 'In terms of the value orientations of the left and right wing unions, I think they emphasize more on collectivism, and neglect individualism and social justice. There are two levels of meaning for this collectivism. The first is the object of loyalty, or the symbol of the 'collectivity' for these two groups ... On the one side it is the Chinese government, on the other is the Taiwanese government, but in neither case the members of the unions. Second, the approaches of the two groups of unions tend to be tailored for the political lines of the two governments. It seems that the opinions of union members do not have much influence on the unions' centrally determined orientations and stands. In the formulation of the unions' directions, it is likely for both left and right wing unions to adopt a top-down approach. I doubt whether there is sufficient prior discussion with the members in the process of formulation [our translation].'
37. See 'Over 200 union members quitting their union', *Sing Tao Daily*, 15 December 1989.
38. See 'The long-run cause of the internal dissent within the TUC', *Hong Kong Economic Journal*, 28 November 1988, in Chinese.
39. See Commissioner for Labour, *Annual departmental report 1993*, p. 29.
40. See Leung, 'Industrial relations in Cable and Wireless: a unionist's view', pp. 123–33.
41. See England and Rear, *Industrial relations and law in Hong Kong*, p. 168.
42. See Turner, 'The prospects for trade unions in Hong Kong', pp. 183–4.
43. See Tsuen Wan District Board, *A report on the survey on the conditions of work for female workers in Tsuen Wan, 1986*. The closest response, given by only 8.7% of the respondents, was 'ask for pay rise from employer'. This leads to the question of how majority of unorganized workers deal with employment problems and grievances. Seeking help through the Labour Department and the Labour Tribunal is a common action when the employment relationship is terminated. Approaching the CIC for help is another strategy. The most common informal means is probably through labour mobility. The other informal means is through ad hoc group bargaining at the place of work when, for example, a group of workers goes on a brief strike. Such bargaining does not necessarily involve trade unions, although unions are sometimes involved in the background giving advice and support, and is typically focused on a specific issue such as piece rates or the sacking of employees. The ad hoc nature of the dispute and of the bargaining process in these cases means that these temporary and spontaneous combinations typically dissolve after the dispute.
44. See Visser, 'The strength of union movements in advanced capitalist democracies: social and organizational variations', p. 23.
45. See Chiu, 'Strikes in Hong Kong: a sociological study', p. 220.
46. Calculated from the unpublished strike records in the Labour Department.
47. This is based on Levin and Chiu's 'Dependent capitalism, a colonial state, and marginal unions: the case of Hong Kong'.
48. The government of the PRC in an early elaboration of its basic policies regarding Hong Kong stated that Hong Kong's capitalist system and lifestyle would remain

unchanged for 50 years after 1997 and that existing rights and freedoms including those of speech, assembly, association, strikes and choice of occupation were to be ensured by the Basic Law. Strong doubts about China's commitment to maintain existing rights and freedoms and to allow Hong Kong autonomy in domestic affairs — exacerbated by the crackdown on students and the democracy movement at Tiananmen Square in June 1989 — contributed to Hong Kong's middle-class brain drain problem.

49. In sharp contrast to the FTU's active participation in the drafting of the Basic Law, the TUC abstained from the process on political grounds. It recognizes the Nationalists in Taiwan as the sole legitimate government of China, so participating in the drafting of the Basic Law would be tantamount to accepting the sovereignty of the Communists over Hong Kong. Thus the TUC had little choice but to boycott the BLCC and the Joint Conference.

50. See Liang, 'Wither the Hong Kong labour movement? On the Lau Chin-shek incident'.

51. See 'Comments of the FTU on the draft Basic Law consultative document,' *FTU Press*, October 1988, p. 1, in Chinese.

52. See 'Mourning our compatriots killed on June 4th in Beijing', *FTU Press*, July 1989, p. 1, in Chinese.

53. See 'Letter to the editor from a group of FTU members', *Ming Pao Daily News*, 30 November 1989, in Chinese.

54. See *The Basic Law of the Hong Kong Special Administrative Region of the People's Republic of China*, Ch. 2, Art. 27, 36.

55. See Lo, 'Colonial policy-makers, capitalist class and China: determinants of electoral reform in Hong Kong's and Macau's legislatures'.

56. Independent trade unionists outside the civil service had the option of running for one of the other functional constituencies. The president of the Hong Kong Professional Teachers' Union chose to run for election for the Education constituency.

57. See Miners, 'The representation and participation of trade unions in the Hong Kong government', p. 45.

58. 'A four-fold increase in FTU candidates', *The Express*, 16 September 1994; and 'A few FTU candidates are going to participate in the Urban Council Election', *Sing Pao*, 7 January 1995.

59. We count only those who had current links to trade unions. This excludes those like Szeto Wah of the Democratic Party who was a former chairman of the Professional Teachers' Union but who was campaigning primarily on a Democratic Party platform.

60. This discussion is based on Chiu and Levin's 'From a labour-surplus to a labour-scarce economy: challenges to human resource management in Hong Kong'.

61. See Ng et al., 'A report on labour supply in Hong Kong'.

62. See *Hong Kong Hansard*, 10/12/88.

63. A number of stop-gap measures were proposed: relaxing restrictions on overtime work by women, examining ways of inducing more people to enter the labour market and expanding the advisory services of the Hong Kong Productivity Council.

64. See Commissioner for Labour, *Annual departmental report 1991*, p. 8.

65. The relaxation of restraints on importation of labour was the government's short-run strategy for coping with a labour shortage and loss of talents due to emigration. Its medium-term strategy was to encourage the return to Hong Kong of former

emigrants. One form this took was a joint venture between the government, the Hong Kong Institute of Personnel Management and the Hongkong Bank to develop an advanced communication network to assist local employers in recruiting suitable staff from abroad (Chan, 'The impact of a changing environment on Hong Kong's human resources policies'). After the Tiananmen Square Incident in June 1989, an additional strategy aimed at encouraging key employees to remain in Hong Kong was to offer them access to foreign passports, most notably the British nationality scheme of granting 50 000 British passports to key persons and their families.

66. The CTU initiated the 'All Circles Against Importation of Foreign Labour' campaign one day before the Joint Committee, but it appeared that the FTU and TUC decided to isolate the CTU in subsequent actions ('Left, right, centre, union all going their own way', *Ming Pao Daily News*, 12 January 1992).

67. See Commissioner for Labour, *Annual departmental report 1994*, p. 69.

68. See *Hong Kong Labour 1995*.

69. See 'Labour organizations protest in front of the Legislative Council against the long-service payment bill', *Ming Pao Daily News*, 19 December 1985, in Chinese.

70. See *Hong Kong Hansard* 1987, p. 34.

71. See Tso, 'Civil service unions as a social force in Hong Kong', p. 24.

72. See ibid., pp. 24–36; also Chiu, 'Labour organizations and political change in Hong Kong', pp. 56–69.

73. See ibid., pp. 62–6.

74. See chapter 3 in this volume.

75. 'CTU isolated because of its close relationship to the Federation of pro-democracy movement', *Hong Kong Economic Journal*, 5 February 1995.

76. See 'Brief report to the General Assembly', *CTU in Solidarity* 15 (February 1995).

77. At its annual general meeting in 1994, the FTU's Secretary-General indicated that due to overlapping membership between the FTU and the Democratic Alliance for the Betterment of Hong Kong, proper coordination of local resources would be arranged in encouraging members' participation in elections. See 'FTU's new Exco elected', *Economic Daily*, 25 April 1994.

78. See Munck, *The new international labour studies: an introduction*; and Seidman, *Manufacturing militance*.

79. The Secretary-General of the FTU noted in an interview that the local branches served three main functions: contacting members, involvement in issues of local livelihood and elections ('A four-fold increase in FTU candidates', *The Express*, 16 September 1994).

80. See Seidman, *Manufacturing militance*.

81. See So, 'The economic success of Hong Kong: insights from a world-system perspective'.

82. See Deyo, Haggard and Koo, 'Labour in the political economy of East Asian industrialization', p. 51; and also Deyo, 'Export-manufacturing and labour: the Asian case' and *Beneath the miracle: labour subordination in the new Asian industrialism*.

83. See England and Rear, *Chinese labour under British rule*, p. 44.

84. See Salaff, *Working daughters of Hong Kong: filial piety or power in the family?*

85. See Levin and Chiu, 'Dependent capitalism, a colonial state, and marginal unions: the case of Hong Kong'.

86. See Podmore, 'The population of Hong Kong', pp. 25–6.

87. See Lau, *Society and politics in Hong Kong*, p. 72.

88. See Lau and Kuan, *The ethos of the Hong Kong Chinese*; and Wong and Lui, 'Reinstating class: a structural and developmental study of Hong Kong society'.
89. See Swidler, 'Culture in action: symbols and strategies', p. 277.
90. See Brockman, 'Theoretical concerns in comparative social movement research'; Larana, Johnston and Gusfield, *New social movements: from ideology to identity*, pp. 3–35.
91. See Lui, 'Work and work values', p. 112.
92. See Lau, *Society and politics in Hong Kong*.
93. See Wong and Lui, 'Reinstating class: a structural and developmental study of Hong Kong society'.
94. See Lui, 'Work and work values', p. 122; and Lau and Kuan, *The ethos of the Hong Kong Chinese*.
95. Studies of the working class in Britain have shown that instrumentalism is not necessarily incompatible with collective action (Goldthorpe et al., *The affluent worker: industrial attitudes and behaviour*; Goldthorpe, 'The current inflation: towards a sociological account'; and Lui, 'Work and work values').
96. See England and Rear, *Industrial relations and law in Hong Kong*, p. 59.
97. See Levin, 'Work and its deprivations', p. 100.
98. See Ng, 'Labour administration and "voluntarism": the Hong Kong case'.
99. See Turner et al., *The last colony: but whose?* p. 114.
100. See Lau, *Society and politics in Hong Kong*, p. 141; and Scott, *Political change and the crisis of legitimacy in Hong Kong*, pp. 152–70.
101. Chiu's study, 'A brief history of the metal industry workers' union', of a metal industry union found union organizers were able to recruit and hold on to members living in the squatter areas by a variety of means including relief to those suffering from fire (a serious and frequent problem in these areas). A veteran union organizer interviewed in the same study also acknowledged that the geographical dispersal of members in the 1960s prevented the union from holding on to existing members.
102. For instance, the impact of the political strikes by the FTU-affiliated union members in 1967 was minimized by the pro-TUC group some of who served as strikebreakers. The failure of a single union to speak for the entire workforce in a particular firm or sector has often been used as a pretext for employers to refuse to negotiate with the unions.
103. See Lange and Ross, *Unions, change and crisis: French and Italian strategy and the political economy, 1945–1980*.
104. See Turner et al., *The last colony: but whose?*
105. An FTU official acknowledged in an interview that enhancing welfare provisions was the principal way of increasing its membership ('FTU hopes to exceed twenty thousand by the end of year', *Sing Tao Daily*, 22 August 1993). Apart from a shopping service and banquets, a major attraction of FTU membership is discounted enrolment in adult continuing education and self-improvement courses organized by the FTU's education centres. Due to the CTU's limited resources, welfare provisions are less important and involvement in industrial disputes are more important in organizing. Even so, the CTU has been able to provide a shopping service to blue-collar union members of its affiliates through agreement with the Professional Teachers' Union to allow use of its supermarket.
106. See Lui, 'The path of development of Hong Kong's popular movements 1994'.
107. See McCarthy and Zald, 'The trend of social movements in America: professionalization and resource mobilization', p. 375.

108. The tendencies for growing professionalization in union administration and centralization in decision-making and their effects were theorized by Michels, *Political parties: a sociological study of the oligarchical tendencies of modern democracy*, in his classic study of the 'iron law of oligarchy'. Lester, *As unions mature: an analysis of the evolution of American unionism*, also drew attention to these processes in his study of the evolution of American unionism.
109. See Visser, 'The strength of union movements in advanced capitalist democracies: social and organizational variations', p. 23.
110. See 'Imported labour plan under threat', *South China Morning Post*, 27 October 1995.
111. The other types are social democratic, pressure group, state-sponsored, and confrontational. There are also signs that Hong Kong's labour movement is moving towards the pressure group type in which 'unions link themselves with a pre-existing party or fragments of it' (Valenzuela, 'Labour movements and political systems: some variations', p. 55), but the political and organizational divisions within the labour movement still have a dominating influence on its development.
112. Ibid., p. 76.

5

Bureaucratic Insurgency: The Public Sector Labour Movement

David A. Levin and Stephen Wing Kai Chiu

❑ Introduction

During the 1970s a trade union growth wave, marked by a continuous increase in the number of unions and union membership, surged through Hong Kong's public sector. This wave persisted into the 1980s and 1990s. Associated with it was collective protest by some unions in the form of wall posters, petitions, marches to Government House, and work-to-rule actions over the employment policies and practices of government, a phenomenon which can be described as 'bureaucratic insurgency'.[1]

The academic writings about this public sector union growth wave have focused mainly on the period up to the early 1980s.[2] We will review what has happened to the public sector union movement since then, and in doing so intend to contribute to the understanding of how and why this public sector union growth wave and its associated insurgency developed and persisted under British colonial rule. Previous writers have located the causes of this growth wave in the institutional framework of staff relations, stressing in particular the role of the civil service consultative machinery and the restructuring of salary scales in the early 1970s. We agree that this institutional framework is an important influence on the generation and persistence of the growth wave. We argue however that it is only a part of a more extensive ensemble of structures that impinge on the public sector employment relationship. These structures include the internal organizational features of the public sector as well as the external political framework within which the public sector is embedded.

We refer to this ensemble of structures that regulates the behaviour and interactions of both management and employees in the public sector as the governance system.[3] We elaborate below on some features of the governance system and how they can influence the industrial relations behaviour of public sector actors. In doing so, we do not assume there is a direct causal relationship between the governance system and collective action. While the governance system imposes constraints on social actors, it also allows scope for choices among alternative lines of action within these constraints.[4] Making sense of these choices requires taking into account not only the context of social action but also the stock of intangible resources available to social actors. These include the ideas, knowledge and perceptions that shape actors' demands and choices. In other words, as new social movement theorists argue, we need to bring culture back in to understand the meanings of the public sector growth wave.[5]

The first section below notes some of the problems in defining the public sector and who public sector employees are. We then outline what we consider to be some of the distinctive features of the public sector as a site for collective employee organization and action. The second section reviews the development and impact of the public sector union growth wave from 1968 to the late 1970s. The third section describes various dimensions of the public sector union movement since the early 1980s. The fourth section turns to three cases involving proposed changes to the governance system and how public sector unions reacted to these proposals. The final section highlights the interactive effects of the governance system and the public sector union movement and its significance from the perspective of social movement theory. We end with brief comments on the future of public sector unionism under the post-1997 government.

❏ The Public Sector

The simplest way of defining the public sector is to equate it with all branches, departments and agencies administered by the Hong Kong government, including for example medical and health services, public works, urban cleansing and public health, education, fire services and the police force.[6] The 'Public Service' is a term used to encompass all staff working in these government departments or other units of the central administration.[7] The Civil Service Branch of the Government Secretariat has overall responsibility for the management of these employees. This branch deals with appointments, pay and conditions of service, staff management, manpower planning, training and discipline. It is also the focal point for consultation with the principal staff associations or unions.

Miners notes that there are other organizations which carry out government policy but without being part of this official government structure.[8] These vary in terms of whether their staff are civil servants or not, what proportion of their finance comes from government, and whether government control over their activities is exercised 'directly by the presence of government officials or appointees, or indirectly through financial pressure, or by the threat of possible sanctions.' These organizations include statutory corporations established by an ordinance, public companies in which government has taken an interest, and private organizations whose activities are subsidized in whole or in part by government.[9] Many schools and hospitals as well as charitable and voluntary organizations are heavily subvented by government and in turn are subject to administrative guidelines with regard to certain policies and practices. The terms of service for staff in the subvented sector are, as Miners notes, generally less generous than those for civil servants since the former group normally does not qualify for housing and education allowances or for overseas leave and training courses.

In this chapter, we shall be primarily concerned with those employed in the Public Service. We shall also make reference to those outside the Public Service who work in the assisted or subvented organizations in the fields of health, education and welfare. To distinguish them from civil servants, we use the term social service sector employees. There are two justifications for their inclusion in the scope of this chapter. The first is that their roles and duties are comparable to those working in similar fields in the Public Service. The second is that the salary scales of those working in subvented organizations are linked to those of the Public Service.

The Public Sector as an Employing Organization

The concept of bureaucratic insurgency suggests a link between the distinctive organizational features of the public sector and collective employee organization and action.[10] A central problem in the analysis of the public sector labour movement thus becomes to identify the 'effects of the peculiarities of the public workplace on the character of public workers' movements.'[11] Three distinctive features of the public sector workplace have significant effects, we contend, on the behaviour of public sector employees and their unions as well as management in Hong Kong.

The first distinctive feature of the public sector is size in terms of number of employees. By October 1997, the Public Service employed some 184 600 persons and they constituted about 5.9% of Hong Kong's workforce. The largest organization in the Hong Kong private sector employs fewer than 15 000 persons. Cheung notes that the civil service is a 'unified service in the sense that a uniform set of appointment procedures and similar disciplinary codes and conditions of service apply to all its employees.'[12] Size and the myriad tasks of government are associated with other structural features: departmentalization, a high degree of occupational differentiation, a hierarchy of ranks, and a high degree of formalization as indicated by programmed activities and extensive rules and regulations prescribing, among other things, job responsibilities and conditions of employment. In July 1994, the 180 064 employees in the Public Service were divided into some 430 separate grades or job categories in the administrative, professional, technical and manual fields, and about 1 256 ranks or job levels.[13]

Following from the above point is a second difference. The public sector has a highly institutionalized internal labour market system characterized by well-defined job groupings or 'families'. It operates as a relatively closed system with entry-level jobs in a job family filled mainly through external recruitment, and higher-level ranks filled mainly by internal promotion or transfer. Most positions are thus sheltered from direct influences of competitive forces in the external market. Moreover, the employment system of public sector organizations approximates what has been called a 'primary labour market' characterized by stable and secure employment, career structures (although with low ceilings for some occupations), and pay scales based on seniority. The internal labour market is also characterized by inequality in the distribution of pay and benefits according to such distinctions as manual/non-manual, type of occupation, rank and whether hired on expatriate or local terms. While similar bases for inequality are also found in private organizations in Hong Kong, what is distinctive about the public sector system of stratified rewards is its visibility and its rule-bound character. In the Hong Kong private sector, pay is usually set by individual negotiation between employer and employee so the outcomes are not known to others. In the public sector, by contrast, the differential allocation of rewards is designed on the basis of administrative criteria and made public.

A third difference between the public and private sectors is the nature of the environment in which they operate. One way of viewing this difference is in terms of Scott's distinction between technical and institutional environments. The former refers to market environments 'in which organizations produce a product or service that is exchanged in a market.' Institutional environments by contrast are 'characterized by the elaboration of rules and requirements to which individual organizations must conform in order to receive legitimacy and support.'[14] For organizations operating in institutional environments, resources do not depend primarily on evaluation of their outputs in a competitive market but instead on political approval. The distinctive feature of the domestic institutional environment of the Hong Kong public sector in this respect is that it is comprised of political bodies including the Legislative Council, its Finance Committee and the Executive Council (the approval of which is needed for general increases in civil service pay scales).[15]

Less obvious but of considerable significance is the external political environment of the public sector. British colonial administration in Hong Kong (as in other colonies) had been subject in its behaviour to guidelines set by the Colonial and Foreign Offices. These guidelines prescribe among other things the manner in which the colonial administrators as managers should deal with their own employees. The Colonial Office has encouraged historically the opening of formal channels of communication and consultation with civil servants and recognition of their trade unions so long as they behave 'responsibly'. It has also been a long-standing principle of British colonial administration that since '[c]olonial Governments themselves are often the largest employers of labour in their territories, a special responsibility is placed on them and they are frequently obliged to initiate and lead wage movements.'[16]

Five implications of these features of the public sector governance system follow for understanding the industrial relations behaviour of public sector employees. First, the scale of the public sector and the commonalities in conditions of service are conducive to public sector employee mobilization within the boundaries of a single organization. As Johnston notes, '[w]hile private sector unionism mobilizes collective action and organization among labor market participants — chiefly, though not exclusively, workers employed across firms in the same labor market — public sector unions mobilize collective action and organization within a single organization.'[17] At the same time, the various forms of structural differentiation within public sector organization generate diverse contexts of collective action as well as interests.[18]

Second, and following from the above, the high degree of occupational and rank differentiation with its associated stratified system of rewards creates numerous bases for the development of group identities and for making inter-group comparisons. The giant organization characterized by a high degree of differentiation makes 'the number of possible categories of distinction quite large, and hence the potential for feelings of relative deprivation enormous.'[19] Whether this potential actually materializes will depend on, among other things, what knowledge employees have about other occupational categories and ranks. In this respect, employees in the public sector have access to considerable knowledge about differences among occupational categories in qualifications, pay structure, benefits, and promotion prospects because of their visibility as public knowledge.

A third consequence for employee behaviour arises from the high degree of employment security and career opportunities offered in the public sector. The overall relatively low turnover or wastage rates among public sector employees can have two consequences for their industrial relations behaviour. First, a relatively high degree of stability in work groups is likely to be conducive to the formation of dense social networks that can be mobilized in support of protest.[20] Second, to the extent many public service employees view their attachment to the public sector as long-term and even permanent — or at least have few external job market opportunities comparable in terms of pay and other employment benefits — they are more likely to exercise the voice than the exit option when dissatisfied with conditions of employment.[21]

A fourth consequence relates to the institutional environment of the public sector. This environment encourages the collective expression of the voice option through the medium of trade unions. While all employment organizations are influenced to some extent by the political environment, the character of the public workplace is more directly shaped by the nature of the polity for two reasons. First, the legal framework set by the Trade Unions Ordinance specifies that trade unions are a socially and politically acceptable organizational form for employees to express their discontents. Second, whereas private sector organizations can counter trade unions by strategies of organizational suppression or by creating alternatives to trade unions,[22] this option was much less feasible for public sector management in Hong Kong so long as public sector unions worked within the parameters of the law. A British colonial government that sought to undermine unions would face considerable internal and external criticism, for both cultural and political reasons, were it to seek to suppress trade union organizations among its own employees.[23] To uphold its own (originally) colonial conceptions of rule of law, a voluntarist system of industrial relations and 'responsible' unionism, it was compelled to serve as a model employer, to adopt a tolerant attitude towards union formation, and to establish communication channels with organizations of its employees.[24]

The system of formalized labour-management relations which evolved since 1968 in the form of consultative machinery at the central and departmental levels is symbolic of the government's adherence to these norms.[25] The domestic political context of the public sector places additional constraints on public sector management in such matters as the setting of salaries and conditions of employment. The filling of some seats in the Legislative Council through elections from functional constituencies has given certain occupational groups a representative spokesperson for their interests since the mid-1980s, and thus creates an interest group 'voice' in the political process which the government must take into account in devising policies.[26]

Finally, as Johnston argues, workers' collective action within the public sector is qualitatively different. While private sector workers rely largely on their market position as a source of power and influence in negotiating with employers, workers' strength in the public sector depends primarily on political-organizational resources. These resources include:

> ... first, legal rights, organizational status, and established procedures; second, strategic alliances within the shifting political universe of the public agency, including clients, constituents, and other participants in that political universe; third, forms of voice that can help mobilize new organization, build or prevent alliances, and, by framing and appealing to 'the public interest,' put a potent political edge on the workers' demands.[27]

Given the difference in the type of the resources vested in public sector employees compared with private sector counterparts, we can expect to find the construction of distinctive strategies and forms of action among public sector worker organizations. Their demands are likely to be presented not simply in terms of advancing the interests of their own group but as a means of serving the wider 'public good'. Hence collective action by public sector unions is normally not simply a struggle over the price of their labour, but a contest over the definition of the public interest and how best to achieve it. Furthermore, given the prevalence of norms of bureaucratic rationality embedded in the public sector governance system, even pay claims are often framed 'in an appeal to principles such as administrative justice or bureaucratic due process.'[28]

These characteristics of the public sector — size, a high degree of occupational and rank differentiation, visibility of the stratified reward system, a relatively weak technical but strong institutional environment, low employee turnover, a formalized system of labour-management consultation, and the application of principles of bureaucratic rationality — constitute key elements of the framework of governance of the employment relationship.[29] This governance system does not however fully account for the timing of union formation or episodes of bureaucratic insurgency, the learning processes involved in mobilizing protest,[30] the particular strategies and tactics adopted by public sector unions or the outcomes of collective protest. But as the critical contexts for collective action they do influence, we contend, the form and content of these processes.

❏ Historical and Institutional Contexts[31]

The roots of the public sector union growth wave lie in the organizational and institutional framework governing civil service employment and employment relations that evolved after World War II. We review three aspects of this framework: unionization among public sector employees, the consultative system and the role of salaries commissions. We then describe aspects of insurgency among public sector employees in the 1970s and how authorities responded to it.

Trade unions of civil servants were among some of the earliest to be formed after 1945 with some 15 staff associations registering as trade unions in 1948 and 1949. They differed in their organizing boundaries. Two were general associations (also called main staff associations) recruiting members across occupational class, grade and department — the Association of European Civil Servants of Hong Kong (AECS) (later renamed the Association of Expatriate Civil Servants of Hong Kong) and the Hong Kong Chinese Civil Servants Association (CCSA). There were ten departmental-based associations and two associations recruiting members from both inside and outside the civil service.

Between 1960 and 1966–67 the number of civil service unions rose from 19 to 27 and membership from 10 831 to 17 403.[32] The number of registered civil service trade unions subsequently increased each year to reach 111 by 1978–79. Civil service union membership climbed from 18 349 in 1969–70 to 51 146 in 1978–79. Union density among civil servants rose from about 25% in 1966–67 to 44% in 1978–79 by one estimate.[33]

The first formal undertaking by the government to consult the main staff associations occurred in 1957 when it agreed not to make any changes in conditions of service affecting a major part of the civil service without prior consultation with the CCSA and the AECS.[34] In 1966, the government and the three main staff associations drafted an agreement which stated that the government will not make any change in conditions of service which affects a substantial part of the civil service as a whole or of the members of an individual main staff association without prior consultation. In June 1968, the government concluded the Agreement with the three main staff associations (including by then the Senior Non-expatriate Staff Association, SNEOA, registered in 1958) that laid the foundations for formal consultation through the Senior Civil Service Council (SCSC) with the dual objectives of improving the efficiency of the public service and securing the well-being of those employed. The Agreement also provided that where agreement could not be reached on certain issues, they could be referred, with the approval of the Governor, to an independent Committee of Inquiry.[35]

In line with British colonial practice, the Hong Kong colonial administration was obligated to be seen as a 'good' employer. It thus had to establish its credentials as a 'model employer' by matching employment conditions including remuneration offered by the more established private sector firms.[36] The primary means for doing so was the appointment of salaries commissions at periodic intervals.

Several commentators have suggested that the Report of the Hong Kong Salaries Commission of 1971 (also called the Mallaby Commission after its chairman) was of considerable importance in triggering discontent among civil servants.[37] On the basis of the Commission's recommendations, the government adopted a new occupational class system.[38] A single Master Pay Scale (MPS) was created to cover most non-manual civil servants. In applying this system, which grouped together a number of grades related to each other by occupational criteria, the Commission used the concept of 'fair comparison' with the private sector as a primary principle for determination of pay scales attached to an occupation. This restructuring of the civil service internal labour market created new bases for grades and occupations to raise arguments about inequities in internal relativities as a way of justifying their claims for improvements in pay structure and promotion opportunities.

By July 1973 demands over pay and grade structures were brewing among civil service occupational groups including teachers, midwives, health auxiliaries, inoculators and clerks who were frustrated by the government's slow pace in dealing with their grievances.[39] These groups tried various means to put pressure on the government to achieve their demands. During its two-year struggle with the government, the Hong Kong Government Clerical Staff Association used tactics such as mass meetings, press conferences, petitioning the Governor, displaying posters in public buildings, and a work-to-rule on two occasions.[40] In 1976 the Demarcators (New Territories Association) called a work-to-rule action after failing to obtain improved conditions of service. The Secretary of the Civil Service proposed to reduce their salaries by 30% on the grounds that participants were performing only 70% of their duties. The demarcators took the case to court which ruled that the government's action constituted a breach of the contract of employment. The government appealed but its action was dismissed by the Court of Appeal.[41] In the same year, the Association of Government Land and Engineering Survey Officers (AGLESO) mobilized 150 members to petition the Governor for the revision of their members' pay structure and title. In February 1977, AGLESO launched two 'no field work' industrial actions to pressure the government to negotiate. The Governor's response was to appoint a Commission of Inquiry, the Willoughby Commission. Industrial action continued until October 1977 when the government applied CSR 611 which states that any civil servant who refuses or omits to perform for any period any part of the usual duties of office may be suspended from duty without pay. Another important case arose in November 1979 when the government suspended 26 dispensers from the Medical and Health Department under CSR 611 for their work-to-rule action. In December more than 30 unions organized a protest action demanding that the government repeal CSR 611. The suspended dispensers then took the government to the High Court for breach of contract, but the case was dismissed in March 1980 on the grounds that the colonial government had the power to dismiss and suspend its employees.[42]

Despite these attempts to curtail certain types of public sector union collective action, the government was facing by 1978 a growing crisis of cumulative disorder in industrial relations as long-running disputes snowballed and unions involved adopted a familiar repertoire of actions: demonstrations at Government House, press conferences, posters, sit-ins, work-to-rules and go-slows.[43] The government attributed this discontent to the rapid growth of the civil service, the growing complexity of administration and a lag in the development of appropriate staff management methods.[44] Whatever its causes, this cumulative disorder appeared to signal the declining legitimacy attached to both the procedural arrangements for determining pay and grade structures and the substantive outcomes of these procedures.

The government was thus compelled to devise a new strategy to deal with this insurgency. In late 1978, it decided to create the Standing Commission on Civil Service Salaries and Conditions of Service.[45] This fit well with the repertoire of British colonial practices of using commissions to solve major problems including industrial relations issues.[46]

The significance of these developments for the governance of civil service employment relationships was threefold. First, the proliferation of trade unions, many organized on an occupational basis and pursuing demands for revision in grade pay and structure that brought them into conflict with the government, both reflected and contributed to the breakdown of normative consensus over the legitimacy of criteria for allocation of occupational status and rewards. Second, civil service unions were learning through trial and error what forms of collective action could bring effective pressure on management to take their claims seriously, but without antagonizing the general public or triggering the application of management sanctions that would cause severe deprivation to members. Civil service management was experimenting with sanctions that could be used in the event of disruptive protest action but without being seen to suppress unions.

Third, bureaucratic insurgency had demonstrated the weakness of the existing consultative system in resolving conflicts of interest over grade and pay structures.[47] Industrial actions had also presented a challenge to the core values of the government's administrative culture: efficiency, neutrality and hierarchical loyalty.[48] The Standing Commission as an independent body 'which both staff and management can approach or consult on all matters of pay, structure, conditions of service and other related matters' was a strategy for attempting to re-establish normative consensus around the governance structure.[49]

Considerable uncertainty thus prevailed at the end of the 1970s over the workability of the civil service governance system. It was not clear whether bureaucratic insurgency had peaked, whether the consultative system was still workable, or whether the Standing Commission could re-establish normative consensus around a set of principles and procedures for designing the internal labour market structure.

❑ Public Sector Unionism, 1980–97

Far from slackening, the public sector union growth wave continued into the 1980s and 1990s. Below we discuss the changing structural features of this wave in terms of union formation, membership and density, and fragmentation and integration, before turning to the character of public sector unionism.[50]

Union Formation

As shown in Table 1, the number of civil service unions rose from 141 in 1981 to 218 in 1997, an increase of more than 50%. The growth was uneven however. The number of unions stabilized between 1982 and 1984 and then began to rise afterwards. The number of social service unions tripled between 1981 and 1997, although starting from a low base. The growth of unions in this sector slackened in the 1983–85 period and accelerated towards the late 1980s.

Changes in the number of public sector unions are the outcome of processes of new union registrations and deregistrations/dissolutions. For the period 1981–97, there were 174 newly registered public sector unions compared with 39 deregistered for a net gain of 135 public sector unions. There was a substantial net growth (new registrations minus deregistrations) in the number of newly registered unions for 1980–82, then a drop to a low of one net union in 1984, followed by a subsequent period of rising net growth.

Table 1: Changes in the Number of Public Sector Unions, 1981–97

	Number of Civil Service Unions (A)	Number of Social Service Unions (B)	Total Public Sector Unions (A + B)	Newly Registered Unions (Public Sector)	Deregistered Unions (Public Sector)
1981	141	19	160	13	2
1982	146	22	168	11	2
1983	147	26	173	8	3
1984	148	26	174	4	3
1985	158	26	184	11	1
1986	163	29	192	9	1
1987	169	28	197	6	1
1988	177	30	207	10	0
1989	181	32	213	8	2
1990	185	38	223	14	4
1991	188	42	230	8	1
1992	191	45	236	7	1
1993	198	50	248	15	3
1994	201	53	254	11	5
1995	212	57	269	15	2
1996	216	64	280	16	3
1997	218	65	283	8	5

Note: Civil service unions include those classified by the Registrar of Trade Unions under International Standard Industrial Classification (I.S.I.C.) division 91 plus other civil service unions classified under I.S.I.C. divisions 72, 92, 93 and 94. Social service unions include non-civil service unions under I.S.I.C. division 93 and some from division 94.

Source: Trade Union Dataset (for description see note 23, Chiu and Levin in this volume)

Several factors likely contributed to the resurgence of public sector union formation around 1985. First, new union formation in the civil service may have been a reaction to the work of the Standing Commission.[51] Second, the changing political environment including the 1984 Sino-British Joint Declaration on the future of Hong Kong and the creation domestically of the Labour functional constituency under which each registered union was entitled to one vote may have encouraged occupational groups to form unions as a way to gain status and voice in the political arena. Third, local factors undoubtedly accounted for some of the proliferation. For example, staff concerns about the loss of civil service status following the recommendations of a consultancy firm (The Scott Report) in late 1985 to establish a Hospital Authority operating outside the civil service triggered off union formation among those employed in the medical field.

Union Membership and Density

Membership trends among unions in the civil and social service sectors differed somewhat from the above patterns of union formation. Union membership in the civil service increased up to 1984 and then stabilized but from 1987 began to grow rapidly, as shown in Table 2. Over the period 1981–97, membership of civil service unions increased 3.1 times. Membership of social service unions rose continuously throughout the period 1981–97 and was about 2.9 times higher in 1995 than in 1981. Public sector union membership (civil and social service sectors combined) as a percentage of all union members increased substantially from about 33% in 1981 to 54.1% in 1997.

England asserts that union density among civil servants 'rose from just one in five in 1961 to one in three in the late 1970s and to one in two in the late 1980s', but does not explain how he arrived at this estimate. Our estimates of the union density (also called the trade union participation rate) in the civil and social service sectors from 1981 to 1997 are shown in Table 2.[52] In the case of the civil service, union density had stabilized at about 53% from 1981 to 1984. It then rose gradually to about 61% in 1987 followed by a sharp increase between 1987 and 1997 as membership soared while civil service employment more or less stabilized.

The meaningfulness of these density measures is open to question however, given that the rates since 1992 exceed 100%. This indicates that an unknown number of civil servants belonged to more than one union. We should note in this connection the extraordinary growth in membership of the CCSA from 17 288 in 1986 to 49 425 in 1988, followed by another doubling of membership to 102 254 in 1993 and then to 126 192 in 1997 when it accounted for about half of total civil service union membership. Since the CCSA is an umbrella organization recruiting members from the entire civil service, it is

Table 2: Public Sector Union Membership and Union Density, 1981–97

	Civil Service			Social Service			Public Sector Union Membership/ Total Union Membership (%)
	Membership	Employment	Union Density (%)	Membership	Employment	Union Density (%)	
1981	80 409	149 638	53.7	32 657	61 667	53.0	32.8
1982	88 474	164 483	53.8	36 585	66 973	54.6	35.6
1983	90 899	169 712	53.6	37 916	71 559	53.0	36.6
1984	93 273	173 452	53.8	40 793	76 105	53.6	37.4
1985	101 949	174 891	58.3	42 677	78 002	54.7	39.3
1986	100 438	178 094	56.4	44 043	81 452	54.1	39.3
1987	111 272	182 199	61.1	48 096	84 078	57.2	41.7
1988	142 994	185 486	77.1	52 939	86 335	61.3	47.1
1989	155 661	187 883	82.8	57 110	87 159	65.5	48.6
1990	169 829	189 868	89.4	60 536	91 159	66.4	49.2
1991	177 631	187 006	95.0	66 610	107 211	62.1	50.1
1992	203 333	182 387	111.5	71 781	107 259	66.9	52.3
1993	212 221	180 675	117.5	76 630	115 057	66.6	53.1
1994	221 234	180 092	122.8	81 139	117 361	69.1	53.8
1995	228 585	181 558	125.9	86 717	117 958	73.5	53.3
1996	245 514	184 242	133.3	92 636	123 315	75.1	54.2
1997	254 021	185 196	137.2	96 540	132 677	72.8	54.1

Notes: 1.   Civil service employment figures refer to persons engaged (*Annual digest of statistics*, various years). Figures up to 1984 are persons engaged in the civil service in the fourth quarter of the year. From 1985 onwards, figures refer to the first of January of the following year.

2.   Social service employment figures are from the Employment and Vacancies Statistics compiled by the Census and Statistics Department as persons engaged in the following sub-sectors in the 'Community, social and personal services' sector: education, research services, research and scientific institutions, welfare institutions, libraries, museums and cultural services. Since civil servants are excluded from the Employment and Vacancies Statistics in this sector, we assume that all persons engaged in sanitary and similar services are in the private sector. We then add the sum total of these sectors to the number of medical professionals engaged by the Hospital Authority to arrive at the total for the entire social service sector. Before the takeover of the management of hospitals by the Hospital Authority in 1991, hospital employees (doctors and nurses, etc.) were mostly civil servants but not after that.

Source: Trade Union Dataset; *Annual digest of statistics*, various years

very likely that its membership overlaps considerably with that of other civil service unions. If CCSA membership for 1997 is deducted from total civil service union membership for that year, civil service membership density would fall to 69%. In the case of the social service sector, union density rose more or less steadily over the period 1981–96.

Sectoral union density figures can mask considerable variation in union density for individual unions (actual membership relative to the potential scope of membership as defined by organizational boundaries specified in a union's constitution). One survey in the late 1980s of 36 civil service unions found that three-quarters (28) claimed to organize over 40% of potential members, one-third (12) claimed to organize from 61% to 80%, and another 28% (10) from 81% to 100%.[53]

Fragmentation and Integration

A characteristic feature of the Hong Kong trade union movement according to a number of observers is its fragmentation, one form of which is the plethora of small unions.[54] The extent to which this applies to the civil and social service sectors is shown in Table 3 which presents data on the size distribution for all public sector unions for 1981, 1991 and 1997. This shows that while the number of public sector unions with 100 members or fewer increased over this period, their relative share among all public sector unions declined from about 42% in 1981 to 39% in 1991. During this period, unions with more than 500 members increased their share of all public unions slightly from about 22% in 1981 to 24% in 1997.

Turning to membership accounted for by the larger unions, we find a very different picture. In 1981, unions with more than 1 000 members accounted for about 75% of all public sector union members. In 1991, the share of the largest unions had risen to about 84% and remained at this level in 1997. The earlier-noted phenomenal growth of the CCSA helps to account for this trend. Of the five public sector unions with over 5 000 members in 1997, shown in Table 4, the CCSA had by far the greatest increase in membership followed by the Hong Kong Professional Teachers' Union (PTU), and then the relatively new Government Employees Association.[55] The PTU and the Association of Hong Kong Nursing Staff are unions of professionals whose membership is primarily from outside the civil service.

One new feature in the structure of the public sector labour movement since the mid-1970s is the emergence of new federations and quasi-federational or strategic alliances as mechanisms of inter-organizational coordination.[56] When the CCSA was advised by the Registrar of Trade Unions that an application to federate with other unions would not be approved (under the 1961 Trade Union Registration Ordinance), it changed its constitution in the mid-1970s to permit

Table 3: Public Sector Unions and Their Membership Grouped by Size of Union, 1981, 1991, 1997

1981	Number of Unions	Union Members	Percentage of Total Members
50 or below	35	1 022	0.9
51 to 100	32	2 409	2.1
101 to 500	58	15 230	13.5
501 to 1 000	14	9 811	8.7
over 1 000	21	84 594	74.8
Total	160	113 066	–

1991	Number of Unions	Union Members	Percentage of Total Members
50 or below	37	1 185	0.5
51 to 100	52	3 728	1.5
101 to 500	84	19 960	8.2
501 to 1 000	22	14 853	6.1
over 1 000	35	204 515	83.7
Total	230	244 241	–

1997	Number of Unions	Union Members	Percentage of Total Members
50 or below	52	1 481	0.4
51 to 100	63	4 462	1.3
101 to 500	109	24 120	6.8
501 to 1 000	36	24 441	6.9
over 1 000	35	298 657	84.6
Total	295	353 161	–

Source: Registrar of Trade Unions, 1982, 1992, 1998

Table 4: Membership Trends in the Five Largest Public Sector Unions, 1980–97

Union	Members 1980*	Members 1997	Membership change 1980–97
Hong Kong Chinese Civil Servants' Association	8 612	126 192	+117 580
Hong Kong Civil Servants General Union	5 715	16 142	+10 427
Government Employees Association	30 (1986)	18 402	+18 372 (1986–97)
Hong Kong Professional Teachers' Union	19 988	67 631	+47 643
Association of Hong Kong Nursing Staff (formerly Association of Government Nursing Staff)	4 397	11 093	+6 696

* as at 31 December 1979

Source: Registrar of Trade Unions

individual unions to have an affiliated status. The CSGU, which was registered as a trade union in 1978, functions in practice as a federation by allowing individual unions to affiliate. The Joint Organization of Unions—Hong Kong (JOU, originally called the Liaison Office of Public Service Unions) was registered under the Societies Ordinance in the late 1970s as a research, education and service organization with membership open to all labour organizations. In 1984, it adopted its present name to broaden its membership to include non-civil service groups. The Federation of Civil Service Unions (FCSU) was registered under the Societies Ordinance in 1984. The Hong Kong Confederation of Trade Unions (CTU) which was registered in 1991 has several public sector unions as affiliates. An example of a strategic alliance among unions, to be discussed in more detail later, was the formation of the League of the Medical and Health Department Staff Unions in April 1986.

Public Sector Union Character

Membership figures by themselves do not tell us about the character of these public sector unions and in particular how they differ from those in the private sector. Generalizing about the character of public sector unions is difficult because of their great diversity in terms of organizational boundaries, histories, affiliations and social composition of membership. A useful benchmark however is Tso's discussion of four distinctive characteristics of civil service unions:
1. short history, with a predominance of young leaders;
2. fragmentation and rivalry;
3. concern with 'domestic' issues of pay structure, promotion and fringe benefits; and
4. few with overt political affiliations.[57]

With regard to the first point, it is true that the proliferation of civil service unions in the 1970s at a time when private sector union formation was more or less stagnant did contribute to the distinctive 'age' profile of civil and social sector unions. But a number of these public sector unions now have histories going back 20 or more years. The characteristic of fragmentation and rivalry, as Tso acknowledges, is not unique to the civil service union movement.

Most observers therefore emphasize Tso's third and fourth points as the key factors differentiating civil and public sector unions formed during the growth wave of the 1970s from those in the private sector. With regard to the third point however, not all civil service unions are equally vocal and aggressive over the advancement of members' sectional or occupational status. A number are relatively quiescent or 'dormant unions'.[58] The more militant unions appear to be those comprised of non-manual employees who are located in the middle ranges of the Master Pay Scale.[59] We lack however solid empirical data about civil and social service sector unions that would enable us to make sound judgements about variations in how union financial resources are allocated among various activities or of leadership or rank-and-file conceptions of union priorities. Cheung's survey of 36 civil service trade unions does however provide some relevant information. One question asked respondents to prioritize the objectives of their union as stated in its constitution, and 27 respondents indicated 'negotiating with the Government on salary and conditions of service' as the most important objective followed by 4 choosing 'promote a sense of solidarity among members'. Another question asked respondents which of four categories — recreational, educational, social and political, and economic — most of the union's activities fell under and to prioritize them (although without specifying any criteria for prioritizing). Twenty-one of the unions ranked organization of recreational activities as the first priority, eight activities of a political nature and six educational activities.[60]

A simple though crude indicator of civil service unions' interest in matters affecting occupational status is the extent to which they respond to invitations from the Standing Commission to comment on various draft consultation documents. In response to its Consultative Document on Principles and Practices Governing the Salary Structure of the Civil Service issued on 14 May 1979, the Standing Commission received some 131 written representations from civil service unions and 1 from the staff side of the SCSC.[61] Since there were 130 registered unions of civil servants in 1979, it appears that nearly every civil service union responded to this document. In response to its 1989 non-directorate salary structure review, the Standing Commission received 563 written submissions in response to the first two phases of its review from staff and departmental management, mostly from the staff side. Over 80 staff associations (including 12 branches of the CCSA) responded to the final phase of the review. These figures suggest the prevalence of a strong interest in matters of grade and pay structure affecting the welfare of occupational groups.

A more robust indicator of the priority civil service unions give to occupational interests and of their degree of solidarity in pursing these matters would be data on overt collective actions (as opposed to simply writing letters) in protest over terms and conditions of employment. We lack time series data on such actions but Arn's data show that between 1977 and 1982 some 16 civil service unions and a unit of the CCSA had engaged in collective protest actions, mainly over pay and grade structure, with some unions mounting more than one protest action.[62] After 1982, sectional actions by civil service unions appeared to have tapered off, in part because a number of long-standing issues had been resolved and the Standing Commission's overall review of grade and pay structures had been completed, but also because the attention of civil service unions was now deflected to the Sino-British negotiations on the future of Hong Kong. Yet, another wave of insurgency swept through the civil service between 1988 and the early 1990s.[63]

Tso's fourth point about the character of civil service unions — the low number affiliated to the established trade union federations (the FTU and TUC) known for their political orientations to the PRC and Taiwan respectively — remains largely accurate. Of the 132 unions classified by the Registrar of Trade Unions under public administration in 1997, 16 were affiliated to the FTU, 1 to the TUC, and 9 to the CTU which like the older peak federations is known for its distinctive political orientation. Three unions of postal workers were affiliated to the FTU and one to the CTU (which also had two government union affiliates classified under transport). In the social and related community services sector, eight unions were affiliated to the FTU, two to the TUC, and eight to the CTU. The larger affiliates of the FTU and CTU are shown in Table 5. Most public sector unions thus remain unaffiliated to the three 'peak' trade union federations.

The lack of affiliation to these three peak federations does not however signify political neutrality. For example, some civil and social service sector unionists have participated since the late 1970s in protest campaigns over community-wide issues.[64] These include the Coalition Against Bus Fare Increase formed in 1981, the Coalition for the Monitoring of Public Utility Companies formed in 1982, the coalition in late 1982 which petitioned the Governor against the setting up of a central provident fund scheme, and the mass rally organized by the Joint Secretariat of Hong Kong and Kowloon Labour Organizations on 1 May 1983, involving some 300 representatives from 80 labour organizations.[65]

The government's 1984 proposed political reforms stimulated another round of trade union joint ventures. In September 1984, unions formed the Joint Conference on Representative Government, with trade unionists who had played a leading role in earlier protest movements among the key figures. Some 88 organizations participated, including 17 independent unions and among them civil service unions.[66] In 1986, the Basic Law Consultative Committee (BLCC) was appointed with 180 members, including 13 representing labour unions in the private sector with 6 from civil service unions and 7 from other labour organizations.[67] Civil and social service sector trade unionists had also been involved in protests over the Daya Bay Nuclear Plant (in 1986), over the right of abode in the UK (1987), in favour of direct elections to the Legislative Council (1988), and in the protests over the events in Tiananmen Square (1989). In the 1990s they had participated in campaigns for a central provident fund and against the relaxation of restrictions on labour importation.[68]

Tso notes that civil service (although not social service) trade unionists' participation in wider community issues is limited by Civil Service Regulation 521 which prohibits civil servants from public debate, either in writing or speech, on government policies and matters of a political or administrative nature.[69] The ideology of civil service political neutrality no doubt also exerts a bias against involvement in community-wide protest campaigns. Civil servants are prohibited from standing for election to the Legislative Council but former civil

Table 5: Civil and Social Service Sector Unions with over 1 000 Members Affiliated to FTU and CTU

1. Affiliated to FTU

Name of Union	Year Registered	Declared Members, 1997
Government Employees Association	1986	18 402
Government Staff Union	1987	4 892
Hospital Authority Staff Association	1992	3 025
Union of Employees of Hospital Services Department and Department of Health	1985	2 936
Government, Armed Forces & Hospitals Chinese Workers Union	1948	2 811
Hong Kong Government Water-Works Chinese Employees Union	1948	1 949
Hong Kong Post Workers Unions	1948	1 153
Hong Kong Customs and Excise Staff General Association	1995	1 077
Hong Kong Urban Services Department and Regional Services Department Employees General Union	1995	1 064

2. Affiliated to CTU

Name of Union	Year Registered	Declared Members, 1997
Hong Kong Professional Teachers' Union	1973	67 631
Union of Hong Kong Post Office Employees	1970	1 653
Association of Government Technical & Survey Officers	1976	1 483
Government Drivers Union	1985	1 278
Traffic Services Employees Association	1983	1 191
Clerical Grade Civil Servants Servants General Union	1979	1 080

Source: Registrar of Trade Unions

servants have stood for election, notably in the newly created (in 1995) community, social and related services functional constituency. Several prominent social sector trade unionists have run for election successfully to the Legislative Council from both the geographical and the functional constituencies.

While the newer independent trade union groupings among civil and social service sector employees are concerned with members' sectional interests, they differ in how far they should broaden their missions. Some have taken the view that trade unions should not fight solely for their own sectional interests, but should play an active part in promoting political and social developments. An example is the PTU. A former vice-president of the PTU has written that the 'primary function of a trade union is to safeguard the members' legitimate professional rights', but he points out that the PTU's goals have evolved to include a keen interest in the quality of education and in social issues beyond the immediate job interests of members.[70] The justification is that

> ... such affairs concern its members as members of society and also because the teaching profession represents the conscience of society and contains a particularly strong intellectual element. The Union assumes these social responsibilities because of society's expectations of teachers. By doing well in this aspect, the Union not only safeguards the members' interests as members of society but also elevates the status of teachers in society.

A similar combination of a concern with professional status and an ideology of responsibility towards community issues involving social and political developments is also characteristic of other social service sector unions.[71] The extent to which leadership support for these broader goals has been internalized by members is a matter that needs further study.

❏ Contention and Controversy in the 1980s and 1990s: Three Cases

Much of the discontent among civil service groups in the 1970s focused on substantive matters, especially over the principles and practices governing the determination of occupational grade and pay structures. This source of discontent continued to flare up from time to time in the 1980s but there had been other contentious issues. Below we discuss three cases involving proposed changes to elements of the civil service governance system as illustrations of the dynamics involved in disputes between public sector unions and management. These cases differ in the type and degree of change proposed and in the resulting scale and nature of union mobilization. The first involves changes to the civil service consultative system, the second, changes in the bases for civil service pay determination and the third, the reorganization of medical services. In reviewing these cases, we consider how effective public sector unions were in achieving their aims.

The Consultative Machinery

As noted above, one of the key governance issues of the late 1970s was whether the consultative arrangements in the civil service could still operate effectively, given that they had failed to resolve the growing tensions over pay and grade structures. In view of the problems with the existing consultative machinery, the Standing Commission earlier on focused on a number of issues involving the scope and structure of the consultative machinery in the civil service. In February 1980, it circulated the 'Consultative Document on Civil Service Consultative Machinery' to all government departments, requesting that it be brought to the attention of all staff associations and individual staff. It outlined existing systems in the civil service and invited comments from both management and staff on how these could be improved.

One issue was the status of employee categories excluded from joint consultation at the central level, mainly the 40 000 Model Scale 1 staff comprised of skilled and unskilled manual workers who then constituted about one-third of all civil servants. The Commission recommended the establishment of a separate council for these employees[72] and in 1982, the government approved the setting up of this new consultative forum at the central level, the Model Scale 1 Staff Consultative Council. Its structure was generally similar to that of the SCSC, with six staff unions — those with a large membership among Model Scale 1 staff — initially making up the staff side. A separate Police Force Council was also created in 1982.[73]

The structure of the SCSC continued to come under criticism from some civil service trade unionists however, especially the restricted composition of the staff side of the SCSC. The first chairman of the Federation of Civil Service Unions pointed out in 1985 that the three staff associations with membership on the SCSC represented only a minority of civil servants on the Master Pay Scale (MPS) due to the growth in the number of trade unions since the 1968 Agreement.[74] The Standing Commission thus decided to re-examine the civil service consultative machinery and in early 1987 it issued the 'Consultative Document on Civil Service Consultative Machinery'. Some 107 written submissions were received in response to this document. A special Committee on Civil Service Consultative Machinery was established by the Standing Commission in March 1988 to consider these responses and formulate recommendations.

On the issue of the representativeness of the existing structure of the SCSC, the Commission noted that as of December 1987, the number of civil servants on the MPS who were covered by the SCSC amounted to about 122 100 out of a total of 181 600 civil servants (excluding members of the Police Force, those on Model Scale 1 and directorate officers). The three staff associations on the SCSC had a total membership of about 25 100.[75] Aside from these three associations, there were 157 other civil service trade unions of which only six were constituent members of the Model Scale 1 Consultative Council and hence directly represented at the central level.[76]

The Commission reported that responses to its consultative document were split on whether the existing structure of the SCSC should be maintained. Proposals for change included admitting representatives of individual grades, creating a body to represent middle-level officers, replacing existing members by elected representatives according to salary bands, and admitting one additional member elected by other unions. Many of the proposals were intended to increase the representativeness for lower- and middle-ranking civil servants.

Another issue was whether the existing system of appointment to the SCSC by the Chief Secretary should continue. One proposal was to replace the existing appointment system by some form of election on the grounds it would make the SCSC more representative and accountable to its constituents. But there were different views about how an election process should operate. One proposal was for a process modelled on the existing Labour Advisory Board and Labour functional constituency for Legco of one union, one vote. Another was a system based on 'one civil servant, one vote' and a third view was that the voting be weighted according to the number of members a union had.

Having considered various alternatives, the Commission rejected any major change since 'the present system has provided a suitable forum for dialogue between management and staff which has operated successfully, and with a high degree of stability, since its inception.'[77] It worried that an electoral system would lead to the 'politicization of the civil service as each association canvasses for votes, and the inevitable breakdown in continuity resulting from possibly frequent changes in the membership of the central council', and viewed such a possibility as a major 'de-stabilizing' factor which might undermine the smooth functioning of the consultative process.[78] It did however recommend that the admission criteria for entry to the SCSC be revised to be more precise and also urged the three constituent members of the SCSC to step up their membership recruitment efforts.[79]

In the case of the Model Scale 1 Staff Consultative Council, the existing requirements for admission to the Council were that any civil service union association applying for membership must have a paid-up Model Scale 1 membership of 1 000 or more. As of December 1987, there were 26 staff associations with Model Scale 1 members. Seven were represented on the Council of which two were service-wide organizations and the other five with membership limited to particular departments or occupational groups. The seven associations on the Council had a combined membership of 12 500 as of December 1987, compared with total membership of about 9 000 for the 19 associations not represented on the Council and 20 800 Model Scale 1 staff who were not members of any civil service union. From the submissions, opinions differed on whether the 1 000-minimum-membership rule should be changed, with some favouring lowering the membership requirement and some raising it. The Commission opposed lowering the membership requirement on the grounds that extending membership would make it more difficult for the staff side to reach a common position on any issue and could make the work of the Council unwieldy if the size increased. Raising the membership requirement would 'seem to be contrary to the objective of improving the representativeness of civil service consultative machinery.'[80]

Another recurring issue is whether the SCSC can be an effective channel for the staff unions to achieve their demands given that the staff side has only consultative but not negotiating status under the terms of the 1968 Agreement. A past president of the CCSA claimed that the distinction between 'consultation' and 'negotiation' was, in practice, blurred partly because of the provision for referring disagreements to a Committee of Inquiry:

> If the Staff Side is strong, the difference between consultation and negotiation is minimal. Sometimes, bargaining does exist in the process of consultation, for example, on the issue of annual pay adjustment [...] The importance of the provision under the 1968 Agreement of referring to a Committee of Inquiry in case of disagreement is often overlooked. This provision in effect gives the Staff Side some negotiating status. The Government is very reluctant to refer any matter in dispute to a Committee of Inquiry since its outcome is uncertain. For this reason, it is forced to 'bargain' with the Staff Side with a view to reaching an agreement.[81]

How widely this view is shared among leaders of civil service unions is not known, although the results from a 1987 mailed questionnaire sent to chairpersons of civil service unions suggest it might be a minority view. Some 93% of the 47 respondents in this survey supported the institution of collective bargaining arrangements. The researcher interpreted these survey findings to indicate that 'the current system of 'consultation' appears to be losing favour with most civil servants, with more opting for better bargaining power through provision of an 'equal partner' arrangement between staff and management.'[82] The chairman of the FCSU stated on a radio discussion programme in April 1990 that

> ... civil servants submit their proposals to the government and the government then passes them on to the Standing Commission. However, the government and the Standing Commission are both evading their responsibility so that we have no way to channel our views. To improve industrial relations, the government and civil service unions should enter into direct collective bargaining. Only by so doing can problems be solved.[83]

Yet during the 1990s, controversy over the composition of the staff side of the SCSC, and its mode of decision-making, subsided without any substantive changes made.[84] One reason was the division among civil service unions themselves, between the 'insiders' represented on the SCSC and the 'outsiders'. Another was that the 1985 agreement among members of the SCSC to specify criteria for admission to the SCSC had opened the door for outsiders to enter if they could meet certain conditions. The issue of representativeness also became moot when the membership of the CCSA subsequently grew rapidly, so it could claim to represent over half of all civil servants. The procedures of the Standing Commission of inviting submissions from disaffected groups, summarizing arguments both for and against change and then providing its rationale for limited change (largely supporting the status quo) also may have defused some of the tensions over this issue. The political situation at the time probably worked against major change as well, since the Sino-British Joint Declaration was geared to preserving the existing governance system of the civil service. Finally, it was questionable whether support among civil service trade union leaders for collective bargaining had extended to rank-and-file members. It seemed doubtful for example that a hypothetical mass rally to pressure the government for collective bargaining status on the SCSC would attract many participants. Even if it did, the government was unlikely to have surrendered its authority to make the final decisions on matters involving the public purse.[85]

The Pay Dispute of 1986–89

Before the government had managed to pacify the civil service unions over issues involving the consultative machinery, serious contention erupted in the mid-1980s over the procedural framework for the determination of the annual pay adjustment. Since the 1968 Agreement with the three main staff associations, the government's policy on civil service pay has always stressed 'a duty and responsibility to maintain a civil service recognized as efficient and staffed by members whose conditions of service are regarded as fair both by themselves and by the public which they serve.'[86] This was to be achieved in practice through 'fair comparison' with the pay of private sector staff employed in broadly 'comparable' work, taking account of differences in other conditions of service. In 1974, a system of annual pay trend surveys was initiated to put into practice this principle of comparability with the private sector and to determine the range of annual pay adjustments for the civil service.[87] A lengthy dispute broke out in the mid-1980s over the conduct of this pay trend survey, leading to a long campaign by the civil service unions for the overhauling of the procedures of public sector pay determination.

The origins of the dispute lay in the Standing Commission's adoption of the views expressed in a private consultancy report in 1982 that the value of the total package of civil servants' pay and other benefits substantially exceeded that of private sector employees.[88] The Commission subsequently recommended that 'future arrangements for determining the general *levels* of civil service pay should take into account the total package of pay and fringe benefits in both the civil service and the private sector.'[89] Then in 1985, the government adopted the recommendations by the Standing Committee on Directorate Salaries and Conditions of Service (the Ross Committee) and raised Directorate grade salaries by between 6.4% and 13.5%. This aroused strong reactions from non-Directorate civil servants, who were pressing for similar adjustments. The pay raise for the Directorate grade also prompted the civil service unions to renew their demand for a compensative pay increase of 3% to make up for the 'shortfall' (the difference between pay trend survey result and the actual adjustment) in the pay adjustment of 1983.[90]

Facing strong staff-side protests, the government first promised as an interim measure a 2.7% pay increase for 1986, and also agreed to conduct a pay-level survey to compare both the salaries and benefits of Directorate and non-Directorate civil servants. The Pay Level Survey Advisory Committee was also established to include SCSC staff-side representatives, the management side and Legco members. Without consulting the staff side however, the Standing Commission appointed Hay Management Consultants to conduct the pay-level survey. The results of the survey showed that 'with the exception of Model Scale 1 Staff (a class of lower paid staff) and senior directorate officers, civil servants on local terms of service were better off than their private sector counterparts when the total package of pay and fringe benefits was taken into account.'[91] The suggestion that non-Directorate civil servants were relatively 'privileged' caused an uproar among the staff side. Both the SCSC and the Police Force Council protested against the Survey's findings by withdrawing from the Pay Level Survey Advisory Committee. The staff side of the SCSC also protested over the recommendations of the 1987-88 Pay Trend Survey which were regarded by the staff side of all three of the central consultative councils as too low. Faced with a huge gap between their views and those of the management side, the staff side demanded the establishment of the independent Committee of Inquiry into the 1988 Civil Service Pay Adjustment and Related Matters to resolve the dispute.[92]

Staff-side representatives made a special effort to influence the proceedings of this Committee of Inquiry from the very beginning. They held several meetings with the management side to determine the Committee's jurisdiction and set up a task force to present their views to the Committee. The bone of contention between the staff side and the government over the Pay Trend Survey was the exclusion of pay increases attributable to merit, promotion and transfer. This, according to the staff side, had led to a systematic underreporting of annual pay adjustments in the private sector, while the proportion of companies adopting merit payment schemes as well as the proportion of merit pay to total pay were both rising.[93]

Regarding the Pay Level Survey, the staff side maintained that comparable job categories had not been used in making pay-level comparisons between the private and public sectors. It had also failed to take into consideration the special characteristics of the civil service, such as seniority, experience and the particular working conditions of disciplined forces. It was also pointed out that some staff benefits (such as the home purchase scheme) were not necessarily 'entitlements' and not automatically awarded to civil servants, hence the actual percentage enjoying a particular staff benefit should be lower in the civil service than in the private sector.[94] The staff side also insisted that they should be consulted before the conduct of pay surveys, including over such matters as the selection of a consultancy firm and the methodology of the surveys. Protest rallies were held and both the Federation of Civil Service Unions and the Civil Servants General Union hinted that industrial action was possible.[95]

In its interim report issued in 1988, the Committee of Inquiry recommended the upward adjustment of the pay trend indicators, taking into consideration those private sector companies which had given over 90% of their employees a merit payment. In January 1989, all civil servants received their back pay in adjusted salaries.[96]

While the methodological framework for civil service pay adjustment as a whole was being reviewed, the case of the disciplined services received special attention from the government. In April 1988 the Standing Commission appointed an independent Review Committee on Disciplined Services Pay and Conditions of Service (Review Committee) before the Committee of Inquiry was even established (in August 1988).[97] In November, the Review Committee released its final report, recommending substantial salary increases for the disciplined services. Correctional Services and Customs staff received a hefty 16.8% increase, Immigration Department staff 14.7%, fire-fighters 10.5% and members of the Police Force 9.4%. Staff turnover and difficulties in recruitment were cited as the major considerations in proposing these differential rates of increase.[98] The police and fire-fighters protested over their lower rates of pay increase. Though they threatened industrial actions, especially the fire-fighters, the Executive Council endorsed the Review Committee's recommendations in December 1988.[99]

The Committee of Inquiry's final report was completed in June 1989. It ruled that the findings of the 1986 Pay Level Survey were insufficient as the basis for the civil service pay adjustment. It took the view that the 1986 Survey had overestimated the value of civil service fringe benefits, especially housing benefits. The principle of job-to-job comparison was also endorsed, whereby jobs in the civil service were compared to ones of a similar nature, instead of basing salaries on an aggregate value of private sector company remuneration. Merit payments were recommended for inclusion in future pay trend surveys. Since the Committee of Inquiry supported many of the staff-side arguments, staff-side representatives naturally endorsed the report.

Apart from substantive changes in the methodology of the pay surveys, perhaps the biggest victory for the unions was a matter of principle since the Committee maintained that the management side should consult the staff side on the methodology and implementation of future pay surveys. In the 1989 Pay Trend Survey, released in March 1990 and incorporating the recommendations of the Committee of Inquiry, the benchmark indicators of private sector increases were between 18.25% (high-level employees) and 16.56% (low-level employees).[100] In April 1990, the government decided on an average civil service pay adjustment of 15%. Major civil service unions objected and demanded a uniform 17% increase for all civil servants, but the government rejected this on the grounds that this might lead to a budget deficit.[101]

With the granting of a hefty 15% increase in civil service pay in 1990, the pay dispute that had lasted for over four years and at one point had threatened the workings of the civil service consultative machinery ended. Civil service unions have subsequently continued to contest the actual ranges of the annual pay adjustment, and the two reports (of the Committee of Inquiry and the Review Committee) did not resolve the thorny issue of internal relativities within the civil service including within the disciplined services. Yet at least after the pay dispute, an overall procedural framework for establishing benchmarks for civil service pay levels and annual adjustments was re-established and accepted by almost all parties concerned. For the staff side, gaining union representation in the implementation of pay surveys was a hard-won victory, while the management side was relieved to rebuild a pay determination mechanism that was viewed as legitimate. Conflicts after that were over the technical details in calculating the pay raise and not over the principles (pay survey indicators subject to the approval of the Governor in Council) underlying the determination of pay. The pay dispute was also an important landmark in the development of civil service trade union solidarity:

> The findings of the Hay pay-level survey brought them [civil service staff associations] together in common cause perhaps for the first time, for *all* on the Master pay scale, irrespective of grade or occupation, were affected, as were the disciplined services. Once the strength of feeling was made manifest, government could not ignore it.[102]

Prior to this, civil service unions were regarded as parochial and narrowly status-conscious. Issues of internal relativities had normally dominated staff relations. The above pay dispute not only brought most of the staff associations into a united front in pressing for concessions from the government, but also demonstrated how effective such concerted actions could be.

The Reorganization of Medical Services

In the late 1980s, a major dispute broke out in the social service sector that again testifies to the power of public sector unions when they unite. The case involved medical service workers, and the main events leading up to the dispute were as follows.[103] In October 1983, during the debate on the Governor's policy address to the Legislative Council, members called for a review of medical services at a time when government hospitals were under considerable pressure due to overcrowding and long queues for treatment in clinics. The Secretary for Health and Welfare agreed on the need for a review, and following approval by the Executive Council (Exco) in May 1984, a firm of Australian management consultants, W.D. Scott Pty Co., was commissioned in February 1985 to conduct a review of hospital services.[104] The consultants submitted their report to the government in December 1985 and made a number of detailed recommendations for change, the major one being that a statutory Hospital Authority (HA) should be established with responsibility for the delivery of medical services in hospitals, and that it should operate outside the civil service but continue to be heavily subsidized by the government.

In March 1986 the Governor in Council took note of the Scott Report and called for a period of public consultation which lasted from March to August 1986. While the public was generally 'enthusiastic' about the recommendations, staff in the Medical and Health Department (M&HD) 'were generally opposed to the proposal and considerable anxiety was voiced about the possibility of reduced fringe benefits and loss of their civil service status and job security.'[105] The Scott Report was published in March 1986. One month later, on 16 April, 22 out of the then 34 registered trade unions of M&HD staff formed the League of the Medical and Health Department Staff Unions (the League).[106] The League eventually included 32 staff unions representing over 90% of all staff in the M&HD. During the public consultation period, meetings were held by the M&HD with the League, the League organized seminars on the Scott Report, and the M&HD organized special Grade Consultative Committee meetings.

In March 1987 a summary of public opinion on the recommendations was published by the Health and Welfare Branch. Of the 27 submissions from civil service staff unions, three-quarters which commented on the proposed HA objected to it. In October 1987, the Governor announced in his policy address to Legco that an independent HA would be set up, with hospital administration hived off from the M&HD to form the Hospital Services Department which would become the executive organ of the future HA.

Further consultation meetings and seminars followed in the M&HD and at government hospitals. A working group was formed between the League and the M&HD to discuss staff concerns. Following six working group meetings with the M&HD, the League voiced dissatisfaction with the lack of firm answers or commitments from the management side (which took the position that it was unable to give guarantees on future conditions of employment under the HA) and halted its participation in the consultation process. Unions in the M&HD announced they would then appoint the League to represent them in all negotiations with the government. In February 1988, the League met senior representatives of the Civil Service Branch (CSB) for the first time and subsequently petitioned OMELCO and urged the government to provide the guarantees it sought.[107] In March 1988, the Health and Welfare Branch set up a special working group headed by a Staff Grade B officer to deal with staff concerns over the setting up of the HA. Other union groups including the CCSA, Public Servants International Hong Kong Co-ordinating Committee, the CSGU, FCSU and JOU supported the League in their demands for the government to provide firm answers about the future status of M&HD staff. The League warned it might take industrial action if its demands were not dealt with satisfactorily. In July 1988, at the initiative of the M&HD, dialogue was reopened between the League and the government; ten meetings had been held by March 1989. Following a meeting between the League and representatives from the M&HD, Health and Welfare Branch and CSB in early September 1988, the convenor of the League announced that they had at last received more details from the government side.

About that time however, trouble was brewing with the Nursing and Allied Grades (consisting of nurses, inoculators, midwives and dietitians and represented by eight staff unions). Consultative meetings between the M&HD and this Grade started in August 1988 and lasted to April 1989 over reorganization matters. However, in late February 1989 the Association of Government Nursing Staff (AGNS) and the Nurses' Branch of the CCSA complained about problems with the nursing grade structure and grade management under the new set-up and about inadequate information and consultation on this matter. Despite walk-outs by AGNS from several of the meetings, the reorganization of the M&HD took place on 1 April 1989 as scheduled. This was possible because the League by that time no longer opposed the move since it had achieved its key aims. A major concern was that all promotion posts under the future HA could be converted to HA posts and that civil servants would have to give up their civil servant status if they were offered promotion. They thus wanted matters of promotion as well as transfer and training to be centrally administered under the new system. The introduction of the Common Grade Management concept was designed to allay their concerns since under this proposal all departmental grades in the 'central pool' would be treated as one common grade whether working in the Hospital Services Department or Department of Health. All eligible staff would be considered for promotion posts whichever of the two departments had the vacancy.

There were other controversies during this period linked to the reorganization of the M&HD and the HA issue. Government doctors had expressed on numerous occasions their grievances over long working hours, low pay compared with doctors in private practice, lack of promotion prospects and overwork. There was a problem of 'exodus' of government doctors to the private sector. The then Senior Assistant Director of Medical and Health Services said in late 1987 that he hoped the new HA would solve the 'exodus' problem by providing more flexible employment terms for doctors, but the then Medical functional constituency representative, Dr Chiu Hin Kwong, stated in June 1988 that the problem of wastage should be tackled immediately. He urged the Government Doctors Association (GDA) to carry out a survey of members. After doing so, the GDA called an open forum in early September in Queen Elizabeth Hospital which was attended by over 500 doctors. A report on the survey findings indicated that one-third of the doctors with 15 years or more working experience in government intended to quit in the coming year. Media sympathy for their case and statements by candidates then campaigning for the Medical functional constituency for 1988 elections added pressure on the government to act. The Secretary for Health and Welfare then initiated a series of meetings among Health and Welfare Branch, M&HD and GDA representatives to discuss the doctors' problems. In March 1989, in the absence of concrete action by the government, the doctors took industrial action by refusing to take up duties unrelated to patient care. Following this action, the government agreed in principle to upgrade 74 medical officers to senior medical officers.

The nurses also raised the matter of a serious wastage problem in the nursing grades in mid-1988, and conducted a survey that showed about 15% of the respondents were in the process of resigning or emigrating and that 55% of the rest were considering leaving the service in two years' time. The AGNS then sought to open discussions over improvements in the nursing grade establishment and training opportunities but no progress was made. In early December 1988, the Nursing and Allied Grades Review Committee was formed within the M&HD to review and improve matters relating to staff, working conditions, salary and structure of the nursing grade, and to make recommendations for retention of nursing-grade staff. The AGNS initiated measures to put pressure on the government including the 'protection of rights of patients' campaign in January 1989. In March 1989, nurses mounted a type of work-to-rule action by refusing to check patients' identity cards or to handle hospital fee matters. On 1 April 1989, the AGNS petitioned the Governor on the staff shortage problem. The frequency of Review Committee meetings was then increased and attended also by representatives from the Health and Welfare Branch, CSB and Finance Branch. After 15 meetings concrete proposals emerged including a review of the existing pay scales of nursing grades, a proposal to create 205 nursing officer posts and several hundred registered nurse posts, as well as extension of pharmacy and shroff services in hospitals. The pay scale for student nurses was also increased substantially.

Cheung's study shows that government doctors and nurses were able on the whole to get what they wanted from the government in 1988–89 and she identifies a number of factors that contributed to their success.[108] The first was the strategic alliance among unions in the form of the League which was possible given that each occupational group faced a common 'threat' to their status and conditions of employment. This gave the League considerable bargaining power over the terms of change, but it depended also on the government's acceptance of the League as representing staff for consultative purposes since the League had no recognized status as a registered union. In the case of doctors, the GDA's mass forum attended by an estimated one-third of government doctors was a clear signal to the government of a high degree of occupational solidarity. The mass meetings held by the AGNS and its mass gathering to present a petition to the Governor on 1 April 1989 were a 'means to exhibit the support behind the union, as well as the power of the union to mobilize staff.'[109]

A second factor contributing to success was the timing of action. The government needed staff cooperation to implement its plans for reorganization of hospital services. It therefore had to solve its industrial relations problems with doctors and nurses in order to proceed with the reorganization of hospital services which had a high priority. It thus acted unusually rapidly in this case.[110] Timing was important in another way — the actions of doctors and nurses coincided with the campaign for election to the legislature. Candidates for both the Medical and the Health Care functional constituencies needed the votes of doctors and nurses respectively. To gain voter support, these candidates came out in support of the demands of doctors and nurses which in turn added to the pressure on the government to act. One of the candidates, Ronald Chow, was a former chairman of AGNS (from 1978 to 1986) and then became an adviser to the AGNS. After his election, he would take up the case of the nurses with the senior levels of government and on one occasion accompanied the representatives of AGNS to petition the Governor.

A third factor contributing to success was the specific tactics used by the unions. The GDA and Nurses used survey results to demonstrate to the public as well as government the seriousness of the wastage problem which was readily understood by the public and gained considerable attention from the media. The press conference was effective in 'attracting public attention and press commentary.'[111] The ability to mobilize support from other groups — other civil service unions but also those from tertiary institutions — demonstrated wider public sympathy with their cause. A fourth factor was persistence in getting the higher levels of the government bureaucracy to take their claims and demands seriously. Since departmental-level officials cannot make policy, pursuing direct contact and discussion with policy branches 'can bring about a more speedy and substantial improvement.' The ability to gain such access was greatly aided by the inherent advantage of providing an essential public service.

❑ Discussion

We have argued in this chapter that a key factor shaping the growth of the public sector union movement is the distinctive nature of the governance system of the public workplace. Let us recap some of its features. First, the public sector employs relatively well-educated employees pursuing careers in internal labour markets (differentiated occupationally and organizationally) located in a relatively sheltered sector of the economy. Second, the public sector has a highly institutionalized character, with norms of bureaucratic rationality and procedural due process embedded within the governance system. Third, within this highly institutionalized governance system, trade unions as the form of collective employee representation have become a legitimatized and taken-for-granted feature of organizational life. Fourth, the broader contours of the polity have also permeated the governance system of the public workplace. Both the domestic changes in the political system arising from democratization in the 1980s as well as the continuing colonial linkages to Britain have imposed significant constraints on public sector actors' industrial relations behaviour.

This governance system has given rise to a public sector union growth wave of greater longevity than similar growth waves which occurred historically in the private sector, with a much higher employee union participation rate and encompassing a much wider spectrum of employees. The impact of this governance system can be demonstrated by comparing white-collar workers in the private sector who, as discussed in the previous chapter, have shied away from joining unions. White-collar and professional employees are by contrast the backbone of the public sector union movement. This suggests that the propensity of employees to participate in collective action is more a function of the organizational (both institutional and instrumental) context of work than of occupational or demographic variables.

Over the past three decades, the interactions between the staff side and the management in the civil service have become increasingly shaped by the 'institutionalization of conflict' in which sectional interests are pursued within a relatively well-defined set of rules. The 1968 Agreement, for example, provided a 'constitutional' framework for the conduct of industrial relations in the public sector, laying down the fundamental although initially largely symbolic rights of consultation of the employees. As a result of interactions between management and unions over time within this framework and also as a by-product of the resolution of disputes such as those discussed above, it can be argued that this framework has become increasingly infused with value by the key participants so that it has become a socially integrative structure.

We have also sought to show the ways in which the public sector governance system has influenced the strategies and demands of the trade unions. We contend that this is a result, in both the strategic and institutional contexts, of the organization of public workplace. Staff-side demands are often couched in terms of 'fairness' as applied to both procedural and substantive matters. The controversy over pay adjustment had been over what constituted a 'fair' comparison between private and pubic sector jobs and what were the 'appropriate' or 'just' procedures for attaining it. Given the government's explicit commitment to 'fair' conditions of service for its employees, staff-side arguments were predictably framed in this language.[112] The distinctive character of the public sector also prompted unions to present their demands as a matter of 'public interest' and to contest the public agenda including government expenditure priorities. They sometimes argued that if their pay demands or demands for representation and participation in matters concerning conditions of service were not met, morale would suffer and the quality of applicants for public sector posts would drop, thus jeopardizing the maintenance of administrative efficiency and stability.

This does not mean that organizational resources are relatively insignificant in the generation and persistence of a union growth wave or in determining public sector union effectiveness. Organizational resources and their mobilization are critical for public sector unions if they are to capitalize on the opportunities offered to them by the public sector governance system. Specific strategies of mobilization among public sector unions, notably strategic alliances over particular issues and avoidance of affiliation to politically charged union federations, can be particularly effective in dealing with the management. Coalition-building, both within the labour movement and with other concerned parties (e.g. legislators and interest groups), not only enhances unions' disruptive potential but can also increase their credibility in the contest over the definition of the public interest. The case of the medical employees best illustrates this point. By avoiding affiliation to the politically oriented trade union federations, their unions were better able to engender trust from the government and from other public sector agencies for purposes of recognition and bargaining, because they were not seen to be mounting fundamental challenges to managerial authority or colonial rule but were seen to be working for change within the existing system.

In following these 'scripts' however, civil service unions are also prompted by their organizational context to delimit their strategies of action. The civil service ideology of 'political neutrality' as well as explicit restrictions on civil servants' political activities mark off unions of the latter from both the social service and private sector unions, which have increasingly pursued a more politicized strategy. Although the activities of civil service unions are political by nature since they directly impinge on the operation of the government, they have not capitalized on their vast organizational resources in participating in electoral and party politics. By contrast, social service sector unions are often at the forefront of campaigns over social issues such as the provision of better medical services and improving the quality of education; they have also been central actors in the forging of political coalitions in the contest for political power. The point is that while civil servants and social service sector employees enjoy broadly similar conditions of service, the difference in their respective institutional frameworks has consequences for the kinds of strategies they pursue both in and outside the workplace.

The application of the concept of a distinctive governance system to the analysis of the public sector union movement can also provide, we believe, a useful vantage point for synthesizing the different strands of the social movement literature. The resource mobilization approach alerts us to how organizational resources engendered by the public sector employment system and the strategic interactions among relevant actors shape the public sector union movement. In examining the impact of broader political changes and alignments as well as the specificities of colonial governance, we are following the lead of the political process models. We have also not overlooked the significance of the symbolic dimensions of the organizational life in the public sector. We have shown for example how the highly institutionalized character of the public sector governance system led to the expression of trade union demands in specific forms. Each of these analytical themes clearly merits a separate study. This paper has attempted to outline in broad-brush strokes how these themes might be further developed in the analysis of the public sector labour movement.

Given the current economic downturn and the Hong Kong government's anxiety over current and future financial solvency, as well as public sector reforms, the ability of public sector unions to pursue instrumental objectives may not be as straightforward as in the past.[113] Civil servants may find it more difficult, for example, to link civil service expansion and their conditions of service to the public interest, which is increasingly being defined in terms of a 'lean but efficient' government.

There is the danger that if civil service unions were to become overly aggressive in the pursuit of their sectional interests, they could arouse strong counterreaction from the SAR government, and thus jeopardize the effectiveness of the established institutional framework for conflict regulation. Civil service unions will therefore have to walk a very fine tightrope between pursuing rank-and-file interests and cooperating with the new administration. In the case of those social service sector unions which have become more deeply involved in electoral and party politics, their room for manoeuvre is likely to be restricted in the future, especially on wider social issues not directly related to their own professions. Still, as broad-based organizations performing critical functions in the society, the public sector union movement is likely to continue to be a force to be reckoned with.

Notes

1. Levi, *Bureaucratic insurgency.*
2. We refer primarily to the work of England and Rear, *Industrial relations and law in Hong Kong,* chapter 6; Turner et al., *The last colony: but whose?* chapter 11; and Arn, 'Public sector unions'.
3. The concept of governance structures derives from several sources. One is the institutional approach to economic behaviour of John R. Commons, who conceptualized the employment relationship as a form of 'industrial government'. This approach has been revitalized by the work of Williamson, *Market and hierarchies* and *The economic institutions of capitalism.* Sociologist Selznick, *Law, society, and industrial justice,* has employed the concept of governance structure in his analysis of organizations, private as well as public, as political systems. For a recent overview of these and other institutional approaches to the study of organizations, see Scott, *Institutions and organizations.*
4. The recognition of the exercise of strategic choices by unions assumes that environmental/structural factors constrain but seldom dictate the process of organizational development and action (cf. Child, 'Organizational structure, environment and performance: the role of strategic choice'). Studies of trade unions are suggestive of the range of strategic choices they confront. These include how narrowly or widely to define organizational boundaries, what priority to give to labour's market interests versus political and social interests, whether to pursue these interests in the economic or political arena and whether to work within or outside established channels, whether to give priority to short-run or long-run achievements, and whether to rely on internal resources or external support for survival and effectiveness (Offe, 'Two logics of collective action'; Siegel, 'The extended meaning and diminished relevance of "job conscious" unionism').
5. See Crozier, *The world of the office worker,* for an early statement of the importance of taking culture into account for understanding the behaviour of white-collar employees.
6. This is the working definition adopted by Turner et al., *The last colony: but whose?* and Arn, 'Public sector unions'.
7. Miners, *The government and politics of Hong Kong,* p. 124, endnote 31, notes that the concept of 'public servants' which appears in the provisions of the Prevention of Bribery Bill (1970) differs from Public Service. 'Public servants' are defined to include not only civil servants but also officials of statutory corporations, franchised utility companies and various other public bodies as listed in the schedule to the ordinance. The possession of assets disproportionate to known sources of income is a ground for prosecution only in the case of civil servants directly paid by government.
8. Ibid., pp. 112–6.
9. The diversity of these organizations is suggested by the following: the Fish Marketing Organization and the Vegetable Marketing Organizations (statutory corporations), the Hong Kong Productivity Council, the Trade Development Council, the Tourist Association and the Consumer Council (established by an ordinance but employing their own staff at commercial rates of pay, though subject to the ruling that 'subvented organizations must not provide conditions of service more favourable than those in government'), statutory corporations involved in commercial activities but whose equity is completely owned by government (the

Export Credit Insurance Corporation, the Mass Transit Railway Corporation, the Industrial Estates Corporation), public utilities granted statutory monopoly by government, boards and committees including 18 standing committees consisting entirely of civil servants. See ibid., pp. 112–3.

10. For attempts to distinguish the character of public and private organizations, see Westrum and Samaha, *Complex organizations: growth, struggle, and change*; and Olson, 'Public and private political realities and the privatization movement'.

11. Johnston, *Success while others fail: social movement unionism and the public workplace*, p. 10.

12. Cheung, 'The civil service', p. 87.

13. Hong Kong government, *Hong Kong annual report 1997*, p. 25.

14. Scott, *Organizations: rational, natural, and open systems*, pp. 132–41. Public sector organizations do however face growing pressures to model themselves along the lines of private sector organizations in order to demonstrate resources are being used effectively. This is one meaning of the rhetoric of 'public sector reform' which has spread to Hong Kong over the past decade.

15. A qualification is that the private sector is also part of this institutional environment insofar as public sector pay is linked through various institutional means with private sector pay levels and pay trends.

16. Central Office of Information, *Labour in the United Kingdom dependencies*, p. 12.

17. Johnston, *Success while others fail: social movement unionism and the public workplace*, p. 11.

18. Lipset, 'Equity and equality in government wage policy', p. 123, notes that 'individuals or groups who are subordinate to the <u>same</u> authority are more likely to use each other as reference groups, than if the reverse were true' and suggests that 'those employed in the public sector...are likely to see comparisons with the rewards of other government employees as legitimate.'

19. Thompson, 'Organizational management of conflict', p. 30.

20. High turnover among workers in the private sector has been hypothesized as one obstacle to the formation of group solidarity (England and Rear, *Chinese labour under British rule*, pp. 69–70).

21. Hirschman, *Exit, voice, and loyalty: responses to decline in firms, organizations and states*, p. 78, argues loyalty is an intervening variable between dissatisfaction and forms of protest since 'loyalty holds exit at bay and activates voice.' In the case of public sector employees, the critical intervening variable may be an ideology of service rather than loyalty. To the extent public sector employees are motivated by an ideology of service, this should dampen their propensity to exit as well as to take militant actions that would be disruptive to the community. On the other hand, the ideology of service can also stimulate public sector employees to define their role as monitoring the policies of government agencies and to voice protest against those policies which they perceive to conflict with the effective delivery of public services. We hypothesize that the stronger the occupational ideology of service to clients, the greater the likelihood that occupational associations will seek to legitimate their demands in terms of serving the public interest.

22. Kochan, 'Toward a behavioural model of management under collective bargaining'.

23. Thus, government actions that appear to threaten trade unions rights of civil servants can evoke strong union counter-reactions. For example, in October 1990 the Postmaster General hinted that powers in the Letters Patent might be used

against postal staff taking part in industrial action. Some post office unions subsequently wrote to the International Labour Organisation to protest that the government's action contravened International Labour Convention No. 151 which says that public employees shall enjoy protection against acts of anti-union discrimination and their organisation protections against interference by public authority. Accounts of this case can be found in *South China Morning Post*, 18, 19, 23 and 27 October 1990. With reference to this and other civil service industrial disputes, Cheung, 'The civil service', p. 39, comments that the Hong Kong government has to 'tread a fine line between recognizing staff's legitimate rights and its own responsibility to provide proper public services.'

24. Comments by the Chief Secretary to the Legislative Council in May 1990 illustrate this point: 'Staff associations within the [Civil] Service are well organized and fight hard for their members. We have encouraged their development because we believe in consultation and the settlement of disputes through frank formal negotiation. With 190 000 people in the Service we must have proper machinery for consultation in all grades and at all levels; the informal style of the private sector simply would not work. The success of our system should be measured by the quiet consensus which ends the majority of disagreements. Not by the few, noisy instances where, for whatever reason, agreement is not possible.' Hong Kong Legislative Council *Official report of proceedings* 9 May 1990, pp. 1494–8.

25. The following statement issued by the Civil Service Branch is indicative of civil service management view of staff unions: 'Government fully recognizes the value of an efficient and responsible Staff Side, and of well organised and fully representative Staff Associations. It is in the interest of the Civil Service and of Government that Staff Associations should be capably and responsibly represented. Departments should therefore ensure that no officer should feel debarred from accepting any office in a Staff Association except for reasons associated with his particular appointment...All officers should feel that a career in the Public Service is in no way incompatible with involvement in Staff Side activities' (Civil Service Branch Circular No. 45/74 of 25 June 1974, reproduced in Hong Kong Standing Commission on Civil Service Salaries and Conditions of Service, *Report no. 4: consultative machinery in the civil service*, p. 34).

26. This illustrates how a change in a constituent element of a political regime can affect the context of collective action within the public workplace.

27. Johnston, *Success while others fail: social movement unionism and the public workplace*, p. 11.

28. Ibid., p. 17.

29. These characteristics do not constitute a complete listing. The governance system is also linked, for example, with the educational system via the production of individuals with appropriate qualifications for entry into various public sector positions.

30. See Conell and Cohn, 'Learning from other people's actions: environmental variation and diffusion in French coal mining strikes, 1890–1935', on the importance of learning from others or 'imitation' in social movements and particularly strikes.

31. We draw in our account in this section from Arn, 'Public sector unions'; Cheek-Milby, 'Staff relations', pp. 192–8; England and Rear, *Chinese labour under British rule*, pp. 268–73; and Ng, 'Staff relations practices in the civil service', pp. 63–78.

32. The largest civil service union was the CCSA with 4 346 members at the end of 1966. The Government, Armed Forces and Hospitals Chinese Workers Union, which

recruited government employees, was larger but also recruited members from outside the civil service.

33. Arn, 'Public sector unions', pp. 238–9.

34. The AECS requested formal negotiating status in 1962. A Colonial Office Principal, C.G. Gibbs, who visited Hong Kong in early 1963, gave some support to this request when he pointed out that the Labour Department's official policy of encouraging joint consultation and collective bargaining in the private sector had a rather hollow ring unless the government was seen to be pursuing this policy in its relations with its own employees.

35. Four categories of staff were excluded from the terms of the 1968 agreement: Directorate Officers (for whom separate machinery existed in the form of the Standing Committee on Directorate Salaries and Conditions of Service), the Royal Hong Kong Police Force, Agreement Officers and Model Scale 1 (labourer and artisan) staff. The membership of the SCSC was comprised of six Official Side members appointed by the Chief Secretary and a maximum of ten from the three main associations appointed from among their members. A Staff Side leader is provided by the associations on a four-monthly rotating basis. The Official Side Secretary is responsible for the production of minutes.

36. See the 1968 government statement on the principles and aims of civil service remuneration quoted in Standing Commission (*First report*, p. 7).

37. See Scott, *Political change and the crisis of legitimacy in Hong Kong*, p. 134; Wong, 'Staff relations in the civil service and the trade union response: review and prospect, 1971–1985', pp. 150–1.

38. The Mallaby Commission defined an 'occupational class' as a number of grades related to each other on the basis of occupational criteria and therefore regarded as having pay links. A 'grade' was a group of job-related ranks, the higher of which are normally filled by promotion from lower ranks, e.g. Executive Officer II, Executive Officer I, Senior Executive officer, Chief Executive Officer. Ranks are thus subdivisions of a grade, normally representing a separate level of responsibility. The Commission also recommended new arrangements for housing, education allowances and other benefits for its staff.

39. *Hong Kong Standard*, 31 July 1973. The pre-existing establishment of networks of activists appeared to have facilitated employee organization and collective action. The CCSA had revised its internal organizational structure in the early 1970s to provide for the formation of occupationally based units which were in effect 'quasi-unions'. Some of these units later became the nuclei for the formation of new unions. Given the large number of these units and the difficulties faced by the CCSA in taking up the grievances of each one, some grades became convinced that they could pursue their cases more effectively as a registered trade union. Ho, 'The government and the clerical workers: a case study of labour-management conflict in the Hong Kong civil service', p. 93, explains as follows why the clerical staff formed a union separate from the clerical unit within CCSA: 'It was believed that the H.K.C.C.S.A. had to look after the interests of a large number of occupational groups in the Civil Service, and that there were conflicts among various occupational groups as to the policies and actions of the union. Thus, it was inevitable that the interests of some groups were better looked after than others... Thus, the decision to form a new union was informed by the desire to create an organizational form that could better protect the interests of the Government clerks.'

40. The Nurses Unit (now the Nurses Branch) of the Hong Kong Chinese Civil Servants'

Association, during their struggle for equal work for equal pay in 1969 and for equivalent pay structure for equivalent grades in 1971, had pioneered in developing protest tactics that came to be widely used by civil service groups in the 1970s. These tactics included holding mass rallies, putting up posters, collecting fighting funds, setting up action groups, threatening industrial actions, making use of the mass media and petitioning the Governor. See Nurses Branch, *20th anniversary issue*, pp. 10–27. We are grateful to Peter H. Wong, former president of the Hong Kong Chinese Civil Servants' Association, for drawing our attention to these points.

41. England and Rear, *Industrial relations and law in Hong Kong*, pp. 109–10.
42. Wong, 'Staff relations in the civil service and the trade union response: review and prospect, 1971–1985', pp. 152–3.
43. See Fox, *A sociology of work in industry*, p. 176, for a discussion of the causes of cumulative disorder in industrial relations. Observers at the time believed — wrongly as it turned out — that these actions by public sector unions were a possible harbinger of widespread labour unrest fuelled by inflation, the rising aspirations of a younger, better-educated workforce, and the demonstration effect of civil service union militancy. See England and Rear, *Industrial relations and law in Hong Kong*, p. 378; and Turner et al., *The last colony: but whose?* p. 159.
44. As the Standing Commission put it in its *First report on principles and practices governing civil service pay*: 'In the years since the 1971 Salaries Commission produced its report the civil service has undergone substantial changes and its size, scope and responsibilities have all increased. To cater for these changes adjustment to grades have had to be made on a piecemeal basis. These ad hoc amendments led to pressure for adjustments from other grades which believed themselves to be related. The basic framework of the civil service salary structure was therefore being eroded and staff associations increasingly felt it necessary to make claims for improved pay in the belief that only those who asked would be considered.' In devising a strategy to defuse the discontent, certain options were closed off. For reasons noted earlier, the government could not suppress staff unions so long as they operated within the parameters of the law. See Scott, *Political change and the crisis of legitimacy in Hong Kong*, p. 153ff., for a discussion of expansion of the civil service.
45. The appointment of a Standing Commission confirms a hypothesis of Thompson's, 'Organizational management of conflict', pp. 30–1, that in circumstances where normative agreement is lacking on the appropriate criteria for resource allocation, management of large organizations is likely to adopt a strategy that seeks to 'enhance legitimacy for its administrative allocation by calling on outside authorities, such as consultants, thus transferring the responsibility for unpopular decisions.' The Standing Commission's terms of reference included reviewing (1) the principles and practices governing civil service class, grade, rank and salary structure; (2) the mechanisms for determining general pay revisions for civil servants; and (3) existing consultative procedures. On the basis of its reviews of these matters, the Standing Commission was to offer advice and recommend to the Governor any changes it considered to be necessary. In January 1979 a small Secretariat was assembled and P. B. Williams, a former Commissioner for Labour, was appointed Secretary-General. Nine individuals with 'extensive links with the business world' (England, *Industrial relations and law in Hong Kong*, p. 90) were appointed as part-time members of the Commission. An exception however was the appointment of Rev. P.T. McGovern who was well known as an advocate of workers' interests.

46. Roberts, *Labour in the tropical territories of the Commonwealth*, p. 374. The appointment of the Standing Commission was however a departure from past practice in Hong Kong in two ways. First, membership was composed entirely of local residents. Second, it was a permanent salaries commission. It differed also in that appointment followed five years of annual pay trend survey awards, Hong Kong Standing Commission on Civil Service Salaries and Conditions of Service, *First report*, p. 4.

47. Aside from creating the Standing Commission, management upgraded the former Staff Relations Unit to a full division in 1978 with responsibilities of advising and assisting departmental management on staff relations matters and 'to provide a conciliatory service to resolve the differences between staff and management' when the consultative process encountered problems, Tso, 'The industrial relations system in the Hong Kong civil service,' pp. 63–4. England, *Industrial relations and law in Hong Kong*, p. 89, suggests the following rationale for upgrading the Staff Relations Division: 'In the belief that many disputes had arisen from breakdowns in communication and in trust, members of this division were given the task of mediating between management in the departments and the staff associations.'

48. Lui, 'Changing civil servants' values', pp. 137–40.

49. Tso, 'The industrial relations system in the Hong Kong civil service,' p. 63. England, *Industrial relations and law in Hong Kong*, p. 91, notes that it had to operate in a context of conflicting expectations: 'In essence, the Standing Commission has to balance the interests of government against those of the staff associations and the civil service against the private sector.' The Standing Commission can thus be viewed as an attempt to deflect some of the heat on the Civil Service Branch. It was also given a critical task of re-establishing a governance system that would protect the core values of the administration.

50. Information on public sector unions is compiled from the Registrar of Trade Union's annual department reports and transformed into a computer database as explained in the previous chapter. We distinguish between civil service and social service unions in the manner described earlier. The figures reported in the tables in this section are based on preliminary analysis of our database and are therefore tentative.

51. Cf. England, *Industrial relations and law in Hong Kong*, p. 92.

52. See the notes to Table 2 on the basis for the calculation of union density figures.

53. Cheung, 'Public sector unions in Hong Kong: a study of the reorganization of the Medical and Health Department', p. 81. She notes that of the 28 unions claiming to recruit more than 40% of potential members, all but 1 recruited from a single profession, grade or rank. Of the 8 unions recruiting 40% or less of potential members, 5 recruited from the same department. This seems to support the proposition that the more narrowly membership boundaries are defined, the higher union density is likely to be. This also has implications for union mobilization.

54. England, *Industrial relations and law in Hong Kong*, pp. 130–1. He notes for the Hong Kong union movement as a whole that in 1987 a majority of unions (230 out of 415) had under 250 members, although they accounted for only 5.5% of all union members. The 12 largest unions with over 5 000 members accounted for close to half of all trade union members. A permissive condition for the proliferation of small unions is the provision of the Trade Unions Ordinance which allows a minimum of seven persons to register as a union. England, ibid., p. 108, argues union proliferation also reflects a 'cultural preference' among Hong Kong Chinese for 'particularistic forms of organization'. Turner et al., *The last colony: but whose?*

p. 134, view proliferation as a rational organizational strategy for pressing section interests. Lam, 'Proliferation and consolidation of trade unionism in the public sector', pp. 159–61, by contrast emphasizes the organizational bases for the proliferation of small unions: 'The rapid growth in the size of the civil service and the complexity of an organization with many departments and numerous occupational differences has produced a distinctive environment which is conducive to the formation of employee unions based on individual departments and particular grades or even ranks within (or sometimes cutting across) departments. From this perspective, the proliferation of unions is thus an inevitable process and the form that the development of unions takes under this type of organizational structure. The social basis conducive to the development of unions with a rather narrow scope of membership is simply the common needs of people of the same rank, the close association that develops in the same workplace and the ease of discussion among friends, and the shared frustrations arising from similar working conditions.'

55. The growth of the CCSA has been explained in terms of the tangible benefits it provides members. England, *Industrial relations and law in Hong Kong*, p. 139, claims the CCSA has grown by luring members with credit cards. The PTU also has an extensive provision of selective incentives for members.

56. England, ibid., p. 132, stresses the rationality of these new forms when he writes that '[a]nother consequence of the proliferation of unions in this sector has been a realization among many small unions that on some issues, such as social and political reform and general improvements to government pay and conditions, collaboration and unity promise better results.'

57. Tso, 'Civil service unions as a social force in Hong Kong', p. 19.

58. Cheung, 'Public sector unions in Hong Kong: a study of the reorganization of the Medical and Health Department', p. 91. She notes that it is difficult to dissolve a trade union because of the relatively high proportion of voting members, whose approval is needed to do so. Kwok, 'Staff representation on the Senior Civil Service Council: consultation, collective bargaining or participation', p. 148, estimated in 1985 that of 150 civil service unions, only about half were active.

59. Scott, 'The Hong Kong civil service and its future', p. 243, endnote 4, shows the distribution of civil servants by pay scales for 1986 as follows: 0.5% on the Directorate scale, 0.9% on MPS points 48–51, 4.6% on MPS points 38–47, 11% on MPS points 30–37, 35.8% on MPS points 1–29, 20.5% on disciplined services scales, 24.9% on Model Scale 1, and 2.1% on training and other pay scales.

60. Cheung, 'Public sector unions in Hong Kong: a study of the reorganization of the Medical and Health Department', pp. 73–5.

61. Standing Commission, *Report no. 2: first report on civil service pay*, appendices IX and X. Some 35 units of the CCSA also made written representations and 5 units of the Government, Armed Forces & Hospitals Chinese Workers Union. There were in addition over 150 written representations from 'Groups of Staff'.

62. Arn, 'Public sector unions', pp. 246–50.

63. Cheung, 'The civil service', pp. 100–2, notes that during 1989–90 industrial actions were undertaken by nurses, midwives, doctors, court interpreters, land and surveying officers and fire-fighters. The fireman's 'hunger strike' in late March 1990 over a demand for reduced working hours 'brought the territory to the verge of partial paralysis.' Other groups threatening industrial actions over pay and conditions included clerical grades staff, court prosecutors, welfare workers, immigration officers and urban services workers. Cheung suggests the following

factors contributed to the upsurge in industrial disputes: the 'dissatisfaction over the results of pay reviews or the lack of them', the tight labour market (which increased employees' bargaining power), rising wastage in government departments (contributing to greater work pressure), and the political climate conducive to 'the general motivation to seek short-term gains in the absence of sufficient confidence in the future.' Perhaps the most influential factor was another point he mentions: the first overall review since 1979 of civil servants' salary structure was then under way, by the Standing Commission.

64. On trade union participation in social and political movements in the 1980s, see Jao et al., *Labour movement in a changing society*; Tso, 'Civil service unions as a social force in Hong Kong'; Chiu, 'Labour organizations and political change in Hong Kong'. England, *Industrial relations and law in Hong Kong*, p. 132, notes 'the increasing numbers of young, well-educated, and socially conscious professionals, such as teachers and medical and social workers, who are organized and who have been willing to use the power of organization to press for social reforms.'

65. A petition was submitted to the Governor for a comprehensive social security plan, laws to protect workers from unfair dismissals, the setting up of a wages compensation fund, and to make Labour Day a paid legal holiday. See Levin and Chiu, 'Dependent capitalism, a colonial state, and marginal unions: the case of Hong Kong', pp. 210–1.

66. Chiu, 'Labour organizations and political change in Hong Kong', pp. 62–6.

67. The nomination of these seven members became a source of controversy within the labour movement. See the account in Levin and Chiu, 'Dependent capitalism, a colonial state, and marginal unions: the case of Hong Kong', pp. 212–3.

68. Chiu and Levin, 'From a labour-surplus to a labour-scarce economy: challenges to human resource management in Hong Kong', pp. 170–3.

69. Tso, 'Civil service unions as a social force in Hong Kong', p. 47.

70. Law, 'White-collar unionism: the case of teachers', p. 166.

71. See Mak, 'White-collar unionism: the case of social workers', p. 167, for the case of social workers.

72. It also recommended that the staff side should be drawn from elected representatives serving on departmental consultative committees (DCCs) but this suggestion was never taken up by the government. The Commission decided no separate council was necessary for directorate grade staff since directorate officers are free to join their own professional or grade associations and/or one of the three main staff associations represented on the SCSC. It is unlawful for police officers to form or join any trade union.

73. Tso, 'The industrial relations system in the Hong Kong civil service', pp. 61–6.

74. Wong, 'Staff relations in the civil service and the trade union response: review and prospect, 1971–1985', pp. 154–5. He proposed that the number of seats allocated to the staff side on the SCSC be increased to ten, with seven seats filled by election among all civil service unions and three reserved for the three staff associations already represented on the SCSC.

75. The Commission noted that if members belonging to the Model Scale 1 were excluded, the membership figure for these three associations would be reduced to about 22 600.

76. Hong Kong Standing Commission on Civil Service Salaries and Conditions of Service, *Report no. 21: consultative machinery in the civil service*, p. 8. Another

13 were registered under the Societies Ordinance including the four police staff associations which had their own central-level consultative forum, the Police Force Council.

77. Ibid., p. 14.
78. Ibid., p. 13. The Commission did not consider it a problem that the three staff associations sitting on the SCSC represented only about 20% of staff on the Master Pay Scale. It noted that the CCSA with 85% of its members below Point 38 on the Master Pay Scale provided a satisfactory channel of representation for the lower and middle ranks.
79. Ibid., pp. 14–6. Authority to admit staff associations to the SCSC lies with the Chief Secretary in consultation with the SCSC. In May 1985, a list of entry criteria which must be met by unions seeking to qualify for admission were drawn up by the SCSC. These criteria covered such matters as:
    1. membership composition: be composed primarily of civil servants, be a service-wide mixed grade, with a majority of paid-up members;
    2. membership size: 'sufficiently large', 'relatively stable and not subject to great fluctuations';
    3. financial position: 'sound as confirmed by the Registrar of Trade Unions', income primarily from membership subscription and 'other proper sources'; and
    4. organization and performance: capacity to 'organize activities, to handle correspondences with the management', 'in existence for a reasonable period', 'adhering to the Union's constitution and the provisions in the Trade Unions Ordinance'.
    The Standing Commission, ibid., p. 15, drew attention to the vagueness of some of the criteria and recommended they be specified in more concrete terms.
80. Ibid., pp. 17–9.
81. Kwok, 'Staff representation on the Senior Civil Service Council: consultation, collective bargaining or participation', p. 149.
82. Cheek-Milby, 'Identifying the issues', p. 112. A 53-question bilingual survey was sent to 155 civil service union chairpersons. The 47 who returned questionnaires represented about 51 000 civil servants.
83. Cheung, 'The civil service', p. 103.
84. Cheung, ibid., p. 104, notes that in protest against the Standing Commission's Report No. 21, some civil service associations boycotted the annual Spring Reception hosted by the Civil Service Branch for civil service leaders on 24 February 1989.
85. See Turner et al., *The last colony: but whose?* pp. 132–3, on this point.
86. Committee of Inquiry into the 1988 Civil Service Pay Adjustment and Related Matters, *Interim report*, p. 10.
87. Ibid., pp. 10–1.
88. Wong, 'The 1986–89 pay dispute', p. 74.
89. Committee of Inquiry into the 1988 Civil Service Pay Adjustment and Related Matters, *Interim report*, p. 13.
90. Wong, 'The 1986–89 pay dispute', p. 74.
91. Committee of Inquiry into the 1988 Civil Service Pay Adjustment and Related Matters, *Interim report*, pp. 15–6.
92. Ibid., pp. 16–7. *Oriental Daily News*, 21 April 1988.
93. *Wah Kiu Yat Po*, 16 April 1988. See also Committee of Inquiry into the 1988 Civil Service Pay Adjustment and Related Matters, *Interim report*, pp. 19–20.

94. Wong, 'The 1986–89 pay dispute', p. 74; and England, *Industrial relations and law in Hong Kong*, p. 93.
95. 'Lower-rank civil servants threaten action', *Wah Kiu Yat Po*, 16 January 1988; and England, *Industrial relations and law in Hong Kong*, p. 93.
96. Committee of Inquiry into the 1988 Civil Service Pay Adjustment and Related Matters, *Interim report*, p. 62, and Wong, 'The 1986–89 Pay Dispute,' p. 76.
97. England, *Industrial relations and law in Hong Kong*, p. 93; and Wong, 'The 1986–89 pay dispute', p. 75.
98. *Oriental Daily News*, 22 November 1988. The police received a smaller increase because it traditionally had higher salary levels than the other disciplined services. The adjustment would narrow the pay gap between the police and these other disciplined services.
99. *Hong Kong Economic Journal*, 21 December 1988.
100. *Ming Pao Daily News*, 24 March 1990.
101. Ibid., 27 April 1990.
102. England, *Industrial relations and law in Hong Kong*, p. 95.
103. See Hong Kong, Provisional Hospital Authority, *Report of the Provisional Hospital Authority 1989*, chapter 1.
104. Its terms of reference included reviewing the organizational structure for managing government and subvented hospitals to achieve better integration between them, examining the internal administration of hospitals, advising whether there were better alternatives to the existing method of staffing hospitals, and devising plans to improve the working environment.
105. Ibid., p. 7.
106. We rely heavily on Cheung, 'Public sector unions in Hong Kong: a study of the reorganization of the Medical and Health Department', chapters 4 and 5, in our subsequent discussion of this case.
107. Cheung notes that the League had five main demands:
    1. existing staff should be allowed to retain their civil service status until their retirement, and their promotion, posting and training etc. should be protected;
    2. existing practice should apply to filling of future vacancies under the Hospital Services Department, i.e., civil servants should be accorded priority and the management should not resort to open recruitment immediately;
    3. civil servants of the Hospital Services Department may apply for and fill posts in the new hospitals managed by the HA without having to give up their civil service status;
    4. promotions in the new hospitals should be recognized as equivalent promotions in the civil service context;
    5. when civil servants leave the civil service establishment and opt to join the HA, their civil service benefits should be preserved.
108. Cheung notes that in the case of nurses, and in particular the AGNS, the actions the AGNS took during this period were less militant than those it took a decade earlier (1978–80), but in that period it was unable, despite more militant actions, to achieve much improvement in promotion prospects and salary scales for nurses.
109. Cheung, 'Public sector unions in Hong Kong: a study of the reorganization of the Medical and Health Department', p. 166. Added to this was the effective communication networks between leaders and members. She notes that the AGNS distributed a one-page newsletter highlighting the latest progress of the union's dealings with the government and action taken.

110. Cheung, ibid., p. 169, comments that 'the complicated procedure of establishment review makes the proposal to create 74 senior medical officer posts and 205 nursing officer posts in a few months a Guinness Record for the Hong Kong Government!'
111. Ibid., p. 174.
112. As Johnston, *Success while others fail: social movement unionism and the public workplace*, pp. 69–70, points out, '[c]laims made by social movements reflect the context within which and against which they emerge. Content aside, demands are framed in distinctive forms, reflecting the institutions within which needs are defined and met, or the way of life within which they are produced and reproduced.'
113. The status of the AECS as one of the three staff associations represented on the SCSC is however likely to become an issue after 1997, as the number of expatriate civil servants dwindles and a uniform set of employment conditions replaces existing differential terms of service for expatriates and locals.

The Rise and Fall of Community Mobilization: The Housing Movement in Hong Kong

Denny Kwok Leung Ho

❑ Introduction

In the 1980s, the housing movement in Hong Kong was viewed by students of social protests as one of the major forces generating social and political changes.[1] It was argued that it had served as a training ground for movement activists who subsequently became politicians, enabling them to gain access to the consultative and legislative bodies at different levels of the political system in the 1980s. As a social force representing the grass roots, it had played a critical role in shaping public housing policy of the colonial state.[2] Together with other community-based collective actions, the housing movement had made a significant impact on the configuration of local politics in the 1980s.

In the early 1990s, however, electoral politics and newly formed political parties seemed to have overshadowed the housing movement in shaping the agenda of community politics. Although issues related to public housing policies occasionally gave rise to heated debate, the significance of the housing movement appeared to have receded. Why did the housing movement assume a marginal role in the political arena after the opening up of the formal political system in the 1980? This essay explores the underlying factors which determine the changing role and the developmental trajectory of the housing movement in Hong Kong.

I shall show that the role and development of the housing movement in

Hong Kong should be understood in terms of the political opportunity structure, forms of organization, resources of the actors, and their ideology and preferences. The examination of the political opportunity structure aims to analyse the political conditions facilitating or hindering collective action. I focus on two aspects of the political opportunity structure: the extent to which it is open to social movement activists attempting to influence the political outcomes, and whether a closed political structure provokes collective action. Next, I explore the relationship between the configuration of political power and the 'conscience constituents' of the social movement in question. I shall argue that activists' strategy preferences depend on the values of the actors. Furthermore, an understanding of the values and ideology articulated by the actors will also enable us to comprehend how the actors of a social movement mobilize participation and design their forms of action and organization.[3] Finally, the availability of resources is another variable determining the extent of movement participation and the continuity of the operation of a social movement.[4] Resource availability determines the continuity and survival of the housing movement.

Before coming to the discussion of the housing movement, I shall first make a brief note on some definitional issues. Community movement is conceived here as an individual community organization 'which make[s] urban demands whatever their level and effects'.[5] The housing movement is conceived as one type of community movement, developing in relation to issues arising from the management and distribution of housing resources.

This chapter consists of four sections. The first two sections examine the development of the housing movement in the period 1970–80 and the 1980s respectively. The third section explores the relations between the political context and the character and trajectory of the housing movement. The fourth section concludes by way of a discussion about the future development of the housing movement in Hong Kong. This, in short, is a brief developmental history of the housing movement in Hong Kong, charting its rise in the 1970s and the marginalization of grass roots mobilization around housing issues in the 1990s.

❑ The Housing Movement Sector, 1970–80

The 1970s witnessed rapid economic growth and the rise of the middle class. The real annual growth rate of the Gross Domestic Product (GDP) was impressive: in the period 1973–79 the average real growth rate in GDP was about 9%, higher than Singapore's and Taiwan's which were 8.7% and 8.6% respectively in the same period.[6] Along with such economic growth, the development of the tertiary sector was phenomenal. The population of the middle class, referring to all non-manual workers, also increased. It made up 41.3% of the total labour force in 1971, increased to 46.8% by 1981.[7]

Meanwhile, after the two riots in 1966 and 1967, the government recognized that its links with the grass roots were inadequate. In response, remedial measures were taken to deal with the discontents revealed during the disturbances. Two major measures were employed to deal with potential social unrests: more provision of social services and welfare, and the formation of a new local administrative structure.[8]

The provision of social services and welfare had significant implications for the structuring of the political environment in the 1970s. It resulted in the expansion of the public sector and brought about greater government intervention into the social life of the grass roots.[9] In particular, public housing policy led to a high rate of geographical mobility in the population. In 1972, the government announced a ten-year public housing programme which sought to rehouse more than a million people to public rental housing estates by the mid-1980s. Such a mass public housing programme was the main engine for relocating a significant proportion of the population to the new towns. The rate of internal geographical mobility was high in the 1970s: in 1971, 81% of the total population of Hong Kong lived in the main urban areas, but by 1981 the figure went down to 73%. On the other hand, the proportion of the total population living in new towns increased from 10% in 1971 to 17% in 1981.[10]

Despite the fact that the development of public housing did not work as smoothly as originally envisaged, the massive rehousing scheme was considered to be a success. Yet, the government's involvement in urban development generated social conflicts throughout the implementation process.[11] There were frequent open conflicts over issues concerning rehousing locations, compensation methods, the speed of development, etc. In the late 1970s, many religious groups, voluntary agencies and student groups worked actively at the grass roots level. They identified problems related to public housing policy, organized social protests and formed residents' groups. According to a study of social conflicts, about 18% of the total number of social conflicts in the late 1970s were related to housing problems and 33% to urban development.[12] Another study also reported that in the period 1966–81, there was a steady increase in the number of conflicts concerning collective consumption problems, from 5 events in 1966 to 30 in 1981. For urban protests, the average number of events per year increased from 3.1 in the 1960s to 18.8 in the 1970s.[13]

In the face of mounting political challenges from the grass roots, the government established a new local administration system in order to strengthen its relationship with local communities. In the early 1970s, it established the Mutual Aid Committee (MAC) Scheme to replace the 'kaifong association network' which had served as a link between the government and the grass roots in the earlier decades.[14] Nevertheless, such new government initiatives failed to pre-empt the further growth of grass roots mobilization. The new government-sponsored local political bodies were occupied by official appointees.

Their compositions were mainly confined to the representatives of traditional kaifong associations, MAC officials, local business people and professionals. Those grass roots representatives who did not share a pro-government attitude were excluded from these local administrative organizations.[15] Such selective consultation and the exclusion of local leaders who were critical of the government created an environment conducive to more protests in the late 1970s.[16]

The housing movement was part of the community movement. Housing issues were articulated by activists at the local level in order to press for concessions from the government. There are two kinds of popular mobilization at the local community level: the community activists, who were excluded from the decision-making process, pressed for more participation opportunities, while the housing movement activists were concerned with the distribution of housing resources and related policy issues. Nevertheless, their relationship was mutually beneficial since community activists also attempted to articulate housing issues in order to fight for political rights. Activists of the political rights movement and the community movement, therefore, consolidated their strength on the basis of grass roots' support. Because of their limited bargaining power, both groups spent long years as 'outsiders' or 'challengers', defending interests that were routinely 'organized out' of institutionalized politics.[17] Confrontation with a bureaucratic polity led to the frequent use of disruptive tactics and dedication to the exposure of social inequalities and injustices in order to exert pressure on the government. In this period, the community movement, the housing movement and the political rights movement went hand-in-hand. Protests arising from social problems and housing problems highlighted not only the poor living conditions of the working class, but also the undemocratic nature of the formal political system.

As regards the social base of the housing and community movements, it is interesting to see that student organizations and welfare agencies played an important part in the mobilization of the grass roots.[18] In the 1970s there witnessed a search for identity among the young and educated people. Critical of the dominance of the colonial regime, students and young professionals attempted to articulate their own radical programmes and put them in practice through collective action.

To some students, participation in community actions was not only a way of challenging the status quo but also a form of self-affirmation. They were attracted to a vague idea of nationalism or sought to articulate their political convictions through an exploration of the dark side of society.[19] Whatever their political orientations at that time, common to their views was the idea that the government was to a large extent non-responsive to popular demands. Pressing for a better social life, in particular for the materially deprived people, became their shared political objective. However, the political outlook of the activists taking part in community politics lacked sophistication. While their ideological claims revolved around anti-capitalism and anti-colonialism, the activists lacked a well-articulated vision of an alternative society. Exposing the dark side of the colonial rule to wider public was adopted as one of the major tactics to discredit the colonial regime. But little effort was invested in the articulation of idea of citizenship. Furthermore, their ideological claims had limited association with political rights or social rights. In short, the activists were to a large extent populist in orientation and adopted a perspective of 'residual social welfare'.

Two common characteristics of these movements can be discerned. First, neither the political rights movement or the housing movement received any recognition from the authority, and both were forced to rely on the use of protest to express people's demands. Most protest organizers adopted the Alinsky-style approach to community development with the use of non-conventional and confrontational methods such as mass gatherings, petitions, demonstrations, sleep-ins, sit-ins, etc.[20] Second, in order to rally communal support for direct action, they employed a *communal mode of mobilization,* putting emphasis on mobilizing substantial personal commitments and community resources, rather than adopting the *market mode of resource mobilization* which relies on paid staff to obtain resources through the solicitation of scattered supporters.[21]

❑ The Housing Movement in the 1980s

The housing movement in the 1980s had a number of features. First, protest actions related to housing issues was the third most frequently organized type of social conflict in the period 1980–91, following labour and political issues. Second, such actions were mainly concerned with local and sectoral interests: 60% of the housing issues were of 'local' scope, whereas 32% were of sectoral scope. Third, as regards the form of organizations, 47% of the organizations involved were loosely organized groups and spontaneously formed organizations whereas 49% were organizations of a permanent nature. Federal form of organizations accounted for a mere 3%.[22] These findings suggest that the housing movement sector was predominately composed of groups and organizations developing on a spontaneous and communal basis, rather than organizations with a higher level of organizing capability.

In my analysis of the development of the housing movement in the 1980s, I discuss the nature of the political opportunity structure with special reference to how housing movement activists responded to the changing balance of political power in the formal political structure. I shall first argue that there emerged a widened gap between political parties and pressure groups because issues concerning political reform became dominant on politicians' agenda, and consequently housing issues were rendered to a position of lesser importance. I also argue that the government had established statutory organizations in order to render itself less likely to be the target of political demands from grass roots. In short, I contend that the housing movement operated and developed in a context where housing issues, especially those concerning local interests, were likely to be edged off the political agenda of political parties and pressure groups.

Changes in the Social Movement Sector

Here I shall first examine two aspects of the institutional context of social mobilization, namely the changing relationship between the political rights movement and the community movement, and the restructuring of the state.

In the 1980s, the bureaucratic polity was opened up, providing more channels for representatives of different interest groups to participate in the management of public affairs. The District Boards were established in 1982. They were primarily advisory in function but a number of the board members were popularly elected. In the mid-1980s, elections were introduced into the Legislative Council. Even if there were still no full direct elections to the Legislature, the previously 'closed' political system became comparatively open and Hong Kong people gained access to the political domain.[23]

In support of candidates of the District Boards, local concern groups sprang up, actively engaging in urban issues such as housing, transport, the environment, etc., in order to mobilize and strengthen local support. A survey found that there were 26 district concern groups in 1986.[24] And it was estimated that about 41% of the elected District Board members in 1985 were associated with pressure groups, electoral alliances or quasi-political groups.[25]

The emergence of pressure groups and political parties in the late 1980s weakened the relationship between the political rights movement and the housing movement. There were three reasons for such a change. First of all, their success in local election to the District Boards convinced the grass roots leaders that they had a chance to get involved in the formal political structure. Subsequently, many leaders of local concern groups shifted their attention from local issues to those at the territory-wide level. Some leaders of local concern groups entered the political arena, developed links with political groups, and became active in actions concerning territory-wide issues such as the drafting of the Basic Law.[26] Second, as politicians, some local leaders considered working through the government-sponsored participatory system to be a better strategy than using non-institutional activities. Hence, once in the political system, the leaders of local concern groups and pressure groups adopted a new strategy, moving away 'from the use of single-issue protests and mobilization tactics to the use of more sophisticated and diversified tactics based on rational arguments, researches and surveys, lobbying and elite coalition.'[27] With the belief that their presence on the District Boards would assist the grass roots to get what they wanted, the local leaders staked a great deal on using institutional access to express their views and grass roots' demands. According to Leung:

> Most pressure groups have chosen to co-operate with government-sponsored institutions instead of being completely dependent on outside mass protest actions. Overt and public protests have been replaced by informal contacts and formal committee work between community spokesmen and public officials. The opening of political channels has resulted in a reduction in the militancy of pressure group activities. To stay within the system, they are more prone to compromise than to seek clear-cut victories.[28]

Lastly, many local leaders became conscious of their vested interests in the existing political arrangements. They had their careers in politics and their re-election became their primary concern.

To sum up, in the 1980s, the opening up of the political system led to a number of changes in the social movement sector. First, with the opening up of the political system which first began with the establishment of District Boards, local leaders appeared to accept the view that securing seats at the local level of the political structure could help to empower the grass roots. Second, the intensity of political debate over the 1997 issue diverted the attention of political and social activists to the struggle for more democracy in the political system and to the question of the future relationship of Hong Kong with mainland China.[29] Third, social and political activists regarded the democratization of the political system as one of the most important processes in ensuring the political autonomy and economic prosperity of Hong Kong after 1997. Accordingly, they invested more of their energy in pressing for the introduction of full direct elections into the Legislative Council and less in issues concerning grass roots' interests and demands.[30] In short, with the opening up of the political structure and the growing involvement of local leaders in electoral politics, the connection between pressure group politics and the community movement weakened.

The Structural Change of the Political System

Another change in the political context is the role of politicians in relation to housing issues. Despite the opening up of the political system, politicians lacked the power to influence public housing policy. This was related to the fact that the restructuring of the political system in the 1970s involved the growth of 'non-departmental appointed public agencies' (NDAPAs) — a term suggested by Johnson that refers to the appointed public agency established by statute or ministerial decision to perform executive tasks in place of a central government Department or elected local authorities.[31]

The nature of the NDAPAs in Hong Kong is slightly different from that of its counterparts in Britain. While those in Britain are designated to perform executive tasks, the NDAPAs in Hong Kong are policy-making or advisory bodies in areas including transport, medical services and public housing.[32] Four distinct features of this kind of NDAPA in Hong Kong can be identified:

1. all the members are appointed by the government;
2. they are responsible for assisting the government in planning and working out policies in the concerned areas;
3. they differ in their degree of autonomy to make policies and/or recommendations; and
4. they are accountable to the government, not to the public.

As regards public housing policies, the Housing Authority is the statutory body responsible for the construction, maintenance and management of all public housing estates. The establishment of the Housing Authority has provided the government with a mechanism to minimize the possible financial burden coming from public housing provision. By restructuring the Housing Authority as a statutory body, the government imposed the principle of self-financing on the Housing Authority. Since then, with the exception that land is provided free and a special interest rate is granted, the Housing Authority has been required to repay all loans obtained either from the government's Loan Development Loan Fund or direct cash injection. On the part of the government, this change ensures that in contrast to social welfare expenditure there is no provision of 'direct outlays of public funds that are not recoverable'.[33] The Housing Authority must rely on rent as the major source of funding for the construction of public housing, recurrent estate expenses, and repayments to the government.[34]

Apart from its economic objective, the Housing Authority also fulfils the political function of countering protest. Not only are professionals and business persons appointed as members of the authority, its composition also includes a small number of grass roots leaders. The inclusion of local leaders creates an image that the Housing Authority represents the public interest, and policies are largely formulated in the grass roots' interest. However, in our view, this is an ideological gloss. The dominance of business interests is revealed by the fact that conservative appointees always outnumber those who have connections with the grass roots.[35] The advantage of this arrangement to the government lies in its capacity for incorporating business interests. Offering business representatives a place inside the Authority avoids provoking protest by the business and construction sectors. By contrast, the small number of grass roots representatives in the Housing Authority makes it difficult for them to develop into a strong opposition against the hegemonic position of the pro-government and business interests. Their power is further curtailed when they are assigned to different subcommittees responsible for different policy areas.[36] This aptly illustrates how the government has taken advantage of setting up the Housing

Authority as a statutory body so as to deal with the increasing tensions in public housing issues.

In 1988 the government granted the Housing Authority administrative and financial autonomy and cancelled the post of Secretary for Housing.[37] The parameters for public housing policy were laid down by the government in the Long Term Public Housing Strategies.[38] This document set the target for total production up to 2001 and the proportion of the types of public housing to be constructed. Working under this basic guideline, the Housing Authority was accountable only to the Executive Council and the Governor of Hong Kong.

Such a relocation of decision-making concerning public housing policies from a government department to a statutory body constitutes an obstacle against external political challenges. The first thing to note is that the Legislative Council has limited authority to influence public housing policy. The Housing Committee of the Legislative Council can summon the Head of the Housing Department to explain specific housing policies, but the ultimate decision remains in the hands of the Housing Authority.[39] Since decision-making in relation to housing issues has been delegated to the Housing Authority, politicians in general and Legislative Councillors in particular, have become less likely to be interested in housing issues. Likewise, District Board members also have little formal political leverage on public housing policies since the scope of influence of the District Boards is confined to issues at the local level.

Second, the division of responsibility between the Housing Department and the Housing Authority leads to confusion over who is responsible for policy. For the public, it is not easy to distinguish between 'policy' and 'administration' matters.

In short, despite the opening up of the political system in the late 1980s, the Housing Authority had kept intact its bureaucratically ruled structure. The establishment of NDAPAs had the effect of circumventing the influence of electoral politics on public housing policies. Faced with the predominance of pro-government members and the absence of democratic procedures in the Housing Authority, external challengers found it difficult to gain access to the decision-making process. In addition, the small number of grass roots representatives in the Housing Authority was powerless to develop an opposing force against the pro-government Housing Authority members.

On urban renewal, the government adopted a similar strategy in dealing with urban planning and development. One of the agencies involved in urban development is the Hong Kong Housing Society which has a long history of administrative and financial autonomy. The grass roots have few means of access to influence the Society's policies and direction. On the other hand, the Land Development Ordinance of 1988 grants the power to a statutory body, the Land Development Corporation (LDC), to acquire private land for profit-seeking development connected with urban renewal.[40] The Ordinance also confers power on the Corporation to evict tenants by force in cases of land resumption. Forced eviction had provoked dissatisfaction and grievances, and disputes about rehousing and compensation have been the most controversial issues arising from urban development. Nevertheless, although urban renewal has been at the core of housing politics, neither the LDC nor the Hong Kong Housing Society offers an open and democratic process which allows for grass roots involvement.

The Reaction of the Housing Movement to the Changing Political Situation

It appears that the issues concerning political reform before and after 1997 absorbed more of the politicians' attention in the 1980s than in the 1970s, and that the Housing Authority has been effectively decoupled from the formal political system. In view of this, I am interested in looking at how the housing movement activists reacted to their weakened relationship with the political rights movement and the autonomous Housing Authority.

In the early 1980s, the housing movement by and large made demands of a sectoral, regional or communal kind. For example, the issue of rooftop heat involved top-floor tenants of public rental housing estates, and the issue of redevelopment was related to the basic living conditions of the tenants of Mark I and II public housing estates. The nature and characteristics of the process of demand-making were similar to those of the community movement in the 1970s. The activists mobilized communities and sought the support of third parties. The People's Council on Public Housing Policy (PCPHP) — a pressure group — undertook the role of an organizer linking up various neighbourhood associations and local concern groups. In 1984, the PCPHP achieved a certain degree of consensus over the issue of public housing review.[41] In the mid-1980s, dissatisfaction with the rental increase policy set in train a series of protests, though the housing movement failed to win any concessions from the Housing Authority.[42] In short, in the early 1980s, the housing movement appeared to be able to maintain its autonomy and independence from those pressure groups which were concerned with political reform.

The expansion of the public housing sector surely created a population of public housing tenants and brought about a critical mass of community social workers who were interested in promoting and defending the welfare of the former. Basically, their concerns were over economic security and a better standard of living. The mode of action of the housing movement continued to concentrate on two domains: the institutionalized channels (for example, the District Boards) and the non-institutionalized means of protests, petitions, etc. At the time, the District Boards appeared to be helpful and '[r]esidents organizations, as a result, have played a secondary, hopefully supplementary, role to the function of the district boards.'[43] As a result of such a change of strategies, non-institutionalized means were relegated to a secondary role within the repertoire of actions. The militancy of protest groups declined in the 1980s.[44]

Demobilization occurred after the housing movement failed in its protest over the 'well-off' tenants issue. This issue was perceived by the activists as critical to the development of the housing movement, since they understood that this was the first move of the government to reduce its commitment to public housing provision.[45] In 1984, the Housing Authority suggested reducing the subsidy to well-off tenants in a document called 'Review of Public Housing Allocation Policies'.[46] In 1985 the Housing Authority suggested that tenants who had resided in public rental housing for more than ten years and whose household income exceeded 1.5 times the application criteria income were required to pay double rent. Some local leaders and politicians fought against this policy by way of direct action, but finally failed.

After this issue, an organizational problem emerged on how to continue the housing movement.[47] The activists lacked a 'dispute frame' which could incorporate the diverse demands put forward by the residents of a wide range of housing types.[48] In the early 1980s, the activists pressed for provision of more public housing flats for those whose incomes were too low to obtain adequate housing through the market. Social actions at that time were based on a framework of residual welfare which had been widely promoted in the 1970s.[49] In the light of a public housing review, the activists were convinced that the government was responsible for the plight of the economically disadvantaged. This claim eventually succeeded in the mobilization of a mass base. In the case of the well-off tenants, however, the activists did not press for any measures for the plight of the poor or disadvantaged, but for the better-off public housing tenants. The activists felt that the policy on well-off tenants was one of the government's strategies in distancing itself from the provision of public rental housing. Therefore, in order to ensure a reasonable production of public rental housing, they decided to take a stand against the government's further withdrawal from its welfare commitment.[50] The activists argued tha well-off had a right to enjoy their benefits, but found it difficult to put forward any convincing framework to support their protest against the new measure imposed on well-off tenants. Eventually, what the protesters asked for was a more lenient criterion for well-off tenants. This case showed that the housing movement activists lacked a new dispute frame for further action, apart from a model of residual social welfare. The lack of a new 'frame of right' or a 'frame of citizenship' provided little in the way of an ideological frame for the housing movement activists to mobilize the masses, especially when the population of the economically disadvantaged had shrunk in the context of phenomenal economic growth.

In addition, with the opening up of the government-sponsored local administration, housing issues appeared to be taken care of by the unofficial members within the District Boards. Different sectors of interests were often represented on the District Boards. Consequently, they often competed with each other for recognition, influence, and control.[51] This further reinforced the tendency for fragmentation within the housing movement.

To sum up, without a new ideological theme serving as the means to incorporate the specific and often contradictory demands of housing protests into its political programmes, the housing movement became fragmented. Most mobilization campaigns thus relied on local organizers and leaders who were inclined to solve community and housing issues through insitutionalized means.

Social mobilization in the late 1980s was dependent on the efforts of local leaders who included MAC members, community social workers, leaders of neighbourhood associations, District Board members, etc. Among these local leaders, the role of the community social workers deserves more attention. The channel for community social workers to become involved in local politics was the Neighbourhood Level Community Development Project (NLCDP).[52] The project was set up in 1977 by the Committee on Neighbourhood Level Community Development Projects which was composed of representatives of social work agencies and government officials. Both the government and the policy-makers of social work agencies regarded this project as an agency for filling the gaps in social service provision. As Wong pointed out, both the government and the social work profession regarded NLCDPs as having no political role in articulating social conflicts.[53] I also found that community social work underwent a process of depoliticization in the late 1980s. Most community social work agencies implicitly avoided being identified as a political force. It was even found that some of the front-line community social workers on the NLCDP teams tended to think that Hong Kong had grown into a prosperous city and that few people were being deprived of basic necessities. Also, they conceived of the government as a very responsive institution in terms of its readiness to tackle social problems and to deliver help. These community social workers, hence, did not find it necessary to use violent and confrontational social action.[54] All in all, while community social workers were involved in community work, they did not identify themselves as local organizers of the housing movement.

The PCPHP attempted to articulate new political claims in the hope of achieving a new unity among local concern groups and neighbourhood associations. Nevertheless, the leaders were unable to build up its social base and a genuinely popular leadership because they served diversified and divided interests. For instance, the tenants of public rental housing estates found it difficult to involve the tenants of other types of settlement, such as the squatters and the Temporary Housing Areas, in their social actions.[55]

To sum up, the housing movement encountered an unfavourable political context in the late 1980s. The political rights movement and the housing movement, though complementary, had different agendas in the context of the decoupling of the Housing Authority from electoral politics. While the political rights movement shifted towards using institutional means to get things done, the housing movement adhered to non-institutionalized means because of the lack of powerful representatives in the Housing Authority. Moreover, the opening up of the formal political system led to a weakened relationship between the political rights movement and the housing movement. The housing movement, furthermore, needed to solve some organizational difficulties. As shown in the case of the protest against the well-off tenants policy, the leaders lacked a new dispute frame for their mobilization campaign.

❑ The Housing Movement in the 1990s

In the 1990s, a number of changes occurred in both the private and public housing sectors. First, the government attempted to further privatize public housing provision.[56] Promotion of home ownership was one of the measures taken by the government to reduce the burden of public housing provision. In July 1991 the Home Ownership Committee of the Housing Authority approved the trial 'Option to Rent or Buy Scheme'. Under this scheme, qualified public rental housing applicants were allowed to opt for buying or renting a flat in the same district. At the same time, some rental blocks were upgraded for sale. In August 1991, the Housing Authority suggested a review of the Sale of Flats to Sitting Tenants policy in order to promote home ownership.[57] In 1992 Governor Chris Patten announced that the government's aim was that 60% of all families would own their homes by 1997.

Second, the government attempted to reduce its commitment to the provision of public rental housing. In the hope of achieving a reduction in demand for public rental housing, the government expected to see a high out-mobility by public rental housing tenants through the purchase of HOS flats. It was anticipated that this measure would lead to a subsequent increase of vacant flats for those on the waiting list. Moreover, the promotion of HOS might lead to a high take-up rate of HOS flats among those affected by resettlement in squatter areas, Temporary Housing Areas and public housing estates under the redevelopment scheme. However, the HOS failed to attract as many clearees and public rental housing tenants as expected. In effect, a shortfall of public rental housing emerged. It was estimated that at least 219 000 households, or roughly 13% of the territory's total population, were still inadequately housed by the end of 1992.[58] The shortfall in the provision of public rental housing was also substantiated by a Housing Authority review, issued in 1993, which estimated that there would be 610 000 families still in need of housing from 1993 up to the end of this century.[59] In addition, the housing needs of the one-person and two-person households, squatters and temporary housing area residents received insufficient attention. Clearly, the shortfall in the annual production of public rental housing became a seed-bed of social conflict.

The third change is related to the private housing sector in which the price of flats increased at a fast rate. In the early 1990s, the general prices of domestic property doubled.[60] The housing needs of lower middle-class people became a social problem in the eyes of social critics. Finally, the urban renewal scheme carried out by the Land Development Corporation gave rise to a number of controversial issues, such as the amount of cash compensation awarded to tenants and owners, rehousing of tenants, etc.

It would be interesting to examine whether these issues sustained the housing movement in the social movement sector. Following our analysis of the housing movement in the 1980s, I examine the political opportunity structure and the reaction of the actors to the rising discontents in respect of housing issues. In the early 1990s, the political scenario remained dominated by political issues concerning the future development of the electoral system and the protagonists of the disputes concerning political reform were the pro-government parties and pro-democracy parties.[61] Although there was a clear line of conflict demarcating these wings, the housing movement activists found it increasingly difficult to rally support from pro-democracy political parties. In the early 1990s, in view of the soaring price of private housing, the pro-democracy wing placed more emphasis on the mobilization of lower middle-class people. This move by the political parties was a reaction to the fact that the political preferences of the lower middle class were uncertain and the middle class had become an important potential constituency base of the political parties. Articulating their issues was a means to gain the electoral support of the lower middle class. In view of the soaring price of domestic units, the Hong Kong United Democrats organized a series of direct actions to press for more public housing flats for lower middle-class people, but the actions were not able to rally mass base support.

Although the 1990s witnessed the government's further privatization of public rental housing by way of the promotion of home ownership scheme (HOS) flats, the housing movement leaders seemed to be less interested in criticizing this move by the government. As reflected in the White Paper issued by the Joint Committee on Public Housing Policy Review, leaders of the housing movement had few disputes with the promotion of home ownership.[62] What the leaders of the housing movement sought to press for was a sufficient supply of public rental housing flats. Their focal concerns were hence confined to the demand for a 'reasonable' level of rental increase and sufficient production of new public housing flats. In 1992 the Sale of Public Rental Housing Scheme was announced by the Housing Authority, and concerted actions were organized by housing movement activists in order to press for the termination of this scheme. In 1992 social actions concerning rent increases were organized by community social workers at local levels.[63] The action focused on the Housing Authority's new criteria for rental increase. The new domestic rent policy put more emphasis on the value of public housing estates and on management and maintenance costs, even though its affordability to the sitting tenants remained one of the principal criteria. The housing movement activists argued that the new method of setting rental increases and rent levels merely would allow the government to generate more revenue from rents.[64] Underlying these disputes was a strong belief that the government should regard public housing policy as a means of ensuring a better distribution of wealth among Hong Kong people, and that lower-income groups should be given decent flats on public housing estates. In reaction to the reduction of governmental commitment to public rental housing provision, the housing movement continued to put pressure on the government to address the outstanding housing needs of the lower-income groups.

Leaders of the housing movement remained committed to the residual social welfare model cherished in the 1970s and the 1980s and, as a result, lacked an alternative belief system which could provide an argument to support the rights of owners in the private housing sector and the housing needs of middle-class people.[65] By virtue of this commitment, issues arising from urban renewal (e.g. compensation arrangements) were unattended. For instance, the housing movement activists showed little interest in the disputes between the LDC and the owners of small shops and property owners affected by the clearance of Kowloon City and the urban renewal policy.[66] One exception was that in 1992 the trade union of social workers organized a series of actions in order to express their discontent with property developers, but it failed to mobilize continuous support.

I found that the housing movement remained a weak social force. It was characterized by a fragmented organizational and membership base. It also failed to secure the responses needed to maintain itself.

Unlike the housing movement leaders in the 1970s, whose demands encompassed both political rights and welfare, the leadership of the movement in the 1980s only made claims in relation to the government's provision of adequate public rental housing. Its scope of concern was restricted to those who were not able to meet their housing needs through the market. This conception, however, posed a challenge to the leaders in the disputes over the promotion of home ownership and the government's suggestion of reducing the subsidy to the 'well-off' public housing tenants. In 1992, the Housing Authority continued to endorse the policy of charging double rent to well-off tenants. However, as shown in this case, the housing movement leaders were weak in presenting a strong argument in support of the well-off tenants. They found it difficult to argue that the well-off tenants were entitled to social welfare by way of public housing provision. This weakened the capacity of the housing movement to mobilize mass support.

Besides the lack of a new dispute frame, the availability of resources was another critical factor shaping the trajectory of the housing movement. According to the resource mobilization perspective, the maintenance of a social movement depends on resources which can be acquired through vertical or horizontal integration. From the point of view of the housing movement activists, integration into coalitions would not only enhance the numerical strength of the movement but also ensure its survival.[67] However, it was difficult for the housing movement to achieve integration. As regards vertical integration, which refers to the connection between the housing movement and agents within the polity (such as political parties, councillors, etc.), the dominance of issues concerning political reform in local political discussion led to a weak connection. Politicians lacked the resources to build up strong connections with community-based social groups. The workload of electoral politics consumed most of the local party members' time. More importantly, local leaders distrusted politicians. Local leaders were sceptical of the politicians' ability in delivering what had been promised in their election campaigns and hence they resisted politicians' penetration into the leadership of local concern groups.[68] As a result, the division between political parties and the housing movement widened. As Lui pointed out, in the 1991 Legislative Council elections the Hong Kong People's Council on the Public Housing Policy 'made a U-turn, ended its "honeymoon" with electoral politics and moved back to its original position of a pressure group on public housing issues.'[69]

Similarly, it was difficult for the housing movement leaders to maintain horizontal integration among interest groups, community social workers and neighbourhood associations. As pointed out earlier, the difficulty in building up a horizontal connection was related both to the lack of a dispute frame, which could link various groups of people who were concerned with, or affected by, housing policies, and to the preference for a communal mode of mobilization strategy of the local groups.

When the housing movement gradually became detached from the political rights movement in the late 1980s, the leadership of the housing movement was then mainly constituted by veterans of the housing movement and community social workers. These actors were accustomed to the communal mode of mobilization, and mobilization was usually carried out by way of articulating single issues. However, the leaders needed to develop links among people affected, who were dispersed over a number of housing estates or areas, into a social force. It was difficult to mobilize people to become involved in a cross-district coalition because this would require a lot of efforts in training indigenous leaders, analysing policies and maintaining participants' commitment. Various coalitions were founded, for instance, those concerning the policy on sales of public rental housing flats, the policy of subsidy to 'well-off' tenants, and the rooftop squatters. However, it was difficult to maintain these coalitions because there lacked trust and solidarity among the members. Even though some coalitions had been established for a longer period (e.g. the Joint Committee of THA Residents Association), they were able to organize only sporadic protest action. Since this type of coalition was mainly composed of the representatives of local concern groups, the leaders encountered difficulties in maintaining solidarity and participation. On the one hand, most local representatives tended to give priority to local concern groups, and their involvement in both the coalition and local concern groups led to competition for time and energy. On the other hand, while the coalition aimed to deal with all the issues arising from housing policies, some local representatives showed little interest in those issues concerning the benefits of other residents.

In the absence of well-established vertical and horizontal organizational integration, the housing movement found it less feasible to rally support through the organizational mode of mobilization. As a result, in the early 1990s activists attempted to rally the support of the public through more direct and radical actions. The housing movement leaders adopted strategies such as sit-ins, road-occupations, blockades, etc. In 1991, the PCPHP hung banners at the venue of the first open meeting of the Boards of Housing Authority, which led to a confrontation between the staff members of the Housing Department and the protesters.[70] In 1992, a group of protesters asking for a reasonable rental increase rate occupied the foyer of the headquarters of the Housing Authority which resulted in a two-day sit-in.[71] In March 1993, a demonstration to the Governor took place at the entrance to Government House. Following a confrontation with the police, the protesters finally blocked the road in front of Government House. As a result, 23 protesters were arrested.[72] In 1994, the protests concerning rooftop squatters included sit-ins, road blockades and refusals to move out, etc. In 1995, furious roof-dwellers were defiant against the evictions carried out by the Buildings Department.[73]

Public reaction to these direct actions was by and large discouraging. The protesters were severely criticized for undermining the social and public order of Hong Kong.[74] Within the social work profession, the confrontational action was interpreted as illegitimate because it was an outcome of manipulation of clients by a few social workers.[75] While some leaders regarded disruptive actions as necessary in order for powerless social groups to win concessions when faced with the lack of organizational and communal support, the unfavourable political climate for the use of disruptive protest actions gave little support to the housing movement leaders and participants.

Despite the fact that there had been a series of social actions concerning housing issues in both the private and public sectors, the housing movement was hardly a coherent social force. Akin to the situation in the 1980s, political parties and trade unions were not interested in housing issues arising from the private and public housing sectors. As a result, community social workers and local leaders of neighbourhood associations became the key participants in the housing movement. They focused on the housing needs of working-class people and pressed for an adequate supply of public rental housing, but lacked a coherent dispute frame and sufficient organizational linkages to achieve a high degree of solidarity and organizational unity.

❏ Conclusion

To start with, I shall summarize my analysis of the development of the housing movement in Hong Kong. In the 1970s the community movement activists challenged the closed bureaucratic structure and at the same time articulated issues arising from the housing problem for the grass roots. Although the government initiated a massive rehousing programme to facilitate urbanization and to contain social discontent, the housing movement activists remained dissatisfied with the rent levels and the quality of public housing flats. Conflicts over various aspects of the public housing policy prevailed. In the 1980s, political reform at the local level institutionalized a large number of conflicts over community issues. The housing movement remained a critical social force outside the formal political structure since the statutory body — the Housing Authority — offered few channels for public participation. This led to an increase in housing protest actions in this period. Nonetheless, the housing movement failed to effect critical change in the political structure because of the lack of third parties' support. Community social workers were active in helping the grass roots to challenge the Housing Authority, but most workers did not regard grass roots politics as a suitable form of action in the 1980s. Meanwhile, demobilization occurred because of the absence of a dispute frame which was important to creating unity among various issue groups related to housing policy.

In the 1990s, the government introduced the policy of privatizing public housing. More flats for sale were built, rental increases were set at a high level, and the Housing Authority continued to impose a higher rental level on well-off tenants. The housing movement activists were not happy with these trends, but were not able to develop the housing movement into a strong social force. Its mode of action remained sporadic, small-scale and localized. The reasons for this character of the housing movement were: the lack of political party support, a fragmented organizational and membership base, and difficulties in building up vertical and horizontal links. The housing movement faced a difficult political situation in the early 1990s. Without well-established horizontal and vertical integration, it sought public support through direct actions. However, disruptive action was discouraging since it resulted in more criticism than support from the public.

In view of this unfavourable political context, I conclude with an admittedly speculative discussion about the future of the housing movement. I believe that the housing movement will continue to play a role in shaping housing policy as long as the government continues its strategy of privatization of public housing.[76] Due to the inadequacy of public rental housing provision, the housing needs of the urban minorities will be left unattended and housing movement activists will have room to continue their work in making claims for the minorities. I do believe that the housing needs of the minorities will continue to be a controversial issue. In fact, in mid-September 1995, the government announced that 13 Temporary Housing Areas were to be retained, although the Governor had previously promised to demolish all Temporary Housing Areas by 1996. The reason for this change in Temporary Housing Area policy, as government officials explained, was to meet the heavy demand for temporary accommodation in the next two years.[77]

The incidence of protests over housing issues relating to the further privatization of public rental housing is strongly associated with two factors: whether political parties are willing to put the housing issue on the political agenda, and the involvement of community social workers and housing movement activists. It will also be important to see the reaction of the SAR government to urban movements and whether the government will increase the supply of public housing flats.

In the light of the above considerations, I arrive at a very pessimistic conclusion. On the one hand, there are few signs indicating that the SAR government would be open to more popular participation in the decision-making processes of housing policy. On the other hand, the incidence of housing protests is strongly associated with the presence of community social workers and pressure groups. In the case of housing protests, pressure groups, such as the Hong Kong People's Council on Public Housing Policy, remain crucial. However, this pressure group has been on the brink of collapse because of financial problems since 1994. It was unable to obtain sponsorship from overseas religious organizations, and was rejected by the Community Chest — a voluntary association which collects donations and distributes them to grass roots organizations — as 'too radical'.[78] The Council now plans to depart from its original role of providing housing rights activism and take up the role of a social service agency. If this were to happen, it would mean that the only radical pressure group on housing policy would give up its function of a pressure group on public housing issues.

The situation of the community social workers is somewhat similar to that of the pressure groups. In September 1995 the government proposed to reduce its support for their programmes — the Neighbourhood Level Community Development Projects — due to budget cuts. Despite a series of protests by community social workers against this proposal, the government has not shown any intention of changing its mind. If community social workers were no longer involved in local politics, the urban minorities would find it difficult to organize their protests, particularly when there are so few intermediary associations in Hong Kong working at the neighbourhood level.

In brief, not only is the political environment in general not conducive to popular actions from below, local urban communities also lack the organizational support to stage sustained mobilization against top-down policy changes.

Notes

1. See Castells, 'Public housing and economic development in Hong Kong'; Lui, 'Urban protests in Hong Kong: a sociological study of housing conflicts'; and Lai, 'The selection of community work models'.
2. See McLaughlin, 'Hong Kong: a residual welfare regime'.
3. See Melucci, *Nomads of the present*; Ferree and Miller, 'Mobilization and meaning: toward an integration of social psychological and resource perspectives on social movement'; and McAdam, *Political process and the development of Black insurgency 1930–1970*.
4. See McCarthy and Zald, 'Resource mobilization and social movement: a partial theory' and 'The trend of social movements in America: professioinalization and resource mobilization'.
5. See Pickvance, 'The rise and fall of urban movements and the role of comparative analysis', p. 32. The definition of urban movement is distinguished from 'Urban Social Movement' which is reserved for denoting urban movements that can achieve high-level changes.
6. See Krause, 'Hong Kong and Singapore: twins or kissing cousins'.
7. See Chau, 'Labour and labour market'.
8. See Scott, *Political change and the crisis of legitimacy in Hong Kong*.
9. Government expenditure per capita at 1980 prices increased from $1 857 in 1971–72 to $4 377 in 1980–81. The public sector workforce on the other hand achieved an average growth rate of 7% per annum.
10. See Yeh, 'Employment location and new town development in Hong Kong'.
11. See Lui, 'Urban protests in Hong Kong: a sociological study of housing conflicts'.
12. See Cheung and Louie, 'Social conflicts in Hong Kong, 1975–1986: trends and implications'.
13. See Lui, 'Urban protests in Hong Kong: a sociological study of housing conflicts'.
14. See Leung, 'Community participation: from kai fong association, Mutual Aid Committee to District Board'.
15. See King, 'The administrative absorption of politics in Hong Kong: with special emphasis on the City District Officer Scheme'.
16. Lau has pointed out that a cloud of mutual suspicion hung over the interaction between the government and the social leaders. In his view, the establishment of the CDOs and the MACs failed to earn the support and active participation of the grassroots. See Lau, *Society and politics in Hong Kong*, pp. 145–8.
17. See Tilly, *From mobilization to revolution*.
18. See Leung, 'Community participation: from kai fong association, Mutual Aid Committee to District Board', 'Problems and changes in community politics'; and

Lau and Kuan, 'The 1985 District Board Election in Hong Kong: the limits of political mobilization in a dependent policy'.

19. See the Hong Kong Federation of Students 1983 edition. See also chapter 7 in this volume.
20. Leung, 'Problems and changes in community politics'.
21. See Lo, 'Communities of challengers in social movement theory'.
22. The findings are based on the database provided by W.T. Chui and O.K. Lai on social conflicts in Hong Kong.
23. See Davies, 'The changing nature of representation in Hong Kong politics'.
24. See Leung, 'Problems and changes in community politics'.
25. See Lau and Kuan, 'The 1985 District Board Election in Hong Kong: the limits of political mobilization in a dependent policy'.
26. See Leung, 'Community participation: from kai fong association, Mutual Aid Committee to District Board'.
27. See Leung, 'Problems and changes in community politics', p. 56.
28. See Leung, 'Community participation: from kai fong association, Mutual Aid Committee to District Board', pp. 366–7.
29. See Cheung and Louie, 'Social conflicts in Hong Kong, 1975–1986: trends and implications'; and Lui, 'Two logics of community politics: residents' organizations and the 1991 election'.
30. The slogan 'Democracy against Communism' used by the mass media to describe the implicit political objective of the political rights movement clearly points to the nitty-gritty of such a movement.
31. See Johnson, 'Accountability, control and complexity: moving beyond ministerial responsibility', p. 207.
32. For example, policy pertaining to transport is delegated to the Transport Consultation Committee, medical services to the Hospital Authority, construction of the new airport to the statutory body known as the Provisional Airport Authority established in April 1990, urban renewal to the Land Development Corporation established in 1988, and education policy to the Education Commission, etc. As far as the provision of public housing is concerned, the Housing Authority is the statutory body responsible for the construction, maintenance and management of all public housing estates. Though the Government Secretary for Transport remains responsible for the overall policy formulation, direction and coordination of internal transport matters, the government-founded Transport Advisory Committee is responsible for giving advice to the Governor in Council on major transport policies and issues. The committee has 17 appointed members, including the chairman and six government officials. The Education Commission is the highest advisory body on education. Its terms of reference includes defining the overall objectives of education, formulating policy and recommending priorities for implementation and coordinating as well as monitoring the planning and development of education at all levels. In 1992, the Commission consisted of 14 members, of whom 12, including the chairman, were appointed from outside the government to bear on the issues under review. Two government members are the Secretary of Education and Manpower, who is the vice-chairman and the Director of Education.
33. Hong Kong Justice of Peace Commission, *The land of Hong Kong: so precious*, p. 64.
34. Lui, 'Urban protests in Hong Kong: a sociological study of housing conflicts', pointed out that the financial constraint imposed by the self-financing policy subjected all

forms of public housing to the need for a constant review of rents and hence this created 'conditions for making the rent issue a tension between the government and the public housing tenants' (p. 75).

35. The *Far Eastern Economic Review*, 7 November 1991, documented that the Hong Kong Housing Authority was dominated by influential professionals and business people who had a direct vested interest in the affairs to be decided upon.

36. This point was borne out by a member of the political party — the United Democrats, Mr Lee Wing Tat. In an interview, he expressed that, even though he was also a member of the Housing Authority, he was of little help to the housing movement because he was not in the Management and Operation Sub-Committee which is the major body responsible for all public housing policy in relation to building and planning.

37. See Yu, 'The nature and implications of the recommodification of public housing in Hong Kong'.

38. See Hong Kong Housing Authority, *Review of the long Term housing strategy*.

39. This point was mentioned by one of the officials of the Housing Department in an interview in 1992.

40. See Lai, 'Urban renewal and the Land Development Corporation'.

41. See Castells, 'Public housing and economic development in Hong Kong'; and Lui, 'Urban protests in Hong Kong: a sociological study of housing conflicts'.

42. See Leung, 'Community participation: from kai fong association, Mutual Aid Committee to District Board'.

43. See ibid., p. 366.

44. See ibid., pp. 366–7.

45. This argument is based on the author's experience of personal involvement in the protest against the well-off tenant policy organized by a pressure group, the Hong Kong Affairs Society.

46. See Castells, 'Public housing and economic development in Hong Kong'; Lui, 'Urban protests in Hong Kong: a sociological study of housing conflicts'; and Leung, 'Housing'.

47. The author was invited in 1989 to attend a meeting which involved leaders of the PCPHP, scholars and social activists. In this meeting, the PCPHP leaders said that they found it difficult to work out the objectives of the housing movement and to articulate issues concerning public rental housing policy. They feared that the lack of future direction would further demobilize the movement in the 1990s.

48. The concept is similar to the concept of 'collective action frames' suggested by Snow et al., 'Frame alignment processes, micromobilization and movement participation'. It refers to the cognitive framework which affirms people commitment to the cause of a social movement and informs people about the causes of injustice. While Snow et al. stress that such a framework is functional to mobilization, we suggest that a dispute frame is mainly used for justifying the cause and actions of a social movement.

49. As Ip pointed out that, in the last two decades, the right to accommodation was seldom promoted by social activists. Most of the struggles revolved around living conditions and rent levels and housing rights were not articulated as an important issue in the housing movement. See Ip, 'Advocating the housing rights and its development'.

50. The activists' view on the significance of the protest against the well-off tenants policy was obtained through informal interviews in 1987 with the activists who were involved in the protest.

51. See Leung, 'Community participation: from kai fong association, Mutual Aid Committee to District Board', p. 366.
52. See Leung, 'Community development in Hong Kong: a study of "top down" and "bottom-up" social policy planning and implementation'.
53. See Wong, *Social movements and Hong Kong*.
54. See Yeung, 'An investigation into the professional ideology of the neighbourhood level community development project community workers.'
55. See Lui and Kung, *City unlimited: housing protests and urban politics in Hong Kong*, pp. 100–1.
56. See Lee, 'From social rented housing to home ownership: the dilemma of housing policy in the nineties'.
57. See Leung, 'Housing'.
58. See ibid.
59. See Hong Kong Housing Authority, *A report on the mid-term review on the long term housing strategy*.
60. See Lau, 'Housing', p. 357.
61. The major cleavage between these two wings was related to the extent of direct election to be introduced to the Legislative Council. Neither wing refused democracy, but the pro-government wing just argued for a slow pace to the introduction of full direct election to the council.
62. See Joint Committee on Public Housing Policy Review, 1992, *The grass roots' White Paper on public housing policy in the 1990s*, Hong Kong: Tang Brothers Resources and Research Publication Company.
63. Informal interviews with Mr Cheng Chun-man, a social worker, who was involved in the Joint Committee on the Sales of Flats to Sitting Tenants Policy.
64. This view was obtained through participation in several protests organized by the Joint Committee on the New Rental Increase Policy in 1992.
65. The Hong Kong Democratic United invited leaders of the Hong Kong People Council on Public Housing Policy to join the coalition concerning middle-class people's housing needs, but the latter refused to become involved in the coalition.
66. Through informal interviews with the leaders of the PCPHP and several community social workers, I found that the leaders and the community social workers regarded the dispute between the LDC and the shop owners as an issue concerning fairness in the market rather than social injustice. Therefore, they decided not to become involved in the dispute.
67. Interviews with community social workers who were involved in the coalition concerning THA policy. In practice, the housing movement in Hong Kong is largely localized, small-scale and sporadic. Yet this form of action was not a direct result of the strategic preference of the actors, but the result of the fact that the activists failed to develop the housing movement as a pressure group. In fact, the PCPHP, the coalition People Council on Squatter Policy, and the Joint Committee of the THA Neighbourhood Associations, etc., played the role of a pressure group.
68. See Lui, 'Two logics of community politics: residents' organizations and the 1991 election'.
69. See ibid., p. 334. The lack of trust was apparent on a number of occasions. First, I observed that some concern groups involved in the housing movement avoided creating any opportunity for political party members to appear at public protests. For example, in one protest, the PCPHP did not allow the politicians to touch the public address system in order to avoid giving the politicians any chance to make

a public speech in front of the protesters. Second, many leaders of the housing movement doubted the loyalty of the politicians to the local concern groups. What the leaders complained of was the politicians' overconcern with votes, rather than the genuine needs and problems of the grass roots. Third, some community social workers who played a crucial role in local mobilization promoted the concept of 'civic society', putting more emphasis on the autonomy of the grass roots and less on working with politicians. The implicit aim of this move was to protect the local concern groups from the encroachment of political groups and parties. All these instances reflected the lack of trust and friendly relations between the two movement sectors.

70. See Chow, 'Angry tenants mob rent policy meeting', *Hong Kong Standard*, 27 September 1991.

71. See 'Public housing tenants' sit-in protest stopped the operation of the Housing Department', *Tin Tin Daily News*, 27 June 1992. See also Leung, 'Changing a new sky for the sun and moon — a reflection on the protest against rental increase for new public rental housing'.

72. See Kam et al., 'The protests at the entrance of Government House and the arrest of 23 people — whose responsibility?' *Sing Tao Daily*, 15 April 1993; T.K. Wong, 'How to conceive the forms of confrontation in social actions', *Hong Kong Economic Journal*, 20 December 1994.

73. See Angel Lau, 'Roof dwellers slam resettlement delays', *Hong Kong Standard*, 4 March 1995; Angel Lau, 'Ex-rooftop dwellers to snub bill for demolition', *Hong Kong Standard*, 13 March 1995; Pamela Leung, 'Roof over their heads', *Eastern Express*, 17 April 1995.

74. Chau, 'Confrontation and protest should be orderly', *Hong Kong Economic Journal*, 21 December 1994.

75. In the case of roof dwellers' protest, community social workers complained that the leaders of this protest were influenced by external agents. See 'SoCO withdrew its assistance for the roof dwellers', *Hong Kong Daily News*, 21 April 1995.

76. In February 1996 the Housing Authority announced that 143 000 home ownership flats should be built in 1996/97, 42 000 more than in the financial year 1995/96. This reveals that home ownership would become the dominant form of public housing provided by the government. See James Kelly and Patsy Moy, 'Critics attacking housing figures', *Hong Kong Standard*, 2 March 1996.

77. See 'Unlucky thirteen', *South China Morning Post*, 23 September 1995. This policy change led to a confrontation between the police and the THA residents. An angry group greeted Governor Chris Patten with a gift of a mouse on 28 September 1995, when the Governor visited three of the THAs he once pledged to close down. See Angela Leary, 'Violent protest greets Governor', *Eastern Express*, 29 September 1995; and also 'Governor runs the gauntlet', *South China Morning Post*, 29 September 1995.

78. See Ng Kang-chung, 'Radical group to adapt or die', *South China Morning Post*, 5 October 1995.

7

The Student Movement in Hong Kong: Transition to a Democratizing Society

Benjamin K.P. Leung

❏ Introduction

Hong Kong's democratization, officially termed the development towards a representative government, began with the introduction in 1982 of the District Board, which had popularly elected members in its composition. The democratization of politics at the district level since then eventually cumulated in the introduction of indirectly elected members in 1985, and directly elected members in 1991, to the Legislative Council. Concomitant with this gradual opening up of the political system have been the rise and proliferation of political parties. Increasing politicization of the community has been one most noteworthy feature of Hong Kong since the early 1980s. It is an irony that students played but a marginal and inconspicuous role in this important period of the territory's political development. And it is puzzling that the student movement, which in the 1970s had been a fervent advocate and agent of social and political reform, should decline into oblivion at a time when reform was the subject of heated debates and acute ideological and political rivalry in the community. In other words, the student movement seemed to have receded into backstage when the drama of reform was being enacted. Is then the student movement in Hong Kong no more than an ephemeral phenomenon of little or no lasting social and political import? Has it any bearing at all on the society's current political development? These questions are the guiding threads of discussion in this chapter.

This chapter is thus essentially an exercise in exploring the significance of the student movement in Hong Kong. It seeks to assess the role of the student movement in generating a public *forum* for political discussion, in carving out a public *space* for political institutionalization, and in fashioning *roles* for professional political participation. It seeks further to explore the *cognitive* significance of the student movement — what it informs us about the Hong Kong ethos. These objectives are premised on the observation that being relatively free-floating intellectuals whose experiences and thinking have not been routinized by occupational and family responsibilities, students are in a particularly privileged position for creative endeavours. We believe that the significance and the career of the student movement have to be understood in terms of its historical location between the aftermath of the 1967 territory-wide riots and the onset of democratization in the early 1980s. The student movement, as we shall argue later in this chapter, was a cognitive articulation of the major concerns and ethos of the Hong Kong people in the wake of the disturbances of the mid-1960s, as well as an attempt to address these concerns and ethos through practice. In so doing, the student activists of the 1970s helped to furnish a direction and to prepare the ground for the territory's democratization in the following decade. Our main thesis is that both in terms of cognition and practice, the student movement was a forerunner and a facilitating factor in the transition to a democratizing society in Hong Kong. The examination below of the career of the student movement revolves around this thesis.[1]

❑ Origins and Rise of the Student Movement in Hong Kong

The student movement in Hong Kong, which involved mainly university students, emerged and gathered momentum around the end of the 1960s. Before that, university students were characterized by an entrenched indifference to social and political issues. A student leader writing in the late 1970s captured succinctly the prevailing mood among university students before the era of student activism:

> [The students] had no sense of belonging to Hong Kong, and only adopted the attitude of an indifferent observer on events in China... A stagnant, totally uncritical and despondent atmosphere pervaded the whole university campus. Material satisfaction and degenerate personal honour and status were what the students looked for...[2]

The description applied aptly to the overwhelming majority not only of university students, but also students in secondary educational institutions. Yet there was an active minority whose activities and concerns helped pave the way for the rise of the student movement in Hong Kong. Some of them were fervent participants in the so-called Literary Associations Movement;[3] others in the Social Service Group of Tertiary Students. Both had their heyday in the 1960s.

The Literary Associations Movement had a quasi-political beginning. As a measure to sustain its cultural influence in the Colony, the United States government founded in the early 1950s a number of US-funded literary organizations to absorb the intellectuals who came to Hong Kong to flee communist rule on the Mainland. Under the sponsorship of the US government, these people produced a large number of publications, the most noteworthy of which included *The Chinese Students Weekly, Nation* and *New Trends in Arts and Literature.* Under the influence of these publications, secondary school students started to organize their own literary associations and produce student publications in the early 1960s. According to one estimate,[4] such literary associations at the height of the Movement numbered around 300 to 400. During the 1966 and 1967 riots, the Movement shifted its orientation, from a focus on arts and literature to current social and political issues. But it faded towards the end of the 1960s. The Movement, however, left behind an important legacy: some of its most committed participants were to play a leading role in the student movement during their university education.

The Social Service Group of Tertiary Students was formed in December 1963. This was a time when the government offered but limited social service and welfare provisions for the poor and underprivileged. Thus when the government decided in August 1963 to resettle a group of squatters, some students from tertiary institutions took up the responsibility of helping the squatters to move and settle down to their new residence. Among their contributions was the building of a road, some 1 000 feet in length, for the resettled residents. This unprecedented project earned the praise of the public, and the participants decided to continue their efforts to serve the deprived segments of the community through establishing an organization for the purpose. The ensuing Social Service Group had the declared objectives of 'practising the ideal of service to the community, disseminating the notion that voluntary service is an honorable deed, and strengthening the bond and friendship among tertiary students through social service'.[5] After the 1967 riots, many members of the Group came to the realization that what the society required was more fundamental changes in its social and political make-up, and that social service was not an effective way to bring about reforms. The Social Service Group thus turned its attention increasingly to analysis and critique of the colonial capitalist system of Hong Kong. Many of its most dedicated members subsequently joined the student movement of the 1970s, and the Group was disbanded in 1973.

For the silent majority of university students, the change in orientation came in the midst of the 1967 riots. The strong nationalist, anti-colonial and anti-capitalist sentiments of the disturbances[6] awakened the university students to issues concerning the colonial status of Hong Kong, the lack of communication between the colonial government and the local Chinese population, and the plight of the poor and underprivileged. Thus at the height of the riots, the student publication *Undergrad* (13 July 1967 issue) of the University of Hong Kong carried an article with the title 'Has Hong Kong a Future?' This article, which was just one of many others of a similar nature appearing in student publications of the time, exemplified the first change of mood and concern among university students. 'If we accept that it is we who have to decide our future', the article stated, '...we will have to strive for more active participation in politics, we will have to campaign for the allegiance of our youth, ...we need to reform our educational system.'[7] Another article which epitomized the burgeoning concern of university students about the need for social and political reforms in the wake of the riots appeared in the *Undergrad* (1 December issue) during the final phase of the disturbances. Carrying the tell-tale title 'The Riots, Public Opinions, and the Adoption of Chinese as an Official Language', the article analysed the riots in terms of the national and cultural identity of the Hong Kong Chinese, and of the gross social and political inequality between the colonizers and the Chinese population. It anticipated the strong nationalist, anti-colonial overtones of the student movement in the following decade. Indeed the seeds of the student movement were sown amid the trauma of the 1967 riots.

The year 1968 was the gestation period of the student movement. It was a year of turbulence in world politics, epitomized in the Soviet Union's invasion of Czechoslovakia, the anti-Vietnam War protests in the United States, and the ongoing Cultural Revolution in China. Youths, particularly students, played a central part in these momentous events, in resisting foreign domination, in the quest for peace, or in reconstructing their country's cultural and political make-up. It was a time when students were seen and expected to assume a prominent or even leading role in domestic and international politics. This international climate of student activism furnished the ideological context for the birth of the student movement in Hong Kong.

While the majority of the university students in Hong Kong carried on with their habitual indifference and complacency, a group of student activists kept alive on campus the budding enthusiasm in social-political affairs through debates and discussions about the role of university students in the larger community. Their concerns, as reflected in the student publications of the two universities (the University of Hong Kong and the Chinese University) and of the Hong Kong Federation of Students, included 'Political Apathy among Hong Kong Youths', 'Living Conditions Among Squatters', 'Student Movements in the West', 'Youth Problems in Hong Kong', and 'Student Movements and Politics'. The subjects of the discourse suggested that the tumultuous political events and the upsurge of student activism in the West in 1968, in addition to problems and deprivations within the local community highlighted by the 1967 riots, set the intellectual and political stage for the emergence of the student movement in Hong Kong. Under the confluence of these circumstances, the students in Hong Kong were going through the first phase of their cognitive liberation[8] from their traditional apathy and quiescence. This cumulated in the *University Reform Movement* staged by the students of the University of Hong Kong in February 1969. The event launched the student movement in Hong Kong.

The main objectives of the *University Reform Movement* were to promote student participation in university administration, and to bring about improvements in university teaching, student welfare and teacher-student relationships. The movement was a localized campaign targeted at the University of Hong Kong, and its achievements were modest — the major gain being student representation on the university's Senate Board. But it changed the atmosphere on campus, and implanted among university students the disposition to confront and challenge established authorities through collective action. An incident which happened several months later served to inculcate a unity among students in various tertiary educational institutions in their struggle against the establishment. This was the so-called Chu Hoi College Student Protest of autumn 1969, which originated from the college authorities' dismissal of 12 students who had criticized in student publications the college's authoritarian control over students. The student unions in several other tertiary institutions — notably the University of Hong Kong, the Chinese University and the Baptist College — issued public statements demanding the reinstatement of the dismissed students. The protest reached its height in September, when some 60 student activists from these tertiary institutions staged a two-day sit-in outside Chu Hoi College, and distributed pamphlets bearing the title 'The Voice of Chu Hai'. While by no means a major incident of student protest in terms of the number of participants and duration, this episode was the first time students from different tertiary institutions took to the streets in concerted action for a cause which was not directly related to issues within their own campus. The foundation of the student movement had now been laid.

❏ The Upsurge of Nationalism in the Student Movement

The early 1970s was a crucial phase in the development of the student movement in Hong Kong. In 1970, university students together with a number of public bodies founded the Special Committee for the Campaign to Make Chinese an Official Language. In the summer of the same year, students of the Chinese University of Hong Kong organized sit-ins and demonstrations to protest against cuts in the budgets of the Chinese University and the University of Hong Kong. But the single most dramatic and long-lasting episode in the student movement

— an episode which fuelled the student movement in the next few years — was the Diaoyutai Islands Protest which started in February 1971.

The Diaoyutai Islands, located near the northeast coast of Taiwan, were originally part of the Taiwan Province, but were somehow included in the Okinawa Territory under the mandate of the United States after World War II. When the United States government announced in 1970 its decision to return Okinawa, together with the Diaoyutai Islands, to Japan in May 1972, the Chinese government protested. This precipitated a dispute between the Chinese government and the Japanese government on territorial rights over the Diaoyutai Islands. To the student activists in Hong Kong, whose nationalist sentiments had already been awakened by the 1967 riots and the ongoing Cultural Revolution in China, Japan's territorial claim signified a revival of Japanese militarism and this invoked memories of Japan's invasion of China during World War II. To defend the territorial integrity of their country, a group of university students in conjunction with other concerned members of the public formed the Action Committee in Defence of the Diaoyutai Islands in February 1971. This launched the *Defend Diaoyutai Movement* in Hong Kong, in which university students played the principal role. In the course of the *Movement*, the students voiced their opposition against the Japanese and the United States governments through organizing a series of public rallies and protest demonstrations. During some of these protest rallies, the students clashed with the police. In particular, the clash between the student demonstrators and the police in the protest rally on 7 July 1971 in Victoria Park was to add a fresh impetus and orientation to the student movement. In an attempt to break up the rally, which did not have the prior approval of the Urban Council, the police resorted to violence against the student protesters. This sidetracked the students' attention to what they now experienced and perceived as repression in a colony. The nationalist sentiments that were already rampant among the student protesters thus speedily developed into a campaign against the colonial establishment in Hong Kong. This campaign became one of the main impetuses of the student movement after the demise of the *Defend Diaoyutai Movement* in May the following year.[9]

❑ Nationalism and Its Ramifications: The Split Within the Student Movement

Two streams of thinking gradually took shape within the student movement in the aftermath of the *Defend Diaoyutai Movement*. Both were ideological continuities of the nationalist and anti-colonial orientations of the *Movement*. The one which emerged as the mainstream in the following few years sought to further and strengthen these orientations through identifying with Socialist

China. The political circumstances were conducive to this trend of development. At a time when the students were highly critical of the legitimacy of the colonial capitalist regime in Hong Kong, Socialist China was making major advancements in its international status. The People's Republic became a member of the United Nations in 1971; President Nixon of the United States made his historic visit to China in 1972; China's table-tennis diplomacy in the early 1970s was forging international goodwill towards the country. To many student activists of the time, Hong Kong's future lay in its reunification with China. They accordingly perceived the mission of the student movement to be preparing the Chinese compatriots in Hong Kong for reunion with the motherland. 'Getting to know Socialist China' and 'identifying with Socialist China' thus became for them the most important objectives of the student movement. The student union of the University of Hong Kong organized its first China visit in December 1971. In the next few years, the student activists undertook further China tours, ran China study groups, and organized China Weeks to carry out their mission of educating Hong Kong students about the achievements of Socialist China. It was under such circumstances that the so-called Pro-China Faction emerged and became the mainstream of the student movement in the first half of the 1970s.

But there was another faction of student actionists who did not identify themselves with Socialist China. They had reservations about the socialist regime in China, and held the view that the student movement should not adopt uncritically a pro-China orientation. To these students, the more important and immediate tasks of the student movement were to rectify the injustices in Hong Kong's colonial capitalist system and to help the deprived and underprivileged members of the community. The ideological division between this faction, then referred to as the Social Actionist Faction,[10] and the Pro-China Faction was later to develop into an internal rivalry within the student movement. Two student protest episodes were instrumental in bringing about this rupture.

The first episode was the Anti-Corruption Campaign of 1973, in which a group of student activists in coordination with a number of concerned public bodies protested against the then widespread corrupt practices within the colonial government, and in particular against the government's mishandling of a case of corruption involving a senior police officer of British racial stock. A number of student protesters were subsequently arrested and prosecuted for illegal assembly. At this point, the Pro-China Faction came to the view that the student movement should refrain from taking radical protest actions against the colonial establishment, for such would not be effective against a recalcitrant colonial regime. They maintained that the movement should instead focus its attention on preparing the Hong Kong compatriots for reunion with mainland China. To the Social Actionist Faction and the prosecuted students, this was a let-down, a betrayal, by the Pro-China Faction. The two factions began to perceive each other as opponents within the student movement.

Then came the Anti-Inflation Campaign of 1974, during which the Pro-China Faction organized a public exhibition on inflation with the objective of demonstrating that Hong Kong's then surging inflation with the corresponding decline in the living standards of the masses was the inevitable outcome of a capitalist economy. The underlying message, which the exhibition sought to demonstrate through comparisons, was that a socialist economy like that of China was spared of such a crisis. To the Social Actionist Faction, the exhibition was but propagandist in nature; to them putting direct pressure on the government to improve the living standards of the poor and deprived was far more worthwhile and urgent than running an exhibition. They distributed pamphlets outside the exhibition hall stating their objections to the exhibition. The incident turned the ideological division within the student body into an open rivalry for leadership and direction of the student movement.

Since then, the Pro-China Faction by and large refrained from taking direct confrontational action against the colonial establishment and concentrated on their mission of educating the students and the public about Socialist China. The Social Actionist Faction, on the other hand, carried on their task of combating the injustices in colonial capitalist Hong Kong. Most of the student protests and social service activities in the following two years — most notably the Protest Against Rise in Telephone Fees (1975), the Protest Demonstration Against the Queen's Visit to Hong Kong (1975), donations and services to fire victims (1976) — were spearheaded by the Social Actionist Faction. Until the end of 1976, however, the Pro-China Faction gained control of the student union of the university and remained the dominant force within the student movement.

❑ Political Developments in China and Their Impact on the Student Movement in Hong Kong, 1976

The year 1976 was a fateful year in the career of the student movement. Events in China proved to have major repercussions on the student movement in Hong Kong. On 5 April, a large crowd estimated at around 100 000 people gathered in Beijing's Tiananmen Square ostensibly to pay the final tribute to the recently deceased Premier Zhou Enlai. On this occasion, members of the gathering voiced their opposition to the Cultural Revolution and its leaders and pledged their support for Deng Xiao Ping who had fallen from power during the Cultural Revolution. The incident developed into a confrontation between the gathering and the police, resulting in a violent suppression of the protest demonstrators. The Beijing government promptly denounced the uprising as anti-revolutionary and Deng once again fell into disgrace. The issue sparked off heated debates within the student body in Hong Kong about the manner in which the Beijing authorities handled the incident. Much to the dislike of many students, the Pro-China Faction who controlled the student union announced their support for the measures taken by the Beijing government. This induced mounting opposition to the Pro-China Faction within the student movement.

But the event that precipitated the collapse of the Pro-China Faction was the downfall in October of the Gang of Four. The Gang of Four had been leaders of the Cultural Revolution, but were arrested and castigated as anti-revolutionary conspirators by their political rivals who came to power after the death of Mao. This drastic reversal in China's political leadership meant that the Pro-China Faction, who had been the main carriers of the student movement in Hong Kong, had unwittingly identified with and followed what now came to be seen as treacherous political operators within the Chinese government. It occurred to most students that the Pro-China Faction had misguided the student movement in the past few years. Disgraced and disoriented, this faction could no longer justify themselves as leaders of the student movement. So since 1976, if there was still a Pro-China Faction in universities and post-secondary colleges, they kept a low profile in the political life of the student body. But as they had been the main carrier of the student movement, with their retreat, the movement lost much of its drive and momentum. Still the tradition of student participation in social-political matters had taken root and lingered on for a few more years. The Boat People Protest Issue of January 1979, in which university student activists backed up and organized the boat people in their demands to the government to be resettled on land, was one good example of student involvement in social issues towards the end of the 1970s. But in terms of the scope of student involvement and of its impact on the public, the Golden Jubilee Secondary School Protest Issue of 1978 was perhaps the most significant since the Diaoyutai Protest of the early 1970s.

❏ The Golden Jubilee Secondary School Protest Issue

Golden Jubilee Secondary School was a Catholic school run by the Precious Blood Order. In early 1977 some teachers of the school discovered irregularities in the school's financial account. Since no satisfactory explanation was offered by the school authority concerning such irregularities, in April 1977 the teachers submitted to the Education Department a report on the information they had collected about the school's financial mismanagement. Subsequent investigation found the school principal Sister Leung guilty of forgery. The Precious Blood Order appointed a new principal, Miss Kwan, for Golden Jubilee Secondary School in August 1977. After taking over, Miss Kwan undertook to reform the school by adopting a number of new measures such as temporarily banning student extracurricular activities, isolating new students from the old teachers and students who had participated in exposing the school's financial mismanagement, searching students' school bags, and threatening to dismiss some of the dissenting teachers. Objections from some of the teachers and students led to a series of confrontations between the two parties. The relationship between Miss Kwan and the dissenting teachers and students deteriorated, and then on 9 May 1978, the dissident teachers and students and some of the students' parents, totalling about 400 people, marched to Government House to petition the Governor to look into the matter and dismiss the school principal. At this point, the student unions of the University of Hong Kong, Chinese University and several other post-secondary colleges declared their support for the protesting teachers and students.

On 14 May, the Education Department announced its decision to close Golden Jubilee Secondary School, effective from the following day, and to start another school to be named Saint Teresa's Secondary School in the old school premises in September. Miss Kwan would continue to be the principal of the new school and the students could carry on with their studies there, but the 16 dissenting teachers would not be employed in the new school. The Education Department's decision sparked off a series of protest actions in which hundreds of university and post-secondary college students expressed their support for the dissident teachers and students of Golden Jubilee Secondary School. The participants held a number of sit-ins, demonstrations, and a two-day hunger strike to demand the immediate reopening of the school and a thorough investigation of the issue. A three-person committee was subsequently appointed by the government to find remedial measures. The committee issued its interim report in July 1978, recommending the setting up of another school to accommodate the dissenting teachers and students. The teachers and students of Golden Jubilee Secondary School could choose to join either Saint Teresa's Secondary School or the new school proposed by the committee. Both parties in the dispute accepted the recommendation and the Golden Jubilee Secondary School Protest came to a close. The episode was a glorious chapter in the history of the student movement in Hong Kong, but it was also the last.

❏ The Eclipse of the Student Movement Since the Early 1980s

Both in terms of commitment and number of participants, student activism since the early 1980s paled in comparison with that in the 1970s. There were still sporadic, small-scale episodes of student activism, but such involved so few students and lasted for so short a duration that they could hardly be regarded as constituting a student movement. Indeed the 1980s and early 1990s were a time of momentous changes in Hong Kong, and it would be incorrect to say that such changes did not catch the attention of students and provoke a response from them. At each major historical moment, students did play a role in voicing an opinion or taking part in collective protest action. During the 1982–84 Sino-British negotiations on Hong Kong's future, for instance, a coalition of student bodies from various local universities and colleges sent a letter to British Prime Minister Margaret Thatcher expressing their views on the matter of Hong Kong's political status after 1997. When an elected element was to be introduced into the 1985 Legislative Council, the Hong Kong Federation of Students in July 1984 voiced their strong preference for direct election. The student body was also not indifferent to the drafting of the Basic Law for the post-1997 Special Administrative Region; from the mid-1980s to the end of the decade, the student unions of the tertiary institutions expressed a series of views about the composition of the Basic Law Consultative Committee as well as the contents of the Basic Law. And students played an active role in the pro-democracy campaigns and demonstrations in connection with the Tiananmen Square Incident of 1989. These are but the more notable examples of student activism since the early 1980s.[11] The question is: why did such incidents of student activism fail to imprint on the public and on the students themselves that there was a recognizable student movement in Hong Kong since the early 1980s?

The small number of student participants, short duration of each episode, and intermittent involvement without a clear and long-term ideological commitment are part of the answer. This decline in student activism has been explained in terms of the rapid expansion of the university student population since the early 1980s.[12] With this expansion, student interest associations proliferated and each was more concerned with competing for resources than with the general unity of the student body. The student union, in other words, has faced mounting problems in controlling the peripheral student associations and forging a consensus among them. This situation has very much weakened the strength of the student body and has seriously crippled the student movement. At the same time, to handle the increasing amount of student affairs, the student union has developed into a much more bureaucratic organization with the result that the relationship between the union and the majority of the students has become more impersonal. Further, like other bureaucracies, the student union has become bogged down in routine matters of management and has found it more and more difficult to spare time on issues that lie outside the daily administration of the bureaucracy. Thus, both in terms of its mobilizing capacity and objectives, the student union of the 1980s and early 1990s could hardly assume a position of leadership in a student movement. The demise of the student movement hence can be attributed to the increasing diversification and competing interests within the student body as well as the absence of a strong leadership.[13]

But a further explanation for the decline of the student movement can be sought in the political changes in the larger society, changes that had the effect of reducing the role of student activists to a subordinate one in social and political issues. In this respect, Cheung and Louie's study[14] of the trend of social conflict and Lui's study[15] of the upsurge and decline of popular social movements in Hong Kong throw light on our discussion.[16]

Encompassing various types of social conflict such as petitions to government, signature campaigns, press conferences, protests, and mass rallies, Cheung and Louie's study is an analysis of the factors accounting for the frequency and nature of social conflict in Hong Kong in the period 1975 to 1986. Their empirical findings indicate that the period was characterized by a rising trend in the frequency of social conflict, as well as by the increasing organizational and mobilizational capacity of the protest participants. They note in addition the growing involvement of students, political activists, community activists and church groups in mobilizing and organizing the grass roots in collective protest action. Indeed, as a number of other writers [17] have also observed, the 1970s were a time of proliferating pressure group activities. The pertinence of this to our discussion is that the upsurge of student activism in the early half of the 1970s should be understood in the larger context of the political awakening of the younger generation and the proliferation of pressure groups in the aftermath of the 1967 riots. Students were arguably the pioneers in the ensuing political activism, but as the decade drew to a close, their role in collective action was increasingly superseded and overshadowed by other pressure groups. As the students lost their pioneering and leadership role in mass mobilization, the student movement became submerged in the growing pressure group activism of the time. This is one explanation for the non-salience of the student movement since the early 1980s. A further explanation can be derived from Lui's study of popular movements.

The popular movements in Lui's study refer to 'protests ... organized by people to make ... claims to state provisions and to challenge the colonial political order'.[18] Such popular movements include protest movements in respect of housing, transport, social welfare, education, and the environment. The 1970s, Lui observes, were the heyday of popular movements in Hong Kong. Like Cheung and Louie, Lui attributes this to the rising anti-colonial sentiments among the local population in the wake of the 1967 riots, and to the rising expectations of the community brought about by the government's expanding role in social service provision. In this context, pressure groups proliferated and mobilized the masses in popular protest movements. For this reason, the rise and decline of popular movements were closely related to the 'career' of the pressure group activists. Hong Kong's development towards a representative government since 1982, and the concomitant opening up of the political system first at the district level and then at the central policy-making level, had the effect of increasingly absorbing pressure group activists into the formal political structure. And as the pressure group leaders found their niche within the formal political system, their concerns and tactics changed from mass mobilization for popular protest movement to mass mobilization for competitive electoral politics. In short, Lui's message is that the decline of popular movements in the 1980s was a by-product of the process of democratization.

The bearing of this for our understanding of the decline of the student movement is that the political climate of the 1980s and 1990s has been different from that of the 1970s. The politics of protest and confrontation in an era of non-democratic government has gradually given way to the politics of institutionalized competition and compromise in a democratizing society. When more and more legitimate channels and institutions are available for the communication and resolution of grievances, the need to resort to protest and confrontational collective action as a means of putting pressure on the government has been correspondingly reduced. If in the late 1970s and early 1980s the student movement was overshadowed by pressure group political activism, then since the mid-1980s it has been rendered insignificant by the burgeoning politicians and political parties that have become the centre of political mobilization and action.

Equally pertinent here is the failure of developing ideological mobilization on college campuses to sustain student activism in the 1980s. From the letter to Margaret Thatcher to participation in the consultation process of the drafting of the Basic Law, student groups were not able to develop a consistent ideological framework to make sense of the political reality and to elaborate on a political programme for action. On the one hand, largely following the established tradition of local student radicalism, they were critical of colonialism. In this regard, their critique of British colonialism and their acceptance of returning Hong Kong to China were inspired by former student activists' response to the talks on Hong Kong's future.[19] They came to see the return of Hong Kong to China's sovereignty as the golden opportunity to launch social reform — reform programmes, such as democratization, which had long been suppressed under colonial governance, would become topics for public debate. Their critical stance towards colonialism led student activists to adopt the position of welcoming Hong Kong's return to China.[20] On the other hand, student activists were also critical of the authoritarian regime in China. They continued to support pro-democracy actions within China. Also, they advocated 'Hong Kong people ruling Hong Kong democratically' in order to keep their distance from the official party line of China and the pro-China groups. Such an ideological position was not that different from other political groups emerging in the context of Sino-British negotiations. As stated earlier, the student movement was soon overshadowed by more formalized political talks and participation of emerging political groups.

❏ The Role of the Student Movement in the Transition to a Democratizing Society

The June 4 Incident had a significant impact on the student movement. Student radicalism once again became a topic of news coverage. Student bodies were seen actively organizing actions for the democratic cause in Hong Kong and China. They were often seen in mass rallies and protest actions against the Chinese government's handling of issues about freedom and democracy in Hong Kong and China. The June 4 Incident had completely changed student activists' earlier sympathetic attitude towards China. Not only were they more openly critical of the political style of the Communist Party, but they were also more prepared to take issues to the streets. Confrontations involving student activists became common after 1989. Their approach was uncompromising and they were ready to test the limits of political tolerance. Some activists saw their new approach as an attempt to stage 'civil society against the authoritarian state'. Some believed that their actions represented some kind of civil resistance against political manipulation.[21] What was evident in the series of radical student actions after 1989 was that the student movement was still firmly committed to ideals such as human rights, freedom and democracy. However, in a political environment of the late transitional period wherein pragmatism and compromise were emphasized, student radicalism was being marginalized.

Meanwhile, college campuses had undergone significant changes. While student activists were becoming more radical in action, their fellow students showed little interests in politics. In fact, even student unions had difficulties in finding active members to form full-fledged executive committees. At the same time, a nationalist territory-wide student organization, the Hong Kong Youth and Tertiary Students Association, was formed to compete with the established Federation of Hong Kong Students. So far, there has not been any indication of a change in the leadership of student bodies (and thus a change in the political orientation of student activism) as a result of the changing political environment. Nor have these new activists been able to use nationalist and patriotic sentiments to challenge pro-democracy student activism. However, that said, the formation of a new student body does illustrate a new environment for the student movement — the student movement will have to encounter competing groups and ideologies.

❏ Conclusion

I have argued in this chapter that the career of the student movement in Hong Kong has to be understood in the context of the changing political climate of the society. It emerged in the aftermath of the 1967 riots, and was geared to issues which these disturbances had unravelled — Hong Kong's political future, national identity, social inequality in a capitalist society, the undemocratic nature of colonial rule, and corruption. It played a pioneering and leading role in mobilizing the grass roots to put pressure on the government to take greater care of the needs of the deprived and underprivileged segments of the community. In this respect, it furnished the climate and gave the impetus for the emergence and expansion of pressure groups.[22]

But as the pressure groups developed and proliferated, they gradually superseded and overshadowed the student movement. Student activists eventually became partners, often junior partners, in their cooperation with pressure groups in confronting the established authorities. It was in this context that the student movement faded away. Its decline was caused also by the paucity of a new generation of student leaders and activists who would carry on the tradition and sustain the fervour of the student movement of the early 1970s. By the first half of the 1980s, the rise of professional politicians and the increased opportunities for the institutionalized resolution of social grievances concomitant with Hong Kong's democratization added further to the eclipse of the student movement. But the student movement did play a significant historical role in Hong Kong's development towards a representative government. It awakened a cohort of the younger generation to some of the most critical issues confronting the society, and remains an organized effort being critical of authoritarianism.

Notes

1. The descriptive account of the student movement that follows is based mainly on the following sources: The Hong Kong Federation of Students, *The Hong Kong student movement: retrospect and examination*; The Hong Kong Federation of Students, *The student movement in Hong Kong: a retrospective examination*; The Student Union of the University of Hong Kong, *Union Journal*, various years; and reports on student activism in local newspapers.
2. Chuek, 'Viewing the Hong Kong student movement through the University of Hong Kong's Student Union', in Chinese, author's translation.
3. There is a paucity of materials on the Literary Associations Movement. The account that follows is based on The Hong Kong Federation of Students, *The student movement in Hong Kong: a retrospective examination*, pp. 9-10.
4. Ibid., p. 9.
5. Ibid., p. 11.
6. For a detailed descriptive account of the 1967 riots, see Cooper, *The colony in conflict*. For a summary and analytic account, see Scott, *Political change and the crisis of legitimacy in Hong Kong*, pp. 96-106.
7. Author's translation.
8. The term 'cognitive liberation' was introduced by Doug McAdam in his 'political process model of social movements.' McAdam considered cognitive liberation to

be an important stage or process in the genesis of social movements. The cognitive dimension of social movements was given a fresh emphasis in Ron Eyerman and Andrew Jamison's book *Social movements: a cognitive approach*. Eyerman and Jamison looked upon social movements as processes of knowledge articulation and knowledge production. They argued that in articulating and fashioning a new cognitive dimension, social movements are important agents of social change. My attempt in this essay to delineate the process and significance of the student movement in Hong Kong is informed by McAdam's and Eyerman and Jamison's conceptual approaches.

9. In making the claim on territorial rights over the Diaoyutai Islands, both the Chinese and Taiwan governments did not adopt a strong stand. The United States government 'returned' the Islands to Japan in May 1972, and the pertinent protest movement in Hong Kong came to an end.

10. The original Chinese label for this faction literally means Society Faction. I translate it into Social Actionist Faction in order to capture the main orientation of this faction.

11. Other noteworthy examples of student activism in the 1980s include:

    a. protests against the Japanese government's revision of textbooks in respect of Japan's invasion of China during World War II (July to September 1982; the student protesters were mainly office-bearers of the Hong Kong Federation of Students and the student unions of The University of Hong Kong and The Chinese University of Hong Kong);

    b. visit to Beijing to present to the Chinese leaders a proposal for democratic self-government in Hong Kong after 1997 (July 1983; 12 representatives from the Hong Kong Federation of Students went on this visit);

    c. visit to Beijing to discuss with the Chinese leaders the matter of Hong Kong's transition to 1997 (June 1984; 30 university students participated in this visit organized by the Hong Kong Federation of Students);

    d. visit to London to solicit the views of the British government on the Hong Kong government's Green Paper on political reforms (July 1987; six students from The University of Hong Kong, The Chinese University of Hong Kong, and the Hong Kong Polytechnic went on this visit);

    e. protest rallies opposing local celebrations of the National Day of the People's Republic of China (annually since the 4 June 1989 Tiananmen Square Incident; student participants from local tertiary institutions on the whole numbered less than 50).

    The small number of student participants in these events is a further testimony that student activism since the 1980s was confined mainly to a negligible minority of student leaders. For this reason, it seems inappropriate to maintain that there was a student movement in Hong Kong in the 1980s and early 1990s. (Source of information: various press reports and student publications.)

12. The arguments in this paragraph are based on an article entitled 'Those were the days' in the *Union Journal* (an annual publication of the Student Union of the University of Hong Kong), 1988 issue, p. 39.

13. This interpretation is based on the analysis of the demise of the student movement in the 1980s in the article 'Those were the days', ibid., pp. 38-9.

14. Cheung and Louie, 'Social conflicts in Hong Kong, 1975–1986: trends and implications'.

15. Lui, 'The path of development of Hong Kong's popular movements'.

16. See Cheung and Louie, 'Social conflicts in Hong Kong, 1975–1986: trends and implications'; and Lui, 'The disintegration of Hong Kong's popular movements in a rapidly changing political environment'.
17. See Leung, 'Problems and changes in community politics' and 'Community participation: past, present, and future'; and Lui, 'The path of development of Hong Kong's popular movements'.
18. Ibid., p. 67.
19. Choi et al. *A common path to divergent destinations: Hong Kong student movement since the Sino-British negotiations*, p. 18.
20. Students' action of sending Margaret Thatcher an open letter triggered heated debates on college campuses. Ibid., pp. 18–20.
21. Ibid.
22. See for instance Chow's study, 'Welfare development in Hong Kong – an ideological appraisal', of the important role of social work graduates from Hong Kong's tertiary institutions in facilitating the formation, and shaping the ideology, of pressure groups in the 1970s. He observed that these young social workers attempted to put into practice the ideals of Fabian Socialism, which was the most favourable school of thinking taught in the social work schools of the two universities at the time. These ideals were equality, freedom and fellowship, and they prompted the social work graduates to promote the formation of voluntary agencies working for justice and equality in the community. These voluntary agencies — the most notable ones include the Hong Kong Christian Industrial Committee, the Society for Community Organization, and the Hong Kong People's Association for Public Housing — were branded by the government as pressure groups. Chow's study is pertinent to our discussion because many of the social work students and graduates were student movement leaders and activists.

Public Discourses and Collective Identities: Emergence of Women as a Collective Actor in the Women's Movement in Hong Kong[1]

Ching Kwan Lee

❏ The Women's Movement and the Politics of Identity

The 'new social movements' paradigm has drawn analytical attention towards what is called the 'politics of identity'. The women's movement, along with the gay and lesbian movement, the peace movement, the environmental movement, youth and countercultural movements, are the most frequently cited examples of identity politics. Although critics have challenged the idea of 'new social movements',[2] questioning the claimed 'novelty' in the form of collective action as well as the assumed distinction between identity and interest as basis for mobilization, almost all sociologists of social movements agree on the analytical and empirical significance of identity politics. Identity politics can be understood as politics either starting from or aiming at claimed identities of their protagonists, and 'politics' here includes the creation of new cultural codes, models and symbolic challenges, not just confrontation with the political system and effects on policies.[3] One way to grapple with the phenomenon of identity politics — explaining how collective identity is created by movement adherents, how grievances are constructed, how issues framing affects recruitment and how frames emerge out of collective action — is through analyses of public discourses. It is because these 'socially sustained discourses about who it is possible or appropriate or valuable to be inevitably shape the way we look at and constitute ourselves'.[4] Or as Jenson explains, the 'universe of political discourse' of a polity functions at any moment to set boundary to a community's political imagination and define the range of meaningful issues and legitimate actors. '[I]ts major impact is to inhibit or encourage the formation of new collective identities and / or reinforcement of older ones. Within a given universe of political discourse, only certain kinds of collective identities can be forged'.[5]

This theoretical perspective, which one writer has called the 'collective identity' approach, informs the discussion here.[6] I look at the women's movement of Hong Kong as a form of identity politics, and I trace the transformation of Hong Kong women's collective identities through analysing public discourses on selected women's issues.[7] These issues were pursued by women's groups and were discussed and contested by various social and political actors. A review of these key areas of struggles informs us as much about the ideal ends (identity) of women's groups as their instrumental objectives (interests). As a matter of fact, many historical examples of social movement defy dichotomous categorization into either interest-oriented or identity-oriented movements. Working class' wage struggles, for instance, entailed both types of ends in that wages were as much about maintaining social honour as preserving families and asserting independence in the face of the newly imposed factory regime. As Somers has observed, 'just as an adequate material life is an essential means of preserving normative relations, so cultural and symbolic relations provide material resources for livelihood.'[8]

The following discussion will map both (1) the agenda of policy reforms that were engaged in by women's groups and that had impact on women's material lives, and (2) the rhetoric of public discourses about these policies. In terms of concrete issues, the women's movement in Hong Kong has pushed for legal and institutional changes affecting different arenas of women's life. Hong Kong's 'feminist' agenda can be reflected in the following key concerns: reform of marriage law and the abolition of concubinage (1947 to 1970), equal pay for equal work (1950s to 1971), legalisation of abortion (1969 to 1981), maternity leave benefits (1979 to present), separate taxation (1981 to 1990), campaign for a Women's Commission and Women's Convention (1990s), and land inheritance right for women (1994). Overall, one can say that women's groups have quite a comprehensive range of concerns that in many ways were pursued by the women's movement elsewhere in the world.

In terms of rhetoric, public discourses about women's issues have, since the 1980s, largely shifted from a language of familial / maternal welfare and needs, to a language of women's rights and gender equality. My discussion here argues that when seen as a cultural phenomenon, the women's movement in Hong Kong has over the years created a new collective actor. Towards the 1990s,

'Hong Kong women' has emerged as a political actor with a collective identity based on women's gender, independent of and superseding their familial roles as wives or mothers, and their class membership as professionals or workers.

This chapter does not claim to present a comprehensive or exhaustive account of all the issues and discourses pertaining to women or women's movement in Hong Kong. Neither do I attempt to explain much about the socio-political setting out of which these discourses arose. These have to be done elsewhere. My purpose is more modest and selective. I aim at a thematic overview of a social movement analytically framed as a case of identity politics, with empirical gaps to be filled in by further collection of historical data. Research and data on women's groups in Hong Kong are scarce, but accounts of their history, organization and strategies are available in Yau et al., Tsang, and Cheung et al.[9] As a background to the following discussion, suffice it to say that the 1980s witnessed the emergence of a number of vocal and grass root women's groups. Prior to the 1980s, the women's movement in Hong Kong was largely the effort made by wives of Chinese elites or expatriate women, including those women founders of the Hong Kong Chinese Women's Club (since 1938), the Hong Kong Council of Women (since 1947) and other service-oriented groups like Zonta Club of Kowloon (since 1977). Then in the 1980s, more grass roots-oriented women's groups were formed, targeting different groups of local Chinese women as their constituencies, while at the same time joined forces with each other in various campaigns. Led by local Chinese women, the Association for the Advancement of Feminism, the Hong Kong Women Workers' Association, the Federation of Women's Centre, the Hong Kong Women Christian Council were among the leading forces which had made women's issues more visible and important on Hong Kong's public agenda.

❑ Issues and Discourses

Marriage Law Reform and the Abolition of Concubinage

This was the earliest and longest struggle waged by women's advocacy groups in Hong Kong. The campaign to reform marriage law, including the thorny issue of abolishing concubinage, started in the 1940s and ended with the passage of the Marriage Reform Bill by the Legislative Council in 1970. Women's groups, including the Hong Kong Council of Women, the Young Women's Christian Association and the Kowloon Women's Welfare Club, fought against opposition from reputable and well-known male Justices of Peace, Urban Councillors and Legislators. While women's groups argued for the abolition of concubinage on the grounds of family welfare and harmony, protection of concubines' children, the out-datedness of the custom, and equal rights for women, those in opposition to legislative reforms defended the practice of taking in concubines in terms of men's rights, protection for the weaker sex, family integration and the need to preserve Chinese customs. From a historical point of view, it was interesting to note that in these debates, family harmony and integration loomed so large that it had eclipsed the issue of women's equal rights as the ground for abolition of concubinage. At times, even women's groups and women leaders foregrounded the advantages of marriage law reform for the family and dependent children, and relegated to a secondary argument women's legal right to a monogamous marriage.

Before the 1970 Marriage Reform Ordinance, as many as six forms of marriage were legally accepted in Hong Kong.[10] Three of these six were most commonly found:

1. Chinese customary marriage was marriage contracted in accordance with the Chinese custom that existed and was recognized in 1843 in Ching Law, which, among other things, allowed men to take in concubines;
2. Chinese modern marriage or open marriage was marriage contracted in conformity with the 1930 Civil Code of the Nationalist Government of China, and did not allow for polygamy; and
3. registry marriage was contracted in accordance with Hong Kong's Marriage Ordinance and was monogamous in nature.

After World War II, the government decided to settle the chaos and confusion brought about by the coexistence of different forms of marriage. In 1953, the Strickland Committee published its report on various Chinese laws and customs. The scarcity of response from the public allowed the government to postpone any policy revision until the publication of the 1960 White Paper on Chinese Marriages and the McDouall-Heenan Report of 1965. Both reports were in response to steady demands made by the Hong Kong Council of Women and other organizations for the abolition of concubinage and for new marriage laws. The McDouall-Heenan Report contained the recommendations jointly submitted by the Attorney General, the Secretary for Chinese Affairs and the Chinese unofficial members of the Executive and Legislative councils, and was later endorsed by the Executive Council. Debates in Hong Kong were intensified during the sixties, coinciding with a series of related reforms in England, leading to the Marriage Reform Law in 1970. This law provided that after 7 October 1971, all marriages must be monogamous. It banned concubinage after that date and made registered marriage the only legal form of marriage in Hong Kong. The status and rights of concubines (and their children) lawfully taken before that date would be protected by law. In the two years after the passage of the Bill, a series of ordinances were enacted, giving legal protection to women in the family and children born out of wedlock: the Matrimonial Causes Ordinance (1972), Married Persons Status Ordinance (1971), the Matrimonial

Proceedings and Property Ordinance (1972), and Affiliation Proceeding Ordinance (1971).

The most prominent theme in this three-decade-long debate, subscribed to by both opponents and supporters of concubinage, was concubines' effect on the unity, harmony and happiness of the Chinese family. For instance, in 1968, the Kowloon Women's Welfare Club argued for the abolition of concubinage because 'it serves no purpose in a modern society and it is harmful, especially with respect to family happiness. Having a concubine in the family does not bring happiness and bliss.'[11] The Club suggested that if a husband had more than one wife, the multitude of conflicts between the principal wife and the concubine would condemn every member of the family to permanent hostility. Moreover, there was the argument that in the past women, lacking social status, were forced to become concubines. By then, in the 1960s, those who were still willing to be concubines were greedy women and if they were allowed into the family, they would probably harass the principal wife or persuade the husband to abandon the principal wife, thereby causing harm to the principal wife.[12]

Although Mrs Ellen Li, the most vocal feminist at that time, took pains to remind the public that marriage law reform was not just about eradication of concubinage, but was part of the project of gender equality and of protecting the legal right of women in marriage matters,[13] the Hong Kong Council of Women which she founded in 1947 argued for law changes also on the ground of family welfare. 'There were many detriments to happiness and a happy home because of concubinage... Many women had sought [our] help in connection with this matter. Some even had said that their husbands had threatened to leave home if their concubines were not accepted,' said Mrs R.T. Eng, chair of the Council, during a signature campaign to abolish concubinage.[14] Similarly, the Human Rights Council of Hong Kong advocated abolition, maintaining that 'as Hong Kong is becoming an industrialized society, if concubinage customs continue, family harmony will dissolve. Concubines and their children will cause tremendous economic and social problems'.[15] Similar opinions were voiced by the Hong Kong International Women's Association and in press commentaries of *Wah Kiu Yat Pao*, reflecting popular sentiments of the day.[16]

Interestingly, male opponents articulated their opposition to legal abolition of concubinage also on the ground of its effect on family unity. Chairmen of various Kai Fong Welfare Associations supported the new marriage law because they believed it could reduce avoidable family conflicts between the wives in inheritance matters.[17] Likewise, in his notorious speech at the Legislative Council debate on the Marriage Reform Bill in 1970, Legislative Councillor Mr Oswald Cheung doubted the superiority of monogamy in preserving marriage unions:

> Is this system of monogamy a complete success? Let me trouble you with
> some statistics. In the United Kingdom in 1968 there was one divorce for

roughly eight marriages celebrated in the United Kingdom that year. In the United States in 1967... there were two divorces for roughly seven marriages which were celebrated in that country in that year. To my mind that evidence suggests not that the system of monogamy as operated is a success...[18]

He went on to suggest that the welfare of concubines and children would be jeopardized by the Marriage Reform Bill:

...[W]hereas she [Mrs Ellen Li] would wish to protect the rights of one class of women, namely those fortunate enough to be principal wives, I would protect all women, including those that do not have the good fortune, who otherwise, if we pass this law, would be deprived of the opportunity of having an honorable and a recognized status.[19]

Opinions among business elites favoured the continuation of concubinage, justifying concubinage as a survival strategy resorted to by women without ability to earn an independent living.[20] Similar opinion along the line of 'protection for the weaker sex' was expressed in a public lecture given by an Urban Councillor and which aroused vehement emotions and outcry from women's groups. Mr P.S. Wu argued that concubinage protected women's interests because men would always maintain extramarital relations with or without legalized concubinage. Not only was this position unsupportive of gender equality, but it also began with the assumption that men's behaviour could not be bound or altered by law. His 'protection for the weaker sex' argument went like this:

If concubinage was abolished, and concubines were not recognized by law, would husbands be restrained from having extramarital unions? The answer was negative. They could not take in concubines but they could have mistresses or underground wives who did not enjoy any legal protection... Neither could their children enjoy legal protection and this often causes tragedy... If concubinage was not abolished, the welfare of these children would be protected... In Chinese societies in the past, the existence of concubinage did not damage society's morality. On the contrary, concubinage works to reduce men's unrestrained indulgence... If concubinage had no more raison d'etre, it would naturally die out.[21]

During these two decades of debate, women's right and gender equality before the law were overshadowed by another argument, besides the one about family harmony and unity. This was the argument against 'cultural imposition' implicit in laws which changed Chinese customary practices. This view found its first authoritative articulation in Sir Man-kam Lo's comments on the Strickland Committee report in 1953. Concubinage was 'an institution ... sanctioned by immemorial Chinese law and customs; it has been preserved by the Colony's Charter; it has received the highest judicial recognition...'[22] Up until the passage of the Marriage Reform Bill in 1970, civic leaders still questioned whether the government should force the Chinese to 'comply with the currently "accepted" laws elsewhere.'[23] Spokesmen of the Reform Club and the Joint Kaifong Research Council argued that 'the Government has no right to stop men having two wives if all parties are in agreement... The new Marriage Reform Bill is wrong, it is senseless to change a system that has existed for more than 2 000 years.'[24] Their views were echoed by Legislative Council member Mr Oswald Cheung, who questioned, '[I]s monogamy so manifestly a superior institution to the traditional Chinese institution of marriage that we should completely deny the right to people to opt out of it if they so wish? Are we right to force this institution upon the people who do not believe in it and who do not want it?' He further argued that the short history of monogamy law did not justify any 'tampering with an institution which has been held honorable for upwards of two thousand years'.[25] Yet some supporters for the Marriage Reform Bill retorted that one should only treasure good customs in the light of the prevalent and local circumstances. Legislative Councillor Wilson T.S. Wang argued:

> The Chinese customary marriage which this bill proposes to bring to an end could well be a good custom a century ago, under the old family structures and the way of life at that time. When slavery was a customary practice, the admission into the family as a new member on the status of a concubine was certainly regarded as one of a more charitable act... We had no need to jeer at the old customs practised at the old time, but what is important is that we must not fall into the habit of accepting any old Chinese custom as being equally fit for the present.[26]

The terms of the debate on concubinage and reform of marriage law were to resurface again in later public discourses about women's issues. The struggle for women's interests and rights was waged not primarily on the grounds of equal rights and gender equality, but also their roles as wives and mothers and their impact on the Chinese family. Moreover, the 'respect for Chinese culture and custom' argument was to return later to counter women's struggle in the 1990s for equal inheritance rights. The tension between the emerging claim by women's groups for universal right for all women based on the general principle of gender equality and opponents' argument for uniqueness of culture and tradition would continue for several decades and probably beyond the 1990s.

Equal Pay for Equal Work

The campaign to change the blatantly sexist government practice of paying female civil servants less than their male counterparts doing the same job at the same rank lasted for 20 years. The first petition asking for review of the salary scales for men and women officers came from the women members of the Chinese Civil Servants Association in 1948. Only in 1969, after many years of incessant mobilization by women's groups and professional associations, did the government finally find justification to adopt the principle of equal pay for equal work, without regard for sex or marital status. In the debates on this issue, the government staunchly defended an argument for differential pay by assuming women's accessibility to husband's financial support and their priority given to family over career. Working women were construed as a different category of employees due to their familial roles as wife and mother. Women's groups and professional associations criticized the government's stance for violating the principle of equality, undermining the status and efficiency of professional employees, and falling behind changes in England.

The salary system for civil servants in post-war Hong Kong was set by the 1947 Salaries Commission which established the practice that 'the remuneration of a woman officer should be approximately 80% of that of a male officer doing comparable work..., that the salary of a male officer should be sufficient under normal circumstances to enable him to support a wife and children and that a female officer will not normally have similar commitments.'[27] Moreover, while married men were entitled to higher rates of cost of living allowances than women and single men, women also suffered from inferior conditions of service. A single woman must retire on marriage and hence lost her status as a permanent and pensionable officer, although she might be reappointed immediately on temporary terms.

Despite the fact that the United Kingdom government had announced in 1955 the implementation of equal pay principle, to be fully realized over a seven years' period, and despite petition from the British Medical Association in 1957 urging the Hong Kong government to introduce equal pay for women medical officers, the Hong Kong government refused to make any changes and referred the question to the Platt Salaries Commission. In its 1959 report, the Commission recommended readjusting women's salary to be 75% of men's, except medical officers who should be paid equally for both sexes. It wrote that '[w]here there are such officers of full professional standing with equal qualifications and doing precisely the same work, we can well understand how unjust and galling a differential in emoluments must appear... The case of Medical Officers clearly comes in this category.'[28] For other non-professional women employees, the Commission found that '[t]heir standard of work may be high; but they cannot be considered of equal value with male officers of the same seniority, who intend to make their career in the Service and can be educated and trained to that end.'[29] These statements spoke volume about the government's persistent attitudes towards working women — no matter how well they performed, their familial roles as wife and mother overrode their work role and should thus be remunerated less than men.

The government adopted the Commission's recommendations and single women medical officers were the first group of women granted with equal pay as men. (Because only those medical doctors on pensionable terms of employment were included in the scheme, married women doctors received 75% of the scale salary.) But such initial changes prompted women's groups to action. Most active among these were the newly formed Association of Women Education Officers and the Association for Married Women Medical Officers. In response to these pressures, the Finance Committee approved a new salary scheme in 1961 which would gradually reduce the differentials for single women officers above a certain salary point, because once an officer passed that salary point, 'she [was] clearly a "career woman".'[30] This new scheme still excluded married women because the government defined them as 'occasional workers' as opposed to 'career workers'. The government's construction of female officers as 'maternal workers' was nowhere more explicit than in the 1962 *Report on Women's Salary Scales in the Public Service*, which stated that,

> The distinction between married and unmarried women is however considered clear-cut since a married woman has a legal claim on her husband to be maintained, whereas an unmarried woman has to maintain herself. Broadly speaking women officers can be divided into two groups: (a) Occasional Workers: Young women (local and overseas) join the Service on leaving school or university. They serve for a few years until they marry: some of them leave. Others continue to serve, their duties being interrupted by maternity leave, until family responsibilities become too pressing, when they resign... (b) Career Women: These are either women who do not marry, or married women whose marriage interferes very little with their duties... The great number of married officers fall into the former category.[31]

Countering this stereotypical views of female civil servants were arguments for equality between the sexes, especially on the grounds that they actually were as committed and career-oriented as men, or that women actually shouldered as much financial responsibility as men. For instance, the chairperson of the Hong Kong Chinese Civil Servants Association Nursing Sub-Committee clarified what their fight was about, 'We do not want to be equal with the man himself, we just don't see why we are not paid the same pay when we do the same work.'[32] The Association of Married Women Medical Officers also argued for equal pay because they were committed workers. 'We have been fighting for the slogan "Equal treatment for equal job" for more than ten years. Although statistically over 60 per cent of us have been in Government service for more than seven years and over 33 per cent more than ten years, yet we are still considered as temporary staff on a month-to-month employment basis.'[33] Elsewhere, the Reform Club supported equal pay for women because 'anyone who is treated unfairly will not try his or her best to work well.'[34] Arguing along similar line on work efficiency of married women, Urban Councillor Alison Bell suggested that married women should be paid the same as single men and women. She said,

Is marriage going to lessen her efficiency or her working hours? Perhaps one can say yes for 'six weeks' while she is granted maternity leave two or three times in the early years of her marriage, but apart from that the answer is surely no. In fact her efficiency may well be increased because she is a contented being and she is happy to rest at home in the evenings instead of 'gallivanting' out to dates, cinemas and dances and walks down lovers' lanes until the early hours of the morning.[35]

Therefore, obviously, even among supporters for equal pay, working women's work performance was considered inevitably tied to their family roles. The above quotation even implied that it was only when women were married would they be happy and efficient. In any case, both sides of the debate did not question the putatively specific nature of female workers and they differed only on whether the family factor exerted a positive or negative impact on women's efficiency.

Another popular argument for equal pay for women was parity with British and international practices. Yielding to mounting societal pressures, the 1965 Salaries Commission Report[36] finally stated that 'we do not consider that personal circumstances, in which are included the sex of the individual as well as his or her marital status and family obligations, provide grounds of principle for the establishment of more than one level of pay for the job.' The Hong Kong government announced in 1969 its plan to achieve equal pay for women civil servants but excluded teachers, nurses and social welfare workers. The Hong Kong Nurses Association petitioned to the Colonial Secretariat: 'Equal pay was granted to female nurses in the United Kingdom 15 years ago by raising the scales of female nurses to those of their male counterparts, and the women nurses of Hong Kong deserve no less, for we share with our colleagues in Great Britain the same code of professional ethics...'[37] The Young Women's Christian Association endorsed the claims of the nurses by noting that as part of a worldwide women's movement, it supported nurses' right to equal pay as other women government employees.[38] Male nurses came out to support female nurses' campaign based on the adverse effect on the professional status of nursing, when the government acceded to teachers' demand for equal pay and excluded nurses alone. As noted by the president of the Hong Kong Nurses Association, equal pay for women nurses had united the entire profession because 'it is the status of the profession that is at stake. If nursing loses its relativity in the pay structure its standing will go down.'[39] Eventually, after threatening strikes, and confronted with mounting pressure from various civil servant associations and international labour organizations, the government agreed to give equal pay to nurses in July 1970, bringing to an end a two-decade-long campaign for equal pay for women in government services.

In retrospect, what was noteworthy of the entire discourse about equal pay was the persistent and almost unquestioned construction of working women as a specific category of workers due to their familial roles. Gender equality *per se* was not the major ground on which the battle for equal pay was fought. Women had to convince the public and the government that they worked like their male counterparts and delivered equal efficiency, in spite of the fact that women did have their unique maternal responsibilities. The collective identity of Hong Kong women was still inextricably tied and confined to their maternity.

Abortion

In the United States, since the 1960s when the women's movement redefined abortion as a women's right issue, and not just a moral and professional control issue, feminists have persistently urged for further liberalization of the American abortion law. They have insisted that the availability of legal abortion realizes a woman's right to have control over her body, her sexuality and reproductive activities. Due to the intense passions and divisions generated by the abortion debate, among Americans in general and American women in particular, abortion has been accorded high priority on American feminist agenda.[40] In Hong Kong, the situation is quite different. Although reforms of the abortion law have intermittently stirred public emotions and controversies, in the period between 1969 to 1981, by and large, women's groups have not taken initiative towards further liberalization of the abortion law. One feminist activist suggested that this relative oblivion of abortion on Hong Kong's feminist agenda was related to the Chinese cultural aversion to talk about sexuality-related issues in public.

Priority of the abortion issue aside, a review of the development of the debate suggests that the discourse on abortion has seldom been framed as a women's right issue. Even among women leaders and activists of women's groups, when they argued for more relaxed abortion laws, the grounds they used were about the welfare of the family and children. These discussions largely construed women needing abortion as those who were victimized by crimes or by misfortune, or as poor mothers unable to support large families. Absent from the discourse was the idea that every woman, even under normal circumstances, should be entitled to the right of terminating a pregnancy she did not want.

Public debates on Hong Kong's abortion law were triggered in 1969 when the Hong Kong government rejected the plea of a 17-year-old rape victim to have a legal abortion. Prior to this case, the government had decided not to follow the reformed British abortion law enacted in 1967. The reason offered was that the change 'might be in conflict with traditional views on this subject in the community.'[41] With the avalanche of criticisms from civic leaders, social workers and legislators regarding the rigidity of the abortion law, the government finally agreed to introduce the Offences Against The Person (Amendment) Bill in 1972, which brought Hong Kong law into line with that in England. This bill provided that a pregnancy might be terminated on the advice of two medical practitioners that the continuance of the pregnancy would involve a greater risk to the life or physical or mental health of the woman than if the pregnancy were terminated. Prior to the introduction of this bill, it was an offence for anyone to attempt to procure a miscarriage. Consequently, a medical practitioner, having performed a therapeutic abortion, would be obliged to rely on the common law defence that the operation was carried out to save the life of the mother or to prevent her from being reduced to a physical or mental wreck. The common law defence left too much room for doubt as to the degree of risk to the mother's health which would justify an abortion. The bill was passed in 1972, reviewed and extended for another two years in 1974, and became statutory law in 1976. In 1981, the bill was further amended to allow for legal abortion when there is substantial risk that a child will be born with physical or mental abnormality, or where the mother-to-be is under 17, or where the pregnancy is the result of incest, rape or intercourse procured by threats, false pretences or drugs.[42]

From the beginning when this so-called 'Abortion Bill' was introduced, the Hong Kong government had emphasized that the objective of the bill was to reproduce the common law in statutory form with provisions that would clarify the circumstances for lawful medical practice, and that 'it does not generally legalize abortion.'[43] Officials also submitted to the public that the change was in response to the Medical Association of Hong Kong and the British Medical Association which asked that the law be clarified. The law 'is intended to do no more than protect doctors who undertake therapeutic abortions in specified circumstances in Government or approved hospitals or clinics.'[44] Supporters for law reform also did not have in mind the advancement of women's right. Social workers, for instance, asked that the government should give care, kindness and help to three classes of women: 'unmarried mothers who are jilted by their boyfriends, married mothers who cannot afford another baby, and girls who become pregnant after a rape attack'.[45] Civic leaders and legislators were concerned about the danger of 'back alley quacks' who performed abortions in unregistered clinics, causing many deaths.[46] Others pushed for legalized abortions so that 'family circumstances and the welfare of existing children could be taken into account'. Arguing on compassionate ground to support the passing of the bill, one legislator associated with the Tung Wah Hospital, a veteran charity establishment, told the Legislature that 'nothing grieved me more than to see sad faces in the maternity ward and to deal with cases of abandoned fatherless babies'. He appealed to the Council to cast a 'sympathetic eye on such victims.'[47]

Women activists likewise saw liberalized abortion law not so much as a safeguard for women's right but as assistance for 'hardship cases'. The leading 'feminist' of the day, Mrs Ellen Li, who founded the Hong Kong Council of Women in 1947 and was the first female member of the Legislative Council, took pains to clarify that she was not advocating 'free choice' in supporting the passing of the bill. Her argument clearly suggested that the language of right for women as individuals had not emerged in public discourses even among those most concerned with women's issues. The predominant imagery of Hong Kong women in this period was still framed in problematic and maternal terms. Her speech in the Legislative debate on the bill was illuminating of this dominant construction of women. The 'woman' Mrs Li had in mind when she argued in the following speeches in support for liberalized abortion law, was not any woman but was either a married mother or a helpless victim of misfortunes.

> [T]he woman herself should be given a chance to decide on her own destiny, not the husband or the mother-in-law, and certainly not a third unknown party in cases of rape. A determined mother who tried very hard but still failed to prevent an unwanted pregnancy should also be given a choice...
>
> ...an avenue of relief must also be provided for those unwanted pregnancies under circumstances beyond their control, such as temporary destitution, sudden illness, physical or mental, of a member of the family who needs special care, or rape. I would like to add here that I am not advocating 'free choice' for all who wish it but only the hardship cases recommended by a qualified social worker. Many may argue that certainly family planning methods should be the answer to all these problems, except rape. The more enlightened and better educated women have adopted this positive and preventive measure for years. It is those sections of the community who are ignorant, superstitious and poor who need our sympathy and consideration.[48]

Similar concern with poor women's welfare was expressed by the president of the Women's Welfare Club-West. The group supported legalized abortion, arguing that its lack would send poor women to charlatans for criminal abortion leaving them in a permanent physical and mental trauma.[49] Other leaders of women's groups urged for legal abortion as a means to control population. The president of the Hong Kong Council of Women maintained that since poverty caused by oversized families created a lot of unhappiness, there was great need for legalized abortion among underprivileged people.[50] One prominent female medical doctor, who was the medical adviser of the Family Planning Association, also favoured legalized abortion so as to reduce population growth rate. She warned that Hong Kong's birth rate was due to soar because so many young women were entering the child-bearing age. 'It is sad that there are a lot of unmarried women who are pregnant. We do not want to encourage promiscuity. We have to face the fact that this is a port and illegitimate births are increasing...'[51]

The abortion debate ebbed and waned throughout the 1970s. The main opponents were church groups, who argued that abortion amounted to murder.

The 'Pro-life Action Group' formed by Catholic organizations staged rallies to fight for the protection of birthright.[52] Public concerns were also directed at the increasing number of legal abortions which rose from 9 400 in 1980 to 14 800 in 1985. There were 76 under-16 abortions in 1980 and by 1984, the number soared to 142.[53]

Since the early 1980s when the abortion bill was further amended and relaxed, women's groups have reframed abortion as a women's right issue. The Hong Kong Council of Women applauded the liberalized abortion law in 1981, saying that women in Hong Kong had the right to choose.[54] The Association for the Advancement of Feminism went a step further to criticize the reformed bill as inadequate because it 'gives the right to registered doctors' and therefore, 'robs women of their rights over their bodies'. 'Since the results of an unwanted pregnancy finally weigh down on women, physically and mentally, we think that women should have the legal right to decide on the abortion.' The role of the doctor was to give advice and the final decision should rest with the woman, and 'the woman alone'. The Association urged the government to provide sufficient, cheap and safe abortion services so that women did not have to seek abortions across the border, in mainland China.[55]

In short, the 12-year-long abortion debate witnessed a transformation of discourse, from one that defined abortion as an issue about welfare of the family and the children to one of women's right. Along with this change was the replacement of the image of a problematic, underprivileged mother or young victim of crime with that of a woman claiming her right to control her body and reproduction.

Maternity Benefits Legislation

The drive to improve legal protection for working women's maternity benefits reached a zenith during the period 1978–81, when paid maternity leave was written into Hong Kong's Employment Ordinance. Yet, since the mid-1960s, unions, civic groups and women activists had already pleaded the government to introduce paid maternity leave for working women. By 1978, when concerted mobilization led by unions occurred, Hong Kong law entitled women to ten weeks of maternity leave without pay after working 26 weeks continuously for the same employer. The government's stance was that the conditions and terms of service conferring maternity benefits as opposed to protection should continue to be a matter of negotiation and agreement between employers and employees.[56] A 1978 survey carried out by the Hong Kong Christian Industrial Committee on maternity protection revealed how local provisions were notoriously behind international standards stated by the International Labour Organization, and that the overwhelming majority of women respondents in the survey wanted maternity leave to be paid leave. Twenty leading church, women and voluntary groups joined the efforts of the Committee to lobby for legislative reform. The government responded by setting up the Working Group on Maternity Leave whose proposal provided the blueprint for the Paid Maternity Leave Bill passed in 1981. This Bill provided for working women covered by the Employment Ordinance to get paid while on maternity leave for not less than two-third of their regular wage, provided that they do not have more than three surviving children and have worked continuously for the same employer for 40 weeks.[57] Throughout the 1980s, unions and women's groups had continuously pushed for changes that shortened the qualifying condition from 40 weeks to 26 weeks, closed the loopholes for employers to dismiss pregnant women staff, lengthened the maternity leave period (12 weeks instead of 10) with full pay, and for paternity leave.

As in the case of the abortion debate, seemingly straightforward 'women's issues' were not always defined in terms of the fundamental right of women. However, over the years, the grounds for supporting maternity benefits legislation have shifted from stressing maternity as a unique women's condition requiring protection and from stressing women's contribution as workers to the economic development of the territory, towards stressing women's right and men's paternal responsibility. The earlier construction of women as mothers with 'maternal instinct' and thus entitled to special treatments, a position which can be called 'familial feminism', was most apparent in the following comments by the leading 'feminist' Mrs Ellen Li. In urging for paid maternity leave for female civil servants in 1967, Mrs Li defined childbirth as a woman's natural duty, provided she did not give birth to more than two children. 'Mrs Li stressed that giving birth to two children was a woman's natural duty to the family, society and humanity. Therefore, she should be given postnatal leave, the length of which can be subjected to government's decision... More than two children could, however, be seen as an additional burden on society, and parents should be more responsible and consider family planning. In any case, a woman needs care after giving birth and it is not an excessive demand that she be paid at 50% of her regular wage during maternal leave for the third and fourth full-term pregnancies... In the past, female civil servants were entitled to maternity leave, on full pay, for their first four full-term pregnancies. That was too much of a benefit and would encourage over-reproduction...'[58]

Likewise, one of the two leading unions at that time, the Hong Kong and Kowloon Trades Union Council asked the government to provide working women with paid maternity leave legislation, so as to 'protect women's maternal instinct' and to improve the quality of 'human health and childrearing as emphasized by eugenicists'. The Union also argued for paid maternity leave as a means to encourage more women to work, so as to further boost industrial output and overall economic prosperity.[59] This reasoning, which linked maternity benefits with the performance of the economy, was also shared by employers. The Hong Kong Chamber of Commerce came out in support of the 1981 amendment of the Employment Ordinance on the grounds that 'since there is no labour shortage at present, we should improve the welfare for local workers and grant paid maternity leave to women.' One women's group, the Zonta Kowloon Club, expressed similar view that maternal benefits were a type of women's welfare. Other supporters of the amendment saw this as a way to improve labour relations and stabilize labour market mobility.[60]

When the Paid Maternity Bill was gazetted in 1981, controversy arose about the two-child limit for a woman to be qualified for the benefits. Church groups and unions objected to this limitation, criticizing the government's intention of using the policy to further family planning. It was then that the issue of human rights appeared in public discourse, with church organizations, labour groups and academics claiming that women had the right to bear more than two children and that the two-child limit might lead to social and legal discrimination against the third child, 'depriving him of his basic rights'.[61]

Among all the groups lobbying for maternity benefits, several women's groups had highlighted the issue as one of women's right, as well as the right of the family and the obligation of the community to protect women's maternity needs. Winifred Lamb of the Hong Kong Council of Women, for instance, emphasized that maternity leave was a family's right and it was not just a women's right or just financial assistance to low-income families, because all members of a pregnant woman's family would be affected by the pregnancy.[62] The Association for the Advancement of Feminism also argued along similar lines that paid maternity leave was a society's responsibility because society depended on women's reproduction for its own labour reproduction. The grounds for maternity provisions were not 'compassion' but collective responsibility.[63]

More recently, as women's groups and unions continued to push for longer periods of fully paid maternity leave, the issue has been redefined as one of gender, that is, one that relates to men. The newly formed (1989) Hong Kong Association of Women Workers has insisted on men's equal share of responsibility in childbirth and therefore should be given paternity leave.[64] Women's groups in new towns are particularly keen on urging for paternity leave, since most families in new towns like Tuen Mun are young couples lacking immediate kin support. Paternity leave was suggested as the solution to reduce family conflicts.[65]

Therefore, as in the abortion debate, the discourse on paid maternity leave was reconfigured from one of women's maternal needs and one of benefits to the family and children, to one of women's rights and men's equal share of responsibility.

Campaign for Separate Taxation

The issue of separate taxation for married women emerged in the early 1980s, when a professional and business women's group initiated and led what was to become a decade-long campaign to change Hong Kong's tax law regarding working wives. Compared with other debates that emerged in the 1960s and 1970s, the one on separate taxation saw women's groups propounding a discourse of women's legal right and individual legal status, terms that were markedly different from other lobbying groups in the campaign. While legislators, government officials and unions linked separate and joint taxation for married couples with issues about harmony of the family and marriage, administrative costs and benefits, monetary benefits to taxpayers and working women, women's motivation to work and labour shortages, women's groups argued for separate taxation on the grounds of women's 'equal legal status' and 'rights'.

Opposition against joint taxation for married couples was first started and led by a body of professional women known as the Ad Hoc Legal Committee, in 1982. The Committee was formed by representatives of such professional women's groups as the Financial Women's Association, the Hong Kong Association of University Women, the Hong Kong Federation of Women Lawyers, the Institute of Chartered Secretaries, Zonta, the Asian Women's Management Association, and the Hong Kong Association of Business and Professional Women. At the time of the campaign, the Inland Revenue Ordinance provided that husband and wife be taxed as a single unit. Section 10 of the Ordinance stated that 'the income of a wife, not being a wife living apart from her husband, shall be deemed to be income of the husband and shall be chargeable accordingly in his name.' Section 15b stated that 'a wife not being a wife living apart from her husband shall be deemed to be one and the same person as her husband.' Women's groups demanded that these two clauses be deleted from the taxation law and recommended that some kind of separate taxation system should replace the old system of joint returns and assessment. The government altered the taxation law in 1983 to allow married women to fill out separate forms of tax returns.[66] Married couples were still to be jointly assessed, though. Then in 1990, the Inland Revenue (Amendment) (No. 3) Bill 1989 provided that working husbands and wives should each receive a basic personal allowance and be charged salaries tax separately.[67]

From the very beginning of the campaign, public debates had variously framed the issue of separate taxation in ways other than that of gender equality before the law. For instance, all three Financial Secretaries who were in office during the course of the campaign objected to separate taxation because of its adverse effect on marriage and family in the local Chinese community. Although English law had allowed the option of separate or joint taxation for married couples since 1971, the Financial Secretary in 1983 declared that 'the adoption of a system of completely separate taxation for husbands and wives would represent a radical departure from our traditional concept of the family unit as the fiscal unit of charge. Hong Kong remains essentially a Chinese community where filial piety and family unity are an integral part of our existence. It would be unfortunate indeed if, in our endeavours to remove an alleged affront to one arguably small sector of our society, we succeeded in giving greater offence to the community at large.'[68] Using the same logic but reaching the opposite conclusion, some legislators and lobbying groups argued that joint taxation encouraged young people to cohabit. Joint taxation amounted to 'marriage tax' and therefore constituted an affront to the marriage system.[69] One Urban Councillor even maintained that joint taxation created a situation in which 'virtuous couples who are married lawfully will be punished with a heavier levy, while the wicked couples who live in sin will be rewarded with a smaller levy.'[70]

A more prominent theme of the debate on separate taxation was economics: its monetary benefits to the middle class, administrative burden to the government, and its implications for Hong Kong's labour market and economic growth. Besides professional women's groups, major support for separate taxation came from a range of pressure groups and unions representing the interests of civil servants, employees in public utilities, teachers and social workers. Members of these unions were the so-called 'sandwich class' who could benefit from a reformed tax system. According to a survey done by one of these unions, it was found that 62% of members polled paid higher taxes when they were taxed jointly with their spouses than if they were taxed separately.[71] The 35 000-strong Hong Kong Professional Teachers' Union calculated that a couple, both working as teachers and each earning a monthly salary of $6 190 in 1987, had to pay 40% more tax under joint taxation than they would under separate taxation.[72] A spokesman of this union also argued more generally that the sandwich class paid higher tax but received very few welfare benefits. 'They are not eligible for public housing nor home ownership scheme. At the same time, their expenses on home mortgage always take up half to 1/3 of their income... If we want to lessen their fiscal burden, we must adopt separate taxation.'[73] On the other hand, tax officials had their own calculations to do. They objected to separate taxation, the implementation of which would not only incur additional administrative costs for handling increased number of files, but would also cause a reduction of government revenue of about $400 million, calculated on the basis of 1986/87 levels of income.[74] This argument was rebutted by others who suggested that separate taxation would encourage more women to join the labour market. This would thus solve the labour shortage problem and create more taxpayers, boosting government revenue.[75] Finally, there were academics who related the separate taxation system as a global trend and joint taxation a hindrance to economic development.[76]

Finally, women's groups offered yet another framing of the issue of separate taxation. Although women's groups also argued on the grounds of real economic benefits and the assurance for women to keep confidentiality of their earnings,[77] most women's groups put on public agenda the clear message that taxation law was related to women's right and women's legal status as individuals. For them, it was about the principle of legal equality and an assertion of women's status as individuals, legally and financially. One of the earliest statements illustrating this position of professional women's groups can be found in their recommendation submitted to the Financial Secretary in 1982. Referring to Section 10 and Section 15b of the then Inland Revenue Ordinance, the Ad Hoc Legal Committee proclaimed that '[i]n the 20th century the concept[s] [that] a woman is not a person and that her income does not belong to herself are not acceptable... In the light of the conclusions from a survey of 20 countries it is clear that Sections 10 and 15b of Hong Kong's Inland Revenue Ordinance are highly anachronistic and do not reflect the equality of married women which is accorded to them in the fast paced and modern economy of the Hong Kong business world.'[78] Another women's group, the Women's Centre, also criticized the Inland Revenue Ordinance under which 'a wife's income is seen as part of the husband's... These unfair clauses mean a humiliation to the female sex, since they reduce married women to financial impotents and advocate the idea that men are the master of a household.'[79] Likewise, the Association for the Advancement of Feminism and the Hong Kong Council of Women called the taxation system discriminatory, unfair, unequitable because of its 'degrading and anachronistic' philosophy which denied women as independent units.[80] In one of its public statements on separate taxation, the Association for the Advancement of Feminism even defined the issue of married women's right to be taxed separately as a human right issue.[81] 'Therefore the struggle for couple's separate tax assessment does not only take into account of economics. It is also based on the principle of gender equality, to ensure that married women are not discriminated against in the present tax system.'[82]

Women's Commission and Women's Convention

The campaign to set up a women's commission and to adopt the International Convention for the Elimination of All Forms of Discrimination Against Women (CEDAW or the Women's Convention) is one of the most recent joint efforts of almost all women's groups in Hong Kong. A joint committee was formed by 18 women's groups in 1989 to collect data and compile a broadsheet on women's situation in Hong Kong. The committee started lobbying the support of the Legislature, issued public statements to urge the government to set up a working group to consider the establishment of a women's commission. The initial response of the government was negative, stating that there was no discrimination against women in Hong Kong. The Legislature was more sympathetic and an ad hoc group was set up in the Legislative Council in 1991 to consider the request. In December 1992, the Legislative Council even passed without dissent a motion calling on the government to extend the Women's Convention to Hong Kong. The government reacted by announcing the publication of a Green Paper to consult the views of the community on the issue, a move which was widely accused by women's groups as a delaying tactic.[83] Eventually, in mid-1994, when the overwhelming response to the Green Paper was to demand government action to ensure gender equality, the government agreed to extend the Women's Convention to Hong Kong, introduce a Sex Discrimination Bill and set up the Equal Opportunities Committee to oversee the enforcement of the Bill.[84] A coalition of 13 women's organizations continues to urge the government to enact more comprehensive anti-discrimination legislation which can address all forms of discrimination, like gender-related age discrimination in employment.[85] Meanwhile, the proposal for a women's commission seemed to have been sidestepped.

One of the most distinguishing features of this round of public debate on Hong Kong women was that women's groups no longer took a piecemeal, remedial approach to women's situations, often posed as problematic. Instead, these groups targeted the state and sought to establish a formal and permanent structure within the polity to deal with women's issues globally and integrally. The debate did not construe a particular group of women as suffering from specific problems needing temporary assistance, as in previous campaigns for legalized abortion and paid maternity leave. Rather, this campaign construed women as an interest group based on their shared gender. Gender defines women as a collective, political subject, separate from and transcending other social divisions like marital status, class, occupation and ethnicity. Gender defines a boundary for women as an interest group to claim legal rights. What was also interesting was that the rights which women's groups were most concerned about were largely economic in nature. Of lower priority to them were women's reproductive and political rights. The relative priority of these issues made interesting comparison with the experience of women's movements elsewhere and was reflective of the specificities of the Hong Kong society in the 1990s.

One prominent theme of the debate on a women's commission was whether 'women's issues' demanded separate treatment. The government opposed to the setting up of a women's commission on the grounds that it would overlap with the work of other advisory bodies already in place and there was no need for a separate women's commission. 'From our experience with youth committees, we've found that with committees dealing with a certain age group or gender, the work would duplicate that of existing advisory committees,' said one government official.[86] According to the government, women should not be viewed as an independent service target because their needs were inseparable from their familial and social roles and duties. On the other side of the debate, women's groups criticized such government stance as 'gender-blind'[87] and insisted not only that women's issues required interdepartmental efforts on the part of the government, but also that women's needs were special to their gender. For instance, women's situations and needs could not be adequately dealt with under the provisions of the Bill of Rights. The Bill regulated the relation between the state and the individual, not between private parties where most women found their rights being violated. Problems like rape, sexual assault, divorce, abortion, women's equal employment right, equal right to qualify for mortgages and child care were all women's special issues not directly protected by the Bill of Rights. Extension of the Women's Convention was supposed to address women's special needs.[88] By then, women were construed for the first time as a special social group that had needs different from other social groups.

Besides the argument that women constituted a distinct social and interest group, public discourses also construed women as a collectivity confronting discrimination and unfair treatments because of their gender. Gender inequality was put forth as a social reality that permeated different arenas of society in which women were unfairly subordinated. Women's groups published data and survey findings attesting to a wide range of gender discrimination: unequal pay, sexual harassment, offensive advertisements, unemployment for women over 30 in the service industry, lack of opportunities for those who were previously part of the manufacturing industry, inadequate child care facilities, etc.[89] Without an institutionalized structure, these women's groups found that the political system also discriminated women in that legislative reforms relating to women were always delayed. Women's groups cited their experience in past campaigns where their efforts were met with delay on the part of the government. 'For example, the Marriage Reform and related ordinances which established that marriages should be monogamous and registered, and that divorce should be based on mutual consent [were] only passed in 1971, almost 20 years after a Committee on Chinese Law and Custom set up by the Home Affairs Secretary recommended a review and reform of the antiquated Chinese Law of marriages in 1953. Similarly, although the Second Report of the Inland Revenue Ordinance Review Committee pointed out in 1967 that subjugating a woman's income as part of her husband's income was out of step with social development, separate taxation for married women was not adopted until 1989.'[90]

Out of a wide range of discriminatory and unfair practices against women, women's groups pressed hardest for changes relating to women's economic right and well-being. In the pamphlet published by the coalition campaigning for a women's commission, one woman's dilemma was described and intended as a composite portrait of a typical Hong Kong woman's problem in the 1990s. The story highlighted sexual discrimination in employment as the primary difficulty Hong Kong women encountered. 'Mei-fun's Dilemma' described a 30-year-old housewife with two children who decided to return to work. In the process, she came across discriminatory job advertisements and sexual harassment in the workplace. Her dilemma was whether to endure all kinds of humiliation imposed on her by her male superiors, or to complain about their misbehaviour and thereby risking her job and promotion opportunity.[91] Moreover, after the government agreed to introduce a Sex Discrimination Bill, the Hong Kong Coalition of Women's Organizations criticized the narrow scope covered by the Bill due to a narrow understanding of gender discrimination. According to the Coalition, age discrimination should also be considered gender-related discrimination based on women's employment experience. 'Often, women who are well qualified for a job are not even considered for it because they are over the age of 30 or 35. This discrimination is gender-related, not only because women are more likely to suffer from it, but because it arises from the sexist notion that women employees should be evaluated on the basis of their appearance rather than their qualifications.'[92] Concerns about the exclusion of women's equality in political right did not gain as much attention, although it had always been recognized that as many as one million women, in their role as full-time housewives, were disenfranchised from having a second vote because there was not a functional constituency for housewives. Political, as opposed to economic, discrimination against women obviously was accorded less priority on Hong Kong's feminist agenda.

New Territories (Exemption) Bill: Land Inheritance Right for Women

While the public was responding to the government's Green Paper on Equal Opportunities for Men and Women in the summer of 1993, the amendment of the New Territories (Exemption) Bill aroused another round of intense and emotional public debate which threw the issues of women's right and gender equality into sharp relief. The fierce opposition against granting women equal legal right to inherit land in the New Territories had the effect of vindicating women's groups' argument that gender equality was far from a *fait accompli* in Hong Kong. Yet, what was apparent was that the rhetoric of 'gender equality' had become the major frame of reference for public debate this time around. Although the amendment to the Bill was diversely construed as an issue of preserving the unity and cultural tradition of an indigenous community, or as a rural-urban conflict, or even a conspiracy of the colonial government, all parties in the debate pledged their support for the principle of gender equality.

At the centre of this maelstrom of protests and furious debates, which pitted women's groups and human rights groups against the clan associations of rural inhabitants, was a proposed amendment to alter the New Territories (Exemption) Bill by Christine Loh, a legislator. The New Territories Ordinance was enacted in 1905 to allow indigenous residents in the New Territories to preserve their custom of male-only land inheritance. Over the years, there were occasional criticism against the Ordinance which deprived women of their inheritance right. But it was only in 1993, after the press revealed that Home Ownership Scheme (HOS) flats in the New Territories were not exempt from the Ordinance, did the government take action and introduce an amendment to the Ordinance to exempt 'non-rural' land from the Ordinance. This would have the effect of granting non-indigenous women living in HOS flats equal inheritance right to the flats with men and with their urban counterparts. However, this amendment still did not address the issue of equal right and inheritance laws for rural women. Loh's proposed amendment in 1994 was to extend the scope of exemption to include 'rural land' as well, so as to allow rural women the equal right to inherit private land, except 'tso' and 'tong', which remained clan property. The indigenous community, led by Heung Yee Kuk, staunchly objected to Loh's amendment and protests were staged, to be met with those mobilized by women's groups from urban areas, indigenous women's groups, church and human rights groups. The media reported cases of indigenous women being pushed out of their family's properties which were seized by male successors in the clans.[93] Actions escalated on both sides: rural inhabitants waged a 'Preserve our Family and Clan Campaign', and 12 women's groups formed themselves into the Joint Committee for Equal Inheritance Right to lobby the support of legislators, political parties and government officials. Finally, in June 1994, the Legislative Council passed a government amendment to the Bill which specified that the Bill covered only rural land inheritance and not other land-related privileges (like the small-house policy and land for burial) of rural inhabitants.

From the start, the amendment drew strong reactions from villagers and the Heung Yee Kuk. They protested against the land rights bill as a serious threat to the unity and cultural tradition of their community. In their marches in downtown areas of Hong Kong, they shouted slogans including 'Against the British-Hong Kong Government' and 'Against ruining our villages and destroying our families'.[94] When the Kuk issued a statement accusing the government of supporting Loh's amendment, it compared the rights of New Territories residents with those of native Americans and other indigenous ethnic groups. It proclaimed that 'respecting and protecting the minorities' social structure, religion, their cultural traditions and their customs are the internationally accepted code of legislative standard. These customs should not be discarded off-handedly on the slogan of sexual equality.' The document further suggested that at issue was a conspiracy of the Governor to incite rural-urban conflict and to divert attention from dissatisfaction with the Governor's performance. 'The latest proposal is nothing but another of his deliberate attempts to incite a hitherto non-existent hostility between the urban and rural population... We will battle to the very end to protect our village, our clan, our way of life...'[95] The soundness of this argument was disputed by women's groups who suggested that the amendment covered only the inheritance of private property, not collective property of 'tso' and 'tong'. Moreover, since male inhabitants had much earlier started selling or renting their property to non-indigenous inhabitants, the clan nature of rural villages had already been transformed well before the introduction of the amendment. [96]

On the other side of the debate, women's groups from urban areas, the New Territories Women Indigenous Residents Committee, feminist legislators and human rights groups like the Movement Against Discrimination defined the issue as one of equal right for women in their mobilization for amendments to the New Territories (Exemption) Bill. The discourse of right was used by these groups to counter an alternative discourse of protection and care used by the rural inhabitants. A public statement by one of the leading women's groups in the campaign explicitly contrasted the two rationales. 'Representatives from the New Territories have emphasized that indigenous women have always been protected by tradition. They have argued that although women do not have the right to inherit land, their livelihood is guaranteed. Unmarried women have their fathers to take care of them. Married women can depend on their husbands. If their husbands die, their children will provide for their needs. Based on this fine tradition, it does not matter whether indigenous women have inheritance right or not... We object to this view completely for two reasons: firstly, depending on fathers, husbands and children is exactly what the 'three subordinations' teaches in feudal society and is a total opposite to the principle of independence for women... Secondly, based on the principle of equality, land inheritance right is the right of every indigenous inhabitant. If women inhabitants are not entitled to it because of their gender, it is blatant discrimination, something we cannot accept.'[97] Legislator Christine Loh also repeatedly stressed that amendment to the Bill was important not because it brought about equality in consequence to men and women, but because it brought about equality in opportunity to inherit land. 'What is important is the principle of equality... This amendment will have limited effect on their customs... A landowner in the New Territories could draw up a will, if he or she so wished, to pass on their land to male relatives only.' 'The idea of human right is that we have to protect every individual's basic right. Not to mention that there are 200 indigenous women complaining, even if there were only two of them, we as legislators still have the responsibility of ensuring their equal right before the law.'[98]

One church group supporting the amendment even accused rural inhabitants of exercising 'patriarchal hegemony'. When the indigenous community retorted Loh's amendment by saying that she did not understand the joy and satisfaction of indigenous women living harmoniously in their community, a Catholic group suggested that these women's consciousness was shaped by the patriarchal society they grew up in, so much so that they were not aware of their oppression. 'It is the result of patriarchal socialization. Even if they are not aware of the problem, it does not mean the situation is not problematic. Moreover, a harmony that conceals injustice is not one to be applauded.'[99]

Even rural inhabitants used the language of gender equality as a legitimate principle, although they saw the amendment as eroding men's equal right. One rural inhabitant wrote that '[a]s a member of the indigenous community, I am for the ideal of equality for men and women. Yet, I strongly object to the amendment because...when women marry, their families give them dowry which is a form of property succession. And when they get married, they naturally enjoy the property and resources of the husband's family... Therefore, the Chinese marriage system already protects them. Now if the Government further allows them to succeed property of their natal families, isn't this unfair to their brothers? ... The amendment to the existing New Territories Ordinance will only deprive male inhabitants of their equal right to inherit property with female inhabitants, and will therefore cause inequality and unfairness.'[100]

All in all, almost all parties in the debate pledged their support for the principle of gender equality and equal right for women. Some women's groups, political parties and legislators disagreed with Loh's 'methodology' or with the inadequate consultation by the government with rural inhabitants and Heung Yee Kuk. Therefore, there was proposal to amend the Intestates Estates Ordinance instead of the New Territories Ordinance so as not to provoke the New Territories people. Women's groups from the New Territories suggested that a Green Paper should be issued to allow more consultation with women and indigenous inhabitants.[101] Despite these dissenting opinions, the overwhelming theme of the debate was about women's right and equality. This unprecedented awareness of the gender issue among different sectors in the Hong Kong society was perhaps understandable. The Bill of Rights had just been passed in 1991 and the government had issued a Green Paper in 1993 soliciting the community's opinion on gender equality. The emergence of the land inheritance issue fit in squarely with the current public discourse while the staunch, and at times violent, objection of the indigenous inhabitants only heightened public attention towards the matter.

❏ Conclusion

In short, after decades of campaigning and struggles, 'gender equality', 'women's rights' and even 'women' have become terms that take on meanings in the popular imagination and the universe of political discourse. In this sense, Hong Kong's women's movement is a new social movement and a cultural phenomenon. This chapter has argued that the postwar women's movement in Hong Kong witnessed a transformation of women's collective identity, from one that construed women chiefly in their maternal and familial roles to one that emphasized the female gender *per se*. This transformation was comprised of and caused by the shift in public discourse on women's issues over the past four decades. Earlier debates[102] construed Hong Kong women as mothers, wives and a particular segment of the working or professional class, and legitimized women's claims in terms of maternal and familial welfare. However, recent debates[103] foregrounded gender equality and universal rights for all women, irrespective of their class and familial conditions. A new collective identity and agency, the 'Hong Kong women', had emerged by the end of the 1980s.

❏ Epilogue: Towards a Politics of Difference

After Hong Kong's return to China as a Special Administrative Region, the local women's movement finds itself in a new political terrain. Although this chapter has focused on the historical evolution of women's collective identity and has thus shifted away from analysing the political economy of the movement itself, the likely development of the former will depend on that of the latter, and a brief digression is in order. A politics of difference is lurking beneath the surface of the new collective identity. Diversity within the movement with women's groups targeting different groups as constituencies and adopting different organizational strategies is exacerbated by the external political terrain, where two major trends operate simultaneously. These are democratization and the impact of the China factor.

Feminist politics and theorization worldwide have increasingly turned to the issue of difference among women. There has been a widespread recognition of the multiple identities of women whose experiences and interests are differentiated by race, ethnicity, class, sexuality, age and citizenship.[104] In Hong Kong, this politics of difference will likely run along three fault lines: class, locality and political faction. From their experience of campaigning for different issues, movement activists were aware that there were class conflicts among women. For instance, in fighting for married women's choice for separate taxation, activists had found that separate taxation benefited middle-class women but not their working-class sisters. Likewise, responses of women's groups towards government policy on foreign domestic helpers divided along class line. 'Regarding the treatment of Filipino maids, there are different voices from women because some women objected discrimination against foreign labourers, while other women looked at the issue from the perspective of the employer and demanded more restrictions on domestics' freedom as contract labourers.'[105] Elsewhere, in a forum jointly participated by different women's groups, the issue of women's class-differentiated identities was raised. One representative of a women workers' group asked the organizers,

In designing this forum, have you considered grass roots women? Should our topic be restricted to those of interest to intellectual women or organizers? Should consciousness be raised only among a small group of women? It's not easy for grass roots women to participate in a public forum on a Saturday morning. Saturday morning is a holiday only for some women. Working-class women have kids to look after, and there is no child care facilities in City University... The way we talk, mingling English with Chinese, makes it difficult for them to feel engaged. How can women earning $4 000 a month feels she is understood by women earning $20–30 000? ... Long after unemployment had become a painful everyday problem for working-class women, did academics publish reports and ask why it was so!'

One representative from the organizers, a women's group with a more middle-class, educated membership, said,

The choice of venue for this forum is a matter of what this organization has at its disposal. Like other women's organizations, we do what we are good at. But there are common interests among all women, like women's entitlement to legal right or legislation against sex discrimination.

Besides class divisions, activists were also aware of localistic differences among women's groups. While some groups talked about their conscious effort to indigenize a social movement inspired by Western feminism, others detected localistic divisions between urban and rural women's groups. The Association for the Advancement of Feminism explicitly stated its goal of indigenization, meaning that it wanted to address local Chinese women's concern. One representative explained their silence on homosexuality as an adaptation to the values and concerns of local Chinese women. Fanny Cheung, a former member of the Hong Kong Council of Women (joined mostly by expatriate women) and the founder of the Women's Center, explained that the purpose of the Women's Center was to involve local Chinese grass roots women. The emphasis of the Center was on leadership by Chinese women and a 'community approach' to feminism that was different from Western feminism. This brand of feminism stressed the need to improve community resources to serve women and avoided polarizing women against men, as well as the militant image of bra-burning women in protest marches in the West.[106]

Beyond this local-and-foreign divide, rural women's groups had articulated their differences from urban women's groups. In an interview with an activist of a Tuen Mun women's organization, the interviewee found that the local communities in the New Territories were more conservative than those in urban areas, and therefore their organization had to cater to the concerns of a 'less progressive' constituency. She compared urban and rural women's groups, saying,

I think our goals are the same, as in improving women's situations and raising their social status. But we do have differences and priorities. For instance, sexual harassment is not much an issue for women in the New Territories. We have no experience with this problem and so we do not raise it as a public issue... Perhaps it's different in urban areas, among women in clerical work... Or about television commercials. They make it a big issue whereas we don't see why they need to go to that extreme... Or with paternity leave demand. We have asked some men in the New Territories about their views and they found it absurd that we would raise such an issue. The difference between us and them is that our community's thinking has not gone as far as they have. We go slower and behind.

Finally, women's groups tended to divide on their stance towards political parties and factions in the polity. Democratization has brought the women's movement closer to formal political processes, as nascent political parties lobbied their support in elections. By and large, women's groups welcomed this opening up of the political opportunity structure and they saw potential for alliance with pro-democracy factions. Indeed, they had lobbied the support of individual legislators who were more concerned with women's interests. Yet, some women's groups preferred to insulate the women's movement from formal politics, insisting that there was a need for an independent women's movement which could maintain autonomy from the state and the parties. They were particularly wary that the women's movement in Hong Kong would follow in the footsteps of those in state socialist countries, in which women's groups became absorbed into the mobilization machinery of the state. On the other hand, the Hong Kong Federation of Women, a 'pro-China' women's group, which was also a branch of the All-China Women's Federation, obviously saw much to learn from the Mainland women's movement. Many of the women leaders of the Federation were wives of powerful pro-China businessmen. Many other women's organizations worried that the Federation's connection to pro-Chinese interests and its political motivation would take precedence over women's interests.[107] How women's organizations will reposition themselves among contending political forces in the new political environment is an interesting issue for further research. Yet, these factional positions are likely to add a further dimension of difference to the women's movement in Hong Kong.

Notes

1. I was lucky to have the excellent research assistance of Leung Hui-tung, Cheung Pui-sze and Lee Wing-yan. They helped me to collect materials that were much more than what I could incorporate in this chapter. I am also grateful for the activists of the women's movement for participating in in-depth interviews. This research was funded by a direct grant from the Social Science and Educational Panel of the Chinese University of Hong Kong.
2. Calhoun, 'Social theory and the politics of identity'; and Somers, 'The narrative construction of identity'.

3. Melucci, 'Getting involved: identity and mobilization in social movements'.
4. Calhoun, 'Social theory and the politics of identity', p. 20.
5. Jenson, 'Changing discourse, changing agendas: political rights and reproductive policies in France', p. 65.
6. Stoecker, 'Community, movement, organization: the problem of identity convergence in collective action', pp. 111–2.
7. These (seven) issues are selected because they were among the major demands urged by women's groups. The reconstruction of the respective public discourses surrounding these issues is heavily constrained by the availability of news clippings and government reports.
8. Somers, 'The narrative construction of identity: a relational and network approach', p. 628.
9. Yau et al., 'Women's concern groups in Hong Kong'; Tsang, 'The women's movement at the crossroads'; and Cheung et al., 'The underdeveloped political potential of women in Hong Kong'.
10. Colonial Secretary of Hong Kong, *White Paper on Chinese marriages in Hong Kong,* p. 5.
11. *Wah Kiu Yat Pao,* 13 August 1968.
12. Ibid.
13. Ibid., 26 December 1958.
14. *South China Morning Post,* 5 July 1957.
15. *Wah Kiu Yat Pao,* date unknown.
16. For example, ibid., 12 February 1958 and 23 May 1970.
17. Ibid., 27 July 1969.
18. Hong Kong Hansard 1970, p. 736.
19. Ibid., p. 737.
20. *Wah Kiu Yat Pao,* 10 July 1961.
21. Ibid., 8 August 1968.
22. *South China Morning Post,* 20 November 1956.
23. Ibid., 19 July 1969.
24. *Star,* 19 June 1970.
25. Hong Kong Hansard 1970, pp. 735, 737.
26. Ibid., p. 734.
27. Colonial Secretary of Hong Kong, *Report on women's salary scales in the public service,* p. 1.
28. Hong Kong Salaries Commission, *Hong Kong Salaries Commission report,* chapter XIII, para. 267.
29. Ibid., para. 264.
30. Colonial Secretary of Hong Kong, *Report on women's salary scales in the public service,* p. 9.
31. Ibid., p. 12.
32. *South China Morning Post,* 27 July 1970.
33. Ibid., 3 November 1969.
34. *Wah Kiu Yat Pao,* 15 February 1965.
35. *South China Morning Post,* 7 July 1957.
36. Para. 99.
37. *South China Morning Post,* 1 June 1970.
38. Ibid., 13 June 1970.
39. Ibid., 2 July 1970.

40. Luker, *Abortion and the politics of motherhood*; and Diamond and Quinby, 'American feminism and the language of control'.
41. *Hong Kong Standard*, 28 August 1969.
42. *South China Morning Post*, 12 February 1981.
43. Ibid., 2 March 1972.
44. Public Records Office, Hong Kong government. Speech by AG in Legco on 1 March 1972.
45. *Star*, 11 January 1971.
46. Ibid., 18 January 1971.
47. *Hong Kong Standard*, 16 March 1972.
48. Public Records Office, speech by Mrs Ellen Li on 15 March 1972.
49. *South China Morning Post*, 28 February 1970.
50. *Star*, 5 July 1965.
51. *South China Morning Post*, 11 September 1971.
52. *Star*, 22 December 1972.
53. *Hong Kong Standard*, 11 February 1982; and *South China Morning Post*, 10 June 1986.
54. Ibid., 12 February 1981.
55. Ibid., 25 June 1986.
56. Ibid., 20 October 1978.
57. Ibid., 30 April 1981.
58. *Wah Kiu Yat Pao*, 3 April 1967.
59. Ibid., 17 May 1965.
60. Ibid., 6 February 1980.
61. *South China Morning Post*, 5 May 1980.
62. *Wah Kiu Yat Pao*, 18 August 1979.
63. Association for the Advancement of Feminism, *Annual report*, 1986–87, p. 27.
64. Hong Kong Association of Women Workers, *Bimonthly*, May 1992, p. 1.
65. *Tun Mun District Women's Association 1989 special report*.
66. *South China Morning Post*, 3 February 1983.
67. Ibid., 31 March 1990.
68. Ibid., 24 February 1983.
69. *Ming Pao Daily News*, 15 March 1987.
70. *Hong Kong Standard*, 15 January 1982.
71. *South China Morning Post*, 6 January 1988.
72. *Hong Kong Standard*, 9 November 1987.
73. *The Express*, 8 February 1988.
74. *South China Morning Post*, 12 February 1987.
75. *Ming Pao Daily News*, 25 January 1988.
76. Ibid., 24 January 1988.
77. *South China Morning Post*, 11 April 1987.
78. The Ad Hoc Legal Committee on Women's Issues, pp. 3–4 of 'A comparative survey of the taxation of married women in twenty jurisdictions and recommendations for amendments to the inland revenue ordinance of Hong Kong', 1982.
79. *Women's Centre News* 6 (June 1988).
80. Ibid., 1 August 1989; and *Hong Kong Standard*, 2 March 1988.
81. Association for the Advancement of Feminism, *Annual report*, 1988–90, p. 43.
82. Ibid., p. 35.
83. *Hong Kong Standard*, 17 December 1992.

84. *Ming Pao Daily News*, 4 June 1994.
85. *South China Morning Post*, 6 May 1995.
86. Ibid., 1 September 1992.
87. Ibid.
88. *A women's commission for Hong Kong: the campaign for a women's commission and for the application of CEDAW*.
89. *South China Morning Post*, 13 December 1992.
90. *A women's commission for Hong Kong: the campaign for a women's commission and for the application of CEDAW*, pp. 5–6.
91. Ibid., pp. 3–4.
92. *South China Morning Post*, 6 May 1995.
93. *Ming Pao Daily News*, 17 March 1994, 7 October 1993 and 16 August 1993.
94. *South China Morning Post*, 9 May 1994.
95. Ibid., 10 May 1994.
96. *Ming Pao Daily News*, 30 March 1994.
97. Ibid., 4 May 1994.
98. *South China Morning Post*, 7 May 1994; *Ming Pao Daily News*, 30 March 1994.
99. Ibid., 29 March 1994.
100. *Ta Kung Pao*, 5 April 1994.
101. Ibid., 22 June 1994.
102. For example, abolition of concubinage, equal pay for equal work, abortion, and separate taxation.
103. For example, women's commission, adoption of CEDEW, and land inheritance right for indigenous women.
104. For example, Farganis, *Situating feminism: from thought to action*; and Mohanty, 'Feminist encounters: locating the politics of experience'.
105. Chan, 'The local women's movement and the women's perspective of new feminism', p. 87.
106. Cheung, 'The women's center: a community approach to feminism in Hong Kong'.
107. *Eastern Express*, 4 February 1994.

Greening of Hong Kong? — Forms of Manifestation of Environmental Movements

On Kwok Lai

❑ Introduction

Environmental movements and their discourse on society and politics have been controversial in many ways. They are not just about how and what the state or the people should do to the degraded environment, but also about the competing ways of governance over the natural world.[1] This chapter examines different forms of environmental movements, focusing on the case of Hong Kong where these differences are manifested.

Before examining the specificity of Hong Kong's environmental movements, two phenomena are identified for the formulation of our research questions. First, social mobilization on environmental issues is infrequent in Hong Kong and is not very visible in terms of media coverage.[2] This might be due to the fact that, compared to their counterparts in other developed countries, local environmental non-governmental organizations (NGOs)[3] have rarely opted for confrontational social protest strategies on environmental issues.[4] Second, local environmental NGOs have had a contribution to the ideological basis of environmental movements in Hong Kong,[5] but most of the environmental protests are articulated at a local level by community groups.[6] The limited involvement of environmental NGOs in community environmental disputes perhaps reflects not only the political opportunities available to them, but also their self-definitions regarding the handling of environmental issues. The important questions are: Why do the environmental NGOs choose such an approach? How do they perceive their role in the environmental movement? And what is the opportunity structure in which they are situated?

In examining the environmental NGOs' acquiescence in community-specific and territory-wide environmental problems, this chapter highlights the differentiated modes of environmental movements and their manifestations in Hong Kong. More specifically, I examine the context and opportunity structure of environmental movements, from the mid-1980s to the early 1990s. In addition, I argue that environmental NGOs' strategic actions are institutionally defined and opportunity-driven.

In the following section, I will outline two main differing forms of socio-political articulation and manifestations of environmentalism, namely, the social mobilization and the lifestyle approaches. These correspond respectively to the *antagonistic* and *consensual* manifestations of environmental movements. Then the antagonistic approach of environmentalism will be illustrated by the not-in-my-backyard (NIMBY) protests on Tsing Yi Island, the anti-Daya Bay Nuclear Plant movement, and the not-in-anybody's-backyard (NIABY) movements against the development in Sha Lo Tung and Nam Sang Wai. The consensual manifestation of environmental movements will then be discussed with reference to state and corporate sponsorships of environmental education programmes, followed by a synoptic account of the emergence of a local environmental NGO (Green Power). The analysis attempts to highlight the transformation process of environmental movements and to map the contours of environmentalism in Hong Kong. This chapter ends with a brief discussion on the development of environmental movements in a new political environment after 1997.[7]

❏ Environmental Movements: Between Collective Action and Lifestyle

The concept of *environmentalism* has been associated with different forms of collective action. These range from social protests characterized by NIMBY and NIABY, to the individually tailor-made green consumerism.[8] To understand the complexity, studies of the new social movements (NSMs) highlight the distinctiveness of environmental movements which are different from the so-called 'old' social movements, e.g. the labour movement. It has been argued that the underlying dynamics, extent and specificity of the NSMs are beyond the confines of class and self-interested politics.[9] More specifically, *green* politics has different sets of praxis-related knowledge and strategies for non-class-specific and non-self-interest-based form(s) of political mobilization, reflecting the significant changes in the state-society relationship within a post-materialistic society.[10] In environmental movements, individuals and groups involved are exposed to more different interpretations of and choices of collective action.[11]

The influences of global environmentalism and their manifestations are far-reaching in many ways. They have been extended to the domains of production, consumption, health and quality of life. On the one hand, the elaboration and interpretation of environmentalism have strong implications for the movement's ideology formation, strategy adoption, organizational form and scope of activities.[12] On the other hand, culturally and ethnically specific interpretations of the synergy of nature, culture and people also shape the contours of environmental movements in the local context.[13] The different manifestations of environmentalism and environmental movements are developed in two key ways. These are the *hard* approach of conflictual NIMBY and NIABY, and the *soft* approach of environmental education and green lifestyles. Methodologically, the distinction between the *hard* and *soft* approaches towards environmentalism lies in the specific forms of manifestation of the movements. The distinction also enables us to examine how environmental concepts are translated into praxis, which in turn appears as environmental movements in the public sphere. Before moving to the empirical analysis, however, a brief overview of the Hong Kong development model is necessary.

❑ Development Without Environmental Considerations — Hong Kong as a Colony

Without long-term planning for resource conservation, Hong Kong represented a classic case of colonial (non)governance of the natural environment, juxtaposed embarrassingly with its economic miracle in the last two decades. As a place with ever-increasing physical construction, the natural environment had been destroyed without any regret from the government.

For the colonial government, urban planning and environmental protection policy initiatives had been developed in a belated way. In most cases, internal initiatives came as a result of the goodwill of past governors Sir Murray McLehose and Lord David Wilson. Externally, Hong Kong was bound to fulfil the requirements of international environment covenants signed by the United Kingdom. Still, Hong Kong's development had been pursued at the expense of the natural habitat. More specifically, engineering, rather than conservation, was the modal environmental protection initiative in the colony. An example of this engineering approach to environmental protection was the Strategic Sewage Disposal Scheme, costing over $10 billion for its construction and operation.[14] In spite of the last-ditch environmental policy initiatives put forward by the colonial government, environmental problems brought about by Hong Kong's economic success had never been fully addressed in policy terms, nor were they on the political agenda of the colonial governance. The first policy paper on environmental protection, *White Paper — Pollution in Hong Kong — A Time to Act*, was published in 1989, following the establishment of the Environmental Protection Department in 1986.[15]

Within the local community, despite belated governmental initiatives, the environmental NGOs' promotion of environmental concerns has become important in the last decade.[16] Yet the environmental NGOs have had difficulties in mobilizing local people to participate in the movement, as their members are mostly from the educated, the upper social stratum and the expatriate community.[17] In other words, environmental consciousness is mainly confined to a selection of social groups in Hong Kong. This is different from the wider appeal of post-materialistic values in Western developed economies.[18]

Due to the fact that environmental conflicts accounted for only a small number of social protests in Hong Kong, they had not been adequately covered in the local media. With the exception of the anti-Daya Bay Nuclear Plant movement (see below), environmental issues had rarely attracted mass media and public attention in the 1980s. A recent study revealed that environmental issues accounted for only 6.2% of all 1 719 identified social conflict issues that appeared in a major newspaper (*Ming Pao Daily News*) for the period 1980 to 1991.[19] In the same study, it was shown, out of a total of 106 identified environmental issue reports, most of them were about community/locality-specific environmental problems (75.5%), followed by territory-wide environmental issues (13.2%) and interest group-specific demands (11.3%). Over time, the occurrence of these social conflicts on environmental affairs seemed to have increased: from 2 issues in 1980 to a peak of 22 cases in 1988, then dropping to 10 in 1989 and later rebounding to 12 and 18 in 1990 and 1991 respectively. In short, environmental protection *per se* received little attention from the government and the local community.

❏ The Antagonistic Manifestation of Environmental Movements

Environmental movements have taken many forms. Their trajectories of development are contingent upon the socio-political constellation of the movements' actors and agencies, and their organizational attributes. For illustrative purpose, all collective actions on environmental affairs can loosely (in the sense of Weberian ideal type) be classified into two distinct modal manifestations, namely, those where conflicting actors/organizations and their counterparts are identifiable — the *antagonistic* manifestation, and those mobilization initiatives in which the involved parties are positioned as if they were not antagonistic (i.e. not in a zero-sum game situation) — the *consensus* manifestation. In order to provide a framework of analysis, I will briefly address the distinction between the antagonistic and consensus modes of environmental movements.

In the antagonistic mode of environmental movement, two modal mobilizations can be further distinguished, namely, the NIMBY mode in which the mobilization is carried out by or for the victims of the site-specific environmental pollution, and the NIABY mode where the third party (those people who have no direct interest in the issue) is the principal initiator of the movement. This distinction between NIMBY and NIABY is important for our study, as they represent two different modes of collective mobilization logic.[20] In the NIMBY type of social mobilization, because they are more locality-specific and the victims can be easily identified, the movements tend to have more involvement from residents of the neighbourhood. They are characterized by mobilizations around the 'avoidance' of a particular polluting or hazardous installation, and/or compensation issues. In contrast, the NIABY type of environmental movements tend to have more participation from 'other outsiders' who are not being victimized nor have a direct interest in the environmental struggle. Rather, nature as such is the prime victim. Therefore, their appeals might be justified in terms of environmental justice and ecological rights.

With reference to the distinction between NIMBY and NIABY, and the site of the environmental issues, the following schematic illustration highlights the different types of societal mobilization for this study:

Mode of Antagonistic Societal Mobilization	Distinction Between Natural Habitat and Built-environment	
	Built-environment	Natural Habitat
Self-Interested NIMBY (victim identity of the people affected and the quest for policy response) Non-Self-Interested NIABY (natural habitat as the victim and the quest for environmental justice)	Siting of hazardous industries — the case of Tsing Yi — Daya Bay Nuclear Plant	— protecting nature for personal consumption or appreciation of nature — property right over use of natural land
	Politics of production — anti-nuclear movement	Protection of wetland — anti-Nam Sang Wai (Mai Po) development — against Sha Lo Tung golf-course

To highlight the different manifestations of environmental movements in Hong Kong, the four case studies below, of social mobilization for environmental protection, will specify the different *modi operandi* and their context: the NIMBY cases of Tsing Yi Island and Daya Bay Nuclear Plant; the NIABY cases of the Sha Lo Tung golf-course development and the Nam Sang Wai (in Mai Po Marshes) development project.

The Not-In-My-Backyard Mode

Two NIMBY protest movements are reported here, including the struggles for the relocation of hazardous industries on Tsing Yi Island and the anti-Daya Bay Nuclear Plant campaign, which are examples of the community environmental protest and territory-wide social mobilization respectively.

The Location of Hazardous Industries on Tsing Yi Island

Tsing Yi Island was originally a fishing village and first developed as a hazardous industries centre in the mid-1960s. It then further developed into a new town, with a population of less than 70 000 in 1980 but increased to more than 200 000 in 1995. The contradictory land use between the hazardous industries and the residential settlement was quite obvious, as highlighted in a confidential government report, *Hazard Potential Consultancy Study* completed in 1982, and another report published in 1989.[21] Here, the potentially hazardous and the contradictory land use patterns provided the context for citizens' NIMBY protests.[22]

The proximity of environmentally hazardous installations, ranging from petrochemical installations to chemical engineering industries, to residential development was and still is the major source of controversy in Tsing Yi Island's development. For instance, the most controversial case was the proximity of the private residential blocks of Mayfair Garden to the Mobil oil depot which was only 50 metres away. The depot stored inflammable petroleum products and liquefied petroleum gas. Tsing Yi's hazardous installations were predominant on the Kwai Tsing District Board (KTDB) meeting agenda for the period 1985 to 1991. In 1983, the leakage to the Tsing Yi Concern Group (TYCG) of the confidential *Hazard Potential Consultancy Study*[23] on the risks to and hazardous exposure of the community served as a catalyst for environmental protests calling for the relocation of hazardous industries on Tsing Yi Island. The protest movement was also reinforced by the concern over chemical disasters in Mexico City in November 1984 and the poison gas leakage of Union Carbide's Bhopal (India) plant in December 1984. The environmental protests lasted for more than a decade and the characteristics of this movement are presented in the following schematic illustration:

Table 1: The Main Characteristics of Environmental Issues on Tsing Yi Island[1]

Period	Major Event	Functions of TYCG	Strategies of TYCG	Goals of TYCG	Governmental Responses
Movement's formation stage (1983–85)	Disclosure of Tsing Yi Hazard Potential Report Mexico Incident Formation of TYCG Involvement in District Board (DB) election and politics	Formation of political will for social actions Put risk issue in context Core leadership formed with social activists' involvement Put issue/candidate on DB agenda and election One TYCG member elected as DB member	Mobilizing residents' consensus Media conference Internal consolidation of core leadership Politicize the issues, via surveys, petitions, exhibitions, etc. External recognition of TYCG — as agency of legitimated speaking right	Encourage participation for consensus Right to know about the risks Have organizational weapon for politicking Formation and consolidation of demands for environmental safety Make the Tsing Yi case visible in media and politics	Government's assurance on safety Set up governmental working group, but refuse to reassess hazardous installations Stop Phase III of Mayfair Garden development Administratively counteracting via propaganda assuring safety
Environmental issues articulation (1986–88)	Relocation of two more oil depots onto Tsing Yi District Board and Town Planning Board's consideration on future development of Tsing Yi District Board Election	Organizing residents and their organizations Advocating change of land use, institutional as well as non-institutional politicking Two TYCG members elected as DB members	Targeting those elected/administrative officials, for change of land use Mobilization via opinion surveys, signature campaigns, petitions, press conferences, demonstrations, and lobbying	Opposition to two oil depots re-siting onto Tsing Yi Formation of Alliance with other potest groups Promote participation and people empowerment	Counteractions from government and their appointed bodies Two more oil depots moved onto Tsing Yi (with conditions) Government started to reassess the hazardous installations in Tsing Yi

Table 1 continued

Period	Major Event	Functions of TYCG	Strategies of TYCG	Goals of TYCG	Governmental Responses
Movement's Maturity Stage (1989–91)	Gas leakage near residential block	Crisis intervention	Militant actions: mass rally, three-day sleep-in petitions, blocking oil depot entrances	Relocation of Mobil and Hong Kong Oil depots away from Mayfair Gardens	Government admitted fault in land use planning
	Town Planning Board and the Executive Council to review on Tsing Yi Hazardous Installation and Contingency Plan	Advocacy for govenmental crisis management/ contingency plan		Reducing the level of risks in Tsing Yi	The 2nd Report of hazardous potential in Tsing Yi released to the public
		Educator and enabler for other NIMBY protests	Extending and strengtheing local and territory networks for crisis management on hazardous installations	Governmental initiative for policy on hazardous installations, contingency plan, etc.	Plan to move three oil depots from residential areas, yet to other parts of Tsing Yi
	KTDB politics and election	Four TYCG members elected to KTDB			

The principal agency of social mobilization on Tsing Yi Island was the TYCG. It was formed in 1983 by a group of community workers to promote grass roots participation in solving community problems. They were prepared to use radical and confrontational community organization strategies, such as protests and demonstrations, to challenge the government.[24] In these protests, community workers played a significant role in the internal operation of the protest group, alongside the media's positive coverage of the protests. Retrospectively speaking, the Tsing Yi mobilization against hazardous installations could be interpreted as an extension of the community's grass roots (for instance, housing) protests in the same period.

The Tsing Yi case highlights four major characteristics of the environmental movements. First and foremost, it was a community and site-/location-specific NIMBY protest movement against the colonial land use planning which did not involve citizens' participation. Since the colonial planning was in favour of corporate interests rather than residents', the TYCG addressed their grievances by petitioning on the streets or appealing through news media. What the TYCG had done in their community organization was in fact quite similar to housing protest groups' mobilization in the 1980s. Second, it was a prototype of the community-based environmental protests in Hong Kong.[25] The TYCG set its own course of action, and it was not supported by the established environmental NGOs nor had their endorsement. At the very least, we cannot find any evidence of their sharing expertise and organizational resources. In other words, the TYCG had to work on their own in their community, engaging in environmental politics with the KTDB and the Town Planning Board. Apparently, there was little networking between community groups and the established environmental NGOs.

Third and following from above, it is quite obvious that this protest movement was considered by established environmental groups to be 'isolated' and self-interested. Because of the view held by the established environmental NGOs on the Tsing Yi case, the protest movement had not enhanced solidarity among environmentalists. This distance between the TYCG and the established environmental NGOs is reflected by this comment from an environmentalist:

> It is fine for the TYCG to have such a strong organizational weapon and continual challenging of the government's decision on land use planning in Tsing Yi, but it's their business [to fight for Tsing Yi's interest]! We don't care much about them, as we [our environmental NGO] want to achieve something different, at least not focusing on self-interested NIMBY [dirty] politics but more on the global issues... Even if we think we should be involved in these protests, I doubt we have those skills to work with the grass roots; in short, it's not our case![26]

Last but not least, the Tsing Yi environmental movement resembles a classic case of the institutionalization of a protest movement, once social activists are involved in local politics. There were some instances of success when the protest movement facilitated some TYCG leaders to become elected KTDB members in the 1985, 1988 and 1991 District Board elections. With their leaders' active participation on the KTDB, backed by confrontational protests, the movement had successfully channelled their grievances to the District Board for hearing and debate. But the limited consultative authority of the District Board had rarely changed the land use of Tsing Yi under the corporatist arrangement of the colonial government.[27] In retrospect, direct involvement in electoral politics had indeed undermined the solidarity of the Tsing Yi protest movement. The involvement of the TYCG in local electoral politics, between 1991 and 1995, generated internal tensions and conflicts. One obvious case was that these conflicts produced a crisis for the TYCG which resulted in the expulsion of some prominent leaders and active members. Those defiant leaders and members later formed the competing Tsing Yi Action Group.

The Anti-Daya Bay Nuclear Plant Campaign

The Daya Bay Nuclear Plant, a joint venture project undertaken by the People's Republic of China (PRC) government and the China Light & Power Co. Ltd. (CLP) in Hong Kong, was aimed to supply electricity to southern Guangdong in the mid-1980s. Because of the risks of nuclear energy, it was the target of the local anti-nuclear movement. The anti-Daya Bay Nuclear Plant campaign was one of the most controversial sagas in the last decade. The campaign reflected many contradictions between Hong Kong and the PRC in their different ways of governance. The controversy was developed under the shadow of the uncertainty of Hong Kong's political future — the problematic drafting process in 1986 of the Basic Law for the Hong Kong Special Administrative Region. The nuclear accidents at Chernobyl in April 1986 also changed people's view on nuclear energy,[28] reinforcing people's critical attitude towards nuclear energy.

The debate was triggered by the uncertainties over the safety of nuclear energy and a generalized doubt regarding the PRC's capability to manage nuclear installations. The environmental NGOs and social activists questioned the necessity for building such a small (in terms of generation capacity) and risky plant near (less than 50km from) Hong Kong. Later, the controversy turned into a polarized and antagonistic mode of political mobilization between the pro-Daya Bay camp of conservatives and business interests, and their opponents, namely environmental NGOs, veteran social activists and environmentally sensitive middle-class liberals. Confrontation and antagonism between the two camps were further reinforced by debates between different segments of the mass media which aligned to different camps.[29]

In the pro-Daya Bay camp, those PRC-oriented conservatives counteracted the environmental protest by emphasizing the patriotic, economic and technological justifications:

> The leftist papers [pro-PRC newspapers] publicized pro-Daya Bay statements by prominent Chinese scholars such as Nobel Laureate physicist Yang Zhen Ning, assured Hong Kong's population that China's nuclear experts were competent and recommended local people to approach the issue with greater calmness and common sense.[30]

In line with the NIMBY protest movement, many politically charged scientific arguments and evidences had been presented. But the pro-Daya Bay arguments could not fully alleviate the community concerns over the safety and risk of the plant:

> the anti-Daya Bay press argued that the effects of a serious accident at Daya Bay would be politically and economically unacceptable. The harbor,

food and water as well as manufactured products would be contaminated by fall-out from the nuclear power plant site. All escape routes for the five-and-a-half million Hong Kong residents would not lead away from Daya Bay but towards it.[31]

More problematic was the fact that both the pro-Daya Bay camp and the colonial administration had not come up with any contingency plan to cope with possible accidents. This had prolonged and intensified the anti-Daya Bay sentiments among people.

Eventually, the mobilization against the Daya Bay Nuclear Plant solicited over one million signatures. This not only indicated the extent of popular outrage against the construction of the plant, but perhaps also reflected the acceptance of the (controversial) leadership of the Joint Conference for Shelving the Daya Bay Nuclear Plant which consisted of 107 local pressure and community groups. In actuality, the Joint Conference was an amalgamation of most of the pressure and community groups of the late 1970s and early 1980s, plus those newly elected politicians (in the District Board election in 1985 and the Urban and Regional Council elections in 1986) who were eager to try out their mandated role as people's representatives. The political challenge of the Joint Conference against the colonial regime and the Chinese government was quite obvious. Although one million signatures did not necessarily amount to very active support by one million people, the extent of popular support for the campaign could not be underestimated.[32]

The Daya Bay issue had two underlying political appeals. First, it was an environmental NIMBY protest movement seeking citizens' participation in the planning of hazardous industries. In the 1980s, people were becoming more environmentally sensitive towards such hazardous installations. This phenomenon could be attributed to the increased coverage of disastrous events by the mass media on the one hand, and the experience of social movement groups in employing confrontational strategies, on the other. Second, there was also a 'lack of confidence' on the part of many Hong Kong citizens regarding the way in which authoritarian scientificism operated in the PRC. The political tensions built up in the mobilization process had further exacerbated the controversies over the project. Historically, this environmental protest movement was the first encounter between the civic forces of Hong Kong and the authoritarian state of the PRC over governance issues affecting Hong Kong. The movement established a strong alliance among a wider range of social activists and community organizations.

The movement was strongly counteracted by CLP's media and public relations campaign and by the explicit endorsement of the nuclear plant by the British colonial state and socialist Chinese state. The movement became more difficult to organize after the Chinese authorities had signed the major contracts in late September 1986.[33] Since then, the retreat of societal support for the NIMBY movement was obvious, which was partly indicative of the transient nature of the social mobilization for the Daya Bay movement. Here, political fatalism and the opportunity structure largely shaped the trajectory of the movement.

Viewed from a historical perspective, the anti-Daya Bay movement had successfully developed a sense of solidarity among the Hong Kong people and the core leadership in the Joint Conference. Their defiant actions against the colonial state and the PRC were a continuation of the social movements in Hong Kong during the 1970s. In fact, the movement was controlled and steered by some veteran pressure groups, such as the Professional Teachers' Union, Christian Industrial Committee, Social Workers General Union, Federation of Students.[34]

Yet the established environmental NGOs, like the FOE and the CA, were not equipped with a strong membership base, leadership nor community organizing skills to engage in a protest movement in 1986. Therefore, their actual influence in the movement was not strong. For instance, the protest leadership (like the spokesperson of the Joint Conference, Reverend Fung Chi-wood) had never been strongly associated with environmental NGOs when the movement developed. The limited participation of environmental NGOs and the maximal steering role of social action groups also affected the life span of the movement. The movement began to subside when other contesting political issues emerged after 1986. In particular, the political struggle for the 1988 direct election distracted the leadership and organizational resources of those veteran social action groups.

To recapitulate, the anti-Daya Bay movement had four salient features. First, the movement was counteracted by the strong colonial and PRC state power. The hegemonies of both British and Chinese states, supported by their allies in the business sector, had been actively engaged in counter-mobilization activities against the movement. They had also disregarded all of the societal and ecological arguments of the movement groups. Second, the fragile and transient nature of the environmental movement in Hong Kong was apparent. The anti-Daya Bay campaign began to fall from its peak quite rapidly after the Guangdong Nuclear Power Plant Joint Venture Company and the (mostly British and French) suppliers signed the contracts for the construction of the plant.

Third, the pragmatic approach of most organizers, leaders as well as participants in the movement led them to abort the movement quickly, being aware that there was little chance to win the struggle. For instance, the withdrawal of most leaders (and their members) from the Joint Conference and a move to other battlefields, such as the struggle for the 1988 direct election for the Legislative Council in 1987, caused the movement to abort abruptly.[35] To a certain extent, the mass media's reporting of the movement also shifted quickly in favour of the winner. In other words, the opportunity structure, including the expected outcome, had shaped the course of the environmental protests. To put it simply, when there was less chance of winning the struggle, all activists were likely to return to their own primary areas of interest. Last but not least, environmental NGOs' lack of adequate community organizing skills and appropriate leadership made it difficult to prolong the environmental struggles in a confrontational mode. These reflected the fundamental constraint of environmental movements in Hong Kong.

The Not-In-Anybody's-Backyard Mode

The controversies of Sha Lo Tung and Nam Sang Wai are presented here to highlight how the environmental NGOs organized and articulated environmental movements. There were three major stages in the Sha Lo Tung case. First, there was a signature campaign (securing around 22 000 signatures) against the golf-course proposal. In the second stage, the Friends of the Earth (FOE) won a judicial review of the High Court against the Country Park Authority (CPA). Finally, complaints were made against government departments. The Nam Sang Wai case had no major public participation because it was handled in the narrowly defined legal-administrative framework. It involved the judicial arbitration of the Town Planning Board and its Appeal Board's ruling. Both cases reveal the peculiar form of the environmental NGOs' mobilization in Hong Kong. The movements appear more like a legal litigation proceeding than a social mobilization for environmental protection.

Golf-course and Low-rise Residential Development in Sha Lo Tung

The Sha Lo Tung golf-course development was originally a local land use dispute. Articulation by environmental groups, however, transformed it into a widely publicized environmental issue. The issues on which they focused were the environmental impact of the project and the problematic governmental land administration.[36] A peculiarity of this protest movement was the complaint to the Commissioner for Administrative Complaints (COMAC) against the administration's impropriety and poor decision-making.[37] After the investigation, the Agriculture and Fisheries Department, the Environmental Protection Department, the Lands Department, and the Planning, Environment and Lands Branch of the Government Secretariat were criticized by the COMAC for wrongful approval of the development of a golf-course within Pat Sin Leng Country Park. It should be pointed out, however, that the condemnation from the COMAC did not have any legal-binding authority.

The following case history highlights salient features of this environmental movement.[38] In 1979, after swiftly assembling village land from the New Territories gentry class,[39] the Sha Lo Tung Development Company (SLTDC) submitted to the Administration a proposal to construct a nine-hole golf-course/ country club/residential development immediately adjacent to Pat Sin Leng Country Park. Initially, the proposal was objected by some government departments. In September 1982, when the SLTDC submitted a revised scheme, the Administration tentatively agreed in principle.[40] Subsequently in January 1983, the 'approval in principle' was given to the developer. After reassessing the development potential, in September 1983, the developer further revised the proposal by expanding the scope of development (totalling 61 hectares). The project then included a 18-hole golf-course, 66 low-density residential houses, 200 apartments, and ancillary facilities transgressing the boundary of Pat Sin Leng Country Park and occupying 31 hectares of government land in the park.

The SLTDC's application was forwarded via the Lands Department (Lands D) to the Planning and Management Committee (PMC) of the Country Parks Board (CPB) and was discussed on several occasions. CPB advised the Country Parks Authority (CPA) to give formal approval under Section 10 of the Country Parks Ordinance (the Ordinance) to the Lands D in March 1990 for the proposed use of the country park land, on the condition that the developer provided certain public recreational facilities for the community. In July 1990, the Lands D approved in principle the land exchange proposal mooted by the developer. Yet, in October 1990, the Environmental Protection Department (EPD) rejected the developer's Environmental Review Report on the grounds of its inadequacy and incompleteness. The developer was then required to commission a professional consultant to conduct a comprehensive Environmental Impact Assessment (EIA) on the terms specified by the EPD.

At this stage, six environmental groups including CA, FOE, GP, WWF, Green Lantau Association and Lamma Island Conservation Society protested against the proposed development. They challenged the Administration's decision to use designated country park land for a private development. More environmental groups joined in the protest against the proposal. Their protest actions included petitions, a week-long campaign obtaining about 22 000 signatures against the development proposal, submissions to both the elected and appointed councillors on District Boards and in Legislative Council and Executive Council, study tours to Sha Lo Tung, and lining-up at the entrance of Pat Sin Leng Country Park. But the Administration maintained that the approval of the proposal was in the public interest.

With vested interests in this development, the District Board (DB) and Rural Committees concerned supported the proposal in the consultation exercise done in December 1991. Their justification was that it would revitalize the deserted village and generally bring potential benefit to the district. In January 1992, the Lands D was ready to confirm the proposal for the development, subject to satisfactory resolution of all issues arising from the EIA study. The

Administration considered that it was unnecessary to change the country park boundary to take account of the proposed land allocation to the developer. The reason was that CPA could then still have some control over the area in addition to the control exercised by the Land Authority under the conditions of exchange.

Dissatisfied with the Administration's explanation, the FOE and other environmental groups applied for a judicial review of the CPA's decision. In April 1992, the High Court ordered that the CPA's approval be quashed on the grounds that CPA had acted *ultra vires* when it offered to grant Section 10 approval to the proposed development. The Administration then announced that the CPA's approval was only 'technically incorrect' in relation to the application of the appropriate Section in the Ordinance. The developer subsequently reduced the scope of its project so that no country park land would be involved. The Administration reconsidered the revised application. In August 1993, copies of the EIA report were sent to relevant departments and interest groups for comment. If the assessment was found to be satisfactory, a submission would be made to the Executive Council to take the project further.

In this case, the COMAC found that there was procedural impropriety and poor decision-making on the part of the Administration. When CPA gave its formal approval in March 1990 to the golf-course development, only a brief environmental review document prepared by the developer's consultants was available. In this process, it was found that no EIA or public consultation had yet been conducted, and the government did not know whether there might be an unacceptable environmental impact or any public objections.[41] For the failure of the colonial administration to listen to the public outcry on the project, the COMAC criticized that 'any Government which operates in the mistaken belief that only it can decide what is best for its citizens without hearing possible dissenting voices cannot be anything but a dictatorship'.[42]

Having completed the investigation, the COMAC suggested to the government departments to implement two sets of recommendations:
1. Appropriate procedures including the requirement of an EIA should be adopted in processing development proposals that would encroach on country parks. The statutory objection procedure should also be invoked before deciding whether the land should or should not be excised from the country park, and if the Administration decided not to amend the park boundary a full explanation should be given to members of the public.
2. Grant of approval-in-principle for future land allocation to a private developer or incompatible use of country park land should take place only after all the important matters of principle — valid objections, objection procedure, EIA, etc. — had been resolved.

In this case, the environmental protest (headed by the FOE) had three achievements. First, the development project was halted because of an application for judicial review and the COMAC was brought in to ensure the compliance of the Administration to the law. Second, with the social mobilization and media exposure, the environmental NGOs successfully brought an environmental perspective to development issues in the New Territories. Last but not least was their achievement in embarrassing the government, which in turn, had prompted the colonial government to propose new amendments to the Country Park Ordinance in 1996.[43] But, these achievements should be viewed against the fact that once the litigation process was brought into the movement, the complicated legal discourses and judicial viewpoints sidelined public participation. In other words, once the case was debated in the courtroom, the legalistic terms, procedures and arguments were rarely appealing to the general public.

In retrospect, this environmental movement was characterized by the intra-networking of the environmental NGOs for legal action, as well as the signature campaign which captured 22 000 signatures. It should be noted, however, that the social mobilization faded out when the case went to court and the COMAC. In this sense, the established environmental NGOs in Hong Kong, particularly the FOE and the WWF (see below), were more inclined to resolve environmental disputes in line with the administratively defined rules of the game. Conversely, the environmental NGOs had rarely utilized confrontational strategy in their campaigns.

Recent initiatives from villagers in Sha Lo Tung may challenge the environmental movement, as they argue for the right to redevelop their village.[44] The villagers' quest for redevelopment of farming is being seen by the environmentalists as a way to destroy the natural habitat, giving legitimate grounds for golf-course and residential property development. Bounded by property rights, environmentalists would then be less likely to stop the development project in Sha Lo Tung. At the same time, the NGOs' engagement in the judicial process has resulted in the demobilization of the movement. In other words, the environmental NGOs' dependence on legalistic interpretation and judgement has created certain inertia for further social mobilization.

The Development Project in Nam Sang Wai

Since 1991, the colonial government had extended its Town Planning Ordinance to the New Territories, aiming to tackle the century-old (since 1898) illegal land use problem which had caused serious environmental degradation. The new policy was generally welcomed by both environmentalists and town planners, but provoked strong protests from New Territories' landowners and the gentry class. The new policy affected the vested interests of the traditional governance bodies in the New Territories, e.g., Heung Yee Kuk and Rural Committees, because they had derived substantial profits from 'informal' land lease or change of the land use. Their common practice was to lease out the agriculture land, fishing ponds and other resources to business operators, who then used the land illegally for container storage, car parks and other undertakings.[45] For instance, a private lychee garden had been established for years partly inside a country park without any consent from the government.[46]

The Nam Sang Wai property development project was subject to the development control of the new planning ordinance. The project site is within the Mai Po Marshes Conservation Zone. The development project aroused much controversy because the proposed private property and golf-course development contradicted the purpose of conservation.[47] The environmental NGOs were very active in soliciting support from non-New Territories residents as well as the Administration. They argued that the proposed development would jeopardize the natural habitat in the region.[48] For this reason, the Town Planning Board (TPB) had rejected the development application from Henderson Property Company on three occasions. But the company made a subsequent appeal to the Appeal Board (established under the Amendment of the Town Planning Ordinance in 1992/93) for review.[49] This was also considered a test case for setting precedents for other applications for property development in the New Territories, as most of the land lots in the region had been assembled by large property developers.[50]

The Appeal Board, composed of a handful of independent appointed members, heard the property developer's case in 1994. When the case was presented to the Appeal Board, environmental NGOs launched a media campaign aiming at influencing the decision of the Board. The Appeal Board, however, was convinced that the original decisions of the TPB were incorrect in both principle and technical terms. Particularly, it was argued that the TPB had *misinterpreted* the essence of the Ordinance. The Appeal Board considered that the burden of proof for any environmental impact of the property development should be on the Administration side, rather than the responsibility of the property developers. Similarly, the Appeal Board review emphasized that the property right for development and for 'a better (built) environment' should be acknowledged. With these considerations, the Appeal Board concluded that the application for development should be granted.[51] Undoubtedly, the ruling of the Appeal Board would have had strong implications for the protection of natural habitat in the New Territories, as many similar property development applications were lining up for further review.

Embarrassed by the Appeal Board's ruling, the colonial government unprecedentedly turned to seek 'expert opinions' and support from the World Wide Fund for Nature (WWF) and other environmental NGOs, and attempted to get a judicial review of the Appeal Board's decision. The protest against the development project then turned to a new direction. Instead of social mobilization and mass participation, the environmental NGOs manoeuvred within the legal and administratively defined town planning protocols. In short, the Nam Sam Wai case demonstrates that the lobbying work of environmental NGOs had exerted some pressure on colonial government decision-making. But their efforts had been mostly directed towards the judicial system and colonial administration at the expense of social mobilization.

What was significant in the Nam Sang Wai case was the emerging consultative role of the environmental NGOs in the colonial land administration. The involvement of environmental groups in the Administration was, however, an exceptional one. They were called upon in a crisis situation to help the colonial government to iron out the problems of amateur town planning in Hong Kong. It followed that the quest for judicial review was only a short-term cooperation between the Planning Department and the environmental groups. This case also revealed a chaotic mix of administrative muddling and the vested interests of property developers and the gentry class in the New Territories.[52]

More controversially, the Nam Sang Wai case also reveals the moral and practical dilemma of some green groups and their leaders. Their integrity was questioned by the radical environmentalists, when one of them became a consultant for the property developer. Ethical issues arose when one environmental group expressed its support for the developer's ecological development contract, and compromised with the developer who offered compensation. To a certain degree, the environmental groups lost their collective identity when some of them accepted the offers from the developer.[53]

In pursuing the case, the developer was very active in soliciting the support of the 'green groups'. Some prominent members of the 'green groups' had been involved in preparing the proposal for the developer. Their opinions did carry weight on the decision of the Town Planning Board at its final hearing.[54]

In the Nam Sang Wai case, it was quite obvious that environmental groups had reacted differently to the developer's offer for compensation. For instance, the WWF published the private developer's advertisement in its environmental newsletter, with its implicit endorsement of the project.[55] More importantly, the temptation of being involved in a profit-driven 'ecologically sound project' initiated by a private developer was difficult, if not impossible, to resist. In addition, the increasingly active engagement of private developers in providing different reward incentives to environmental groups had expanded the scope of opportunities for the latter to manoeuvre. In short, the new opportunity structure, including the various potential rewards for environmental groups and individual environmental leaders, did, do and will, shape the trajectories of environmental movements.

An Interim Analysis: Networking, Opportunity and Directions

In the early 1990s, media exposure of global environmentalism brought more environmental issues to community attention. This was also a result of environmental groups' endeavours. For instance, a number of development proposals similar to that of the golf-course in Sha Lo Tung had been challenged by environmental NGOs, e.g., the Royal Hong Kong Jockey Club project in Kau Sai Chau and another one in Luk Keng.[56] In all these cases, the most important factor shaping the manifestations of environmentalism was the networking of environmental NGOs in a given opportunity structure. The manifestations of environmental issues also reflected certain peculiar relationships and dynamics between those environmental NGOs and governmental agencies, the *modi operandi* of the environmental NGOs and the political opportunity structure and networking under which they operated.[57]

The networking among the environmental NGOs, as well as between the environmental NGOs and community groups, should be noted here. Two major characteristics of the networking in the antagonistic environmental movements in Hong Kong can be observed. First, there is a lack of networking between grass roots protest groups and environmental NGOs. Second, individual environmental NGOs prefer to work on their own projects, as they each have different definitions of and orientations towards environmentalism. The FOE approaches environmental disputes in the institutional arena, including litigation. The CA works on scientifically defined conservation issues. The WWF is mostly engaged in its conservation project in Mai Po Conservation, while the GP has extended their alternative lifestyle focus to include environmentalism.

The difficulty for territory-wide social mobilizations on environmental issues stems from the incompatibility of world-views between environmental NGOs and community groups, and their different political and ideological alignments. In contrast to the *left-libertarian* tradition of green political groups in Europe,[58] the environmental NGOs in Hong Kong have not been in favour of the *left* political ideology. This can be partly seen by their non-involvement in most local social issues and struggles for social justice. The environmental NGOs' apathy towards local social protests is a result of their middle-class leadership, which has opted for a consensual approach to environmental movements. In addition, there is also a strong element of participation by expatriate and middle-class professionals in the environmental movement, which in turn reduces the extent of grass roots radicalism.[59] To recapitulate, the environmental and grass roots protests groups have more inherent differences than similarities, and they rarely work together in socio-environmental movements; therefore environmental movements are separated from social movements.[60]

Instead of mass mobilization, lobbying of the colonial administration and taking environmental disputes into the courtroom had been the dominant activities of the environmental NGOs. Three main factors accounted for this mode of environmental movements. First, the environmentalists' middle-class background and their social networks with the colonial government had shaped their preference for lobbying and litigation. These activists and the colonial officials obviously felt more comfortable working in a legal and lobbying framework. Second, most of the environmental leaders had no grass roots mobilization experience, nor did the NGOs have the skills to organize mass mobilization, which in turn shaped their preference to work with the Administration and/or the legal proceedings. Last but not least was the colonial government's active pursuit of governance-by-consultation since the 1980s. As a result of the consultative co-optation, environmental issues had limited public participation and were non-confrontational in nature.

❏ The Consensual Manifestation — Sponsored Environmental Education

Since the 1990s, many environmental NGOs have been involved in the promotion of green lifestyles and have been drawn into sponsored environmental education campaigns. Both external and internal factors account for this development. They are the influence of global environmentalism on Hong Kong society, and the increase of corporate and governmental sponsorships. More fundamentally, there is a change in corporate and governmental attitudes towards the environmental NGOs. The latter are no longer considered as hostile pressure groups but possible partners.[61] The cooperation also reflects the mutual interest of both parties. Therefore, many environmental NGOs have been granted green funds to promote environmental education programmes.

Green funds available from public and private sectors have become a major force in shaping Hong Kong's environmental movements. In the 1993/94 government financial year, the colonial government established the Environment and Conservation Fund amounting to $50 million and the Environmental Education Committee.[62] This corresponds to the burgeoning of green funds available in the private sector, with the providers of such funds including the Overseas Trust Bank, Caltex, Shell, Esso Green Fund, China Light & Power Co. Ltd., and the Provisional Airport Authority.

Perhaps because of the availability of green sponsorships, the environmental NGOs have adopted a softer approach to environmentalism in order to capture the new opportunities. This new approach has a strategic meaning for the major environmental NGOs. Similarly, other smaller environmental groups have followed this approach towards environmental education under a new sponsorship regime. The main providers of sponsored environmental education include the four established environmental NGOs (CA, FOE, GP and the WWF) and smaller groups, such as the Green Lantau Association, the Lamma Island Conservation Society, the Ping Chau Conservation Society, green groups in universities (Green Union of Students), in secondary schools (Joint School

Environmental Protection Association) and in social service centres (e.g. the Caritas Social Service).[63] Despite the estimated total membership of all environmental groups being less than 10 000, the influence of environmental education programmes should not be underestimated.

Raising environmental consciousness was, and still is, the primary focus of the environmental NGOs. This is recently reinforced by the full-fledged recognition of environmental education programmes as part of extracurricular activities in schooling, civic education in the community, and one of the fashionable themes in television and radio programmes.[64] Through various sponsorship arrangements, environmental NGOs have been very active in promoting environmental education programmes in various social settings. Since these campaign activities are mostly through the mass media, these programmes usually attract a substantial number of transient and passive participants.

My observations indicate that there are four major benefits for the environmental NGOs' acceptance of green sponsorship. First, they can get financial support through sponsorship and more revenue for organizational operations. The financial consideration is an important one for the survival of most environmental NGOs, as membership subscriptions are rarely sufficient to support them. Second, green sponsorship has provided credibility and media exposure for the environmental NGOs' experimental projects,[65] for example, Green Power's projects of Green University, Green Primary School and Eco-tours. Third, the enhancement of the NGOs' public image in the mass media has in turn helped their membership recruitment. This can be seen from the exponential growth of the NGOs' membership through sponsored educational programmes. The final benefit is the publicity for environmental leaders, raising their own profiles in the mass media.

Yet, green sponsorship is also a source of conflict and tension for the environmental NGOs. For instance, the Friends of the Earth (FOE) in Hong Kong has lost their affiliation to the worldwide FOE movement as a result of receiving sponsorship from environmental polluters. In addition, the marriage of green sponsorship and environmental movements has been controversial among environmentalists. An eco-fundamentalist questioned the extent of environmental NGOs' independence and the trivialization of environmentalism. In most cases, the environmental NGOs have to realign their modes of operation in accordance with state or corporate sponsorships.

More problematically, this phase of the development of environmentalism in Hong Kong reflects the 'softness' (if not weakness) of the environmental movements. Indeed, the term 'environmental' has been used as a magic catchword for most educational and entertainment programmes in the cultural and media industries. Though these programmes have gained public attention with a large audience, they have not generated actual participation in environmental movements.[66] Consequently, the manifestation of Hong Kong's environmental movements in the early 1990s can be termed as the paradigmatic turn to the *'soft' modi operandi*.

To conclude, the increasing amount of green sponsorship has been a strong influence on the environmental movements. There appears to be a high degree of mutual dependency between the environmental NGOs, their green sponsors and the mass media. The dependency is expressed in terms of the budgetary consideration of the NGOs, the public image of the sponsors, and the 'political correctness' of the media.[67] Newly emerged environmental NGOs and those with a strong environmental education profile are more likely to be influenced by green sponsorship. For business corporations, green sponsorship is not uncommonly used as a strategy for public relations and corporate image-building. For the mass media, environmental education programmes can be used as a kind of community service. More importantly, sponsored environmental education has been instrumental in keeping the *soft* environmental movements alive!

The Cognitive Praxis of Green Power

The self-identified world-views of respective environmental NGOs are fundamental in shaping their cognitive praxis for environmental movements.[68] There are different modes and interpretations of environmentalism, which can be categorized in terms of their orientations (i.e. following the centre-of-gravity principle) towards people (anthropo-centric), technology (techno-centric) and nature (eco-centric).[69] To highlight the interpretative aspect of environmentalism, the cognitive praxis of one environmental NGO is examined here. The phenomenal development of Green Power (GP) deserves special attention, for its 'indigenization project' in exploiting Chinese cultural values and putting them into an eco-alternative lifestyle approach to environmentalism.[70] Because of its frequent media exposure, GP has had an environmental appeal to the Hong Kong middle class which has resulted in a high membership growth rate.

Green Power Ltd. (GP) was established in 1988 under company registration by a dozen 'activators' with a middle-class socio-economic background.[71] Politically, they were more like the liberal right than the left. More specifically, they were a group of people seeking for self-actualization through a green lifestyle. GP began as an environmental observer articulating environmental issues in the mass media, and later gradually diversified its activities because of leadership change and demand from the mass media. Since its inception, there have been seven major areas of GP's engagement in Hong Kong's environmental movements:

1. Alternative policy commentary and advocacy in the mass media, yet not necessarily politically charged.

2. Green opinions' formation and representation in the mass media, via writing columns in the print media or being interviewed, etc.
3. Environmental education programmes, e.g., regular seminars, outdoor nature activities — organic farming, organizing Summer Green Primary School and the Green University's programmes, etc.
4. Membership activities (recreational and educational).
5. Publication and translation of foreign green literature.
6. Involvement in other mobilizations or in lobbying for environmental policy change.
7. Gathering information for Eco-data bank.

In contrast to other established environmental NGOs (WWF, FOE and CA), GP is very successful in recruiting new members through their programmes. It can be seen from the following statistics:

Year	1988–89 (first year)	1991–92 (fourth year)	1992–93 (fifth year)
Membership	35	1 200	1 400
Annual Expenditure*	$110 000	$1 340 000	$1 800 000
Full-time Staff	0.5	3.5	6
No. of Activators	5	11	15

*   Revenue derived from project-based corporate sponsorship and individual donation.[72]

More strategically, GP has utilized the mass media to attract public attention. Its advocacy has been for a green consumption lifestyle as a means of saving the world. Many green promotional programmes have been carried out under the themes of:
*   paper saving and recycling;
*   Bring Your Own Bag (BYOB) — use fewer plastic bags;
*   others pertaining to green consumption;
*   organic farming (GP supports one such farm in the New Territories) which provides a taste of green life for urban residents;
*   nostalgia through eco-tours to tropical rain forests;
*   the movement for vegetarianism coupled to that for no or decreased consumption of shark's fin, swallow's nests, snakes and all kinds of wild creature following the Buddhist teaching.

- advocacy of polluters-pay-principle (green tax) on certain selected consumption items
- collaboration with Chinese religious bodies to promote greener lifestyles

To recapitulate, GP's activities have been mostly educational in nature with an alternative lifestyle appeal to the middle class. Their advocacy highlights green and sustainable ways of life, as well as promoting a new model of quality of life for individuals and the community. GP has been successful in building up a good public image of its environmental expertise. The prominent 'activator', Simon Chau, had also become an environmental celebrity in Hong Kong in the early 1990s.[73] Therefore, GP is not just popular among environmentally conscious individuals, but is also attracting many green sponsorships.

More specifically, the ecological reasoning of Simon Chau resembles the lineage of Chinese Buddhist ideas on nature and culture, people and environment. His view has been echoed in *The Light of Dharma* (publication of a local Buddhist group — Fa Ju Xue Wu) and by Fok Tou-hui.[74] Chau and Fok share similar viewpoints on the futuristic cognitive praxis for Hong Kong environmental movements. In short, they strive for a personal lifestyle approach to environmental movements.

There are several reasons which account for GP's success. First, GP's attempt to promote 'quality of life' coincides with the middle class's deep concern for their individual physical and spiritual health.[75] Second, GP's quality of life approach has highlighted its project of indigenization of environmentalism. In other words, its advocacy for a Chinese way of green consumption and a green cosmology is attractive to local mass media also because of the sympathy of the editorial personnel.[76] Third and following from above, since GP's advocacy of cognitive praxis for environmentalism is in line with Chinese religious beliefs (e.g. Buddhism and Taoism), they are likely to have a good response from local Chinese. To conclude, the phenomenal emergence of GP clearly indicates that a new mode of environmentalism has taken shape in the Hong Kong Chinese community.[77]

In this regard, the rise of GP should be understood as a process of mixing Eastern and Western environmentalisms under the new mass media hegemony. The new environmental cognitive praxis has taken shape within a short time span in Hong Kong, bridging Chinese traditionalism and Western post-materialistic values. For example, the most obvious manifestation of this brand of environmentalism is the discursive and praxis embedment of the vegetarian diet in Chinese (Buddhist and Taoist) rituals.

The Lifestyle Approach to Environmentalism

Strongly supported by environmental groups, the emergence of alternative lifestyles reflects the socio-economic dynamics in a post-materialistic society. Environmentalists argue that each individual has a duty towards global sustainability by adopting green consumption. The advocacy for a green lifestyle and consumption pattern involves the reasoning that the process of consumption and the product cycle can influence the rate of environmental degradation and environmental conservation.[78] Hence each individual should consume ecologically. The business sector is also exploiting green consumerism by providing more green or eco-labelled products.[79] Since the 1990s, Hong Kong has been catching up with the new fashion of consumption based on ecologically sound principles in marketing and retailing of goods and services, such as the Body Shop movement.[80] In short, the striving for *lifestyle* or the *quality of life* approach to environmental issues is structurally embedded in and enabled by the development of a green economy. All these reinforce the *soft* environmental movements.

In response to global environmentalism and the burgeoning green market, there are various business initiatives to foster green lifestyles. For instance, the recent establishment of the Private Sector Committee on the Environment and the Centre for Environmental Technology indicates the responsiveness of the business sector to the opportunities in a greening economy. More strategically, the private sector environmental institution is also a counter-mobilization instrument against eco-fundamentalism, such as that of the Green Peace. Usually the private sector initiatives are in the name of environmental management. Yet, their environmental management is in fact a strong lobbying force against radical and progressive environmental policy initiatives. For example, they have organized media campaigns against the introduction of the polluter-pay-principle in sewage treatment.[81] Put simply, the key expression for this phase of development is the coupling of green economy with the *soft (or consensus)* approach for environmental movements.

Institutionalization and Professionalization of Green Groups

Environmental NGOs had actively promoted the conservation of the natural habitat in the New Territories. But their endeavours had encountered many difficulties, as the politics of development was controlled by a handful of colonial officials and the gentry class who had vested interests in land and property development. Furthermore, the environmental NGOs' legal proceedings in environmental disputes were beyond the comprehension of the general public and thus rarely contributed to social mobilization for environmental justice. Nevertheless, with the rise of the *soft* approach of environmentalism and the exposure of environmental problems through the mass media, there was no doubt that more people, especially the younger generation, were exposed to informed knowledge regarding environmental protection. This was indeed the major contribution of the environmental NGOs in Hong Kong.

In the 1990s, a growing green economy demanded the involvement of the environmental NGOs in both the consumption and production spheres. Parallel to this, the colonial government also involved the environmental NGOs in their consultation exercises. These two developments had led to an emerging consultancy role for the FOE, WWF and CA in environmental affairs.[82] This marked a new era of environmentalism, with an exponential growth of professional (some were profit-oriented) and amateur green groups. Similarly, more green groups had been establishing in universities and secondary schools. Consequently, they had become more vocal and visible in environmental affairs in the public sphere.

More importantly, the institutionalization of the environmental NGOs in the consultation process demanded professionalism in environmental debates. This development followed much of the absorption process of environmental groups into the colonial consultative framework for governance since the 1980s.[83] The 'absorption' corresponded to the compliance of the environmental NGOs' to colonial governance. Their compliance, in contrast to other social protest groups, enabled them to be more readily accepted by the colonial government. The environmental NGOs had rarely constituted any threat to the colonial regime. Except in the anti-Daya Bay protests movement, they had not been involved in mass mobilization to challenge the legitimacy of the colonial regime during the past two decades. In addition, their cognitive praxis in environmental movements was somewhat apathetic towards politics but in favour of legal proceedings. Obviously, this enabled them to work closer with the colonial administration.

Moreover, the political apathy of environmental NGOs was reflected in their non-engagement in other social movements, such as housing protests and the NIMBY type of environmental struggles at the community level. Influenced by their idiosyncratic interpretations of environmentalism, they seldom formed strong alliances among themselves to challenge the colonial regime. Comparatively speaking, their apolitical position was distinctly different from their Western counterparts' political radicalism, and was also far from those militant community protest groups in Hong Kong, such as the Tsing Yi Concern Group.[84] Therefore, it was not surprising that the environmental NGOs in Hong Kong had virtually no grass roots base, and did not challenge the colonial governance.

Furthermore, the administrative absorption of some environmental leaders was likely to have enhanced their sense of importance and euphoria in their movement 'career'. The institutional arrangements of the EPCOM (Committee for Environmental Protection) and the ACE (Advisory Committee on Environment), and the formation of the Council for Environmental Education (CEE) mirrored the institutionalization process of environmental movements with absorption of the groups and co-optation of the leaders. Co-optation of the movements' leaders might lead to the neutralization of the political appeals of the green groups and the undermining of the environmental movements. In other words, appeals for environmental protection were overshadowed by the public image of environmental leaders. Under the institutionalization influence, Hong Kong's environmental movements had had a strong public image of environmental leadership yet without much social mobilization.

Functional specialization to achieve professionalism by the environmental groups was an obvious outcome of their seven-year-long involvement in policy consultation. The professionalization process had developed along the environmental NGOs' respective areas of interest and specialities. For instance, the FOE had focused their work on the New Territories' natural habitat conservation, while the WWF had concentrated on their Mai Po conservation project. The professionalization was also a result of the niche development of the environmental NGOs. Due to organizational survival, they had to develop some form of specialism in environmental protection, which was distinctive from others. Captured under the professional hegemony, the environmental NGOs had developed a new set of terminology in their environmental projects. For instance, some environmental NGOs referred to the general public and polluters as their 'clients' or 'customers'. One prominent chief executive had argued that this represented the progressiveness of those environmental groups and their readiness to accept consultancy offers, regardless of the clientele's background. On the other hand, as shown in the Nam Sang Wai case study, there was the temptation for some environmental group leaders to act as consultants for private developers. Alternatively, they might present themselves as advocates for nature, accepting compensation for ecological destruction.[85]

The institutionalization of environmental movements also reinforced the professionalization of the environmental NGOs. This was more obviously facilitated under a new regulatory regime of environmental impact assessments (EIAs). An EIA required inputs from both technical consultants and environmental NGOs. The latter requirement had had a strong influence on the environmental NGOs' scope of activities. The environmental NGOs might be driven into the administratively defined arena, following the defined rules of the game. This was in line with the procedural requirement of EIAs, which prescribed a solicitation of the NGOs' views. As a result the environmental NGOs' public advocacy was likely to fade out and be replaced by in-house consultancy.

As clearly shown in the above analysis, there were two interrelated developments for the environmental NGOs which might change the course of environmental movements. First, there was their professionalization and functional specialization. The FOE and WWF seemed to have opted for this approach. Second, there was their quest for the reinforcement of public exposure through the mass media and a *soft* approach to environmental issues. Indeed, this was also an eco-populist 'Catch-All' strategy (to get maximum support from people) to secure public attention. For instance, GP was a typical group which took this symbolic appeal approach but without much substantial threat to the political institutions. Yet the quest for a strong public image of environmental groups had ironically become a burden for the movement because their leaders might emerge as celebrities in the entertainment and media industries, and at the detriment of the social mobilization momentum.[86] If both approaches were to continue to be pursued in future, the environmental movements would be strongly influenced by the professionalism and the media industries. The result of a populist, soft environmentalism would be the apoliticalization of environmental movements.

❏ Post-1997 Environmental Movements

With the greening of the global market, the colonial government had been belatedly meeting the challenge of environmentalism with some policy initiatives. For instance, in the *Territorial Development Strategy* (1993), the government brought back the limit-to-growth concept, such as the assimilative *capacity of the environment*. In addition, it had introduced environmental auditing with the symbolic appointment of 'green managers' in all government departments in 1994.

In retrospect, environmental movements of the last decade in Hong Kong were characterized by their *softness* in form, style and presence in the public sphere, and their distinct separation from other social protest movements. In addition, the environmentalists had their middle-class world-views about environmentalism, which were distant from the grass roots. Since 1990, most of them had shown a readiness to be incorporated into the institutional opportunities structure of the business sector and the colonial government.[87] Despite their fragility and transience, the movements had some achievements. For the general public, their environmental awareness had increased substantially; for the environmental groups and their leaders, they had gained a public profile through the mass media and a professional image through policy consultation.

To end this chapter, I shall attempt to sketch the emerging contours of environmentalism in Hong Kong. There are four different, albeit related, sets of dynamic factors which would shape the manifestations of environmentalism and have an impact on the course of environmental movements. They include the increase in environmental consciousness, the degree of emphasis on environmental quality in the regional economic restructuring, cross-border pollution, and lastly the role of social groups in environmental movements.

First, people's world-views of environmental affairs are contingent upon their quality of life. Owing to the environmental movements, people in Hong Kong have apparently acquired more environmental knowledge over the last decade.[88] Recent studies indicate that Hong Kong people are not happy with the state of the environment. Their attitudes on environmental issues, their knowledge, participation and readiness to participate in environmental protection, seem to suggest a shift of people's orientation towards a *new environmental paradigm*.[89] A tentative conclusion is that people have become less tolerant of environmental problems than in the previous decade. At the very least, they have changed, or attempted to change, their immediate environment, arguably by adopting a *green lifestyle*-oriented approach to environmentalism. The new lifestyle approach is exemplified by the Body Shop movement, which indicates alternative choices for middle-class cosmetic and body care consumption.[90]

But the emergence of environmental consciousness is paradoxical. People may expect more proactive public policy to eradicate the environmental problems, but they may not be willing to give up some individual freedom in favour of a regulatory regime. For instance, Hong Kong's people might support the Polluters-Pay-Principle (PPP) for the sake of environmental protection; but when the PPP actually was implemented in April 1995 as a sewage charge proportional to the volume of fresh water consumption, many people and organizations were actively against such a preventive measure. Here, people's readiness to accept environmental protection policies was questionable, regardless of their attitudes and knowledge on environmental issues. The logics of free riders and NIMBY became clear in this situation.

Second, unlike other Western developed economies, there has not been much advocacy for green production in Hong Kong. The main reason was the shift of manufacturing industries to southern China. The emergent regional division of labour in the Pearl River Delta (PRD) had facilitated not just the relocation of labour- and land-intensive industries across the border, but also the pollution-intensive production process. The unintended consequence of the economic restructuring was the temporary halt to the deterioration of environmental quality in Hong Kong. This could be seen from the drastic decrease of (stationary source) pollutants, such as sulphur dioxide, in the air, chemical waste and discharge from dyeing and electroplating industries in the early 1990s.[91] On the other hand, the restructuring of Hong Kong from a manufacturing to a service economy had generated a different set of environmental problems, which might be easily overlooked or underestimated, e.g. the increase of traffic noise and solid waste from over-packaging.

Third and following from above, the successful development of the Shenzhen Special Economic Zone (SZSEZ) had, in contradiction, become an environmental threat to Hong Kong's ecological system. The SZSEZ industrial land use and its built-environment of skyscrapers encroaching the border area of Hong Kong had generated new environmental problems, e.g., toxicity in the PRD's rivers and soils which had entered into the food chain, and the regional acid rain. It was quite obvious that the temporary improvement of environmental quality in Hong Kong would be offset by cross-border pollution and hazards. Cross-border pollution was, and will be catastrophic for Hong Kong! But the complexity and extent of the pollution problems were and are beyond the coping capability and jurisdiction of the past colonial government and the present Special Administrative Region (SAR) government. Furthermore, because of the differences in socio-economic, technological and political institutions between Hong Kong and southern China, the opportunity appears to be slim for the development of a set of compatible terms and institutions to deal with the environmental problems.

The last set of factors is the role of environmental NGOs and their independence in the environmental movements. Assuming, in future, all environmental NGOs can still operate as they do now,[92] they are less likely to find any independent counterparts in the PRC for partnership. Without partnership with the independent NGOs in China, environmental NGOs in Hong Kong cannot effectively address to the cross-border pollution. In other words, there will be more difficulties to develop environmental movements in Hong Kong and China. Under these conditions, any confrontational social movement or conflicting manifestation of environmentalism will be less likely to flourish. This pessimistic prognosis on the future development of environmental movements can be substantiated by two historical facts. First, there had been an acquiescence in basic human rights issues (either neglected or forgotten) among most environmental NGOs in Hong Kong in the last two decades. Without a liberal regime safeguarding civil and political rights, there was a reduced probability of the development of an independent environmental movement. Second, the experience of the protests against the Daya Bay Nuclear Plant and its aftermath highlighted the difficulties for the pursuit of environmental protection against the PRC's national agenda for economic development. In other words, the national agenda for economic development is and will be, more important than ever. To put it simply, under the Hong Kong SAR governance, the opportunity for full-fledged social mobilization on environmental issues is very slim. On the contrary, there will be strong forces for the development and reinforcement of the *soft* and *consensual* approach to environmentalism.

In the attempt to stage a smooth transfer of sovereignty to the PRC, the quest for stability had been the dominant concern of the ruling elite. Consequently, confrontational politics and large-scale protest movements had been contained. By putting all these considerations into our prognosis, it is likely that environmental movements will be shaped into a soft and consensual mode of environmentalism which is found acceptable by the new administration.

The environmental cognitive praxis might be turned into fashionable green consumerism, or it might be rejuvenated into different lifestyles under the influence of Chinese traditionalism of health and wholesomeness.

To conclude, the paradoxical Hong Kong environmentalism in future will be shaped by the emerging opportunity structure in a green market and the predicaments of the socio-political systems. Market forces are likely to promote green lifestyles but without a substantial contribution to the improvement of environmental quality. The socio-political systems will not be capable of solving pollution problems, and will not tolerate large-scale antagonistic NIMBY or NIABY protest movements.

Acknowledgements

The author wishes to thank all those colleagues and students, in institutions he has been affiliated to, for their support and assistance generously provided, especially for the generous sharing of findings by Fung Kam-kong, Hung Ho-fung, Lee Yok-shiu, Man Si-wai, Ng Hang-sau, and all participants of the First Workshop on Asia's Environmental Movements in Comparative Perspective (organized by the University of Hawaii at Manoa and the East-West Centre, 29 November to 1 December 1995); and the continuous encouragement from Yunn-ya Chen and both editors of this volume.

Notes

1. See Dobson, *Green political thought*; Lai, *The snergy of nature, people and technology* and 'Community, environment and sustainable development'; Canan, 'Bringing nature back in: the challenge of environmental sociology'; and Brulle, 'Environmental discourse and social movement organizations'.
2. See Chui and Lai, *Patterns of social conflicts in Hong Kong*, for an empirical account on social conflicts.
3. For example, four major environmental NGOs in Hong Kong are Conservancy Association, Friends of the Earth (FOE) [Hong Kong], Green Power and World Wide Fund (WWF) for Nature [Hong Kong].
4. For a comparison, see Dalton and Kuelcher, *Challenging the political boundary*.
5. For this, the critical observation of Man, a local academic environmentalist, was half right when she pointed out that environmental issues had never been put in terms of conflicting socio-political mobilization and hence, no such category of environmental movement might be included in the spectrum of social movements. See Man, 'In search of the community' (in Chinese), pp. 17–20.
6. See Chan and Hills, *Limited gains*.
7. For a detailed discussion, see Lai, *The synergy*.
8. See Canan 'Bringing nature back in', Lai 'Community, environment and space', and Goodin, *Green political theory*, for a detailed discussion.
9. Refer to Dalton and Kuechler, *Challenging the political boundary*.

10. See Dobson, *Green political thought*, Goodin, *Green political theory*, and Kitschelt, *The logics of party formation*.
11. For instance, the concept of the 'Tragedy of the Commons' captures such a variety of people's responses to environmental problems, see Harding, 'Tragedy of the Commons', for conceptual discourse, and Goodin, *The politics of rational man*, Herring, 'Restructuring the Commons', and Shiva, 'Coming tragedy of the Commons'.
12. See Kitschelt, *The logics of party formation*, for details.
13. Cf. Engels and Engels, *Ethics of environment and development*.
14. The recent Port and Airport Development Strategy (PADS) represents only one of these building/engineering projects. On environmental protection in Hong Kong after the *1989 White Paper on environment*, see Hong Kong government, *2nd review of progress on the 1989 White Paper*.
15. For an official chronology of environmental protection in Hong Kong, see Environmental Protection Department, *Environment Hong Kong 1994*.
16. See Lee, 'Local NGOs and community-based urban environmental initiatives', for comparative studies.
17. This is derived from a draft paper by Fung, 'Draft on the environmentalists' profile', and the author's own observation.
18. This assessment is drawn from a comparison between Chau and Fung's 'Ancient wisdom and sustainable development' and Inglehart's *Cultural shift*.
19. See Chui and Lai, 'Pattern of social conflicts', for details.
20. I have developed this distinction in detail in two of my forthcoming works, 'Community, environment and sustainable development' and 'The politics of environment and space'. For analytical and empirical accounts on the distinction between NIMBY and NIABY, see Armour, 'The sitting of locally unwanted landuse', Heiman, 'From Not-In-My-Backyard to Not-In-Anybody-Backyard', Hsiao, 'The character and changes of Taiwan's local environmental protest movement', Hsiao, Milbrath and Weller, 'Antecedents of an environmental movement in Taiwan', and Szasz, *EcoPopulism*.
21. See Environmental Resource Ltd., *Tsing Yi hazardous potential* for details.
22. This Tsing Yi case study has drawn many original materials from Ng Hang-Sau's published and unpublished works on Tsing Yi Concern Group (he was under the author's supervision for his Master of Social Work dissertation in 1991–92), apart from the author's own participation in Tsing Yi affairs when he was an elected District Board member of the Kwai Chung & Tsing Yi District Board 1985–88. Naturally, disclaimer and acknowledgment apply here.
23. In spite of its exposure to most of the concerned parties, the confidential *Consultancy study* has never been released.
24. Adapted from Ng, 'Mobilizing Tsing Yi residents against environmental hazards', pp. 78, 79, 81.
25. See Leung, *Community development in Hong Kong*, for community organization strategies to strive for citizens' welfare in Hong Kong; in this respect, the TYCG was not different from other community work groups' attempt to confront the colonial government for social justice. For housing issues and their mobilization, see chapter 6 in this volume.
26. See Chan and Hills, *Limited gains*, for discussion.
27. From a conversation with an environmentalist.
28. See Kwok, 'Political exchange network of Kwai Tsing District Board', for a detailed analysis on the local politicking process in Kwai Tsing and its District Board.

29. The author has to confess that he was involved in this protest campaign as one of the members in the Joint Conference. Perhaps, this provides some more reflection on the case. For a detailed contextual account of the anti-Daya Bay Nuclear Plant protests, see Yee and Wong, 'The politics of the Daya Bay Nuclear Plant debate'. Discussion here follows much of their empirical findings and our exposure, yet our interpretation is very much different from theirs, as I argue that this movement, in spite of its differential political meanings for different interest groups as appeared in media coverage, is a more typical NIMBY case than a political quest for 'autonomy' case.

30. News media, following their political world-views, had (un)intentionally aligned themselves with both camps, respectively; for the anti-Daya Bay media group, they were: *Ming Pao Daily News, the Express, Hong Kong Economic Journal, Hong Kong Times, Oriental Daily News, Sing Tao Daily, Wah Kiu Yat Pao*, and the two English dailies: *Hong Kong Standard, South China Morning Post*; and the pro-Daya Bay camp was represented by the PRC-funded newspapers: *Wen Wei Po, Ta Kung Pao* and *Sin Wen Pao*.

31. Yee and Wong, 'The politics of the Daya Bay Nuclear Plant debate', p. 622.

32. Ibid., p. 619.

33. One of the comparable mass mobilizations might be the pro-democracy movement in 1989, see chapter 3 in this volume.

34. Cheng, 'Hong Kong: the pressure to converge', p. 283.

35. See chapter 2 in this volume for an overview of the networking of pressure groups against the colonial (and PRC) governance in Hong Kong, since the 1970s. Yet, it should be pointed out that the Joint Conference (and other territory-wide mobilization) with such a variety of pressure groups had one common, apart from the logistic, problem of organizing. That is the one that I refer to as the 'Phantom of the Anarchism' which reduced the trust level among partners as many organizers suspected some form of anarchist infiltration in the movement, the latter was politically unacceptable for both the British colonial and the PRC governments.

36. See chapter 2 in this volume.

37. See Hong Kong Council of Social Service (HKCSS), *Case analysis on building a golf-course at Sha Lo Tung*, for background information.

38. This section has drawn much from the *COMAC case file no: OCAC 35/93*.

39. For details, refer to the COMAC case file.

40. There are strong evidences in favour of the speculation that, in New Territories, the gentry class (mostly represented by the male-dominated Rural Committees and the Heung Yee Kuk) and the local colonial officials had been in certain form of collaboration. In exchange for local governance, the colonial officials (mostly in the District Office) turned a blind eye to land use abuse and district land mismanagement, prior to the mid-1980s; not mentioning those special privileges enjoyed by the 'indigenous residents of New Territories' (i.e., their ancestors had been settled there prior to the arrival of British colonialists in 1898).

41. Despite the Water Supplies Department's objection that the project would affect the water quality in the reservoir catchment.

42. At that time, support for the project was far from unanimous — reservations had been voiced by a number of departments and certain PMC and CPB members that using country park land for a private project might run against the objective of catering for the recreational needs of ordinary citizens.

43. The COMAC report further noted that since the Administration was responsible

for making a balanced choice having regard to all relevant considerations, it was duty-bound to observe the objection procedure so as to afford the public an opportunity of airing their views. As a matter of procedure, approval-in-principle given to applicants in complicated land grant cases should be given only if all the fundamental issues of principle had been resolved. In the case under complaint, the EIA study, public objection, consultation with CPB/the relevant DB, etc. were clearly not only technical or procedural matters, but were matters of importance that ought to have been addressed prior to the grant of approval-in-principle. If the Administration simply wished to express interest in a private development proposal, then a simple statement to that effect would suffice. COMAC file no. OCAC 35/93.

44. *Sing Tao Daily*, 20 May 1996 on WWW: http://www.singtao.com/news/mon/0520a010.html.
45. The 're-farming' is in fact a step to destroy the natural habitat, see *Ming Pao Daily News*, 11 June 1995, p. B2 and *South China Morning Post*, 9 October 1994.
46. Siddall, 'The environment'.
47. *South China Morning Post*, 30 August 1994, p. 5.
48. According to Hung, 'The environment', p. 261, the proposal included a land exchange of Lut Chau (situated next to the Mai Po Marshes and fell within the Zone I buffer) owned by the developer for an equivalent piece of crown land adjacent to the Nam Sang Wai development. The developer also promised to preserve and maintain Lut Chau in future.
49. See Conservancy Association, *Land use and environmental quality in north west New Territories*.
50. The Town Planning Board, membership appointed by the Governor, was formed under the provision of the Town Planning Ordinance and is empowered to have the authority of development control over land use via statutory zoning plan and other administrative instructions empowered in the Ordinance.
51. The land assembly in the New Territories was controlled by less than ten large property groups.
52. It had been pointed out by the author, 'Urban redevelopment and community work', that both the Town Planning Board (TPB) and its Appeal Board were not representative nor professional, they just represented a 'social club' of those powerful property developers and the comprador class in a colonial regime; in short, they acted for the interests of land capitalists and the colonial state. Yet, there are some speculative explanatory theses on the TPB's refusal to grant any consent for redevelopment in Nam Sang Wai. One of them attributes to the 'special relation' between the global WWF (their most active principle patron is Duke Edinburgh) and the colonial government.
53. See case analysis by the *Hong Kong Economic Journal Daily*, 10 June 1995, p. 5; and Leung, Sung and Kwok, 'The case of golf-course development'.
54. Succinctly noted by Hung (a veteran environmentalist in Hong Kong), 'The environment', p. 262.
55. Ibid., pp. 261–2.
56. If we examine the positional change of the WWF, as shown by their serial publication, *The extension of life*, from 1993 to 1995, it is quite surprising that they changed their stand on the Nam Sang Wai issue, even by accepting the advertisement of the new proposal from Henderson Property Development Co. to be printed in their publication.

57. Refer to Hung, 'The environment', p. 261.
58. See Kriesi, 'The political opportunity structure of new social movements', for discussion. For local protest movements networking, see chapter 2 in this volume.
59. See della Porta and D. Rucht, 'Left-libertarian movements in context', for elaboration.
60. See Ng and Ng, 'The environment', p. 367.
61. This resembles the 'noises' in Luhmann's *Ecological communication*. He argues that the differentiation of the sub-system of environmental movements into further subdivided more separated entity, but they can not become resonance with each other. See Luhmann, *The differentiation of society* and *ecological communication*, for details.
62. See Chau, 'The environment', for discussion.
63. See Hung, 'The politics of the environment', and Ng, 'Environmental education'.
64. See Lai, 'Environmental education'.
65. See Hong Kong Council of Social Service, 'A situation report on voluntary agencies' environmental educational protection activities', and Lai, 'Environmental education'.
66. See Ng, 'Environmental education'.
67. The mass media in Hong Kong has been arguably developed in line with the entertainment industries. The promotion of environmental education programmes by the mass media is considered as a pretentious way to put more civic conscience (rather than business profits) into their broadcasting and publicity.
68. See Eyerman and Jamison, *Social movement: a cognitive approach.*
69. The following analytical scheme highlights certain domains of the differential world-views, with reference to the inclination to or the importance placed on people (A), ecology (E) and technology (T):
    I.   A > T > E = Anthro-Centric Scientific Modernism (European Culture)
    II. A > E > T = Anthro-Centric Holism (Chinese Culture: Buddhism/Taoism)
    III. E > T > A = Eco-Centric Scientificism
    IV. E > A > T = Eco-Fundamentalism (Myth, Deep Ecology)
    V.   T > A > E = Techno-Centric Modernism (Rationalization *per se*).
    VI. T > E > A = Techno-Fundamentalism (Systematic modernization)
       * World-views orientation: A = Anthropo-Centric, E = Eco-centric, T = Techno-centric.
       * The > sign symbolizes the dominance of the left domain over the right one. According to the author's analysis, the colonial governance style and the development orientation of economic powers in Hong Kong were mostly economic one, similar to modes (I), (V) and (VI) of the scheme; whereas the world-view version (II) and its variations are found among many Chinese. The author considers that the WWF, CA and the FOE are more or less following the (I) and (V) domains in their interpretation (or the *Shallow Green* version) of environmentalism, while GP has adopted the (II) dimension with a very strong articulation for changing the lifestyle.
70. For detailed elaboration, see Lai, *The synergy of nature, people and technology* and 'Community, environment and sustainable development', Canan, 'Bringing nature back in: the challenge of environmental sociology', and Brulle, 'Environmental discourse and social movement organizations'.
71. This was according to Simon Chau, one of the 'famous' eco-lifestyle experimenters, as well as a Green Power activator. He was once the celebrity of the environmentalism in Hong Kong. For reference, see Chau, 'Changing environmental

attitudes in Hong Kong' and 'Environmental education and environmental ethics in Hong Kong', and his work with Fung, 'Ancient wisdom and sustainable development from a Chinese perspective'.

72. Source from Chau, 'Letters to activators'.

73. Green Power has chosen the term 'activator' to symbolize their anti-hierarchy and anti-organizational orientation.

74. See Fok, 'Where is the green movement going?' and the regular column on green issues in *The light of Dharma* for reference.

75. See Chau, 'Letters to activators', and Fung, 'Draft on environmentalists profile' for detailed description.

76. See Chau and Fung, 'Ancient wisdom', for elaboration.

77. It might be argued that those ideological appeals have been embedded in 'Chinese' culture for centuries. This can be shown by the use of herbal medicine and other eco- and environmentally based rituals to deal with the body and mind of Chinese.

78. The socio-political implication derived from this discussion on the intricate relations between consumption and environmental quality is two-fold. First, it is believed that by changing consumption patterns, say, consuming less and using recycled materials, the depletion rate of natural resources could be reduced in the long run, or at least, the problem of waste could be lessened. The state's procurement policy to foster the 'green' sector of production is thus advocated. Second, environmental problems, as argued, could largely be controlled by the use of (not just) market mechanisms, such as government-imposed pricing, or indirect means to reduce demands for non-environment-friendly production and consumption.

79. In Hong Kong, another related fashion which was associated with the nostalgia identity of consumable products (hence consumerism) was the less-than-18-month life span of the LOFT (Looking Out for Thing, the name of an avant-garde shop, managed by an eco-friendly legislator). See Pang, 'Influence of environmentalism on consumer behavior' and also Bourdieu, *Distinction*, for analysis on the symbolic meaning of consumption.

80. Body Shop sells (and promotes consumption of) green products. According to their advertisement, the products are not harmful to the environment, and are safe and healthy for people. Yet, this might be questioned by those eco-fundamentalist or product life cycle analysts that there is no such thing as 'no harmful effect' on nature.

81. See Howroyd and MacPherson, 'Business, environment and the community', for the business community's interest and their approach to environmental protection.

82. It should be noted that a handful of environmental NGO leaders did literally work as freelance consultants for government or environmental consulting companies. This might be argued that they had rested interests in soft approach to environmental movements.

83. An important concept coined by King, 'The administrative absorption'.

84. See Princen et al., *Environmental NGOs in world politics*, and Lee, 'A comparative look at the environmental movements in Taiwan and Hong Kong', for comparison.

85. Accordingly, at least one of the environmental NGO leaders has his own private business in environmental consultancy.

86. The obvious examples of media-made environmental celebrity are Simon Chau and green legislator Christine Loh. See also the critical position of Man, 'In search of community'.

87. See the critical position in Man, 'Too soft', versus a technologist's version of environmental movements by Montgomery, 'Too hard'.

88. See Environmental Campaigns Committee, 'A survey on environmental attitude', Ng, 'The environmental attitude', and Lai, 'Environmental attitude' for change in the environmental attitude in Hong Kong.
89. See Catton and Dunlap, 'A new ecological paradigm', for elaboration.
90. See Cheng, Lim and Ng, 'Green consumption', for brief analysis.
91. As expected, the official line of explanation argued that environmental quality improvement was a result of the government's environmental protection programmes. See Environmental Protection Department, *Environment 1994.*
92. The author is doubtful about this assumption due to the fact that, on several occasions, some environmentalists from Hong Kong had been requested 'not to present certain views' by their 'NGO' counterparts in China.

Bibliography

❑ Documents and Periodicals

Amnesty International.

Association for the Advancement of Feminism. *Annual report.* Various years.

The Basic Law of the Hong Kong Special Administrative Region of the People's Republic of China. 1992. Hong Kong: One Country Two Systems Economic Research Institute.

Census and Statistics Department. *Hong Kong annual digest of statistics.* Various years.

———. December 1996. *Monthly digest of statistics.*

———. 1997. *Quarterly report on general household survey: October to December 1996.*

Cheng Ming.

The Chinese Democracy Movements Information Centre, ed. May 1990. *Newspaper advertisements on the democratic movements of China '89.*

———, ed. May 1990. *Witness reports on the democratic movement of China '89.*

Colonial Secretary of Hong Kong. 1962. *Report on women's salary scales in the public service.* Hong Kong: Colonial Secretariat.

———. 1967. *White Paper on Chinese marriages in Hong Kong.* Hong Kong: Colonial Secretariat.

Commissioner for Administrative Complaints (COMAC) of Hong Kong. 1994. *The sixth annual report of the COMAC.* Hong Kong: Hong Kong Government Printer.

Commissioner for Labour. *Annual departmental report.* Various years. Hong Kong: Government Printer.

Committee of Inquiry into the 1988 Civil Service Pay Adjustment and Related Matters. 1988. *Interim report*. Hong Kong: Government Printer.

CTU in Solidarity.

A draft agreement between the government of the United Kingdom of Great Britain and Northern Ireland and the government of the People's Republic of China on the future of Hong Kong. 1984.

Eastern Express.

Economic Daily.

Environmental Campaign Committee. 1993. *A survey of environmental attitudes in Hong Kong* [a study commissioned by the Education Working Group, undertaken by the Social Science Research Centre of the University of Hong Kong].

Environmental Protection Department. 1994. *Environment: Hong Kong 1994*. Hong Kong: Hong Kong Government Printer.

Environmental Resources Ltd. 1989. *Tsing Yi hazard potential*. Hong Kong: Hong Kong Government Printer.

The Express News.

Far Eastern Economic Review.

FTU Press.

The grassroots White Paper on public housing policy in the 1990s. 1992. Hong Kong: Tang Brothers Resources and Research Publication Company.

HKPTU News.

The Hong Kong Alliance in Support of the Patriotic Democratic Movements of China, ed. *Annual report of the general committee of the Alliance*. Various years.

Hong Kong Association of Women Workers. *Bimonthly* (May 1992).

Hong Kong Commission on Salaries. 1971. *Report*. Hong Kong: Government Printer.

The Hong Kong Council of Social Service. *Community development resource book*. Various years.

Hong Kong Daily News.

Hong Kong Economic Daily.

Hong Kong Economic Journal.

Hong Kong Government. *Hong Kong*. Various years.

———. *Kowloon disturbances 1966: report of Commission of Inquiry*. Hong Kong: Government Printer.

———. 1989. *White Paper: pollution in Hong Kong — a time to act*. Hong Kong: Hong Kong Government Printer.

———. 1993. *2nd review of the White Paper on environment*. Hong Kong: Hong Kong Government Printer.

Hong Kong Hansard.

Hong Kong Legislative Council. *Official report of proceedings*.

Hong Kong Provisional Hospital Authority. 1989. *Report of the Provisional Hospital Authority 1989*. Hong Kong: Government Printer.

Hong Kong Salaries Commission. 1959. *Hong Kong Salaries Commission report*. Hong Kong: Salaries Commission.

Hong Kong Standard.

Hong Kong Standing Commission on Civil Service Salaries and Conditions of Service. 1979. *First report on principles and practices governing civil service pay*. Hong Kong: Hong Kong Standing Commission on Civil Service Salaries and Conditions of Service.

———. 1980. *Report no. 2: first report on civil service pay*. Hong Kong: Hong Kong Standing Commission on Civil Service Salaries and Conditions of Service.

———. 1980. *Report no. 4: consultative machinery in the civil service*. Hong Kong: Hong Kong Standing Commission on Civil Service Salaries and Conditions of Service.

———. 1988. *Report no. 21: consultative machinery in the civil service*. Hong Kong: Hong Kong Standing Commission on Civil Service Salaries and Conditions of Service.

Inrasia Pacific Ltd. Survey reports: H-03, May 1989; OP 19, 29 October 1988; OP 6a, August 1989.

Joint Committee on Public Housing Policy Review. 1992. Hong Kong: Tang Brothers Resources and Research Publication Company.

Joint Committee on the Promotion of Democratic Government. 16 May 1989. 'An urgent statement concerning the students' hunger strikes in Beijing and in Hong Kong' [unpublished statement].

Ming Pao Daily News.

The minutes of no. 38 general meeting of the JCPDG [unpublished internal document]. 16 May 1989.

New York Times.

The Nineties.

Nurses Branch, Hong Kong Chinese Civil Servants' Association. 1989. *20th anniversary issue*. Hong Kong: Nurses Branch.

October Review.

Oriental Daily News.

Planning, Environment and Land Branch of the Hong Kong Government Secretariat. 1993. *A green challenge for the community — the 2nd review of the White Paper on pollution in Hong Kong*. Hong Kong: Hong Kong Government Printer.

Registrar of Trade Unions, Hong Kong. *Annual department report*. Various years. Hong Kong: Government Printer.

Review Committee on Disciplined Services Pay and Conditions of Service. 1988. *Final report*. Hong Kong: Government Printer.

Sing Pao.

Sing Tao Evenings News.

Sing Tao Jih Pao.

South China Morning Post.

Students of the Capital. 'Letter to Hong Kong compatriots [Gao Xianggang tongbao shu]'. Republished in *The Selection of Source Documents from the Chinese Democracy Movement* 1, p. 14.

The Student Union of the University of Hong Kong. *Union Journal.* Various years.

Ta Kung Pao.

Tin Tin Daily News.

Tun Mun District Women's Association 1989 special report.

United Daily News.

University Line.

The Urban Council White Paper 1971. Hong Kong: Government Printer.

Wah Kiu Yat Po.

Washington Post.

Wen Wei Po.

A women's commission for Hong Kong: the campaign for a women's commission and for the application of CEDAW. March 1993.

❏ Books and Articles

Armour, A.M. 1991. The sitting of locally unwanted landuse: towards a cooperative approach. *Progress in Planning* 34.

Arn, Jack. 1984. Public sector unions. In *The Hong Kong civil service: personnel policies and practices*, eds. Scott, Ian and John P. Burns. 227–57. Hong Kong: Oxford University Press.

Barbalet, J.M. 1989. Social movements and the state: the case of the American labor movement. In *Politics of the future: the role of social movements*, eds. Jennett, Christine and Randal G. Stewart. South Melbourne: The Macmillan Company of Australia.

Baum, Richard. 1994. *Burying Mao*. 69–79. New Jersey: Princeton University Press.

Bourdieu, Pierre. 1984. *Distinction: a social critique of judgement of taste.* London: RK Paul.

Brand, Karl-Werner. 1990. Cyclical aspects of new social movements: waves of cultural criticism and mobilization cycles of new middle-class radicalism. In *Challenging the political order: new social and political movements in Western democracy*, eds. Dalton, Russell J. and Manfred Kuechler. Cambridge: Polity Press.

Brockett, Charles D. The structure of political opportunities and peasant mobilization in Central America. *Comparative Politics* 23, no. 3 (1991): 253–74.

Brockman, Vicky. Theoretical concerns in comparative social movement research [paper presented at the XIII World Congress in Sociology, International Sociological Association, Bielefeld, Germany, 18–23 July 1994].

Brulle, Robert J. Environmental discourse and social movement organizations. *Sociological Inquiry* 66, no. 1 (1996): 58–83.

Calhoun, Craig. 1994. Social theory and the politics of identity. In *Social theory and the politics of identity*, ed. Calhoun, Craig. 9–36. Oxford: Blackwell.

Canan, Penelope. Bringing nature back in: the challenge of environmental sociology. *Sociological Inquiry* 66, no. 1 (1996): 29–37.

Canel, Eduardo. 1992. Democratization and the decline of urban social movements in Uruguay: a political-institutional account. In *The making of social movements in Latin America*, eds. Escobar, Arturo and Sonia Alvarez. 276–90. Boulder, CO: Westview Press.

Castells, M. 1988. Public housing and economic development in Hong Kong. In *Economic development and housing policy in the Asia Pacific Rim: a comparative study of Hong Kong, Singapore, and Shenzhen Special Economic Zone*, eds. Castells, M. et al. Berkeley: Monograph 37, Institute of Urban and Regional Development, University of California at Berkeley.

Catton, Wiley and Raph Dunlap. A new ecological paradigm for post-exuberant sociology. *American Behavioral Scientist* 24, no. 1 (1980): 15–47.

Central Office of Information, Reference Division. 1956. *Labour in the United Kingdom dependencies*. London: Central Office of Information.

Chan, Cecilia and Peter Hills, eds. 1993. *Limited gains*. Hong Kong: Centre of Urban Planning and Environmental Management, the University of Hong Kong.

———, eds. 1997. *Community mobilizations and the environment*. Hong Kong: Centre of Urban Planning and Environmental Management, the University of Hong Kong.

Chan, John. The impact of a changing environment on Hong Kong's human resources policies. Hong Kong Institute of Personnel Management 12th Annual Conference, 9 October 1991.

Chan, King-cheung. A review of the Hong Kong students' participation in the Chinese democracy movement. In *Democratic China*, ed. the Student Union of the Chinese University of Hong Kong. (In Chinese.)

Chan, Ming K. and David J. Clark, eds. 1991. *The Hong Kong Basic Law: blueprint for stability and prosperity under Chinese sovereignty?* Hong Kong: Hong Kong University Press.

Chan, Ming K. and Tuen-yu Lau. Dilemma of the Communist press in a pluralistic society. *Asian Survey* 30, no. 8 (August 1990): 738–44.

Chan, Po-king. 1987. The local women's movement and the women's perspective of new feminism. In *Popular cultural studies and sexism*, eds. Sze, Stephen M.H. et al. Hong Kong: Youth Literary Books.

Chan, R. Yee-kwong. A study of the environmental attitudes and behaviors of customers in Hong Kong. *International Journal of Environmental Education and Information* 12, no. 4 (1993): 285–96.

Chau, L.C. 1989. Labour and labour market. In *The economic system of Hong Kong*, eds. Ho, H.C.Y. and L.C. Chau. Hong Kong: Asian Research Service.

Chau, Simon S.C. 1990. The environment. In *The other Hong Kong report 1990*, eds. Wong, Richard Y.C. and Joseph Y.S. Cheng. Hong Kong: The Chinese University Press.

———. 10 November 1992. Letters to activators of Green Power Limited [unpublished].

———. 'Changing environmental attitudes in Hong Kong. Conference paper, Environmental Education and Environmental Ethics — Asian Perspectives, organized by the Centre of Urban Planning and Environmental Management, the University of Hong Kong, 22–23 February 1994, Hong Kong.

———. Environmental education and environmental ethics in Hong Kong. In *Community mobilization and the environment in Hong Kong*, eds. Chan, Cecilia and Peter Hills. Hong Kong: Centre of Urban Planning and Environmental Management, the University of Hong Kong. (Forthcoming.)

——— and Kam-K Fung. 1990. Ancient wisdom and sustainable development from a Chinese perspective. In *Ethics of environment and development*, eds. Engel, J. Ronald and Joan G. Engel. London: Belhaven Press.

Chau, W.S. Confrontation and protest should be orderly. *Hong Kong Economic Journal* (21 December 1994). (In Chinese.)

Cheek-Milby, K. 1984. Staff relations. In *The Hong Kong civil service*, eds. Scott, I. and J.P. Burns. 187–226. Hong Kong: Oxford University Press.

———. 1988. Identifying the issues. In *The Hong Kong civil service and its future*, eds. Scott, I. and J.P. Burns. 109–30. Hong Kong: Oxford University Press.

Cheng, Joseph Y.S., ed. 1984. *Hong Kong: in search of a future*. Hong Kong: Oxford University Press.

———. Hong Kong: the pressure to converge. *International Affairs* 63, no. 2 (1987): 271–83.

Cheng, Tun-jen. Democratizing the quasi-Leninist regime in Taiwan. *World Politics* 41 (July 1989): 481.

Cheng, Wai-ling, Mei-kei Lim and Wing-han Ng. Green consumption — a new phase of consumerism [unpublished project report, Department of Sociology, the Chinese University of Hong Kong].

Cheng, Y.T. 1988. The role of a trade union centre in a changing society: the case of the Hong Kong Federation of Trade Unions. In *Labour movement in a changing society: the experience of Hong Kong*, eds. Jao, Y.C. et al. 113–6. Hong Kong: Centre of Asian Studies, the University of Hong Kong.

Cheung, Anthony B.L. The rise of the new middle class and its political implications. *Ming Pao Monthly* 253 (1987). (In Chinese.)

———. 1990. The civil service. In *The other Hong Kong report 1990*, eds. Wong, Richard Y.C. and Joseph Y.S. Cheng. 87–112. Hong Kong: The Chinese University Press.

———. 1991. The civil service. In *The other Hong Kong report 1991*, eds. Lee, Ming-kwan and Yun-wing Sung. 27–54. Hong Kong: The Chinese University Press.

Cheung, Bing-leung and Kin-sheun Louie. 1991. Social conflicts in Hong Kong, 1975–1986: trends and implications [occasional paper no. 3, Hong Kong Institute of Asia-Pacific Studies, the Chinese University of Hong Kong].

Cheung, Fanny. The women's center: a community approach to feminism in Hong Kong. *American Journal of Community Psychology* 17, no. 1 (1989): 99–107.

Cheung, Fanny M. et al. 1994. The underdeveloped political potential of women in Hong Kong. In *Women and politics worldwide*, eds. Nelson, Barbara J. and Najma Chowdhury. 327–46. New Haven: Yale University Press.

Cheung, Kit-fung, Wing-hung Lo, Kin-hing Yeung and Lucie Chan, eds. 1991. *No change for fifty years! The wrestle among China, Britain and Hong Kong for the Basic Law*. Hong Kong: Wave Publishers. (In Chinese.)

Cheung, Lilian Suet-mui. 1989. Public sector unions in Hong Kong: a study of the reorganization of the Medical and Health Department [M.Soc.Sc. dissertation, the University of Hong Kong].

Child, John. Organizational structure, environment and performance: the role of strategic choice. *Sociology* 6 (1972): 1–22.

The Chinese Democracy Movements Information Centre, ed. February 1991. *Concerned organizations on Chinese democratic movement '89.* (In Chinese.)

Chiu, K.Y.P. 1986. Labour organizations and political change in Hong Kong [M.Soc.Sc. dissertation, the University of Hong Kong].

Chiu, Stephen W.K. 1986. A brief history of the metal industry workers' union. In *Dimensions of the Chinese and Hong Kong labor movement*, eds. Chan, M.K. et al. 138–44. Hong Kong: Christian Industrial Committee. (In Chinese.)

———. 1987. Strikes in Hong Kong: a sociological study [unpublished M.Phil. thesis, the University of Hong Kong].

———. 1992. The reign of the market: economy and industrial conflicts in Hong Kong [occasional paper no. 16, Institute of Asia-Pacific Studies, the Chinese University of Hong Kong].

——— and David A. Levin. From a labour-surplus to a labour-scarce economy: challenges to human resource management in Hong Kong. *The International*

Journal of Human Resource Management 4, no. 1 (February 1993): 159–89.

——— and Ho-fung Hung. 1997. The colonial state and rural protests in Hong Kong [occasional paper no. 59, Institute of Asia-Pacific Studies, the Chinese University of Hong Kong].

——— and David A. Levin. 1997. Private sector unionism. In *Social movements in Hong Kong*, eds. Chiu, S.W.K. and T.L. Lui. Armonk: M.E. Sharpe.

Choi, C.K. et al. 1998. *A common path to divergent destinations*. Hong Kong: Hong Kong Humanities Press. (In Chinese.)

Chow, Ming-fai. Angry tenants mob rent policy meeting. *Hong Kong Standard*, 27 September 1991.

Chow, Nelson. 1994. Welfare development in Hong Kong — an ideological appraisal. In *25 years of social and economic development in Hong Kong*, eds. Leung, Benjamin K.P. and Teresa Y.C. Wong. Hong Kong: Centre of Asian Studies, the University of Hong Kong.

Chuek, Chai. 1978. Viewing the Hong Kong student movement through the Hong Kong University Student Union. In *The Hong Kong student movement: retrospect and examination.* Hong Kong: the Student Union of the University of Hong Kong. (In Chinese.)

Chui, W.T. and O.K. Lai. 1994. Patterns of social conflicts in Hong Kong in the period 1980 to 1991 [mimeo].

Chui, Wing-tak and On-kwok Lai. 1995. *Patterns of social conflicts in Hong Kong in the period 1980–1991* [monograph no. 1, Department of Applied Social Studies, Hong Kong Polytechnic University].

Chung, Eun-sung. 1990. Transition to democracy in an authoritarian regime: a case study of South Korea [Ph.D. thesis, City University of New York].

Chung, Robert T.Y. 1994. Public opinion. In *The other Hong Kong report, 1994*, eds. Choi, Po-king and Lok-sang Ho. 401–24. Hong Kong: The Chinese University Press.

———. 1994. Public opinion. In *The other Hong Kong report*, eds. McMillen, Donald H. and Si-wai Man. 103–24. Hong Kong: The Chinese University Press.

Cohen, Jean. Strategy or identity: new theoretical paradigms and contemporary social movements. *Social Research* 52, no. 4 (1985): 663–716.

Collier, David and Deborah L. Norden. Strategic choice models of political change in Latin America. *Comparative Politics* 24, no. 2 (1992): 229–33.

Conell, Carol and Samuel Cohn. Learning from other people's actions: environmental variation and diffusion in French coal mining strikes, 1890–1935. *American Journal of Sociology* 101, no. 2 (September 1995): 366–403.

Conservancy Association. September 1994. *Land use and environmental quality in north west New Territories.*

Cooper, John. 1970. *The colony in conflict.* Hong Kong: Swindon.

Cottrell, R. 1993. *The end of Hong Kong.* London: John Murray Ltd.

Crozier, Michel. 1971. *The world of the office worker*. Chicago: University of Chicago Press.

Dahl, R. 1971. *Polyarchy*. New Haven: Yale University Press.

Dalton, Russell and Manfred Kuechler, eds. 1990. *Challenging the political boundary*. Cambridge: Polity Press.

Darayani, Renu. 1995. *Hong Kong 1995: a review of 1994*. Hong Kong: Government Printer.

Davies, S.N.G. 1989. The changing nature of representation in Hong Kong politics. In *Hong Kong: the challenge of transformation*, eds. Cheek-Milby, K. and M. Mushkat. Hong Kong: Centre of Asian Studies, the University of Hong Kong.

della Porta, Donantella and Dieter Rucht. 1995. Left-Libertarian movements in context. In *The politics of social protest*, eds. Jenkins, J. Craig and Bert Klandermans. Minneapolis: University of Minnesota Press.

Deyo, F., S. Haggard and H. Koo. Labor in the political economy of East Asian industrialization. *Bulletin of Concerned Asian Scholars* 19, no. 2 (1987): 42–53.

Deyo, Frederic C. 1984. Export-manufacturing and labor: the Asian case. In *Labor in the capitalist world-economy*, ed. Bergquist, Charles. Beverly Hills: Sage.

———, ed. 1987. *The political economy of the new Asian industrialism*. Ithaca: Cornell University Press.

———. 1989. *Beneath the miracle: labor subordination in the new Asian industrialism*. Berkeley: University of California Press.

Di Palma, Giuseppe. 1990. *To craft democracies: an essay on democratic transitions*. Berkeley: University of California Press.

Diamond, Irene and Lee Quinby. 1988. American feminism and the language of control. In *Feminism and Foucault: reflections on resistance*, eds. Diamond, Irene and Lee Quinby. 193–206. Boston: Northeastern University Press.

Diamond, Larry. 1990. Beyond authoritarianism and totalitarianism: strategies for democratization. In *The new democracies: global change and U.S. policy*, ed. Roberts, Brad. 227–49. Cambridge, Mass. : MIT Press.

———. 1993. Global economic transformation and less developed countries. In *Global transformation & the Third World*, eds. Slater, Robert O., Barry M. Schutz and Steven R. Dorr. 31–70. Boulder, Colo.: L. Rienner.

———. Toward democratic consolidation. *Journal of Democracy* 5, no. 3 (1994): 4–17.

Dobson, Alan. 1990. *Green political thought*. London: Unwin Hayman.

Donald, Share. Transitions to democracy and transition through transaction. *Comparative Political Studies* 19, no. 4 (1987): 532–48.

Dunlop, J.T. 1977. *Industrial relations systems* (2nd ed.). Carbondale IL: Southern Illinois University Press.

Eisinger, Peter K. The conditions of protest behavior in American cities. *American Political Science Review* 67 (1973): 11–28.

Elliott, D. The numbers don't lie. *Newsweek* (13 July 1998).

Engel, Ronald J. and Joan G. Engel, eds. 1990. *Ethics of environment and development*. London: Belhaven Press.

England, Joe. 1989. *Industrial relations and law in Hong Kong* (2nd ed.). Hong Kong: Oxford University Press.

———— and John Rear. 1975. *Chinese labour under British rule*. Hong Kong: Oxford University Press.

———— and John Rear. 1981. *Industrial relations and law in Hong Kong*. Hong Kong: Oxford University Press.

Eyerman, Ron and Andrew Jamison. 1991. *Social movements: a cognitive approach*. Cambridge: Polity Press.

Farganis, Sondra. 1994. *Situating feminism: from thought to action*. Thousand Oaks: Sage Publications.

Ferree, M. and F.D. Miller. Mobilization and meaning: toward an integration of social psychological and resource perspectives on social movement. *Sociological Inquiry* 55 (1985): 38–61.

Fok, Tou-hui. Where is the green movement going? *The Light of Dharma* 81 (February 1989): 1. (In Chinese.)

Foweraker, Joe. 1994. Popular political organization and democratization: a comparison of Spain and Mexico. In *Developing democracy*, eds. Budge, Ian and David McKay. London: Sage.

Fox, Alan. 1971. *A sociology of work in industry*. London: Collier Macmillan.

Friends of Rooftop, ed. 1997. *The moonlight on rooftop: lessons of the Tsuen Wan rooftop squatters incident*. Hong Kong: Shi-lin Publisher. (In Chinese.)

Fung, Kam-kwong. 1994. Draft on the environmentalists' profile in Hong Kong [unpublished].

Fung, Siu-yin. 1995. Social dynamics in Cathay Pacific strike [unpublished M.Phil. thesis, Department of Sociology, the Chinese University of Hong Kong].

Fung, Wai-hing. 1993. Vegetarian diet and the green belief system [unpublished project report, Department of Sociology, the Chinese University of Hong Kong].

Fung, Yuk-lin. 1990. *Approaching 1997*. Hong Kong: Cosmos Books Ltd. (In Chinese.)

Gamson, William. 1975. *The strategy of social protest*. Homewood, Ill: Dorsey Press.

Gastil, Raymond. 1978. *Freedom in the world*. Westport: Greenwood Press.

Gilley, Bruce. Jumping the gun. *Far Eastern Economic Review* (6 February 1997): 16.

————. Security for whom? *Far Eastern Economic Review* (24 April 1997): 17.

Goldthorpe, J. 1978. The current inflation: towards a sociological account. In *The political economy of inflation*, eds. Hirsch, F. and J. Goldthrope. London: Martin Robertson.

—— et al. 1968. *The affluent worker: industrial attitudes and behaviour.* Cambridge: Cambridge University Press.

Goodin, Robert. 1976. *The politics of rational man.* New York: John Wiley & Son.

——. 1992. *Green political theory.* Cambridge: Polity Press.

Hambro, Edward I. 1955. *The problem of Chinese refugees in Hong Kong.* Hong Kong: Macmillan Publishers Ltd.

Harding, G. Tragedy of the Commons. *Science* 162 (13 December 1968): 1243–8.

Harris, P. 1978. *Hong Kong: a study in bureaucratic politics.* Hong Kong: Heinemann Asia.

Heiman, M. From not-in-my-backyard to not-in-anybody-backyard. *American Planning Association Journal* (Summer 1990): 359–62.

Herring, R.J. Restructuring the Commons: collective action and ecology. *Items* 44 (4 December 1990): 64–8.

Hirschman, Albert O. 1970. *Exit, voice, and loyalty: responses to decline in firms, organizations and states.* Cambridge, MA: Harvard University Press.

Ho, Kwong-ming. 1979. The government and the clerical workers: a case study of labor-management conflicts in the Hong Kong civil service [unpublished M.Phil. thesis, Department of Sociology, the University of Hong Kong].

Hoadley, Stephen. Hong Kong is the lifeboat: notes on political culture and socialization. *Journal of Oriental Studies* 8 (1970).

The Hong Kong Council of Social Service (HKCSS) — Editorial Board of the *Quarterly*. A situation report on voluntary agencies' environmental protection activities. *HKCSS Quarterly* 18 (Winter 1991): 11–8.

The Hong Kong Council of Social Service (HKCSS) — Resource Group on Town Planning. 1992. *Case analysis on building a golf course at Sha Lo Tung* [unpublished].

The Hong Kong Federation of Students, ed. 1983. *The student movement in Hong Kong: a retrospective examination.* Hong Kong: Wide Angle Publisher. (In Chinese.)

Hong Kong Housing Authority. 1987. *Review of the long-term housing strategy.* Hong Kong: Hong Kong Housing Authority.

——. 1993. *A report on the mid-term review on the long-term housing strategy.* Hong Kong: Hong Kong Housing Authority.

Hong Kong Justice of Peace Commission. 1979. *The land of Hong Kong: so precious.* Hong Kong: Hong Kong Justice of Peace Commission.

Hopkins, Keith, ed. 1971. *Hong Kong: the industrial colony.* Hong Kong: Oxford University Press.

Howroyd, S. 1997. Business and the environment in Hong Kong. In *Community mobilization and the environment in Hong Kong*, eds. Chan, Cecilia and Peter Hills. Hong Kong: Centre of Urban Planning and Environmental Management, the University of Hong Kong.

Hsiao, Michael Hsin-huang. The character and changes of Taiwan's local environmental protest movement: 1980–1991. In *Environmental protection and industrial policies*, ed. Taiwan Research Fund. 555–73. Taipei: Vanguard Publication Co. (In Chinese.)

———, Lester M. Milbrath and Robert Weller. Antecedence of an environmental movement in Taiwan. *Capitalism, Nature, Socialism: A Journal of Socialist Ecology* 6, no. 3 (1995): 91–104.

Hung Wing-tat. 1993. The politicization of the environment. In *Limited gains*, eds. Chan, Cecilia and Peter Hills. 41–50. Hong Kong: Centre of Urban Planning and Environmental Management, the University of Hong Kong.

———. 1994. The environment. In *The other Hong Kong report 1994*, eds. McMillen, Donald H. and Si-wai Man. 253–64. Hong Kong: The Chinese University Press.

———. The politics of the environment. In *Community mobilization and the environment in Hong Kong*, eds. Chan, Cecilia and Peter Hills. Hong Kong: Centre of Urban Planning and Environmental Management, the University of Hong Kong. (Forthcoming.)

Huntington, Samuel P. 1991. *The third wave: democratization in the late twentieth century*. London: University of Oklahoma Press.

Inglehart, Ronald. 1990. *Cultural shift*. Princeton: Princeton University Press.

Ip, C.P. 1995. Advocating the housing rights and its development. In *A symposium on housing policy in Hong Kong*, eds. Kam, P.K. et al. Hong Kong: Joint Publishing (H.K.) Co., Ltd. (In Chinese.)

Jao, Y.C. et al., eds. 1988. *Labour movement in a changing society*. Hong Kong: Centre of Asian Studies, the University of Hong Kong.

Jarvie, I.C. 1969. A postscript on riots and the future of Hong Kong. In *Hong Kong: a society in transition*, eds. Jarvie, I.C. and J. Agassi. London: Routledge & Kegan Paul.

Jenkins, J. and B. Klandermans, eds. 1995. *The politics of social protest*. London: UCL Press.

Jenson, Jane. 1987. Changing discourse, changing agendas: political rights and reproductive policies in France. In *The women's movements of the United States and Western Europe: consciousness, political opportunity and public policy*, eds. Fainsod Katzenstein, Mary and Carol McClurg Mueller. 64–88. Philadelphia: Temple University Press.

Johnson, Nevil. 1982. Accountability, control, and complexity: moving beyond ministerial responsibility. In *Quangos in Britain: government and the networks of public policy-making*, ed. Baker, A. London and Basingstoke: The Macmillan Press Ltd.

Johnston, Paul. 1994. *Success while others fail: social movement unionism and the public workplace.* Ithaca NY: ILR Press.

The Joint Associations Working Group. 1989. *Report on Hong Kong's labour shortage.* Hong Kong: the Joint Associations Working Group.

Jones, Carol. 1995. The New Territories inheritance law: colonization and the elites. In *Women in Hong Kong*, eds. Pearson, Veronica and Benjamin Leung. 167–92. Hong Kong: Oxford University Press.

Kam, P.K. et al. The protests at the entrance of Government House and the arrest of 23 people — whose responsibility? *Sing Tao Jih Pao*, 15 April 1993. (In Chinese.)

Kelly, James and Patsy Moy. Critics attacking housing figures. *Hong Kong Standard*, 2 March 1996.

King, Ambrose Y.C. Administrative absorption of politics in Hong Kong. *Asian Survey* XV, no. 5 (May 1975): 422–39.

———. 1981. The administrative absorption of politics in Hong Kong: with special emphasis on the City District Officer Scheme. In *Social life and development in Hong Kong*, eds. King, Ambrose Y.C. and Rance P.L. Lee. Hong Kong: The Chinese University Press.

———. 1981. The political culture of Kwun Tong. In *Social life and development in Hong Kong*, eds. King, Ambrose Y.C. and Rance P.L. Lee. Hong Kong: The Chinese University Press.

Kitschelt, Herbert P. Political opportunity structure and political protest: antinuclear movements in four democracies. *British Journal of Political Science* 16 (1986): 57–85.

———. 1989. *The logics of party formation.* Ithaca, NJ: Cornell University Press.

Kochan, Thomas A., Harry C. Katz and Robert B. McKersie. 1994. *The transformation of American industrial relations* (2nd ed.). Ithaca, NY: ILR Press.

Kochan, Tom. 1982. Toward a behavioral model of management under collective bargaining. In *Conflict management and industrial relations*, eds. Bomer, Gerald B.J. and Richard B. Peterson. 194–211. Boston: Kluwer-Nijhoff.

Kong, T.C. 1988. The strikes at the Mass Transit Railway: causes and implications. In *Labour movement in a changing society: the experience of Hong Kong*, eds. Jao, Y.C. et al. 143–6. Hong Kong: Centre of Asian Studies, the University of Hong Kong.

Krause, L.R. Hong Kong and Singapore: twins or kissing cousins. *Economic Development and Cultural Change* 36, no. 3 (1988): S45–S66.

Kriesi, Hanspeter. 1995. The political opportunity structure of new social movements. In *The politics of social protest*, eds. Jenkins, J. Craig and Bert Klandermans. Minneapolis: University of Minnesota Press.

——— et al. 1995. *New social movements in Western Europe: a comparative analysis.* London: University of College London Press.

Kuan, H.C. 1979. Political stability and change in Hong Kong. In *Hong Kong: economic, social and political studies in development*, eds. Lin, T.B., R.P. Lee and U. Simonis. New York: M.E. Sharpe.

Kwok, Ngai-kuen. 1994. Political exchange network of Kwai Tsing District Board [unpublished M.Phil. thesis, Department of Sociology, the Chinese University of Hong Kong].

Kwok, Y.H. 1988. Staff representation on the Senior Civil Service Council: consultation, collective bargaining or participation. In *Labour movement in a changing society*, eds. Jao, Y.C. et al. 147–9. Hong Kong: Centre of Asian Studies, the University of Hong Kong.

Lai, On-kwok. 1992. Opinion survey report on environmental problem in Kwai Chung and Tsing Yi [unpublished report to the Kwai Chung and Tsing Yi District Board].

———. 1994. The selection of community work models. In *Community work: theory and practice*, eds. Kam, P.K. et al. Hong Kong: The Chinese University Press.

———. The synergy of nature, people and technology [unpublished research seminar paper, Centre of Urban Planning and Environmental Management, the University of Hong Kong, 8 November 1994].

———. 1995. Green consumption: towards a new modernity? [Occasional paper no. 5, Department of Applied Social Studies, Hong Kong Polytechnic University.]

———. 1995. The social goal of public housing under the Hong Kong style of capitalism. In *A symposium on housing policy in Hong Kong*, eds. Kam, P.K. et al. Hong Kong: Joint Publishing (H.K.) Co., Ltd. (In Chinese.)

———. 1995. Urban redevelopment and community work. In *Community work in Hong Kong*, eds. Mok, Henry T.K. et al. Hong Kong: Chung Hwa Publisher.

———. 1997. Community, environment, and sustainable development. In *Community mobilization and the environment in Hong Kong*, eds. Chan, Cecilia and Peter Hills. Hong Kong: Centre of Urban Planning and Environmental Management, the University of Hong Kong.

———. The politics of environment and space. In *Sustainable development and the future of city*, eds. Hamm, Bernd and R. Muttagi. Paris: UNESCO Press. (Forthcoming.)

Lai, Wai-chung. 1993. Urban renewal and the Land Development Corporation. In *The other Hong Kong report 1993*, eds. Choi, Po-king and Lok-sang Ho. Hong Kong: The Chinese University Press.

Lai, Wing-hoi. 1993. Environmental education in Social Welfare Agency [unpublished MSW dissertation, Department of Social Work and Social Administration, the University of Hong Kong].

Lam, Wah-hui. 1988. Proliferation and consolidation of trade unionism in the public sector. In *Labour movement in a changing society*, eds. Jao, Y.C. et al. 157–62. Hong Kong: Centre of Asian Studies, the University of Hong Kong.

Landsberger, Stefan R. 1990. Chronology of the 1989 student demonstrations. In *The Chinese people's movement: perspective on spring 1989*, ed. Saich, Tony. New York: M.E. Sharpe.

Lane, Kevin P. 1990. *Sovereignty and the status quo*. Oxford: Westview Press.

Lange, Peter and George Ross. 1982. *Unions, change and crisis: French and Italian strategy and the political economy, 1945–1980*. London: George Allen and Unwin.

Larana, Enrique, Hank Johnston and Joseph R. Gusfield, eds. 1994. *New social movements: from ideology to identity*. Philadelphia: Temple University Press.

Lau, Angel. Roof dwellers slam resettlement delays. *Hong Kong Standard*, 4 March 1995.

———. Ex-rooftop dwellers to snub bill for demolition. *Hong Kong Standard*, 13 March 1995.

Lau, K.Y. 1991. Housing. In *The other Hong Kong report 1991*, eds. Sung, Y.W. and Ming-kwan Lee. Hong Kong: The Chinese University Press.

Lau, San-ching. A journey without regret. *Hong Kong Economic Journal* (10 February -3 March 1992).

Lau, Siu-kai. 1982. *Society and politics in Hong Kong*. Hong Kong: The Chinese University Press.

———. 1985. Political reform and political development in Hong Kong. In *Hong Kong and 1997*, eds. Yao, Yu-ching et al. Hong Kong: Centre of Asian studies, the University of Hong Kong.

———. 1987. Decolonization without independence [occasional paper no. 19, Centre of Hong Kong Studies, the Chinese University of Hong Kong].

———. 1988. Basic Law and the new political order of Hong Kong [occasional paper no. 26, Centre of Hong Kong Studies, the Chinese University of Hong Kong].

——— and Hsin-chi Kuan. 1985. The 1985 District Board election in Hong Kong: the limits of political mobilization in a dependent policy [occasional paper no. 8, Centre for Hong Kong Studies, Institute of Social Studies, the Chinese University of Hong Kong].

——— and Hsin-chi Kuan. 1988. *The ethos of the Hong Kong Chinese*. Hong Kong: The Chinese University Press.

———, Ming-kwan Lee, Po-san Wan and Siu-lun Wong. 1991. *Indicators of social development: Hong Kong 1988*. Hong Kong: The Chinese University Press.

Law, P. 1988. White-collar unionism: the case of teachers. In *Labour movement in a changing society*, eds. Jao, Y.C. et al. 163–6. Hong Kong: Centre of Asian Studies, the University of Hong Kong.

Leary, Angela. Violent protest greets Governor. *Eastern Express*, 29 September 1995.

Lee, James K.C. 1992. From social rented housing to home ownership: the dilemma of housing policy in the nineties [paper presented at the conference on residential housing in Hong Kong, jointly organized by the Department of Business Studies, Hong Kong Polytechnic, and the Department of Economics, the Chinese University of Hong Kong].

Lee, Ming-kwan. 1987. Pressure groups and party politics. In *Hong Kong politics and society in transition*, ed. Lee, Ming-kwan. Hong Kong: Commercial Press. (In Chinese.)

———. 1998. Hong Kong identity — past and present. In *Hong Kong economy and society*, eds. Wong, S.L. and Maruyo Toyojiro. Tokyo: Institute of Developing Economies.

Lee, Yok-shiu F. Local NGOs and community-based urban environmental initiatives. Conference paper presented at the 2nd International Workshop on Community-based Urban Environmental Management in Asia, at the Centre of Urban Planning and Environmental Management, the University of Hong Kong, 6–10 September 1993.

———. A comparative look at the environmental movements in Taiwan and Hong Kong [conference paper presented at the Hong Kong Baptist University, sponsored by Green Power, 1 June 1996].

Lester, Richard A. 1958. *As unions mature: an analysis of the evolution of American unionism*. Princeton: Princeton University Press.

Leung, Sai-wing. 1993. The 'China factor' in the 1991 Legislative Council election: the June 4th incident and anti-communist China syndrome. In *Hong Kong tried democracy: the 1991 elections in Hong Kong*, eds. Lau, Siu-kai and Kin-sheun Louie. 187–235. Hong Kong: The Chinese University Press.

Leung, Benjamin K.P. 1982. Who protests [unpublished Ph.D. thesis, York University].

———. 1996. *Perspectives on Hong Kong society*. Hong Kong: Oxford University Press.

——— and Teresa Y.C. Wong, eds. 1994. *25 years of social and economic development in Hong Kong*. 252–69. Hong Kong: Centre of Asian Studies, the University of Hong Kong.

Leung, C.B. 1982. Community participation: from kai fong association, Mutual Aid Committee to District Board. In *Hong Kong in the 1980s*, ed. Cheng, J.Y.S. Hong Kong: Summerson (HK) Educational Research Centre.

———. 1986. Community participation: the decline of residents' organizations. In *Hong Kong in transition*, ed. Cheng, Joseph. Hong Kong: Oxford University Press.

———. 1990. Community development in Hong Kong: a study of 'top-down' and 'bottom-up' social policy planning and implementation [unpublished Ph.D. thesis, Department of Social Work and Social Administration, the University of Hong Kong].

———. 1990. Problems and changes in community politics. In *Social issues in Hong Kong*, ed. Leung, Benjamin K.P. 43–63. Hong Kong: Oxford University Press.

———. 1994. Community participation: past, present, and future. In *25 years of social and economic development in Hong Kong*, eds. Leung, Benjamin and Teresa Wong. 252–69. Hong Kong: Centre of Asian Studies, the University of Hong Kong.

Leung, C.Y. 1994. Changing a new sky for the sun and moon — a reflection on the protest against rental increase for new public rental housing. In *Searching for a path for grassroots organizations*. Hong Kong: Tsuen Wan Ecumenical Social Services Centre.

Leung, Pamela. Roof over their heads. *Eastern Express*, 17 April 1995.

Leung, P.L. 1988. Promoting workers' interests outside the trade union system: the experience of the Christian Industrial Committee. In *Labour movement in a changing society: the experience of Hong Kong*, eds. Jao, Y.C. et al. 117–9. Hong Kong, Centre of Asian Studies, the University of Hong Kong.

Leung, S.H. 1983. Industrial relations in Cable and Wireless: a unionist's view. In *Contemporary issues in Hong Kong labour relations*, eds. Ng, S.H. and D. Levin. 123–33. Hong Kong: Centre of Asian Studies, the University of Hong Kong.

Leung, Siu-han, Siu-kwok Sung and Min-yee Kwok. 1994. On environmental protection and economic development — the case of golf course development [unpublished students' report, Department of Sociology, the Chinese University of Hong Kong].

Leung, Trini and Apo Leung. 1988. *At the crossroads: Hong Kong's independent trade union movement and the international trade secretariats*. Hong Kong: Hong Kong Trade Union Education Centre and Asia Monitor Resource Center Ltd.

Leung, Wai-tung. 1993. Housing. In *The other Hong Kong report 1993*, eds. Choi, Po-king and Lok-sang Ho. Hong Kong: The Chinese University Press.

Levi, Margaret. 1977. *Bureaucratic insurgency*. Lexington, MA: Lexington Books.

Levin, David A. 1990. Work and its deprivations. In *Social issues in Hong Kong*, ed. Leung, Benjamin K.P. 85–113. Hong Kong: Oxford University Press.

——— and Stephen W.K. Chiu. 1993. Dependent capitalism, a colonial state, and marginal unions: the case of Hong Kong. In *Organized labor in the Asia-Pacific region: a comparative study of trade unionism in nine countries*, ed. Frenkel, Stephen. 187–222. Ithaca NY: ILR Press.

——— and Stephen W.K. Chiu. 1994. Decolonization without independence: political change and trade unionism in Hong Kong. In *The future of industrial relations: global change and challenges*, eds. Niland, John, Russell D. Lansbury and Chrissie Verevis. 329–48. Thousands Oaks and London: Sage Publications.

Li, W.W. The tension in labour relations is about to explode. *Pai Shing* (16 January

1990): 9–17. (In Chinese.)

Liang, S.X. 1986. Wither the Hong Kong labor movement? On the Lau Chin-sek incident [student's report, the University of Hong Kong]. (In Chinese.)

Lipset, Seymour Martin. 1976. Equity and equality in government wage policy. In *Public employee unions: a study of the crisis in public sector labor relations*, ed. Chickering, Lawrence A. 109–30. San Francisco: Institute for Contemporary Studies.

Lipsky, M. Protest as a political resource. *American Political Sciences Review* 62 (1968): 1144-58.

Lo, Clarence Y.H. 1992. Communities of challengers in social movement theory. In *Frontiers of social movement theory*, eds. Morris, Aldon D. and Carol McClurg Mueller. New Haven and London: Yale University Press.

Lo, S.H. Colonial policy-makers, capitalist class and China: determinants of electoral reform in Hong Kong's and Macau's legislatures. *Pacific Affairs* 62 (1989): 204–18.

Luhmann, Niklas. 1982. *The differentiation of society*. New York: Columbia University Press.

———. 1989. *Ecological communication*. Cambridge: Polity Press.

Lui, Tai-lok. 1984. Urban protests in Hong Kong: a sociological study of housing conflicts [unpublished M.Phil. thesis, Department of Sociology, the University of Hong Kong].

———. 1989. Pressure group politics and political participation. In *Hong Kong in transition*, ed. Cheng, Joseph. Hong Kong: Joint Publications. (In Chinese.)

———. 1990. Back to basics: rethinking the roles of residents' organizations. *Community development resource book 1989 and 1990*. Hong Kong: The Hong Kong Council of Social Service. (In Chinese.)

———. 1992. Work and work values. In *Indicators of social development*, ed. Lau, Siu-kai. 105–28. Hong Kong: Hong Kong Institute of Asia-Pacific Studies, the Chinese University of Hong Kong.

———. 1993. Two logics of community politics: residents' organizations and the 1991 election. In *Hong Kong tried democracy: the 1991 elections in Hong Kong*, eds. Lau, Siu-kai and Kin-sheun Louie. Hong Kong: Hong Kong Institute of Asia-Pacific Studies, the Chinese University of Hong Kong.

———. The path of development of Hong Kong's popular movements. In *Hong Kong Journal of Social Sciences* 4 (Autumn 1994): 67–78. (In Chinese.)

———. What is to be done? *Outspoken* (June 1996). (In Chinese.)

——— and J.K.S. Kung. 1985. *City unlimited: housing protests and urban politics in Hong Kong*. Hong Kong: Wide Angle Publications. (In Chinese.)

——— and Stephen W.K. Chiu. Industrial restructuring and labour-market adjustment under positive noninterventionism: the case of Hong Kong. *Environment and Planning* 25 (1993): 63–79.

Lui, Ting Terry. 1988. Changing civil servants' values. In *The Hong Kong civil service and its future*, eds. Scott, I. and J.P. Burns. 131–66. Hong Kong: Oxford

University Press.

Luker, Kristine. 1984. *Abortion and the politics of motherhood*. Berkeley: University of California Press.

Mak, Hoi-wah. 1988. White-collar unionism: the case of social workers. In *Labour movement in a changing society*, eds. Jao, Y.C. et al. 167–74. Hong Kong: Centre of Asian Studies, the University of Hong Kong.

Man, Chi-sum. The inadequacy of legislation on environmental impact assessment. *Hong Kong Economic Journal Daily* (14 October 1994).

Man, Si-wai. 1993. The environment. In *The other Hong Kong report 1993*, eds. Choi, Po-King and Lok-Sang Ho. 327–44. Hong Kong: The Chinese University Press.

———. 1995. The environment. In *From colony to Special Administrative Region*, eds. Cheng, Joseph Y.S. and Sunny S.H. Lo. Hong Kong: The Chinese University Press.

———. 1995. In search of community, the breakthrough of the discussion on public and private. In *Public and private: the development of human rights and civic society*, eds. Man, Si-Wai and Chan-Fai Cheung. 3–22. Hong Kong: Humanities Press.

———. Too soft — lashing the greens. *One Earth* [quarterly of the Friends of the Earth] (Summer 1995): 35.

McAdam, Doug. 1982. *Political process and the development of Black insurgency 1930–1970*. Chicago and London: University of Chicago Press.

———. 1982. Political process model of social movements. In *Political process and the development of Black insurgency 1930–1970*, McAdam, Doug. Chicago and London: University of Chicago Press.

———. 1988. Micromobilization contexts and recruitment to activism. In *International social movement research, vol. 1: from structure to action: comparing social movement across cultures*, eds. Klandermans, Bert, Hanspeter Kriesi and Sidney Tarrow. 125–54. Greenwich: JAI Press.

———. 1994. Culture and social movements. In *Ideology and identity in contemporary social movements*, eds. Gusfield, Joseph, Hank Johnston and Enrique Larana. 36–57. Philadelphia: Temple University Press.

———, John D. McCarthy and Mayer N. Zald. 1988. Social movements. In *Handbook of sociology*, ed. Smelser, N. 695–738. Newbury Park: Sage.

———, John McCarthy and Mayer Zald. 1996. *Comparative perspectives on social movements: political opportunities, mobilizing structures, and cultural framing*. Cambridge: Cambridge University Press.

——— and David Snow. 1997. Social movements: conceptual and theoretical issues. *Social movements*, eds. McAdam, D. and D. Snow. xviii–xxvi. Los Angeles: Roxbury Publishing Company.

McCarthy, John and Mayer Zald. Resource mobilization and social movement: a practical theory. *American Journal of Sociology* 82 (1977):1212–41.

McCarthy, John D. and Mayer N. Zald. 1987. The trend of social movements in America: professionalization and resource mobilization. In *Social movements in an organizational society: collected essays*, eds. Zald, Mayer N. and John D. McCarthy. 337–92. New Brunswick: Transaction Books.

McLaughlin, Eugune. 1993. Hong Kong: a residual welfare regime. *Comparing welfare states: Britain in international context*, eds. Cochrane, Allan and John Clarke. London: Sage Publications in association with the Open University, Hong Kong.

Melucci, Alberto. 1988. Getting involved: identity and mobilization in social movements. In *From structure to action: comparing social movement research across cultures*, eds. Klandermans, Bert, Hanspeter Kriesi and Sidney Tarrow. 329–48. Greenwich, Conn: JAI Press.

———. 1989. *Nomads of the present*, eds. Keane, John and Paul Mier. London: Hitchinson Radius.

———. 1995. The process of collective identity. In *Social movements and culture*, eds. Johnston, Hank and Bert Klandermans. 41–63. Minneapolis: Minnesota University Press.

Michels, Robert. 1968. *Political parties: a sociological study of the oligarchical tendencies of modern democracy* (2nd ed.). Glencoe III: Free Press.

Miners, Norman. 1975. *The government and politics of Hong Kong*. Hong Kong: Oxford University Press.

———. 1981. *The government and politics of Hong Kong* (3rd ed.). Hong Kong: Oxford University Press.

———. 1988. The representation and participation of trade unions in the Hong Kong government. In *Labour movement in a changing society: the experience of Hong Kong*, eds. Jao, Y.C. et al. 40–7. Hong Kong: Centre of Asian Studies, the University of Hong Kong.

Mohanty, Chandra Talpade. 1992. Feminist encounters: locating the politics of experience. In *Destabilizing theory: contemporary feminist debates*, eds. Barrett, Michele and Anne Phillips. 74–92. Stanford: Stanford University Press.

Montgomery, Mark. Too radical — lashing the greens. *One Earth* [quarterly of the Friends of the Earth] (Summer 1995): 34.

Morley, James W., ed. 1993. *Driven by growth: political change in the Asian-Pacific region*. New York: M.E. Sharpe.

Munck, Ronald. 1988. *The new international labour studies: an introduction*. London: Zed Press.

Nathan, Andrew. 1985. *Chinese democracy*. 3–30. New York: Alfred A. Knopf.

Neher, Clark D. 1991. *Southeast Asia in the new international era*. Boulder: Westview Press.

Ng, Cho-nam and Ting-leung Ng. 1992. The environment. In *The other Hong Kong report 1992*, eds. Cheng, Joseph Y.S. and Paul C.K. Kwong. 365–82. Hong Kong: The Chinese University Press.

Ng, Hang-sau. 1992. Grassroots mobilization for environmental protection [MSW dissertation, Department of Social Work and Social Administration, the University of Hong Kong].

———. 1993. Mobilizing Tsing Yi residents against environmental hazards. In *Limited gains*, eds. Chan, Cecilia and Peter Hills. 63–82. Hong Kong: Centre of Urban Planning and Environmental Management, the University of Hong Kong.

Ng, Kang-chung. Radical group to adapt or die. *South China Morning Post*, 5 October 1995.

Ng, Kwai-yan and Louis Wong. PWC firm on Bill of Rights dilution. *South China Morning Post*, 8 November 1995.

Ng, Mayer. 1983. Staff relations practices in the civil service. In *Contemporary issues in Hong Kong labour relations*, eds. Ng, S.H. and D.A. Levin. 63–78. Hong Kong: Centre of Asian Studies, the University of Hong Kong.

Ng, Mei. 1997. Environmental education in Hong Kong. In *Community mobilization and the environment in Hong Kong*, eds. Chan, Cecilia and Peter Hills. Hong Kong: Centre of Urban Planning and Environmental Management, the University of Hong Kong.

Ng, S.H. Labour administration and 'voluntarism': the Hong Kong case. *Journal of Industrial Relations* 24, no. 2 (June 1982).

———, F.T. Chan and K.K. Wong. 1989. A report on labour supply in Hong Kong [mimeo., sponsored by the Hong Kong Economic Research Centre].

Ng, Ting-leung. 1991. *Environmental attitudes in Hong Kong*. Hong Kong: Conservancy Association.

The Observers of Far Eastern Affairs, ed. 1982. *The student movement*. Hong Kong: the Observers of Far Eastern Affairs. (In Chinese.)

O'Donnell, Guillermo A. 1986. Introduction to the Latin American cases. *Transitions from authoritarian rule: prospects for democracy*, eds. O'Donnell, Guillermo A., Philippe C. Schmitter and Laurence Whitehead. 3–18. London: Johns Hopkins University Press.

———, Philippe C. Schmitter and Laurence Whitehead, eds. 1986. *Transitions from authoritarian rule: prospects for democracy*. London: Johns Hopkins University Press.

Offe, Claus. 1985. Two logics of collective action. In *Disorganized Capitalism*, ed. Offe, C. 170–220. Cambridge: Polity Press.

Olson, David J. 1992. Public and private political realities and the privatization movement. In *Language, symbolism, and politics*, ed. Merelman, Richard M. 67–81. Boulder, CO: Westview Press.

Ono, Keitaro. 1992. A Japanese view of nature. In *Voices from Kyoto forum in earth summit times*, ed. Kyoto Forum. Osaka: Kyoto Forum.

Pang, Sin-fun. 1994. Influence of environmentalism on consumer behaviors [unpublished project report, Department of Sociology, the Chinese University of Hong Kong].

Pickvance, C.G. The rise and fall of urban movements and the role of comparative analysis. *Society and Space* 3 (1985): 31–53.

Podmore, D. 1971. The population of Hong Kong. In *Hong Kong: the industrial colony*, ed. Hopkins, Keith. 21–54. Hong Kong: Oxford University Press.

Princen, Thomas, Mathias Finger, M.L. Clark and J. Manno. 1992. *Environmental NGOs in world politics*. London: Routledge.

Przeworski, Adam. 1986. Some problems in the study of the transition to democracy. In *Transitions from authoritarian rule: prospects for democracy*, eds. O'Donnell Guillermo A., Philippe C. Schmitter and Laurence Whitehead. 53–4. London: John Hopkins University Press.

Roberts, Ben. 1964. *Labour in the tropical territories of the Commonwealth*. London: Bell and Sons.

Robinson, T.W. 1991. *Democracy and development in East Asia*. Washington: AEI Press.

Rueschemeyer, D., E. Stephens and D. Stephens. 1992. *Capitalist development and democracy*. Oxford: Basil Blackwell Ltd.

Rustow, Dankwart A. Transitions to democracy: toward a dynamic model. *Comparative Politics* 2, no. 3 (1970): 352–3.

Salaff, J. 1981. *Working daughters of Hong Kong: filial piety or power in the family?* Cambridge: Cambridge University Press.

Scalapino, Robert A. Democratizing dragons: South Korea and Taiwan. *Journal of Democracy* 4, no. 7 (1993): 70–83.

Scott, Ian. 1988. The Hong Kong civil service and its future. In *The Hong Kong civil service and its future*, eds. Scott, Ian and John P. Burns. Hong Kong: Oxford University Press.

———. 1989. *Political change and the crisis of legitimacy in Hong Kong*. Hong Kong: Oxford University Press.

Scott, W. Richard. 1992. *Organizations: rational, natural, and open systems* (3rd ed.). Englewood Cliffs: Prentice-Hall International.

———. 1995. *Institutions and organizations*. Thousand Oaks CA: Sage.

Security Branch (Security B) of the Hong Kong government. *Hong Kong government's contingency plan for dealing with serious accidents involving potentially hazardous and industrial installations on Tsing Yi Island* [press release and report to the Kwai Tsing District Board on 13 September 1993].

Seidman, Gay. 1994. *Manufacturing militance*. Berkeley: University of California Press.

Selznick, Philip. 1969. *Law, society, and industrial justice*. New York: Russell Sage.

Sender, Henny. Bubble vision. *Far Eastern Economic Review* (3 July 1997): 66–7.

Shanzhong, Ren. The Chinese University of Hong Kong and the 1989 democracy movement. *Newsletter of The Hong Kong Alliance in Support of the Patriotic Democratic Movements of China* no. 24 (January 1994): 9–10.

Shapiro, Thomas M. Structure and process in social movement strategy: the movement against sterilization abuse. *Research in Social Movements, Conflicts and Change* 8 (1985): 87–108.

Share, Donald. Transitions to democracy & transition through transaction. *Comparative Political Studies* 19, no. 4 (1987): 527–30.

Shiva, V. Coming tragedy of the Commons. *Economic and Political Weekly* XXI: 613–4.

Sida, M. 1994. *Hong Kong towards 1997*. Hong Kong: Victoria Press.

Siddall, Linda. 1991. The environment. In *The other Hong Kong report 1991*, eds. Sung, Yun-wing and Ming-kwan Lee. 403–19. Hong Kong: The Chinese University Press.

Siegel, Abraham. 1965. The extended meaning and diminished relevance of 'job conscious' unionism. In *Proceedings of the eighteenth Annual Winter Meeting*, ed. Somers, G. 166–82. Madison WI: Industrial Relations Research Association.

Sing, Ming. 1993. The democracy movement in Hong Kong 1986–1990 [unpublished Ph.D. thesis, University of Oxford].

———. Democratization of Hong Kong 1984–90: an anomalous case. Berlin: Berlin World Congress, International Political Science Association, August 1994.

———. Democratization & economic development: the anomalous case of Hong Kong. *Democratization* [mimeo] 3, no. 3, 1996: 343–59.

———. Survey report on the public towards Chris Patten's reform [mimeo]. 1996.

Skrentny, John D. Concern for the environment. *International Journal of Public Opinion Research* 5, no. 4 (Winter 1993): 335–52.

Snow, David A., E. Burke Rochford, Jr., Steven K. Wordon and Robert D. Benford. Frame alignment processes, micromobilization, and movement participation. *American Sociological Review* 51 (1986): 464–81.

So, Alvin Y. The economic success of Hong Kong: insights from a world-system perspective. *Sociological Perspectives* 29 (1986): 241–58.

Somers, Margaret R. The narrative construction of identity: a relational and network approach. *Theory and Society* 23 (1994): 605–49.

Stepan, Alfred. 1989. *Democratizing Brazil: problems of transition and consolidation*. New York: Oxford University Press.

———. On the tasks of a democratic opposition. *Journal of Democracy* 1, no. 2 (1990): 41–9.

Stoecker, Randy. Community, movement, organization: the problem of identity convergence in collective action. *The Sociological Quarterly* 36, no. 1 (1995): 111–30.

Swidler, Ann. Culture in action: symbols and strategies. *American Sociological Review* 51 (1986): 273–86.

————. 1995. Cultural power and social movements. In *Social movements and culture*, eds. Johnston, Hank and Bert Klandermans. 25–40. Minneapolis: Minnesota University Press.

Szasz, Andrew. 1995. *EcoPopulism: toxic waste and the movement for environmental justice*. Minneapolis, MN: University of Minnesota Press.

Tarrow, Sidney. 1989. *Democracy and disorder: protest and politics in Italy 1965–1975*. Oxford: Clarendon Press.

————. 1989. Struggle, politics, and reform: collective action, social movements, and cycles of protest [Western Societies Program, occasional paper no. 21, Centre for International Studies, Cornell University].

Thatcher, Margaret. 1993. *Thatcher's memories, the Downing Street years*. New York: Harper Collins.

Thompson, James D. 1976. Organizational management of conflict. In *Organizations and beyond: selected essays of James D. Thompson*, eds. Rushing, William A. and Mayer N. Zald. 23–39. Lexington MA.: Lexington Books.

Tilly, Charles. 1978. *From mobilization to revolution*. New York: Random House.

Ting, K.Y. 1988. The impact of containerization on seamen's employment: the Hong Kong experience. In *Labour movement in a changing society: the experience of Hong Kong*, eds. Jao, Y.C. et al. 120–3. Hong Kong: Centre of Asian Studies, the University of Hong Kong.

Tong, James. 1994. *1989 democracy movement in China: a preliminary spatial analysis*. Hong Kong: Universities Service Centre, the Chinese University of Hong Kong.

Tsang, Gar-yin. 1995. The women's movement at the crossroads. In *Women in Hong Kong*, eds. Pearson, Veronica and Benjamin Leung. 276–91. Hong Kong: Oxford University Press.

Tsang, Shu-ki. 1979. An exploratory analysis of Hong Kong's class structure. In *Between Hong Kong and China* (2nd ed.), ed. Tsang, Shu-ki. Hong Kong: Seven Hills Book Shop. (In Chinese.)

————. 1993. Income distribution. In *The other Hong Kong report 1993*, eds. Choi, Po-king and Lok-sang Ho. 361–8. Hong Kong: The Chinese University Press.

Tso, M.T.T. 1983. Civil service unions as a social force in Hong Kong [M.Soc.Sc. dissertation, the University of Hong Kong].

————. 1988. The industrial relations system in the Hong Kong civil service. In *Labour movement in a changing society*, eds. Jao, Y.C. et al. 61–6. Hong Kong: Centre of Asian Studies, the University of Hong Kong.

Tsuen Wan District Board. 1987. *A report on the survey on the conditions of work for female workers in Tsuen Wan, 1986*. Hong Kong: Tsuen Wan District Board.

Turner, H.A. 1988. The prospects for trade unions in Hong Kong. In *Labour movement in a changing society: the experience of Hong Kong*, eds. Jao, Y.C. et al. 177–90. Hong Kong: Centre of Asian Studies, the University of Hong Kong.

———— et al. 1980. *The last colony: but whose?* Cambridge: Cambridge University Press.

————, P. Fosh and S.H. Ng. 1991. *Between two societies: Hong Kong labour in transition*. Hong Kong: Centre of Asian Studies, the University of Hong Kong.

Valenzuela, J. Samuel. 1992. Labour movements and political systems: some variations. In *The future of labour movements*, ed. Regini, Marino. 53–101. Thousand Oaks CA: Sage.

Visser, Jelle. 1992. The strength of union movements in advanced capitalist democracies: social and organizational variations. In *The future of labour movements*, ed. Regini, Marino. 17–52. Thousand Oaks CA: Sage.

Walsh, Edward J. Resource mobilization and citizen protest in communities around Three Mile Island area. *Social Problems* 29: 1–21.

Wang, Jennhwan. 1988. Political movements against the state: the transition of Taiwan's authoritarian rule [Ph.D. thesis, University of California, Los Angeles].

Westrum, Ron and Khalil Samaha. 1984. *Complex organizations: growth, struggle, and change*. Englewood Cliffs: Prentice-Hall.

White, Gordon. Civil society, democratization and development: clearing the analytical ground. *Democratization* 1, no. 3 (1994): 375–82.

Williamson, Oliver E. 1975. *Market and hierarchies*. New York: Free Press.

————. 1985. *The economic institutions of capitalism*. New York: Free Press.

Wong, C.K. 1988. *Social movements and Hong Kong*. Hong Kong: Twilight Books. (In Chinese.)

Wong, Hyo. 1989. The 1986–89 pay dispute. In *Hong Kong Chinese Civil Servants' Association 75th anniversary commemorative volume*, ed. Hong Kong Chinese Civil Servants Association. 74–6. Hong Kong: Hong Kong Chinese Civil Servants' Association.

Wong, Pik-wan, ed. 1990. *Some Christian reflections on the June 4 massacre and the democratic movement*. Hong Kong: Hong Kong Christian Institute. (In Chinese.)

————. 1991. Nationalism and the democracy movement in Hong Kong [unpublished M.Phil. thesis, Department of Government and Public Administration, the Chinese University of Hong Kong].

————. 1993. Workers' participation in the 1989 democracy movement in China [unpublished paper, Department of Political Science, UCLA].

Wong, Richard Y.C. and Joseph Y.S. Cheng, eds. 1990. *The other Hong Kong report 1990*. Hong Kong: The Chinese University Press.

Wong, T.K. How to conceive the forms of confrontation in social actions. *Hong Kong Economic Journal* (20 December 1994). (In Chinese.)

Wong, Thomas W.P. and Tai-lok Lui. 1992. Reinstating class: a structural and developmental study of Hong Kong society [occasional paper no. 10, Social Sciences Research Centre, the University of Hong Kong].

Wong, Wai-hung. 1988. Staff relations in the civil service and the trade union response: review and prospect, 1971–1985. In *Labour movement in a changing society*, eds. Jao, Y.C. et al. 150–6. Hong Kong: Centre of Asian Studies, the University of Hong Kong.

Worcester, Robert M. Public and elite attitude to environmental issues. *International Journal of Public Opinion Research* 5, no. 4 (Winter 1993): 315–34.

World Bank. 1984. *World development report.* New York: Oxford University Press.

Wu, M.M. The political conjuncture of contemporary Hong Kong and the development of popular movements. *Equator Monthly* no. 5 (1978). (In Chinese.)

Xu, Jiatun. 1993. *Memories of Hong Kong.* Taipei: Lianjing Publishers. (In Chinese.)

Yan, Jiaqi. 1992. *Toward a democratic China: the intellectual autobiography of Yan Jiaqi.* Honolulu: University of Hawaii.

Yau, Betty et al. 1992. Women's concern groups in Hong Kong [occasional paper no. 15, Hong Kong Institute of Asia-Pacific Studies, the Chinese University of Hong Kong].

Yee, Herbert S. and Yiu-chung Wong. Hong Kong: the politics of the Daya Bay Nuclear Plant debate. *International Affairs* 63, no. 4 (1987): 617–30.

Yeh, A.G.O. 1985. Employment location and new town development in Hong Kong. In *State policy, urbanization and the development process: proceedings of a symposium on social and environmental development, October 1984,* ed. Hills, P.R. Hong Kong: Centre of Urban Studies and Urban Planning, the University of Hong Kong.

Yeung, S. 1989. Looking at the trade union movement as a social movement. In *The directions of the Hong Kong trade union movement,* ed. Hong Kong Federation of Trade Unions. 17–24. Hong Kong: New City Cultural Service Ltd. (In Chinese.)

Yeung, Vincent F.Y. 1987. An investigation into the professional ideology of the neighbourhood level community development project community workers [unpublished MSW thesis, Department of Social Work and Social Administration, the University of Hong Kong].

Yip, Hung-sang, ed. 1979. *Where is China heading?* Taipei: Cheng Wen. (In Chinese.)

Yu, W.K. 1995. The nature and implications of the recommodification of public housing in Hong Kong. In *A symposium on housing policy in Hong Kong*, eds. Kam, P.K. et al. Hong Kong: Joint Publishing (HK) Co., Ltd. (In Chinese.)

Zald, Mayer N. and Bert Useem. 1987. Movement and countermovement interaction: mobilization, tactics, and state involvement. In *Social movements in an organizational society*, eds. Zald, Mayer N. and John D. McCarthy. 247–88. New Brunswick, New Jersey: Transaction Books.

Index